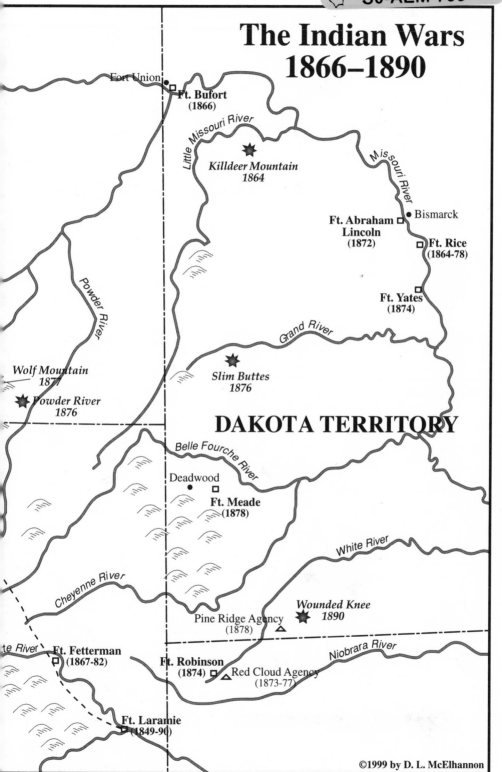

The Indian Wars 1866–1890

Fort Union

Ft. Bufort
(1866)

Little Missouri River

Killdeer Mountain
1864

Missouri River

Ft. Abraham
Lincoln
(1872)

Bismarck

Ft. Rice
(1864-78)

Ft. Yates
(1874)

Powder River

Grand River

Wolf Mountain
1877

Slim Buttes
1876

Powder River
1876

DAKOTA TERRITORY

Belle Fourche River

Deadwood

Ft. Meade
(1878)

White River

Cheyenne River

Wounded Knee
1890

Pine Ridge Agency
(1878)

te River

Ft. Fetterman
(1867-82)

Ft. Robinson
(1874)

Red Cloud Agency
(1873-77)

Niobrara River

Ft. Laramie
(1849-90)

©1999 by D. L. McElhannon

CRAZY HORSE

CRAZY HORSE
THE LIFE BEHIND THE LEGEND

MIKE SAJNA

John Wiley & Sons, Inc.

New York • Chichester • Weinheim • Brisbane • Singapore • Toronto

This book is printed on acid-free paper. ∞

Copyright © 2000 by Mike Sajna. All rights reserved

Published by John Wiley & Sons, Inc.
Published simultaneously in Canada

Photos on pages 16, 45, 181, and 327 courtesy of Jim Schafer. Photos on pages 28, 116, 157, 235, 243, 254, 262, 266, 270, 298, and 323 courtesy of Nebraska State Historical Society. Photo on page 3 courtesy of Western Historical Department, Denver Library. Photo on page 236 courtesy of South Dakota State Historical Society. Photo on page 325 courtesy of Sandoz Collection, University of Nebraska.

This publication is designed to provide accurate and authoritative information in regard to the subject matter covered. It is sold with the understanding that the publisher is not engaged in rendering professional services. If professional advice or other expert assistance is required, the services of a competent professional person should be sought.

Library of Congress Cataloging-in-Publication Data:

Sajna, Mike
    Crazy Horse : the life behind the legend / Mike Sajna.
      p. cm.
    Includes bibliographical references and index.
    ISBN 0-471-24182-2 (cloth : alk. paper)
    1. Crazy Horse, ca. 1842–1877. 2. Oglala Indians–Biography. 3. Dakota Indians–History.   I. Title.
    E99.O3 C7274   2000
    978'.0049752'0092–dc21

                                         99-045547

Printed in the United States of America

10 9 8 7 6 5 4 3 2 1

For Jim Schafer, "High Plains Drifter,"
photographer supreme, and friend.

CONTENTS

PREFACE

WINSTON CHURCHILL once described the Soviet Union as a riddle wrapped in an enigma. The same might be said of Crazy Horse. Finding the living person buried beneath a myth powerful enough to inspire the largest sculpture ever undertaken (never mind that there is no absolutely verifiable photograph of the subject and that he would have been horrified to see such a desecration of his sacred Black Hills) is a difficult task. Add the fact that Crazy Horse was a quiet, even shy person who came from a preliterate people, and so left behind no letters, diaries, speeches, or account books to tell his side of the story, and it becomes even tougher. Then consider that the handful of the primary sources who actually knew the war chief did not record their memories of him for from roughly twenty-five to more than fifty years after his death, and the task begins to verge on the impossible.

Confronted by such barriers, as well as vagaries of translations and the Native American habit of telling stories without consideration for chronology, the only way I could find to approach the subject was to try to match the primary sources to the historic record. Except for pointing out well-known stories for which no basis in fact could be found, I avoided secondary sources as much as possible. Secondary sources are rich in colorful incident but seem to run the gamut from pure fiction to assumption with very little or no support in the existing record.

Instead of relying on secondary sources, I have attempted to fill in the gaps of Crazy Horse's life, and they are many and yawning, by placing him within the historical times that so shaped his life. Using those facts and what is known about his personality, readers can decide for themselves what Crazy Horse might have been thinking, how he felt, or why he reacted the way he did when certain events occurred. Hopefully they will be able to see not only the smart and brave war chief with the good of his people at heart, but also the mesmerized lover and cautious warrior who at times made mistakes and was as frightened as anybody when confronting death.

To undertake any biography, even one with such limited primary sources as those available on Crazy Horse, requires the help of a great many people. First among those are my agent, Gerard McCauley, who was willing to listen to my idea and steered me in the proper direction; my editor, Hana Umlauf Lane, who was so understanding and patient when problems involving my health brought the project to a temporary halt and slowed progress for several months; and finally my friend Jim Schafer, who is always full of interesting conversation, traveled with me to many of the places that played a role in Crazy Horse's life and never let me down.

Others whose help, encouragement, good wishes, and prayers were indispensable during the tough times that descended as the book neared conclusion include: my wife, Lisa Baxter, my parents, Mike and Leona Sajna, Peggy Schafer, Laurie and Dave Hanson, Fritz Huysman and all of my other friends at the *Pittsburgh Post-Gazette*, as well as the readers of the paper's outdoors pages, Bob and Mary Jane Dragovich, Rebecca Cook, Lindsay and Lacy Thomas, Eric Weiss, Jack Hess, Jim Skrabski, Lou Patrick, Don and Margaret Fox, Elmer and Bobbi Brewer, Bob Burnett, and Dr. Delynne Myers and all of the other wonderful doctors and nurses who work at the Pittsburgh Cancer Institute and on the seventh floor of UPMC Shadyside Hospital. I don't mention all of their names only because there were so many and I fear leaving out somebody.

In the research arena I wish to thank the librarians at the University of Pittsburgh's Hillman Library for their assistance in tracking down some of the more obscure material. Pitt faculty and staff who aided my work included Dave Brumble, author of *American Indian Autobiography*; Lee Gutkind, for putting me in contact with Gerard McCauley; Nancy Brown, for putting me in contact with Lee; and Linda Howard, for some last-minute research assistance.

Outside of my Pittsburgh base, help came from the Archives and Special Collections departments of the University of Nebraska at Lincoln; the staff at the Nebraska State Historical Society (who never ran out of the endless change needed to photocopy the Ricker tablets and other material); the Fort Robinson Museum; the archives of Marquette University's Memorial Library; the Western Historical Manuscript Collection of the University of Missouri; the South Dakota State Historical Society; the Western History Collection of the University of Oklahoma; the Western History Collection at the University of Wyoming; and the people who spoke with me or provided help at the Pine Ridge and Rosebud reservations, the Little Big Horn National Battlefield, Fort Laramie, the Custer State Park and Bear Butte State Park visitors' centers, the Platte Bridge museum, Fort Phil Kearny, Ash Hollow, and other locations pertinent to Crazy Horse's life.

The life of an Indian is just like the wings of the air.—*Black Elk*

We must try to distinguish friendly from hostile and kill the latter, but if you or any other commanding officer strike a blow I will approve, for it seems impossible to tell the true from the false. —*General William Tecumseh Sherman, in a letter to Colonel Henry Carrington*

1

"Crazy Horse with Us"

Slowly the column made its way down the wide valley between two long, sloping bluffs. It was about ten o'clock in the morning.[1] The sky was clear and bright, the plains gleaming with the night's rain and the first tender green of spring.

About a mile in advance of the column rode Lieutenant J. Wesley Rosenquest with a detachment of the 4th U.S. Cavalry.[2] Five days earlier, on May 1, 1877, Rosenquest had left Camp Robinson in northwestern Nebraska to meet the "hostiles," the band of the Oglala Lakota Sioux leader Crazy Horse, on Hat Creek. At the request of the Oglala Lakota Red Cloud, who had been out in the Powder River country negotiating Crazy Horse's surrender since mid-April, Rosenquest brought the band ten wagons of supplies and a hundred head of cattle.[3] Rosenquest would later become known as the first army officer to shake hands with Crazy Horse, but interpreter William Garnett, who accompanied him on the mission, said that is a "mistake."[4] He does not, however, elaborate.

To meet Rosenquest and accept the surrender of Crazy Horse, Lieutenant William Philo Clark, known to the Indians as White Hat, had ridden up Soldier Creek from Camp Robinson with twenty Cheyenne scouts and a reporter for the *Chicago Times*, most likely L. F. Whitbeck.[5] The reporter would write of Clark:

> There is a personal magnetism about the man that attaches a person to him as soon as one meets him. This is used to great advantage with Indians. His Indian soldiers perfectly worship him. His word is law to them. His perfect control of them shows that Indians can easily be got along with if dealt with honestly, treated kindly, and with a firm hand. Clark may well be proud of the splendid reputation he is getting in the Indian war.[6]

Clark's interest in the plains tribes would later lead him to write *The Indian Sign Language.*

Five miles outside of Red Cloud Agency, which stood one and one-half miles east of Camp Robinson, Clark's detail encountered Rosenquest and the advancing column of Indians. Alone at the head of the Indians rode Crazy Horse on a light-colored pony. Clark and his men waited until the column was about a half mile away and then rode forward to meet it. As they did, Crazy Horse dismounted and sat on the ground.[7] According to Short Buffalo or Short Bull, youngest brother of Crazy Horse's close friend He Dog: "Crazy Horse spread out his blanket for Red Cloud to sit on and gave his shirt to Red Cloud; He Dog did the same for White Hat. This meant that they gave up to these two. He Dog gave his war-horse and saddle to White Hat. You can see by this that there was no ill feeling toward the whites."[8]

Halting his men, Clark moved ahead alone. When he was within a few yards of Crazy Horse, he dismounted and sat down facing the Oglala leader.[9] For five minutes the two men remained in that position. What was said was not recorded, but the talk could well have been a reiteration of Crazy Horse's thoughts on the location of the agency he had been promised. Short Buffalo said: "In all the talk they had that day, Crazy Horse said, 'There is a creek over there they call Beaver Creek; there is a great big flat west of the headwaters of Beaver Creek; I want my agency put right in the middle of that flat.' He said the grass was good there for horses and game."[10]

According to Short Buffalo, Crazy Horse originally wanted his agency located near what is now Gillette, Wyoming, or on the edge of the Big Horn Mountains where Sheridan, Wyoming, stands. If he could not have an agency in either of those locations, he was willing to accept one on Beaver Creek east of Camp Robinson. This was the only cause of misunderstanding at that time, Short Buffalo said. Crazy Horse wanted to have his agency established first. Then he would go to Washington to talk with the president. White officials wanted him to go to Washington before he was given an agency.[11]

The talk over, Clark rose, stepped closer to Crazy Horse, and extended his left hand. According to Garnett, Clark had been instructed to use his left hand because the Indians believed the "left hand is next to the heart, but the right hand does all manner of wickedness."[12]

Crazy Horse and his band of Indians on their way to surrender at the Red Cloud Agency. From *Frank Leslie's Illustrated Newspaper*, June 6, 1877.

Clark's action broke the tension, and Rosenquest, the *Times* reporter, and several of the most important Lakota warriors moved forward to exchange handshakes. "Most of them gave a good hearty grip, and seemed to mean it," the *Times* noted. "Three gave the left hand, a few just touched their fingers very politely, not even saying 'How koola?' But nearly all gave good hearty evidence of submission." About a hundred yards behind the group sat another three hundred warriors divided into five bands, with a headman at the front of each. Darkening the bluffs above the scene were the band's women, children, old men, and young warriors.[13]

During the entire ceremony, according to the *Times*, Crazy Horse remained seated alone where Clark had first met him. When the party returned, he was joined by Little Hawk and He Dog. Like Crazy Horse at one time, He Dog was an appointed leader of the highest rank, officially called *wicasa yatapike*, "owners of the tribe" or "supreme headmen," but commonly known as "shirt wearers."[14]

In his reminiscences recorded more than twenty-five years later, Garnett reported that Crazy Horse then presented Clark with "a war bonnet, war shirt, pipe and beaded sack for tobacco and kinni kin-nick and pipe. Clark was told to put on his Indian clothing, being assisted by some of his new friends, and made an imposing appear-ance."[15] The *Times* reporter, writing that same day, though, reported that He Dog opened the council by saying: "I have come to make peace to those only I like and have confidence in. I give these."[16] He Dog, not Crazy Horse, then removed his ceremonial bonnet and heavily beaded and embroidered war shirt. He hung the shirt over Clark's shoulders and placed the war bonnet on the lieutenant's head. Clark responded by sitting next to Crazy Horse.

"We have come to make a lasting peace, never to be broken," Clark said. "We had a rain last night that has washed out all bad feel-ings that have ever been between us. The sun is now shining brightly. All shows the Great Spirit is pleased with our actions. To ensure this lasting peace it is necessary to give up arms and ponies. This after-noon, when we reach camp, I will take the names of all Indians who turn in ponies and arms, and will send them to the great father at Washington. General Crook is now in Washington, looking out for your interests. We want to count the Indians so as to provide them with rations, and keep them supplied."[17]

Well-known among the Lakota for holding his tongue at councils, Crazy Horse replied: "I have given all I have to Red Cloud."[18] It was his only recorded comment at the surrender council. The *Times* reporter and many writers since have taken Crazy Horse's words to mean that he had given his possessions to Red Cloud. But that might be too literal an interpretation or even a mistake in translation, since Crazy Horse remained in possession of such things as his Winchester rifle and pony. As Short Buffalo indicated, the remark probably meant that he had ceded his authority to Red Cloud.

In response, Red Cloud told Clark: "Crazy Horse is a sensible man. He knows it is useless to fight longer against the whites, and is now willing to give himself up." Through Red Cloud, the warriors then asked to be allowed to surrender their arms voluntarily at Red Cloud Agency and not have them forcibly taken away. Clark agreed and laid out a plan that called for each warrior to deposit his guns on the ground at the agency and then give his name.[19]

By noon the council was over and the march begun to Red Cloud Agency. Clark and Rosenquest led the column, followed by their Cheyenne soldiers, and a quarter of a mile back Crazy Horse and his warriors, as the *Times* reported, "marching with the regular order of troops."[20] The Lakota horses were brightly painted, and all but Crazy Horse, who wore his customary plain shirt and single eagle feather, were dressed in their best shirts, ceremonial bonnets, blankets, and leggings heavily ornamented with glass beads, brass, silver, and tin. "The sun shining on them made such a dazzling show as almost to blind the eyes," the *Times* noted. "Behind the warriors [came] the two thousand ponies then tepees and lodge poles. It was a grand and imposing sight."[21]

As the column approached Red Cloud Agency at 2:00 P.M., there was none of the parading, wild firing of weapons, whooping, or celebrating that had followed some earlier surrenders. From one end to the other of the two-mile-long column arose a solemn peace chant. Watching the band of 899 Lakota approach through field glasses, one officer was moved to exclaim: "By God! This is a triumphal march, not a surrender!"[22]

On a wide plain bordered by bluffs along the White Earth River (White River), the band pitched their lodges in a crescent about three-fourths of a mile from Red Cloud Agency and two and three-fourths of a mile from Camp Robinson. When they turned in their ponies, chief packer Thomas Moore stopped counting after seventeen hundred, according to the *Times*. Other sources report the final total to have been about twenty-two hundred horses and a few mules.[23]

Before the warriors would turn in their arms, they asked that all whites withdraw. The request was made "apparently meaning to convey the idea that their pride was so crushed that they did not want the further humiliation of having spectators at the scene," the *Times* reported. "They were humored in this, all white people and Indian soldiers making themselves scarce and leaving a large open place in which they could deposit their arms." Only Clark, Rosenquest, Lieutenant Charles Johnson (the acting agent for Red Cloud Agency), and two interpreters remained to watch Crazy Horse and his warriors give up their arms.[24]

The collection of arms caused the only hitch in the surrender. According to the *Times*, the band's warriors turned in only forty-six rifles and seventy-six pistols. Believing there were more, Clark refused to accept the arms and told Crazy Horse he knew the band had more weapons and it was a requirement of the agreement that all arms be surrendered at once.[25] Garnett said the Cheyenne soldiers had mingled among the band on the way in to Red Cloud Agency, "watching for guns and counting those the Indians carried; these scouts were most active, industrious and faithful in their new capacity."[26]

Confronted by Clark on the issue of guns, Crazy Horse remained stoic and did not reply. The warriors picked up their arms and went to their lodges. Clark immediately ordered up a wagon and with Rosenquest, two interpreters, and a detachment of Cheyenne soldiers, began searching every lodge for arms, "taking everything of the kind he could find." By 8:00 P.M. the search had produced 113 guns, 9 less than the warriors originally had turned in. According to the *Times*, "two fine Winchester rifles were taken from Crazy Horse's tent. No objections were made, no assistance given. Nearly half the guns are Winchesters; a good many are Sharp's carbines." Frustrated by the search, Clark ordered that no rations be issued to the band until all arms were surrendered.[27]

The date was Sunday, May 6, 1877. As the *Times* reporter telegraphed his story on Crazy Horse's surrender for the next day's newspaper, only Sitting Bull, of the important plains Indian leaders, remained free, in Canada. Scattered, small-scale fighting between whites and Indians would continue for more than a dozen years, finally ending when Hotchkiss guns overlooking Wounded Knee Creek, a tributary of the same White Earth River where Crazy Horse pitched his camp that day, were fired on a band of Miniconjou Lakota of Big Foot on the bleak winter morning of December 29, 1890.

But it was the surrender of Crazy Horse that was the epochal event in the plains Indian wars and in the history of the West. The arrival of Crazy Horse at Red Cloud Agency marked the end of more than three and a half centuries of massive Indian resistance to the white takeover of North America. And the whites were well aware of it. "CRAZY HORSE WITH US. . . . End of the Last of Our Great Indian Wars Practically Reached," blared the headline on the *Times* story.[28]

Despite what had happened at the Little Big Horn River just ten months earlier, most white Americans, long certain of their eventual triumph over the Indians, already had shifted their attention to other things. News of Crazy Horse's surrender made only page seven of the *Chicago Times*. Page one belonged to the approaching war between Russia and Turkey over the treatment of Christians in Turkish Armenia. There also was a note on the appropriation by the Illinois General Assembly of $27,000 for the Lincoln monument in Springfield, and two stories of suicides. John T. Daly, a New York millionaire, hanged and shot himself in a dilapidated Long Island house. Embarrassment over financial problems was believed to be the cause. And Frank Fisher of Torch Lake, Michigan, hanged himself in the Houghton, Michigan, jail. Fisher had been confined in the jail after cutting off his hand with an ax and attempting to kill himself by driving a chisel into his brain.

Even a story by "Romeo" about how William F. "Buffalo Bill" Cody once helped to tame the "decadence of romantic Indian fighters on the frontier" by presiding over a marriage ceremony appeared before the story of Crazy Horse's surrender. The author lamented:

> I fear that the heroes of the west, the fellows who knew the western life and had imbibed much of its natural wildness in their dress and speech and manners are fast falling away. . . . The necessities when rough men were needed to fight Indians, and fully as savage white men, are fast passing away, and, with the necessities of the time, the men whom the necessities created.[29]

Among the more thoughtful commentators on the surrender was Lieutenant John Gregory Bourke. Stationed at Fort Laramie, Bourke had been part of the long hunt for Crazy Horse after Custer's defeat. In his diary, Bourke wrote:

> If our Government will only observe one-half of its promises, the Indians will comply faithfully with their agreement, I am certain; the great danger of the future is not from the red man's want of faith so much as from the indifference of our Government to the plainest requirements of honor. Our own faith is worse than Punic; yet, we always prattle about treachery. . . . If the Government will only keep its promises and treat these red men with justice, we shall have no more Indian wars.[30]

For Crazy Horse, though, it would never end. In fewer than four months, fear, jealousy, and misunderstanding would drive the bayonet of a middle-aged cipher of a white private into his back while his arms were being held by an old friend.

2

BUFFALO PEOPLE

In the beginning, before there was a beginning, there was only Inyan (Rock), which had no beginning. Inyan was the first of the superior Gods and his spirit was Wakan Tanka (The Great Mystery). Inyan then was soft and shapeless like a cloud and had all the powers and was everywhere.

Being all-powerful, Inyan longed to use his powers. But there was no other upon whom he could do so. To make another, he gave his blood, which was blue, spreading it about him in the shape of a great disk, beyond which there is no beyond. He named the disk Maka (Earth) and gave it the spirit Maka-akan (Earth Goddess), the second of the superior Gods and a part of Inyan.

To create Maka required all of Inyan's blood and he shrank and became hard and powerless. His blood became the blue waters and the sky, and Nagi Tanka (Sky God), the Great Spirit who is all-powerful and called Skan (Most Holy), the third superior God. And so in the beginning there was Inyan and Maka and the waters, which are the world, and Nagi Tanka, named Skan, which is the sky.

When Inyan created Maka, he gave her discontent, which made her chide him for not making her a separate being and because Han (Darkness) was everywhere. But Inyan could do nothing. He had used all his powers to create Maka. He told Maka: "We shall take our contention before Skan, who is the possessor of all the powers that have departed from me, and we shall abide by his decision."

After listening to Maka's complaints, Skan decreed that Maka must remain joined to Inyan as part of the Earth. But he would make it so she could see herself and control the waters. So Skan divided Han and created Anp (Light). But the light had no shadows or heat and made Maka cry: "How bare I am and how cold and ugly!" Then Maka beheld the waters and found them blue and beautiful and decided she would adorn herself with them. She divided the waters into seas and lakes and streams that she wore as ornaments.

But Maka was weary of viewing herself in the same glaring light. She complained that the brightness of the light was unbearable and cold. Skan then took from Maka and Inyan, the waters and from himself, that which he made into a great shining dish he named Wi (Sun) and gave the spirit Wi-akan (Sun God), the fourth superior God.

Skan commanded Wi to shine upon the Earth and give it heat. But Maka was not satisfied. She wanted shadows and argued with Wi. Skan heard the fighting and commanded Wi: "Give a shadow to every material thing, but do not make a shadow for a spirit thing. The shadow of each thing shall be its spirit and shall be with it always." But Maka still was not happy. She was hot and begged Skan to return Han to cool her. Wi then complained he had no rest and was weary. So Skan divided time into day and night. In that way Maka was made comfortable.

But Maka and Wi continued to quarrel. So Skan assembled the Gods and gave each a rank. Wi, because he was above all, was given the highest rank. Maka, the ancestress of all things upon the Earth, was given the third rank, and Inyan, the source of all, the fourth. Skan kept for himself the second rank, but as the source of all spirit retained for himself authority over all.

After the Gods were given their places, Skan gave each a domain over which to rule. Wi was given all above the Earth. Maka was given all lands, save the mountains and high hills. Inyan was given all rocks, mountains, and high hills. But still Maka complained that she was dull and drab, while Wi was bright red and Skan a beautiful blue. To pacify her, Skan gave Maka the color green, the color of all growing things on Earth, and to Inyan, the ancestor of all, the color yellow. Since Wi was the highest of the Gods, red became the color of all that is sacred. Skan retained the color blue for himself so all that can be seen of him is the blue of the sky.

Skan and the other superior Gods then created Wi-win (Moon), Tate (Wind), Wakinyan (Thunderstorm), and Unk (Passion). Then they created Ksa (Wisdom) and Wohpe (Peace). Skan said: "All the Gods are as one God and that one is Wakan Tanka, the Great Mystery.

So as it is the will of the Great Mystery that there should be beings to do his will such beings shall be created."

Skan then took from Inyan that from which he created bones and from Maka that from which he created flesh and from the waters he created blood. Then Wohpe brought to him the white fruits from which he made entrails. Skan molded the Earth about the bones and the entrails and placed blood in all the parts. Then he gave to each of his creations a spirit.

"You have been created to serve the Gods," Skan told the beings. "Therein lies your happiness. Should you ever cease to do so, great will be your punishment. . . . Your offspring shall be as you are; and as long as they continue to do the will of the Gods, they will be happy, and their increase shall be many. You and your offspring shall be known as the Oyate Pte (Buffalo People)." And so, according to the old Lakota medicine men interviewed at the turn of the century by James R. Walker on the Pine Ridge Reservation, were created the Sioux.[1]

MORE EARTHLY SOURCES point to the East and the South, particularly North Carolina, as the original homeland of the Sioux.[2] The Oglala Lakota holy man Black Elk, a cousin through marriage of Crazy Horse, several times mentions his people living in the south:

> A long time ago before we have history, as far as the Sioux could remember back, it used to be they had seven bands and in these bands there was a chief by the name of Slow Buffalo. I figure they were living way out toward where you always face (south) along the edge of the ocean.[3]

The historic record, however, reaches back for certain only to the sixteenth century and the headwaters of the Mississippi River.

Before they settled on the northern plains, the Sioux consisted of seven tribes that sometimes called themselves the Otchenti Chako-win or Seven Council Fires. They had never assembled as one, but claimed to be related on the basis of a shared culture, history, and language. In the dialect of the eastern tribes they called themselves Dakota, and of the western tribes Lakota. The term means "ally" or "friend." Any people with whom peace had been made could fall under the meaning of Dakota or Lakota, while any people with whom peace had not been made were enemies. Sioux was the name applied to the Dakota and Lakota by French traders and later adopted by the Indians themselves. It is a corruption of the derogatory Ojibwa word *nadewisou*, which means "treacherous snake."

Pressed by Ojibwas, Algonquians, and Crees armed with weapons obtained from the French and English to the east, the Sioux first retreated to the plains about the middle of the seventeenth century. That initial wave of migration was followed by a second, larger one, in about 1735. According to Black Elk, the decision to move west was made by Slow Buffalo after a vision in which he saw that the people had become too numerous and needed to disperse throughout the land. He called a council and divided the people into seven bands, appointed a chief for each band, and gave each a share of the common fire.[4]

As with any move involving a people, the Lakota's shift from the hunting-agriculture life they developed on the prairies of Minnesota to the nomadic hunting life of the high plains was a gradual affair that occurred in a haphazard fashion in different ways in many locations. Left Hand, an Oglala Lakota, told of how one band made the crossing of the Missouri River on to the high plains while pursuing buffalo near where Platte Creek enters the Missouri in what is now Charles Mix County, South Dakota.

Before the Lakota acquired horses, according to Left Hand, they sometimes would hunt buffalo that wandered near their camps in the winter by driving them out onto the ice of the river or stream along which they had erected their lodges. The buffalos' smooth hooves would find little purchase on the slick ice and the animals would slip and fall, making them relatively easy targets for hunters on foot.

When the band hunting along Platte Creek made its kill on the frozen Missouri, they found themselves closer to the western bank than the eastern bank of the river. Instead of dragging the hides and meat back across the river, they set up camp on the western bank to finish butchering their kill. While they were completing their work over the next few days, a warm chinook wind arose and caused the ice to become thin and break up, stranding the party and the villagers who had joined it on the western bank of the Missouri. Gradually, as winter turned to spring, the people moved out of the Missouri Valley and began to explore the plains above the river.[5]

LIFE FOR THOSE early Lakota migrants to the plains was extremely difficult. For the most part they simply drifted about in quest of food. Dogs carried most of the camp equipment on their backs, and even tiny girls of six and seven had to carry bundles while their band was on the move. Under such conditions, a village could travel only about five miles a day.

The first great turning point in the lives of the Lakota came when they acquired the horse. Exactly when that happened is unknown, but it is believed to have occurred about the time of the first migration in the mid-seventeenth century. As with the move across the Missouri River, it occurred in a piecemeal, haphazard fashion. According to Black Elk, the Lakota first acquired the horse from the Cheyenne, who found it in the South. A medicine man had a vision of the animal and two hunters found it after following a strange set of tracks to a spring. The Sioux swapped bows and arrows and other valuables for the horse.[6]

Left Hand also reports that the Lakota obtained the horse from the Cheyenne. Two scouts from the hunting party that had followed the buffalo across the icy Missouri River one day saw two strange objects on the horizon. As the objects came closer, they appeared to be men riding giant dogs. The men were friendly, but spoke a language the Lakota did not understand. Finally, the Cheyenne drew signs on the ground showing that the hunters should follow them to their camp.

The Lakota followed the scouts and in two days came to the White River, where they found the largest camp they had ever seen. Because the Cheyenne had horses to drag long poles, they also had bigger lodges than the Lakota. The Cheyenne treated the Lakota with great friendship and at the end of the visit gave them several horses. From that day on, according to Left Hand, the Lakota and the Cheyenne became friends and allies.[7]

Through such friendly encounters, raids, thefts, trades, and the occasional capture of wild animals, the horse spread among the Lakota until by the start of the nineteenth century it was so abundant that Meriwether Lewis, during the Lewis and Clark Expedition of 1803–1806, envisioned the animal as a means of developing commerce in the West. He wrote: "This abundance and cheapness of horses will be extremely advantageous to those who may hereafter attempt the fir trade to the East Indies by way of the Columbia River and the Pacific Ocean."[8]

Once established on the high plains, the original seven Sioux groups divided. In the West they became known as the Teton Sioux and included seven tribes: the Sans Arc (Without Bows), the Hunkpapa (Campers at the Opening of the Circle), Miniconjou (Planters by Water), Two Kettle (Two Boilings), Sihasapa (Blackfeet, but different than the Blackfeet tribe), Brulé (Burned Thighs—the name came from a raiding party that was caught in a fire set by a band of Arapahos the party had intended to attack), and Oglala (Scatters Their Own, for the group's habit of camping in small bands). The largest of the seven tribes were the Oglala and the Brulé.

Fierce, persistent warriors, the Lakota drove the Crow, Pawnee, Shoshone, and other tribes from their hunting grounds, expanding their territory until it stretched from the North Platte River in Nebraska, west and north to the Powder River of Montana and the Black Hills of South Dakota. In 1840, the Lakota living in that territory numbered about eleven thousand. The population of white America was approximately seventeen million.[9]

EMPTY AND ALIEN was the impression most whites had of the plains during the first half of the nineteenth century. Major Stephen Long, commander of the Yellowstone Expedition launched from Pittsburgh in 1819 to secure American rights to the northern plains in the face of British claims, wrote: "In regard to this extensive section of the country, I do not hesitate in giving the opinion, that it is almost wholly unfit for cultivation, and of course uninhabitable by a people depending on agriculture for their subsistence." Dr. Edwin James, the expedition's scientific leader, agreed. The lack of water and timber, James felt, made the land "an unfit residence for any but a nomade population." He said that the region should "for ever remain the unmolested haunt of the native hunter, the bison, and the jackall."[10]

Descriptions of the plains brought back by the Yellowstone Expedition caused white Americans to label the heart of the continent "The Great American Desert." Supported by other reports, the description became fixed in the minds of whites of the period and to a large extent prevented them from settling in the region until after the Civil War. But, as Francis Parkman reveals in *The Oregon Trail*, it was quite a different land to the Lakota once they acquired the horse:

> About noon horsemen suddenly appeared into view on the summit of the neighboring ridge. They descended, and behind them followed a wild procession, hurrying in haste and disorder down the hill and over the plain below; horses, mules, and dogs, heavily-burdened *travaux*, mounted warriors, squaws walking amid the throng, until, as if by magic, a hundred and fifty tall lodges sprung up. Of a sudden the lonely plain was transformed into the site of a miniature city.[11]

Parkman's *The Oregon Trail* is one of the two most extensive accounts of the lives of the plains Indians in the first half of the nineteenth century. The other great work of the period is *North American Indians* by George Catlin.

Although neither Catlin, an artist from Pennsylvania who became enthralled by the plains Indians when he saw a group of them pass through Philadelphia in the early 1830s, nor Parkman, an adventurous member of a prominent Boston family, were immune to white attitudes of their time that labeled Indians as "savages," a term generally applied by whites of the period to all non-white, non-Christian native peoples, both attempted to present an honest portrait of tribal life. And what they found, while there certainly was jealousy, feuds, insanity, fear, greed, prejudice, war, disease, and bad times, as in all cultures, was a generally happy, hospitable people whose camps were pleasant places in which to live.

"Look into our tent, or enter, if you can bear the stifling smoke and the close atmosphere," Parkman besieged his readers.

> There, wedged close together, you will see a circle of stout warriors, passing the pipe around, joking, telling stories, and making themselves merry, after their fashion. We were also infested by little copper-colored naked boys and snake-eyed girls. They would come up to us, muttering certain words, which being interpreted conveyed the concise invitation, "Come and eat." Then we would rise, cursing the pertinacity of Dahcotah hospitality, which allowed scarcely an hour of rest between sun and sun.[12]

Catlin wrote:

> There has gone abroad . . . an opinion that is all too current in the world, that the Indian is necessarily a poor drunken, murderous wretch. I have traveled several years already amongst these people and I have

not had my scalp taken, nor a blow struck me; nor has my property been stolen . . . to the value of a shilling; and that in a country where no man is punishable by law for the crime of stealing; still some of them steal, and murder too; and if white men did not do the same, and that in defiance of the laws of God and man, I might take satisfaction in stigmatizing the Indian character as thievish and murderous. That the Indians in their *native state* are "*drunken*" is false; for they are the only temperance people, literally speaking, that ever I saw in my travels, or ever expect to see . . . for these people manufacture no spirituous liquor themselves, and know nothing of it until it is brought into their country and tendered to them by Christians. That these people are "*naked*" is equally untrue, and as easily disproved; for I am sure that with the paintings I have made . . . and with their beautiful costumes which I have procured . . . I shall be able to establish the fact that many of these people dress, not only with clothes comfortable for any latitude, but that they also dress with some considerable taste and elegance. Nor am I quite sure that they are entitled to the name "*poor*," who live in a boundless country of green fields, with good horses to ride; where they are all joint tenants of the soil, together; where the Great Spirit has supplied them with an abundance of food to eat; where they are all indulging in the pleasures and amusements of a lifetime of idleness and ease, with no business hours to attend to, or professions to learn—where they have no notes in bank or other debts to pay—no taxes, no tithes, no rents, nor beggars to touch and tax the sympathy of their souls at every step they go.[13]

LAKOTA CAMPS were erected along rivers or streams where the people could obtain water and find shelter from the plains weather beneath high banks and wood from the chokecherry, aspen, willow, and cottonwood that grow in such areas. The tipi was the main form of housing, the comforts of which in winter Luther Standing Bear described: "If snow fell heavily, it banked up all around the outside of the tipi, which helped us keep warm. On nights when there was a cold, sleeting rain, it was very pleasant to lie in bed and listen to the storm beating on the sides of the tipi. It even put us to sleep."[14]

Sleeping robes, clothing, and other necessities were stored along the base of the walls. On the poles hung storage bags and a tanned hide on which was painted the history of the family. Called a "brag hide" by some, the skin was to the Indians what paintings and photographs were to white families.

A plains Indians lodge or tipi at the Little Big Horn reenactment.

Backrests made from tripods of willow branches covered by a reed mat or buffalo hide were arranged opposite the entrance. There guests were entertained and the father rested and smoked his pipe, an important part of life for Lakota men. "There may be two good reasons for this," Catlin wrote, "the first of which is, that the idle and leisure life that the Indian leads . . . induces him to look for occupation and amusement in so innocent a luxury, which again further tempts him to its excessive use, from its feeble and harmless effects to the system. There are many weeds and leaves, and barks of trees, which are narcotics, and of spontaneous growth in their countries, which the Indians dry and pulverize, and carry in pouches and smoke to great excess—and which in several languages . . . is called *k'nick k'neck*."[15]

Although smoking appeared to be an amusement and innocent luxury to Catlin, it was far more to the Lakota. "In filling a pipe," according to Black Elk,

all space (represented by the offerings to the powers of the six directions) and all things (represented by the grains of tobacco) are contracted within a single point (the bowl or heart of the pipe) so that the pipe contains, or really *is*, the universe. But since the pipe is the universe, it is also man, and the one who fills a pipe should identify himself with it, thus not only establishing the center of the universe but also his own center; he so "expands" that the six directions of space are actually brought within himself. It is by this "expansion" that man ceases to be a part, a fragment, and becomes whole or holy; he shatters the illusion of separateness.[16]

IN THE WINTER, the tribes would break up into small bands that were easier to feed than larger bands and the people would pass the days listening to tales of creation, love, heroism, and betrayal. In good weather the camp bustled with activity. Everywhere barking dogs roamed, snarling and fighting for scraps of food, while naked children played, racing from tipi to tipi. Women busied themselves with preparing hides, drying meat, picking berries and herbs, digging wild turnips and other roots, and cooking while they gossiped among themselves. Gossip was an important way of asserting social pressure and getting people to follow tribal customs and ways.

While the women busied themselves with domestic chores, men tended their ponies, hunted, fished, mended old weapons and made new ones, smoked, and went on raiding parties. Because women performed all of the hard labor, most whites looked upon them as little more than slaves. Lieutenant Colonel Richard Irving Dodge, a noted frontier officer, wrote in 1877 in *The Plains of the Great West and Their Inhabitants:*

> The life of an Indian woman is a round of wearisome labour. Her marriage is only an exchange of masters. . . . She cooks his [her husband's] food, makes or mends his clothing, dresses skins, dries meat, goes after and saddles his horse. When making a journey, she strikes the lodge, packs the animals, and superintends the march. On arriving at the camping place she unpacks the animals, pitches the lodge, makes the beds, brings wood and water, and does everything that ought to be done.

In Dodge's eyes, the Indian woman was "more absolutely a slave than any negro before the war of the rebellion." But, at the same time, he admitted, "a happier or more contented woman cannot be found," and acknowledged that "the women are not without their weight and influence in all the affairs of the tribe."[17]

Actually, neither sex was looked upon as superior or inferior in Lakota culture. Although men were permitted to have up to six wives, polygamy in no way implied a lower status for women. Instead, it was a way to maintain family and tribal stability by eliminating conflicts caused by wandering husbands. In many instances it was a man's first wife who suggested her husband take a younger wife to lighten her household burden. A second wife also added to the status of the first wife by making her the senior spouse of a wealthy man, since only a wealthy man could afford more than one wife. That economic burden kept all but a very few Lakota men from ever having more than two wives. Sometimes a man would marry two sisters. Such a marriage had the advantage of bringing together two women already bound by family and close friendship.

For their part, women dominated family life. The wife, not the husband, owned the lodge and all of the family's possessions and had the ultimate authority over the children, boys until they reached puberty and girls until they married. Lakota women also had the right to leave their husbands at any time, which Dodge admitted was "a sure remedy against all conjugal ills," and unmarried women had the right to reject arranged marriages.

On the whole, the Lakota woman of the mid-nineteenth century may have led a more comfortable life and had more rights than white women of the period, who could not vote and generally did not own property. As for working as a slave, diaries and letters written by white women of the time reveal how hard they labored. Mary Jane Megquier, who moved to San Francisco during the California Gold Rush, explained the situation in a letter to her daughter in November 1849:

> Some days we have made fifty dollars but I have to work mighty hard, a family of twelve boarders in two small rooms with very few conveniences. We came to this house the third of July. I have not been into the street since. . . . I intend to stay only long enough to make a small pile of the [gold] dust which will not overrun two years . . . it is the most God foresaken country in the world, not one redeeming trait excepting the gold. . . . I do not sit down until after eight o'clock at night and three nights out of the week I have to iron. I do not go to bed until midnight and often until two o'clock.[18]

WITH THE ARRIVAL OF SPRING, the winter bands would gather in a tribal circle to prepare for the year's activities. Each band had its own chiefs and soldiers, but these men had no authority outside of their own group. When the tribal circle was formed, four *wakincuzas* (camp leaders) were chosen by the tribal council to take charge of affairs, such as decisions to move the camp. The wakincuzas were not chiefs, but prominent warriors. Their orders were enforced by the *akicita* (Warrior Society), which acted as a sort of police force. A willingness to follow leaders, though, was never a strong suit of the Lakota.

Parkman noted:

Each village has a chief, who is honored and obeyed only so far as his personal qualities may command respect and fear . . . Courage, address, and enterprise may raise any warrior to the highest honor . . . but when he has reached the dignity of chief . . . let it not be imagined that he assumes any of the outward semblances of rank and honor. He knows too well how frail a tenure he holds his station. . . . Many a man in the village lives better, owns more squaws and more horses, and goes better clad than he. . . . He ingratiates himself with his young men by making them presents, thereby often impoverishing himself. Does he fail to gain their favor, they will set his authority at naught, and may desert him at any moment; for the usages of his people have provided no sanctions by which he may enforce his authority. Very seldom does it happen . . . that a chief attains much power, unless he is the head of a numerous family.[19]

Bravery, generosity, wisdom, and fortitude were the four great virtues of the Lakota. War and, to a lesser degree, the hunt were the main ways to practice them, and the great preoccupations of the tribe, especially the men. War, better described as raids, was a relatively frequent occurrence. Lakota winter counts, calendars that record tribal history from one spring to the next, are full of violent encounters with other tribes. In White Bull's winter count, 1770–1771 is the year an unknown tribe "attacked the camp from both sides"; 1773–1774 the year "they burned the Mandan lodges"; in 1774–1775 "they killed three who went for wood"; in 1776–1777 "they killed a man who went on a hill"; in 1785–1786 "four returned home after counting coup"; and in 1786–1787 "Lone Man, a warrior, came home dead."[20]

Such encounters go on and on through the eighteenth century and most of the nineteenth century. Wars were fought in self-defense; to defend hunting grounds; to obtain horses (the chief measure of wealth among the plains tribes); in retaliation for wrongs, both real and imagined; and for glory.

Although war between plains tribes most often involved what whites would consider small encounters, they could be bloody and involve atrocities. White Bull's winter count records 1779–1780 as the year "Skinned Penis used in the game of Haka winter." Skinned Penis was a Lakota who had been circumcised. When he was killed by a group of Pawnees, his friends hid his body, but the Pawnees found it, cut off his penis, and used it in a game of Haka, a hoop and stick game. Another example occurred in 1795–1796, when "they made Has A Bucket stand up." Has A Bucket was a Lakota who was killed by the Arikaras, who then propped up his body in their village and hung a buffalo paunch water pail from the corpse's hand to mock it.[21]

Generally, though, individual valor was valued more than victory by a tribe. And rarely did two sides fight until one was helpless. To count coup—strike a live enemy with a stick, lance, bow, or rifle—showed more daring and brought more honor than actually slaying him. A man who counted coup before witnesses boasted of it, reveled in public acclaim, and was allowed to wear an upright golden eagle feather as a sign of his feat.

Standing Bear related one such encounter with a party of Pawnees who entered Lakota hunting grounds. He and other braves of his camp rode out to drive off the intruders. When the Pawnee saw the Lakota coming, they fled, all except one man, who became separated from the hunting party and was encircled by the Lakota. "He was a big man and very brave," Standing Bear recalled. "When our men would shoot an arrow at him and it struck, he would break the arrow off and throw it away. If they shot at him and missed, he would pick up the arrows and defy the Sioux to come on."

The Pawnee exhibited such strength and power that even though they outnumbered him the Lakota were afraid of him. Then Standing Bear announced he was going to count coup on the man, and rode up and touched him with his lance. The Pawnee responded by shooting Standing Bear in the arm with an arrow. "After the Pawnee had wounded me," Standing Bear wrote,

> the other men expected to see him get excited, but he did not lose his nerve. As soon as I had passed him with an arrow through my arm, the Pawnee had a second arrow all ready for the next man. The second man was shot in the shoulder, and the third man in the hip. As the last man

touched the enemy, he received an arrow in the back. In this manner the Pawnee shot all four men who had touched him with their lances. We had all gained honor, but we were all wounded. Now that all four of our men had touched the enemy, he was so brave that we withdrew from the field, sparing his life.

On another occasion, Standing Bear remembered a group of Pawnee prisoners brought into his village after a raid. Among the prisoners was a tall, slim youth whom the Lakota boys wanted to play with very much "just so we could touch him." It was the first opportunity that Standing Bear and his friends had to touch an enemy. The Lakota boys coaxed the Pawnee boy out of the tipi where he was being held and asked him to show them how fast he could run, and touched him. Then the chiefs held a council and decided to send the prisoners home. "Each man who had captured a prisoner was to give that person clothing and a horse," Standing Bear wrote. "It cost something to capture a man or woman in those days."[22]

After counting coup, the most praiseworthy act a plains warrior could perform was stealing an enemy's horse from outside his tipi. That was followed by the recovery of an enemy's weapon from the battlefield, the riding-down of an enemy, and finally the slaying of a enemy. Sometimes the warrior who actually killed an enemy received no recognition because others had already counted coup on the warrior involved. It was a concept of war that would leave the plains tribes at a distinct disadvantage when confronted with white armies bent on their destruction by whatever means possible.

SCALPING, the custom that so horrified readers of nineteenth-century Western adventures, was not invented by the Indians. In fact, it probably is as old as the human race. Anthropologists have uncovered evidence of scalping on Bodo man, a predecessor of *Homo sapiens*, and the historical record goes back all the way to the fifth century B.C.E. Herodotus reported that the Parthians took the hair of slain enemies and used it to decorate their weapons and clothing.

A few generations later, the Greek general Xenophon noted that the hair was removed from the heads of some of his men who were attacked while traveling to the Mediterranean Sea, while the Byzantine historian Procopius wrote of the practice among the soldiers of Count Belisarius. After first torturing their captives, some of the count's men removed their scalps "by making a series of short slashes about the victim's skull below the line of the ears, removed the entire upper skin portion of the skull. This they treated with oils and stuffed with padding, making a most grisly trophy."

In the Americas, the tradition may have crossed the Bering Strait with the first migrants. Spanish conquistadors found Caribbean natives removing the heads and hair of their enemies when they arrived in the New World. And Jacques Cartier reported the practice among tribes living along the St. Lawrence River in the sixteenth century.

Whatever its origins, by the nineteenth century, scalping was a tradition on the Great Plains. Both Indians and whites took scalps as trophies. Dating back to the Pilgrims, white governments also frequently encouraged the practice by offering a bounty on Indian scalps. The territorial government of Arizona at one time paid as much as $250 for an Apache scalp.

That human hair in the nineteenth century held a special cultural significance for both whites and Indians that it does not today also played a role in the taking of scalps. Hair was looked upon as a special, deep connection to the person to whom it belonged, a place where the human spirit was housed. So white women grew their hair to fantastic lengths, wove miniature pictures using different colors and textures of hair, exchanged bracelets and other gifts made of hair, and preserved the locks of their children, lovers, and spouses in elaborate frames. White men wore watch chains of braided hair and sent clippings to their wives and lovers as signs of devotion. Generally, though, white men who fussed too much with their hair were derided and drew speculative glances. Custer was labeled "Fanny" by fellow cadets at West Point because of the length of his hair. When he began to use a scented pomade, they called him "Cinnamon" and later "Curly," a somewhat ironic choice of names in light of the way his fate collided with that of Crazy Horse, who as a boy also was called Curly.[23]

Unlike whites, the Indians admired beautiful hair on both women and men. They tied locks of hair representing the people of the tribe to the shirts worn by the *wakincuzas*, the prominent warriors who had sworn to protect the people of their camp. They also presented the scalp of a warrior who had died in battle to a relative of that fallen warrior. The gift was given because the hair was believed to hold the spiritual essence of the lost relative.

Such was the world into which Tasunke Witko—Crazy Horse—was born. It was an old, richly cultured world well suited to its environment; a world that, though at times could be dangerous, full of sadness and pain, also was a place of great love, contentment, and happiness, far more so than the world of many whites.

3

INDIAN BOYHOOD

CRAZY HORSE was born sometime between 1838 and 1840. He Dog reported on July 7, 1930: "I and Crazy Horse were both born in the same year and at the same season of the year. . . . I am now ninety-two years old." That would mean Crazy Horse was born in 1838. Chips, also known as Horn Chips and Encouraging Bear, spiritual adviser to Crazy Horse, reported that the war chief was born in the fall "in the year in which the band to which he belonged, the Oglalas, stole one hundred horses." According to winter counts kept by Cloud Shield and White Bull, the year would have been 1840.[1]

The medicine man's remarks are strengthened by a story about Crazy Horse's death in the September 14, 1877, *New York Sun* in which Worm, the war chief's father, is described as lamenting: "Crazy Horse was his last and only living child. He had another boy, equally brave and renowned, but he was killed by the Shoshoni. Neither had any children. . . . His family and name would become extinct with his own death, and he was sixty-six years of age. His son would have been thirty-seven, having been born on the South Cheyenne River in the fall of 1840."[2]

Like the year, the location of Crazy Horse's birth is also open to some debate. The *Sun* story gives it as the South Cheyenne River. But that could be a mistake caused by confusion involving Rapid Creek, a southern tributary of the Cheyenne River. All other sources point to either Rapid Creek, near present-day Rapid City, South Dakota, or near Bear Butte outside Sturgis, South Dakota. Chips said: "Crazy Horse was born at the foot of Bear Butte, near the present Fort Meade," which is just outside of Sturgis.[3]

GLIMPSES OF Crazy Horse's future as a renowed warrior prone to powerful emotions are evident in his lineage. He has been described as a descendant of a line of holy men named Crazy Horse. While that is possible, Oglala sources who actually knew him do not indicate that his father or grandfather were holy men. Neither do they reveal Crazy Horse to be the name of Crazy Horse's grandfather. Chips said only that Crazy Horse's father was named Crazy Horse and that his "grandfather, Makes The Song, had a dream that Crazy Horse would be called Crazy Horse."[4] The name itself denotes more a spirited horse than one that has gone mad.

Worm, the name taken by Crazy Horse's father after he passed on the name Crazy Horse, probably was born in 1811 and his mother, Rattle Blanket Woman, in 1815.[5] His mother may have been a member of the One Horn or Lone Horn family, leaders of the Miniconjou, who are often mentioned in winter counts. If she was a member of the One Horn family, her brother, One Horn, like Crazy Horse three decades later, was a shirt wearer.[6]

George Catlin painted One Horn's portrait during his 1832 visit to Fort Pierre, South Dakota. Catlin described him as a

> superior chief and leader, a middle-aged man, of middling stature, with a noble countenance, and a figure almost equalling the Apollo . . . who has risen rapidly to the highest honours in the tribe, from his own extraordinary merits, even at so early an age. . . . This extraordinary man, before he was raised to the dignity of chief, was the renowned of his tribe for his athletic achievements. In the chase he was foremost; he could run down a buffalo, which he often had done, on his own legs, and drive his arrow to the heart. He was the fleetest in the tribe; and in the races he had run, he had always taken the prize. It was proverbial in his tribe, that Ha-wan-je-tah's [One Horn] bow never was drawn in vain, and his wigwam was abundantly furnished with scalps that he had taken from his enemies' heads in battle.[7]

Blaming himself for the accidental death of his only son, One Horn in 1836 mounted his favorite war pony and with his bow in hand dashed off at full speed across the plains vowing, Catlin wrote, to "slay the first living thing that fell in his way, be it man or beast, friend or foe."

No one in the camp dared follow One Horn until his horse returned covered with blood and with arrows in its flanks. A party of warriors trailed the horse back to the mangled body of One Horn lying next to a bull buffalo. According to Catlin:

> He had incensed the animal by shooting a number of arrows into him. The chief had dismounted and turned his horse loose, having given it a couple of arrows from his bow, which sent it home at full speed. He then had thrown away his bow and quiver, encountering the infuriated buffalo with his knife alone. Many of the bones of the chief were broken. He was gored and stamped to death, but his huge antagonist lay by his side, weltering in blood from a hundred wounds made by the chief's long, two-edged knife.[8]

THE MARRIAGE OF Worm and Rattle Blanket Woman produced two children: a daughter born in 1838 whose name has been lost to history, and Crazy Horse. The marriage ended in 1844. It is possible that Rattle Blanket Woman terminated the union and returned to her Miniconjou relatives, since Crazy Horse retained close ties with the Miniconjou all of his life. A February 2, 1875, story in the *Omaha Weekly Bee* even identified him as a Miniconjou. However, Victoria Conroy, the granddaughter of Big Woman, a paternal aunt of Crazy Horse, wrote in 1934 that Rattle Blanket Woman hanged herself after Worm's brother was killed in a raid on the Crows.[9]

In the spring of 1844, an Oglala raiding party set out from the Platte River to steal horses from the Crows. While traveling across the Laramie Plains of southeastern Wyoming, they were discovered by their intended victims. During the running fight that ensued, as many as thirty-eight Oglala were killed, among them He Crow, leader of the raiding party and the younger brother of Worm. According to Conroy, Rattle Blanket Woman "thought a good deal of her young brother-in-law [and] in her grief she took a rope and herself to a tree." Hanging was a common method of suicide among Lakota women.

Left with two young children, Worm probably remarried soon after Rattle Blanket Woman hanged herself or ended the marriage by returning to her Miniconjou family. Like some other Lakotas who could afford it, he eventually married two sisters, siblings of the Brulé Lakota chief Spotted Tail. One of the women bore him a son, Little Hawk, in about 1846.[10]

FOLLOWING THE LAKOTA CUSTOM, Crazy Horse had different names at different times in his life. Names were given to a person for a variety of reasons, including to honor a relative, commemorate a father's deeds in battle, or in recognition of a particular event, personal habits, appearance, or actions.

Chips reports that Crazy Horse's birth name was Light Hair. He Dog says that Crazy Horse was called Curly or Curly Hair until he was about ten years old, when Worm changed his name to His Horse On Sight (also translated as Horse Stands In Sight, His Horse Looking, and His Horse Partly Showing), in recognition of his son's role in the capture of a wild horse in the Sandhills of Nebraska.

But that name did not stick, and finally Worm passed on the name of Crazy Horse. He Dog says that happened after Crazy Horse showed bravery in a fight with the Arapahos when he was about eighteen years old. Chips says it happened a few years later, when Crazy Horse was about twenty-one years old, and in a fight with the Shoshone.[11] Since Crazy Horse was a name that was passed down from father to son, it would seem that He Dog and Chips are correct about the way Curly became Crazy Horse. Many Lakota fathers would change a son's name after he performed a noteworthy feat. That Worm followed the practice is evident from the fact that he tried to change Curly's name after his son's capture of a wild horse. Black Elk, though, claims that Crazy Horse's name came from a vision the war leader had as a teenager. In that vision, Curly's "horse was standing still there, and yet it danced around like a horse made only of shadow, and that is how he got his name, which does not mean that his horse was crazy or wild, but that in his vision it danced around in that queer way."[12]

Since both He Dog and Chips were close friends of Crazy Horse, their stories about the origin of Crazy Horse's name probably are the more accurate. The variations in them might be attributed to old age. Both men were interviewed long after the fact and could have

Interviews with Crazy Horse's longtime friends He Dog and Chips (here with his wife) provide valuable information about his life.

confused the details. Black Elk's story of Crazy Horse's name came to him secondhand from his father after he was an adult, by which times Crazy Horse was dead and passing into legend.

During his lifetime, Crazy Horse also is said to have carried the nicknames Crushes Man, possibly in reference to some feat in battle, and Buys A Bad Woman, probably a reference to his relationship with Black Buffalo Woman, an affair that nearly got him killed by a jealous husband.[13]

As a boy, Crazy Horse had very fine, sandy brown hair and a complexion so light he is said to have been mistaken for a white child by many settlers heading west past Fort Laramie in the 1840s and early 1850s, a strange irony in light of the way he resisted the white world his entire life. According to numerous accounts by people who knew or met him, Crazy Horse would grow to be a man of medium stature, about 5 feet, 8 inches tall and 140 pounds, with a narrow face devoid of prominent cheekbones and a sharp, straight nose. Chips said: "He was born with light hair and was called by the Indians the Light Haired Boy. His hair was always light. It did not reach the ground . . .

but did reach below his hips. . . . Crazy Horse was a man small in stature, rather light in frame and weight, light complexion."[14]

Mrs. Charles Tackett, the wife of a scout and clerk at Camp Robinson who encountered Crazy Horse after his surrender, described him as

> a very handsome young man. . . . He was not so dark; he had hazel eyes, nice long light brown hair. His scalp lock was ornamented with beads and hung clear to his waist; his braids were wrapped with fur. He was partly wrapped in a broad blanket, his leggings were also navy blue broad cloth, his moccasins were beaded. He was about medium height and slender.[15]

Although it would seem normal for a light-haired person to have hazel eyes, Short Bull, a friend of Crazy Horse, contradicts Tackett's description by giving the war chief black eyes.[16]

ALONG WITH Crazy Horse's relatively slight stature went a quiet, shy, many report "strange" or "queer" personality that avoided attention off the battlefield but nevertheless inspired awe, excitement, jealousy, and fear. Perhaps his mother's suicide or abandonment of her family when Crazy Horse was a young child, and his light skin, which would have set him off and so could have inspired teasing by other boys, played roles in his shyness and "strange" nature. Like a boy today who feels he does not fit in and seeks to overcome the pain, anger, and loneliness that grow out of such a situation by throwing himself into sports or rock 'n' roll, Crazy Horse might have sought relief and acceptance by becoming a renowned warrior. Chips said: "When we were young all we thought about was going to war with some other nation; all tried to get their names up the highest, and whoever did so was the principal man in the nation; and Crazy Horse wanted to get to the highest rank."[17]

He Dog said: "He never spoke in council and attended very few. There was no special reason for this; it was just his nature. He was a very quiet man except when there was fighting." Short Buffalo reported that Crazy Horse "usually wore an Iroquois shell necklace; this was the only ornament he wore." He also says the war chief had eyes that "hardly ever looked straight at a man, but they didn't miss much that was going on all the same," while Chips notes that other

Lakota kept their distance from Crazy Horse and "had no use for him except when there was fighting."[18]

The most detailed description of Crazy Horse's character comes from Black Elk, though some of it may be the rose-tinted memories of old age and the legends that sprout around the famous after their death. This is evident when he reported, in the 1930s, that "everybody liked" Crazy Horse, which is contrary to Chips's assessment of the war chief and later contradicted by Black Elk himself. According to Chips: "Crazy Horse was not accounted good for anything among the Indians but to make war; he was expected to do that; he was set apart in their minds to make war, and that was his business."[19]

Envy and jealousy are twin emotions that, to varying degrees, shadow everybody who obtains notoriety. They frequently are intensified by a shy personality misinterpreted as aloof. While it is likely that Chips goes too far when he says the Lakota had no use for Crazy Horse except when there was fighting, there always were factions and individuals within the tribe who were envious of and angered by the war chief's fame.

Black Elk reports that Crazy Horse sometimes summoned him to eat and

> would say things to tease me, but I would not say anything back, because I think I was a little afraid of him. I was not afraid that he would hurt me; I was just afraid. Everybody felt that way about him, for he was a queer man and would go about the village without noticing people or saying anything. In his own tipi he would joke. . . . But around the village he hardly ever noticed anybody, except little children. All the Lakotas like to dance and sing; but he never joined a dance, and they say nobody ever heard him sing. But everybody liked him, and they would do anything he wanted or go anywhere he said. . . . He never wanted to have many things for himself, and did not have many ponies like a chief. They say that when game was scarce and the people were hungry, he would not eat at all. He was a queer man. Maybe he was always part way into that world of his vision.[20]

CRAZY HORSE SPENT his childhood in an immediate family that was smaller than the typical white family of the mid-nineteenth century. "If there were anything like an equal proportion of deaths amongst the Indian children, that is found in the civilized portions of the world,

the Indian country would long since have been depopulated . . . "
Catlin noted. "It is a very rare occurrence for an Indian woman to be
'blessed' with more than four or five children during her life; when in
civilized communities it is no uncommon thing for a woman to be
the mother of ten or twelve."[21]

Considered the greatest gifts from Wakan Tanka, the Great Spirit,
children were doted upon by the Lakota. Roots of the freedom Crazy
Horse enjoyed and fought so hard to preserve can be seen in Parkman's description of the behavior of his Indian hosts toward their
children:

> Both he and his squaw, like most other Indians, were very fond of their
> children, whom they indulged to excess, and never punished except in
> extreme cases, when they would throw a bowl of cold water over them.
> Their offspring became sufficiently undutiful and disobedient under
> this system of education, which tends not a little to foster that wild idea
> of liberty and utter intolerance of restraint which lie at the very founda-
> tion of the Indian character.[22]

White culture's misunderstanding and disapproval of Indian ways
are evident in Parkman's use of the words "undutiful" and "disobe-
dient," and in the phrases "wild idea of liberty" and "utter intoler-
ance of restraint." But in truth Sioux children were taught to be
extremely dutiful to their people. The training of a Sioux child in the
ways of his or her people began while the child was still in the womb.
George Eastman, a Santee Dakota Sioux who was born in 1858, educated at Dartmouth University, and served as a doctor on the Pine
Ridge Reservation during the 1890s, wrote:

> The expectant parents conjointly bent all their efforts to the task of giv-
> ing the new-comer the best they could gather from a long line of ances-
> tors. A pregnant Indian woman would often choose one of the greatest
> characters of her family and tribe as a model for her child. This hero
> was daily called to mind. She would gather from tradition all his noted
> deeds and daring exploits, rehearsing them to herself when alone. In
> order that the impression might be more distinct, she avoided company.
> She isolated herself as much as possible, and wandered in solitude, not
> thoughtlessly, but with an eye to the impression given by grand and
> beautiful scenery.[23]

From birth, a Sioux boy was serenaded with lullabies that told of
wonderful exploits in war and the hunt. He might learn the story of
his people almost every evening as he grew older, and he also was

regaled with tales of the tribe's triumphs and sufferings and required to repeat them. According to Eastman, who might be romanticizing his own boyhood a bit: "This sort of teaching at once enlightens the boy's mind and stimulates his ambition. His conception of his own future career becomes a vivid and irresistible force. Whatever there is for him to learn must be learned; whatever qualifications are necessary to a truly great man he must seek at any expense of danger and hardships."[24]

EASTMAN ALSO is the source for the earliest anecdote involving Crazy Horse. Eastman heard the story in the 1890s from Lakota elders on the Pine Ridge Reservation. Whether it is true or legend is impossible to determine. But the tale does reflect generosity, one of the great virtues of the Lakota that was exhibited by Crazy Horse in later life. A certain credence is added, too, by the doubt Eastman expresses over the excesses of one storyteller. And then, as every parent is well aware, children are capable of saying or doing practically anything, so the story could be true on that basis alone.

The incident supposedly occurred during a severe winter when Curly was four or five years old. The band to which his family belonged was snowed in and very short of food. Buffalo were not to be found. But Curly's father was a tireless hunter who went out every day. Finally, after many days of hunting, he returned home with two pronghorn.

No sooner had his father appeared with the meat than Curly ran off to spread the word. Without the knowledge of his parents, he invited all the old people in camp to come to his family's tipi. Old men and women lined up outside the Crazy Horse lodge, and Curly's mother was forced to distribute nearly all of the meat, keeping only enough for two meals for her family. The next day, when Curly's stomach began to growl and he asked for meat, his mother had to tell him that the old people had taken it all. "Remember my son," she added, "they went home singing praises in your name, not my name or your father's. You must be brave. You must live up to your reputation."[25]

As SIOUX BOYS grew older, games became an important part of their education. According to Black Elk:

> All the boys from five or six years up were playing war. The little boys would gather together from the different bands of the tribe and fight each other with mud balls that they threw with willow sticks. And the big boys played the game called Throwing-Them-Off-Their-Horses, which is a battle all but the killing; and sometimes they got hurt. The horsebacks from the different bands would line up and charge upon each other, yelling; and when the ponies came together on the run, they would rear and flounder and scream in a big dust, and the riders would seize each other, wrestling until one side had lost all its men, for those who fell upon the ground were counted dead. . . .
>
> We were always naked when we played it, just as the warriors are when they go into battle if it is not too cold, because they are swifter without clothes. . . . I thought that when we all grew up and were big together, maybe we could kill all the Wasichus [white men] or drive them far away from our country.[26]

While still a boy, Crazy Horse most likely also was initiated to the real horrors of war. But how, where, or when that may have occurred is impossible to know. As with his contemporary White Bull, it might have happened after a failed raid by another tribe on his village. White Bull was only six years old when a raiding party came to his village one fall day to steal horses. He heard the yells and shooting, and when it was over saw blue beads and a brass armlet taken from two dead enemies.

The trophies aroused the curiosity of all the boys in the village. The next day they were told they could go and see the two dead enemies from whom the items had been taken. White Bull followed the bigger boys and was startled when he saw the two enemies standing upright on the plains. Then the adult warriors laughed and told him: "Do not fear! They are dead." The frozen bodies had been propped up with sticks by the adult warriors, who urged the boys to go on and "count coup" on their enemies.[27]

Other boys' games were Buffalo Hunt and Fire Throwing. Buffalo Hunt used a cactus out of which the center had been cut to mark the buffalo's heart. One boy would carry the cactus on a stick, while the other boys would shoot arrows at it. When an arrow pierced the heart of the "buffalo," the boy carrying it would chase the marksman until he poked him in the buttocks with the cactus. In Fire Throwing, teams of boys would set fire to a brush pile, from which each member of a team would pick a few flaming sticks. The boys would then "attack" each other with the sticks. The object of the game was to drive the other team away from the brush pile.[28]

The most popular of all boys' occupations, though, was shooting their bows and arrows. In one game, an arrow was shot randomly into the air. Before the arrow struck the ground, the boys playing the game would note its direction and fire their arrows in the same manner. The boy whose arrow struck closest to the first arrow was the winner. "It was considered out of place to shoot by first sighting the object aimed at," noted Eastman. "This was usually impracticable in actual life, because the object was almost always in motion, while the hunter himself was often upon the back of a pony at full gallop. Therefore, it was the off-hand shot that the Indian boy sought to master."[29]

THE HORSE was so important to the Lakota that every boy whose family could afford it was given a pony of his own with which to learn horsemanship as soon as his legs were long enough to straddle the animal. Boys whose families were too poor to provide them with a pony shared those of more fortunate youngsters. The loaning of horses was common even among Lakota adults. As boys grew older, they also were charged with caring for their family's herd. In that way, every boy was guaranteed to grow up with the knowledge of horses he would need to prosper as an adult.

Several sources report that Crazy Horse—or Curly, as he was then known—was given a pony with all the trappings by his father while very young. Eastman says he became a fine horseman while still a boy. It is a claim that would appear to be supported by the efforts of Worm to change the name of his son to His Horse On Sight after Curly was involved in the capture of a wild horse when he was about ten years old.[30]

Capture of a wild horse was an event worthy of a name change because it was so difficult. Even though the horse played a central role in the culture of the plains tribes, the Indians never had an extensive breeding program. Herds were replenished by stealing horses from other tribes or by capturing wild horses. Stealing was the preferred method because it allowed a man to obtain several horses at one time.[31]

Catlin describes the habits of wild horses that made capturing one such an accomplishment. "There is no other animal on the prairies so wild and so sagacious as the horse; and none other so difficult to come up with," he wrote. "So remarkably keen is their eye, that they will generally run 'at sight,' when they are a mile distance; being, no doubt, able to distinguish the character of the enemy that is approaching when at threat distance; and when in motion, will seldom stop short of three or four miles."[32]

Standing Bear remembers the capture of a wild horse by his father. It started when word arrived in camp that horses had been spotted nearby. As an old man moved through the village urging the men to wait until everybody was ready and not ride off on their own, Standing Bear's father rode to a nearby creek and returned with a willow stick about fifteen feet in length. He tied a thin strip of buckskin to one end of the stick and another piece about four feet from the first. Then he made a loop with a long, braided rawhide rope and tied it to the strings.

After the men had prepared their willow sticks, they headed off after the horses. As they neared the herd they split up to circle it at a distance of two or three miles and drive the animals to the men with the willow sticks, all of whom remained hidden behind a hill. While they waited, the men with the sticks ran their horses back and forth to warm them up for the chase, and then moved to a spot where they could watch the herd without being seen.

"There were forty or fifty of them, all busy eating the green grass," Standing Bear recalled. "Among them was one animal which would raise his head very high very often and look all around in a very proud way. My father pointed out this particular animal to me. 'Do you see that horse with his head in the air?' he said to me. 'Well, that is the stallion—the leader of the herd.'"

While the men with the sticks watched, the drivers appeared to the west. The herd immediately made a dash to the north, where another party of drivers appeared, causing them to wheel to the south, where a third group rode forward, leaving the herd no choice for escape but the east.

"The animals had already run quite a distance and were not very fresh for a long chase," Standing Bear wrote. "Our men with the sticks were all ready for them; our horses were fresh and anxious to go, so our men whipped up and gave chase. . . . As we went up a hill and down the other side, I observed my father was after a buckskin horse, a very pretty animal. It was a good runner in spite of the fact that it had already covered considerable ground."

When the horses reached the catchers, the men raised their willow sticks, threw the rawhide loops over a horse's head, and gave it a jerk. The buckskin strings broke and the ropes tightened around the horse's neck, cutting off the wind of the exhausted animal, and causing it to stagger and fall. Once a horse was down, a catcher would tie a rope halter-style around its nose and wrap the other end around his own horse, from tail to shoulders, so that when the wild horse jumped to his feet, he was tied to the other animal, and was pulling against its own nose.[33]

Although Curly may have been so good with horses that his father was moved to change his name to His Horse On Sight, the adult Crazy Horse is said to have been very hard on his animals. According to Black Elk:

> Horses couldn't go far with him for some reason. He was small and slender. Warriors think that the stone he carried with him had something to do with this. [Chips had given Crazy Horse a small stone on a thong that he wore under his left arm when he went into battle.] They think he had a vision about a rock and that he was as heavy as a rock. That's why no horse could pack him.[34]

AS A YOUNG BOY, Curly also would have accompanied his father on buffalo hunts during which he would scout the herd, tend the packhorses, and watch the hunters. In that way he was kept out of harm's way while gaining valuable training in the dangerous art of hunting buffalo from horseback with a bow and arrow. Black Elk recalled the end of a hunt when he was a young boy: "When the butchering was all over, they hung the meat across the horses' backs and fastened it with strips of fresh bison hide. On the way back to the village all the hunting horses were loaded, and we little boys who could not wait for the feast helped ourselves to all the raw liver we wanted. Nobody got cross when we did this."

Back at camp, the women set up drying racks made out of forked sticks and long poles, and laid down blankets of leaves. When the hunters arrived in camp, they would throw the meat down on the leaves. Then the advisers who had planned the hunt retired to the council lodge and people came from all directions bringing gifts of meat. The advisers would thank the people and sing for those who had brought the gifts. Then they would eat their fill and send the crier out to call the people to return for what remained of the meat.

After the women had cut the meat into thin strips and hung them on the drying racks the people would feast, dance, and sing all night, while the young boys would build grass tipis on the edge of the village and pretend they were the enemy. "We had an adviser, and when it got dark he would order us to go and steal some dried meat from the big people," Black Elk remembered.

> He would hold a stick up to us and we had to bite off a piece of it. If we bit a big piece we had to get a big piece of meat, and if we bit a little piece, we did not have to get so much. Then we started for the big people's village, crawling on our bellies, and when we got back without getting caught, we would have a big feast and dance and make kill talks, telling of our brave deeds like warriors.

In the summer, the kill talks would be followed by a chapped breast dance. The adviser would select the boy whose chest was sunburned the worst from not wearing a shirt during the day and have him lead the dance while the other boys sang: "I have a chapped breast. My breast is red. My breast is yellow." Sometimes, too, the adviser would put dry sunflower seeds on the wrists of his "warriors" and light them. "We had to let them burn clear down to the skin," Black Elk recalled. "They hurt and made sores, but if we knocked them off or cried Owh!, we would be called women."[35]

With other Lakota boys, Curly also on occasion would wait in the field for orphaned buffalo calves to return, searching for their mothers. The boys would then mimic the adult hunters by chasing calves and lassoing them or driving them into camp. After one successful hunt, Eastman reports, the older boys teased Curly into riding one of the larger calves. Surrounded by shouting and laughing boys on their ponies, he somehow managed to hang onto the calf until it tired. Whether the incident actually happened cannot be determined. It seems possible, though, since quiet and shy boys such as Curly have been known to accept the dares of older boys to fit in.[36]

4

MANIFEST DESTINIES

By the time of Curly's birth, the vast majority of white Americans subscribed to the belief that the history of the world was a progressive phenomenon marked by a series of steps or turning points that had brought the human race ever closer to realizing the ultimate ideals of humanity—the equality, fraternity, and liberty of the French Revolution. And at the pinnacle of that progress, as the culmination of all history in the minds of white Americans, stood the United States. "This is his chosen land," the Reverend Benjamin Tefft announced in 1845, echoing a sentiment that was constantly repeated during the period. "For this He has been for ages watching and preparing. . . . All climes and countries have been working for us. The elements of a glorious order of civilization are now ready."[1]

Naturally, there were some dissidents among the faithful. Henry David Thoreau dared to ask: "Is a democracy, such as we know it, the last improvement possible in government?" But, as usual, Thoreau stood in the minority of a nation that believed it was a divine gift to the world. As essayist Thomas Low Nichols noted: "We were taught every day and in every way that ours was the freest, the happiest, and soon to be the greatest and most powerful country in the world. . . . We read it in our books and newspapers, heard it in sermons, speeches, and orations, thanked God for it in our prayers, and devoutly believed it always."[2]

White America's belief in its destiny poised it to transform the continent in countless, far-reaching ways as the nineteenth century approached its midpoint. By the end of the 1840s more than nine thousand miles of railroad track had been laid and the nation's first telegraph line strung between Washington, D.C., and Baltimore, Maryland. Charles Goodyear had learned how to vulcanize rubber; the first air conditioner was installed in a Broadway theater and chewing gum sold commercially for the first time; gold was discovered in California; and the word "millionaire" was coined.

During the 1840s, Thoreau also moved into his cabin at Walden Pond; James Fenimore Cooper published *The Pathfinder* and *The Deerslayer*; Edgar Allan Poe, *The Raven and Other Poems*; Herman Melville, *Typee*; and Stephen Foster, "Susanna." The University of Notre Dame was chartered, and the Smithsonian Institution was dedicated. Thomas Edison was born near Cleveland, Ohio, and coal baron Henry Clay Frick near Pittsburgh.

On the political front, William H. Harrison, James K. Polk, and Zachary Taylor were elected to the presidency; Texas gained its independence from Mexico, and the United States fought a war with Mexico; the slave Dred Scott filed a lawsuit to obtain his freedom; and the journalist John L. O'Sullivan captured the mood of the nation in a single sentence when he wrote in 1845 that nothing must interfere with the push west and "the fulfillment of our *manifest destiny* to overspread the continent allotted by Providence for the free development of our yearly multiplying millions."[3]

But such "progress" came at a heavy price to the freedom paid so much lip service in the press and from the pulpit. In sharp contrast to the mostly contented lives that Catlin reported the plains Indians living, white Americans existed in a near constant state of struggle, agitation, and expectation that left them no time to enjoy their labors. Michel Chevalier, a French engineer who traveled through the country in the late 1830s, caught the mood in his 1839 book *Society, Manners and Politics in the United States*:

> The manners and customs are altogether those of a working, busy society. At the age of fifteen years, a man is engaged in business; at twenty-one he is established, he has his farm, his workshop, his counting-room, or his office, in a word his employment, whatever it may be. He now also takes a wife, and at twenty-two is the father of a family, and consequently has a powerful stimulus to excite him to industry. A man

who has no profession, and . . . who is not married, enjoys little consideration; he . . . who contributes his share to augment the national wealth and increase the numbers of the population, he only is looked upon with respect and favour. The American is educated with the idea that he will have some particular occupation, that he is to be a farmer, artisan, manufacturer, merchant, speculator, lawyer, physician, or minister, perhaps all in succession, and that, if he is active and intelligent, he will make his fortune. He has no conception of living without a profession, even when his family is rich, for he sees nobody about him, not engaged in business. The man of leisure is a variety of the human species, of which the Yankee does not suspect the existence, and he knows that if rich today, his father may be ruined tomorrow. Besides the father himself is engaged in business . . . and does not think of dispossessing himself of his fortune; if the son wishes to have one at present, let him make it himself!

From the moment he gets up, the American is at his work, and he is engaged in it till the hour of sleep. Pleasure is never permitted to interrupt his business; public affairs only have the right to occupy a few moments. Even meal-time is not for him a period of relaxation . . . it is only a disagreeable interruption of business, an interruption to which he yields because it cannot be avoided, but which he abridges as much as possible. In the evening, if no political meeting requires his attendance, if he does not go to discuss some question of public interest, or to a religious meeting, he sits at home, thoughtful and absorbed in his meditations, whether on the transactions of the day or the projects of the morrow. He refrains from business on Sunday, because his religion commands it, but it also requires him to abstain from all amusement and recreation, music, cards, dice, or billiards, under penalty of sacrilege. On Sunday, an American would not venture to receive his friends; his services would not consent to it. . . . Nothing is therefore, more melancholy than the seventh day in this country; after such a Sunday, the labour of Monday is a delightful pastime.[4]

By the time of Curly's birth, too, most white Americans long believed that the Indian was inferior and destined to vanish in the face of white Christendom. European diseases and warfare, aided by such things as blankets infected with smallpox that the British used as a form of germ warfare, and bounties paid for Indian scalps, so rapidly decimated native populations that the image of the vanishing Indian was accepted by the majority of whites as early as the American Revolution. The tragedy of the last living member of a tribe was a staple in American literature beginning with the poems of Philip Freneau in the 1780s and made its mark on world literature with the publication of James Fenimore Cooper's *The Last of the Mohicans* in 1826.[5]

White America's image of the Indian can be traced to the arrival of the *Nina*, *Pinta*, and *Santa Maria* in the New World and the picture of the "good Indian" and the "bad Indian" created by Columbus. The "good Indian," while lacking in technology, was generous, pleasant, and enjoyed life. Sounding amazingly like Catlin almost 350 years later, the explorer wrote:

> They are so guileless and so generous with all they possess, that no one would believe it who has not seen it. They refuse nothing that they possess, if it be asked of them; on the contrary, they invite any one to share it and display as much love as if they would give their hearts. They are content with whatever trifle of whatever kind that may be given to them, whether it be of value or valueless.[6]

In contrast, Columbus created the "bad Indian," the hostile and depraved "red devils" the *Bismarck Tribune* would report massacred Colonel Custer, when he passed on a hearsay story about "Carib," an island inhabited by "a people who are regarded in all islands as very fierce and who eat human flesh. They have many canoes with which they range through all the islands of India and pillage and take whatever they can."[7]

Depending on their personal needs and how they viewed their own society or conditions, the Spanish, French, English, and white Americans who followed Columbus used the image of the "good Indian" or the "bad Indian" as it suited their purpose. Writing in the aftermath of a war that grew out of the Jamestown colony's continued encroachment on Powhatan land, a Virginia poet in 1622 proclaimed the Indians as "Rooted in Evill, and opposed in Good; errors of nature, of inhumane Birth, The very dregs, garbage and spanne of Earth." Three years later, Samuel Purchas, another Virginian, wrote of the Indians living across the James River as a bad people, "having little of humanitie but shape, ignorant of Civilitie, of Arts, of Religion; more brutish than the beasts they hunt, more wild and unmanly than that unmanned wild country, which they range rathen then inhabite; captivated also to Satans tyranny in foolish pieties, mad impieties, wicked idlenesse, busie and bloudy wickednesse."[8]

Depending upon the need, images of the "good Indian" and the "bad Indian" could appear in the same person. Seeking donations for the conversion of the Indians to Christianity, Alexander Whitaker, a minister in Virginia, resorted to the "bad Indian" and hearsay evidence in his 1613 pamphlet *Goode Newes from Virginia*, when he described the people he met as "naked slaves of the divell" who "serve the divell for feare, after a most base manner, sacrificing sometimes (as I have heere heard) their own Children to him. . . . Their priests . . . are none other but such our English witches are." But lest such bad images keep whites from contributing to his cause, Whitaker quickly switched to the "good Indian" and added: "Let us not think that these men are so simple as some have supposed them: for they are bodie lustie, strong, and very nimble: They are very understanding generation, quick of apprehension suddaine in their dispatches, subtile in their dealings, exquisite in their inventions, and industrious in their labour."[9]

Parkman continued the dual tradition more than 230 years after Whitaker when he wrote of the great hospitality of the Oglalas who dragged him from feast to feast. Hospitality often was one of the first impressions that whites had of the Indians, at least until the whites encroached too much on Indian land. As one Jamestown colonist noted in 1607: "The [native] people used our men well untill they found they begann to plant & fortefye. Then they fell to skyrmishing & kylled 3 of our people."[10]

So, after regaling his readers with the hospitality of the Oglala, Parkman turned on the plains tribes, hardening his views to proclaim:

> For the most part, a civilized white man can discover very few points of sympathy between his own nature and that of an Indian. With every disposition to do justice to their good qualities, he must be conscious that an impassable gulf lies between him and his red brethren. Nay, so alien to himself do they appear, that having breathed for a few months the magic air of this region, he begins to look upon them as a troublesome and dangerous species of wild beast, and if expedient, he could shoot them with as little compunction as they themselves would experience after performing the same office upon him.[11]

New York Tribune publisher Horace Greeley was even more blunt and derogatory in his assessment of the Indians. He summarized the views of most whites toward the plains tribes when he wrote in *An Overland Journey, from New York to San Francisco in the Summer of 1859:*

> To the prosaic observer, the average Indian of the woods and prairies is a being who does little credit to human nature—a slave of appetite and sloth, never emancipated from the tyranny of one animal passion save by the more ravenous demands of another. As I passed over those magnificent bottoms of the Kansas which form the reservations of the Delawares, Potawatamies, etc., constituting the very best corn-lands on earth, and saw their owners sitting around the doors of their lodges at the height of the planting season and in as good, bright planting weather as sun and soil ever made, I could not help saying, "These people must die out—there is no help for them. God has given this earth to those who will subdue and cultivate it, and it is vain to struggle against His righteous decree."[12]

ON THE NORTHERN PLAINS and in the Rocky Mountains, the point guards for white America's restless energy, expectations, desires, and prejudices were the mountain men who headed west in the 1820s and early 1830s. According to White Bull's winter count, the Lakota first came in contact with traders from 1765 to 1767, the year "when we first had knives,"[13] a reference to steel knives acquired from an English trader. But contact remained relatively minimal until the appearance of the mountain men who headed west in search of beaver, adventure, escape from the confines of society, or the pain of a broken heart. Mixed in with the mountain men were traders carrying rifles, beads, household goods, and whiskey, followed by government explorers seeking to secure the nation's right to the Missouri River country and the Pacific Northwest.

The abundance of worldly goods that the traders dangled before the plains tribes with the promise of better times was so powerful that many Indians quickly succumbed to the point where they were willing to threaten their successful way of life in order to acquire the products of the white man's world, especially whiskey.

It is commonly believed that buffalo were plentiful throughout the plains before professional market hunters began slaughtering them in the early 1870s. The commercial exploitation and annihilation of the buffalo, however, began at least fifty years earlier. It started when white Americans discovered the fine warming qualities of carriage robes made from buffalo hides and the tastiness of buffalo tongues. That led the fur companies to shift their sights from beaver to buffalo. As early as 1825, an estimated 25,000 buffalo hides annually were being floated down the Missouri River. By the 1840s, between 85,000 and 100,000 buffalo robes a year were being shipped to St. Louis.

Contrary to the popular image of the free Indian as an exemplary conservationist who utilized every part of the buffalo and never wasted a hoof, the plains tribes were intimately involved in the slaughter. Since only several thousand whites lived in buffalo country, the fur companies had to rely on the Indians to keep them supplied with hides. About 110,000 cow buffalo hides were shipped to St. Louis in 1847. Of that total, only 5,000 were killed by white traders, trappers, and migrants. The plains tribes killed the remainder, as well as hundreds of thousands of others to supply their own subsistence needs. According to historian George Hyde, the image of the free Indian as a conservationist was "set forth by the reservation Indians after the last of the buffalo herds had been destroyed by white hunters. Men who saw the wild Indians at work among the herds were under no such delusions."[14]

Among those men was Catlin, who wrote of what happened in May 1832 when a trader wanted to ship a boatload of salted tongues to St. Louis and an immense herd of buffalo appeared along the Missouri River near Fort Pierre, South Dakota:

> A party of five or six hundred Sioux Indians on horseback forded the river about mid-day and spending a few hours amongst them [the buffalo], recrossed the river at sun-down and came into the Fort with *fourteen hundred fresh buffalo tongues*, which were thrown down in a mass, and for which they required but a few gallons of whiskey, which was soon demolished. . . .
>
> This profligate waste of the lives of these noble and useful animals, when, from all that I could learn, not a skin or a pound of meat (except for tongues), was brought in, fully supports me in the seemingly extravagant predictions that I have made as to the extinction [of the buffalo],

Contrary to the popular image of them as exemplary conservationists, the plains tribes were intimately involved in the slaughter of the buffalo.

which I am certain is near at hand. In the above extravagant instance, at a season when their skins were without fur and not worth taking off, and their camp was so well stocked with fresh and dried meat, that they had no occasion for using the flesh, there is a exhibition of the improvident character of the savage, and also of his recklessness in catering for his appetite, so long as the present inducements are held out to him in his country, for its gratification.[15]

Catlin generally may have been a sympathetic observer of the plains tribes, some say overly romantic, but his assessment of the Indian character as "improvident" seems to be one of those instances when the "bad Indian" took over. The image of the Indian as "improvident" and "childlike" actually is as old as the "good Indian" and "bad Indian" images. Thomas Jefferson wrote that the Indian could not survive in the face of advancing white civilization because "the Indian could only be considered a child." Thomas L. McKenney, U.S. superintendent of Indian affairs during the 1820s and 1830s, echoed that thought, going so far as to use the impersonal pronoun "it" when he noted that "Indians, I have found out, are only children, and can be properly managed, only by being treated as such. It requires care, and a knowledge of their character to guide them—but it can be guided."[16]

Far from being children, of course, the Indians possessed cultures as complex and rich, though less technologically advanced, as whites. And the Indians were no more improvident than the whites who clear-cut eastern forests, hunted the passenger pigeon into extinction, and destroyed Atlantic salmon runs in New England. More than anything else, perhaps, the Indians' acceptance of a few kegs of whiskey as payment for fourteen hundred buffalo tongues is an indication of the place alcohol held in American life in the mid-nineteenth century and the eagerness of traders to exploit the Indians' naïveté about the drug. Whiskey traders killed and demoralized far more Indians than the most rabid Indian-hunter ever produced by the U.S. Army.

BRANDY WAS FIRST INTRODUCED into the Indian trade by the French around the Great Lakes in the middle of the seventeenth century. After the Hudson Bay Company was formed by the British in 1670, rum began to compete with brandy. By the end of the eighteenth century the tribes of the western Great Lakes were awash in alcohol. Then, in the 1820s, American traders began carrying it up the Missouri River to compete with British traders out of Canada already at work in the Rocky Mountains. For many plains Indians, the acts of trading and drinking soon became synonymous.[17]

Aware of what was happening, the federal government passed legislation banning the use of liquor in trade with the plains tribes. But it provided a loophole by allowing traders to carry one "gill," a quarter of a pint, of alcohol up the Missouri River per day, per employee. When Congress moved to completely prohibit the use of whiskey in Indian country, John Jacob Astor of the American Fur Company complained: "If the Hudson's Bay Company did not employ ardent spirits against us, we would not ask for a single drop. But without it, competition is hopeless; for the attraction is irresistible."

After a shipment of American Fur Company trade goods containing liquor was confiscated at Fort Wayne, Indiana, in 1824, Astor filed suit and began lobbying Congress to change the law. When Astor lost his suit in the District Court of the United States for the

District of Ohio, he appealed the ruling to the U.S. Supreme Court, claiming there was no evidence that the liquor was intended for sale to the Indians. In 1829 the Supreme Court overruled the Ohio court on the grounds that an improper charge had been given to the jury regarding the meaning of the term "Indian country." The term was becoming more and more difficult to define. It was in essence a moving target because of the rate at which Indians were being forced or persuaded to cede their lands.

The American Fur Company further responded to federal restrictions on transporting liquor into Indian country by building a distillery at Fort Union on the upper Missouri River, which technically meant it was not transporting liquor into the region. It operated the distillery until it was discovered and dismantled by government agents. Then the company began smuggling whiskey up the Missouri from the numerous distilleries that had sprung up in St. Louis to supply the Indian trade. The vastness of the plains, its tiny population, and the lack of an adequate number of troops to enforce prohibition laws made smuggling a simple matter. The Jesuit missionary Father De Smet found barrel after barrel of liquor sitting on the docks at Council Bluffs, Iowa, in 1839 awaiting sale to the Indians. Throughout his life, De Smet characterized Indian liquor merchants as the "tools of hell" and crusaded against the "abominable traffickers." But all efforts at prohibition were useless, since a gallon of whiskey that sold for one dollar in St. Louis could be sold for thirty dollars in Indian country.

Even the federal government was not above using whiskey in its dealing with the plains tribes. At the same time that Congress was passing laws prohibiting the trading of liquor in Indian country, the government's paternalistic approach to dealings with the tribes called for them to be rewarded with gifts when they acquiesced to the will of the "Great White Father" in Washington and gave up their land or signed treaties. Those gifts included flour, pork, guns, ammunition, plows, blankets, beads, pots, pans, missionaries, schools, new land for old land, and liquor. The powerful hold that whiskey came to have on the Indians is evident by the fact that they referred to it as "milk" or "our father's milk." Used as a reward, it was a powerful incentive to do what the federal government wanted.

LIQUOR'S EXPLOSIVE EFFECT on the plains Indians is reported again and again in nineteenth-century accounts. One migrant diarist described the scene in 1841 at Fort Platte near the junction of the Laramie and North Platte rivers in southeastern Wyoming:

> Men, women and children were seen running from lodge to lodge with vessels of liquor, inviting their friends and relatives to drink; while whooping, singing, drunkenness, and trading for fresh supplies had evidently become the order of the day. Soon individuals were noticed passing from one to another, with mouths full of the coveted fire-water, drawing the lips of favored friends in close contact, as if to kiss, and ejecting the contents of their own into the eager mouths of others.[18]

Father De Smet reported fourteen Indians in a camp on the Missouri River "being cut to pieces in a most barbarous manner" within a few weeks of a shipment of whiskey being delivered by a boat in 1856:

> A father seized his own child by the legs and crushed it, in the presence of its mother, by dashing it against the post of his lodge. Two others most cruelly murdered an Indian woman, a neighbor of ours, and mother of four children. . . . The passion of the savages for strong drink is inconceivable. They give horses, blankets, all, in a word, to have a little of this brutalizing liquid. Their drunkenness only ceases when they have nothing more to drink.[19]

The father of Crazy Horse's rival Red Cloud died of alcoholism. Red Cloud devotes a chapter of his autobiography to the whiskey peddler. That tale starts with a drunken mother and son. As the mother chatters on, a gray-haired man on an old pony rides past. Seeing the old man, the mother breaks into a hysterical whine, telling the son: "Do you see that man riding there? Thirty years ago that man made me cry, and he made you and your brothers and sisters cry also, for he killed your father."

Angered by his mother's words, the drunken son grabs his rifle and shoots the old man. As the old man falls from his pony, witnesses scream, and several men rush to the scene with their rifles. Suddenly aware of what he has done, the son starts to run. He dodges between the lodges to avoid the shots being fired at him, but is wounded several times before he makes it to a hill above the village.

On a rocky ledge, the son makes a stand, forcing his pursuers to circle around the rear of the hill to try to reach him from above. Blood streaming down the rocks makes it clear that he is mortally wounded. As his brother pleads with him to surrender, the drunken son drags himself into the open. There he sits motionless until several shots are fired at him. Then slowly he places the muzzle of his gun to his head and fires.

After the drunken son's death, his pursuers turn their attention to the trader who has been staying in the village and had provided the whiskey. In the confusion, the trader had fled up a gulch to a hiding place in a stand of cedars. From there he watches as the Indians set fire to his wagon and trade goods, sending a shower of bullets "whizzing through the kegs, spilling the liquor upon the ground and increasing the blaze." When the Indians learn the trader has run off with a rifle, they fear an ambush and are reluctant to follow him. Instead, they gather along the brow of the hill above the gulch and begin firing into the brush. "They kept this up until evening," according to Red Cloud, "and in some places the brush was fairly mowed to the ground."[20]

PART OF THE REASON why liquor was so destructive to the plains Indians stems from the fact that, as Catlin noted, they were a people who "in their native state" never made or used liquor.[21] Without a history involving alcohol and centuries of warnings and condemnations about the dangers of its use, many Indians were totally unprepared, culturally, morally, or psychologically, to deal with the drug. Even with a long history, many whites of the period could not withstand the temptations of the bottle. Writing in the 1830s, Englishman William Corbett devoted several pages in his book *A Year's Residence in the United States of America* to white Americans floundering in a sea of alcohol. "You cannot go into hardly any man's house, without being asked to drink wine, spirits, even IN THE MORNING," he noted. "Even little boys at, or under, TWELVE years of age, go into stores and tip off their DRAMS!"[22]

Whiskey became America's national drink in the first half of the nineteenth century for a number of reasons. Clear spring water was scarce and considered to have little value when it came to digesting the average citizen's heavy diet of bread, meat, and potatoes. Milk was avoided because people feared that cows transmitted disease through it. What supplies were available also generally were reserved for children. Then, too, local supplies of milk were irregular and expensive, and could not be kept long without refrigeration. Whiskey, on the other hand, produced no hazards. It did not spoil, and it was believed to stimulate digestion. Even more importantly, it was a lucrative way to use the abundant corn and rye being produced by farmers in Indiana, Ohio, Pennsylvania, and other midwestern and Appalachian states. Whiskey also was considered a patriotic drink. Gin and rum were drinks of the British, of whom many Americans were suspicious, and wine of the French. As one American distiller noted: "[A]nd why should not our country have a national beverage?"[23]

Besides lacking a history that involved alcohol, the Indians were susceptible to liquor because the whiskey sold to them usually was of the worst imaginable quality. Often it was not whiskey at all, but pure alcohol, which was the cheapest way to transport liquor into Indian country. Traders could double, triple, quadruple, and more their supply of "whiskey," and so their profits, by cutting the alcohol with water and adding tobacco juice for color and flavor. In an attempt to calm the fury unleashed by frontier whiskey, but without harming sales or profits, some traders also added laudanum, or opium, which was the leading trade good in the world, to their alcohol concoctions.

Western artist Charles Russell described frontier whiskey as "the kind that makes a jackrabbit spit in a rattlesnake's eye." White mountain men themselves often lost all control after drinking frontier whiskey. At rendezvous, rifles, knives, and other weapons were cached to keep their owners from killing each other. Rufus B. Sage, in *Rocky Mountain Life*, captured the scene among mountain men and traders at Fort Platte in 1841:

> The night of our arrival at Fort Platte was the signal for a grand jollification to all hands . . . who soon got gloriously drunk. . . . Yelling, screeching, firing, shouting, fighting, swearing, drinking and such like interesting performances, were kept up without intermission. . . . The scene was prolonged till near sundown the next, and several made their egress from this beastly carousal, minus shirts and coats—with swollen eyes, bloody noses, and empty pockets . . . liquor, in this country is sold for four dollars per pint.[24]

While there always were whites, such as Father De Smet, who spoke out against the liquor trade and its effect on the Indians, most simply were too busy seeking elusive prosperity to care about or even pay any attention to what was happening. Some white Americans actually used the image of the drunken Indian as further proof of the inferior, degenerate nature of the "bad Indian." They pointed to it as a reason to kill the Indian in order to save the man.

STARTING IN THE MID-1830s, the center of liquor and other trade with the Lakota was Fort Laramie, near the confluence of the Laramie and North Platte rivers in southeastern Wyoming. Fort Laramie was established on May 31, 1834, when William Sublette, a descendant of French Huguenots from Virginia, arrived at the site with a thirty-four-man trading party. Sublette had first traveled up the Missouri River on a fur-trading expedition eleven years earlier. Since that trip, he had returned on many other occasions and had become well known to the mountain men and the Indians, who called him "Cut Face" because of a scar on the left side of his chin.[25]

Named for French trapper Jacques La Ramee (also spelled Loremy, Laremais, and Laramie), a shadowy figure whose claim to fame was being killed in the area by a party of Arapahos in 1821, the Laramie River was on the eastern edge of the Rocky Mountains, which location made it ideal for a trading fort. Even before the untimely demise of its namesake, the river was an established trading and council site. Fur trader Robert Stuart followed it out to the plains on his 1812 expedition from Fort Astoria at the mouth of the Columbia River, during which he located South Pass, the passage through the Rockies that made the Oregon/California Trail possible.

Although innocent enough on the surface, Sublette's trading fort, dubbed Fort William in his honor, marked a turning point in Indian/white relations on the northern plains. Until then, the western fur trade had been the domain of free-spirited mountain men who lived as guests of the Indians. Most embraced the dress and ways of their hosts, often taking Indian wives and raising families, even though many such marriages were business decisions, since a trader gained control of a village's market by marrying into it.

By the mid-1830s, however, control of the fur trade was slipping from the hands of the mountain men who gathered at annual rendezvous to barter and sell their catch into those of hardened businessmen in fixed outposts and settlements. Astor's American Fur Company started the trend in the 1820s and early 1830s when it established several trading forts on the upper Missouri River. Fort William was both the first trading settlement and permanent white enclave in the heart of the northern plains. While the mountain men had once lived openly among the Indians, Fort William's palisade walls stood as a barrier between the two cultures. Its inhabitants were not guests willing to adapt, but intruders determined to live as they had back in the states.

For such expensive permanent settlements to survive in the highly competitive fur trade, the companies that owned them needed to obtain large quantities of pelts. The several thousand mountain men living in the Rockies could not meet the demands of the trading forts. But experience had shown that there were always Indians willing to supply furs for whiskey.

To lure the Lakota to Fort William, Sublette sent two experienced traders, John Sabille and Charles Galpin, north to the Black Hills even before the fort was completed. Near Bear Butte, the pair found an encampment of Oglala Lakotas, to whom they described the abundance of the country around the North Platte River: buffalo as countless as the needles of the pine, grass to satisfy the hunger of even the largest pony herd, and more trade goods than they imagined the world held.

Even though the Oglalas to that point had never been regular visitors to the North Platte country, they were vulnerable to the blandishments of Sabille and Galpin. In the late summer of 1834, Bear Bull moved his band of approximately a hundred lodges, about a thousand people, south. They were followed in 1835 by a band of Brulés, and the fort near the mouth of the Laramie River was on its way to becoming the center of white trade with the Lakota.

IN THAT SAME YEAR OF 1835, Sublette and his partners sold Fort William to Fontenelle, Fitzpatrick & Company, who renamed it Fort Lucien in honor of Fontenelle. In 1836 Fontenelle, Fitzpatrick &

Company in turn sold Fort Lucien to the American Fur Company. To compete with Fort Platte, which had been established about a mile downriver by trader Lancaster Lupton, the American Fur Company during 1841–1842 replaced Fort Lucien with a new adobe structure it named Fort John in honor of stockholder John Sarpy. But to most trappers and traders, the fort was known as Fort Laramie, although that would not become its official name until 1849, when the U.S. Army purchased it for $4,000. The army bought the fort because of its strategic location near the intersections of the Great Platte River (or Oregon/California) Trail to the West Coast, the Mormon Trail into Utah, and the Bozeman Trail north into Montana.

To the Indians, the trails leading to Oregon and California became mainly sources of confusion and concern. The reaction of one group on first sighting the "Great Route to Oregon" is described by Father De Smet, although his use of the word "admiration" seems to be more a reflection of his own feelings than those of his fellow travelers:

> Our Indian companions, who have never seen but the narrow hunting-paths by which they transport themselves and their lodges, were filled with admiration on seeing this noble highway, which is as smooth as a barn floor swept by the winds, and not a blade of grass can shoot on it on account of the continual passing. They conceived a high idea of the countless White Nation, as they express it. They fancied that all had gone over that road, and that an immense void must exist in the land of the rising sun. Their countenances testified evident incredulity when I told them that their exit was in nowise perceived in the lands of the whites. They styled the route the "Great Medicine Road of the Whites."[26]

Like other Oglala, Curly and his family periodically would visit Fort Laramie and Fort Platte to trade. So, while a young boy, the future chief would have been exposed to the fur and liquor trade, and seen how whites tended to separate themselves and look down upon the Indians. As children are prone to experiment with all manner of things, Curly might even have tried whiskey as a youngster. Since he came from a respected family, though, it is likely that his father early on would have lectured him on the dangers of alcohol, though no firsthand account of that exists. But the Indians never were ignorant victims of the liquor trade. From the start, wiser heads among them repeatedly issued warnings about whiskey. Lakota chief Bull Tail did so in 1841, when his band encountered a supply party carrying alcohol to Fort Platte: "Brothers: Why would you drink the firewater, and become fools? Would it not be better that the Long-knife no more bring it to us? We give for it our robes and our horses—it does us no good. It makes us poor. We fight our own brothers and kill those we love, because firewater is in us and makes our hearts bad! The firewater is the red man's enemy."[27]

Exactly what impression the liquor trade and the attitudes of whites at Fort Laramie might have had on Curly and how it may have colored his view of whites is impossible to know. But it seems likely that an observant, introspective person who, as Chip noted, "wanted to get to the highest station and rank"[28] in his culture, like Crazy Horse, early on would have become suspicious of whites and their effect on his people. It might have been at Fort Laramie and Fort Platte that the seeds of the war chief's resistance to whites were planted.

5

PRAIRIE TRAVELERS

ALONG WITH the possible birth of Crazy Horse, the year 1840 was monumental in the history of the Lakota and other plains tribes for the appearance at Fort Laramie of farmer Joel Walker, his wife, and five children. Spurred by an economic panic that began three years earlier when a land speculation bubble was burst by President Andrew Jackson's specie circular order requiring that all public land be purchased with gold or silver instead of credit, they were the first avowed overland migrants to Oregon.[1]

While Divine Providence in the guise of Manifest Destiny may have been seized upon by politicians, clergy, and the press to justify white America's march across the continent, the practical driving force behind overland expansion was somewhat less than divine. Migrants already had been trekking west for almost five years before the term "Manifest Destiny" was coined to describe the movement.

Politics and patriotism that could be ascribed to Manifest Destiny did play a role in the decision of some migrants to head west at the start of the 1840s. Great Britain and the United States were contesting Oregon. More Americans in Oregon aided the claim of the United States. For that reason, combined with the economic and "spiritual" benefits expansion would bring to their region, or themselves, western newspapers, businesses, missionaries, landowners, and politicians, especially Missouri senator Thomas Hart Benton, who wanted to help his state's lead and fur industries, became ceaseless proponents of expansionism.

The migrants themselves, though, most often pointed to financial difficulties, the possibility of improving their economic lot, and the desire for a more healthful climate as their reasons for heading west. Underlying those prosaic factors, they also confessed in their journals and diaries to traveling to Oregon and California with a wish to escape the increasingly virulent passions surrounding slavery, a hope to avoid arrest for a crime, a call to serve as missionaries to the Indians, a broken heart, a need to escape the restraints of society, and a general restlessness or desire for adventure. A few migrants even reported that they were traveling to Oregon for the fishing.[2]

Despite the claims of Manifest Destiny, many Americans originally opposed overland expansion. In particular, residents of eastern cities where the Industrial Revolution was gaining steam were against expansion for fear of losing their labor force or harming established industries such as whaling and textiles. They argued that there still was plenty of good land available east of the Mississippi River and that the center of the continent was nothing but a desert of hardship and suffering best left to the Indians.[3]

Among the most ardent opponents of overland expansion was Horace Greeley. In editorial after editorial in his *New York Tribune* in 1843, Greeley argued against overland migration to Oregon. While acknowledging the validity of American claims to the region, he cautioned against courting trouble with Great Britain by attempting settlement. He believed that such a course of action also was prohibitively expensive "at a time when the Treasury is already destitute of funds, the Federal Revenue inadequate to the demands upon it, and the prospect of any speedy augmentation at best exceedingly precarious." The land, too, Greeley maintained, was not as valuable as many people claimed.[4]

But at the same time, and to his credit as a newspaperman, Greeley also ran positive letters from people who already had made the trip. P. H. Burnett's dispatch ran in the December 28, 1843, edition of the *Tribune* and was typical of many such letters of the time. It contained information on the best starting time for a trip, the type of wagon and supplies needed, and travel conditions. "The most serious difficulty we have had to meet has been made by ourselves, and that is the grumbling and quarreling in camp; but this is just as harmless as you ever witnessed." Burnett also describes Oregon as a "beautiful region" and notes that "we have seen some beautiful and striking objects on the way."

STANDING IN OPPOSITION to Greeley and other antiexpansionists were zealots such as Senator Benton and members of the Oregon Provisional Emigration Society, a Methodist group organized to promote the migration of Christian settlers to Oregon and the Christianization of the Indians. Through its newspaper, *Oregonian, and Indian's Advocate,* the society dispelled doubts and concerns about the hardships of a journey west by noting that "wagons have repeatedly crossed the Rocky Mountains." It assured readers that women and children would thrive on the overland journey, which it claimed was much safer than a sea voyage to Oregon, and confidently predicted that the health of all would improve while crossing the country.[5]

By 1839 there were hundreds of such migration societies scattered throughout the country feeding "Oregon Fever." They played on the universal human aspirations for wealth, health, happiness, and patriotism. In the skillful hands of such eager promoters, the land not only became fertile beyond imagining but also available in vast quantities. Much was made of a homestead bill pending in Congress to give every Oregon settler 640 acres of land.

Through such promotion and letters sent East by people who already had made the journey and who often wanted to brag to friends and relatives about their accomplishments, Oregon and California became the Promised Land.

FOLLOWING JOEL WALKER and his family west was the Bidwell-Bartleson party, the first migrant wagon train. Led by mountain man and fur trader Thomas Fitzpatrick, the party set out in May 1841 from Westport Landing on the Kansas River near Independence, Missouri. It included seventy-seven men, women, and children, among them a group of Catholic missionaries under Father De Smet.

By the end of 1841 about a hundred migrants had made their way west through Fort Laramie. That number doubled to about two hundred in 1842, jumped to an estimated thousand in 1843, and continued to grow until it reached five thousand in 1845. The outbreak of the Mexican War and its manpower demands slashed the total to a thousand in 1846. Among the migrants that year was the Donner party, which would enter western legend when it became trapped during the winter in the Sierra Nevadas and resorted to cannibalism to survive.

Victory over Mexico, which added the territories of Utah, Nevada, California, New Mexico, and Arizona to the United States, and a treaty with Great Britain that settled the dispute over Oregon, pushed migrant numbers to two thousand in 1847 and to four thousand in 1848. The number of migrants also rose in 1848 because of the mass migration of the Mormons from Omaha, Nebraska, to Utah's Great Salt Lake region. But those numbers were flurries compared to the blizzard that raged out of the East when gold was discovered at Sutter's Mill in California.

Driven by desperation, greed, adventure, or a naive belief in a better life over the horizon, thirty thousand migrants made their way west in 1849. The plains tribes could not believe there were so many people in the world. And still they came. As Curly entered his second decade of life in 1850, more than fifty-five thousand migrants passed through Fort Laramie, or about three times the population of the entire Lakota nation. Another ten thousand came in 1851; fifty thousand in 1852; twenty thousand in 1853; and ten thousand in 1854. Even as Curly was learning to hit a moving target with an arrow, playing Buffalo Hunt, and raiding the meat racks to acquire the skills needed to prosper in the world of the Lakota, the most basic elements of that life were unalterably changing.[6]

GENERALLY, THE INDIANS greeted migrants entering their lands in the early days of the overland migration with curiosity, seeing them mainly as new sources of trade goods, often free goods. Many migrants overpacked for the journey and were forced to discard items along the way, starting a trend of trashing the Great Plains that continues today with the countless abandoned cars, ranch equipment, barns, homes, and churches that dot the landscape. The Indians would visit the migrants' abandoned campsites and collect everything of use or curiosity. "They filled their pouches with knives, forks, spoons, basins, coffeepots and other cooking articles, axes, hammers, etc.," Father De Smet noted. "The countless fragments of conveyances, the heaps of provisions, tools of every kind, and other objects with which the emigrants must have provided themselves at great expense."[7]

Beginning with the Bidwell-Bartleson party, the Indians also often trailed wagon trains as they passed through their lands, a sight that for some migrants, such as Nicholas Dawson, could be disconcerting. A member of the Bidwell-Bartleson party, Dawson decided to go hunting one morning shortly after the party reached the Platte River, only to return running a few hours later minus his mule, rifle, pistol, and most of his clothes. Claiming that he was being pursued by Indian hordes, Dawson sent the party dashing headlong toward the river until Fitzpatrick managed to head them off and form the wagons into a circle.

As the party anxiously awaited its fate, about fifty Cheyenne appeared and began to make camp. Puzzled, Fitzpatrick rode out to talk to them. The Cheyenne told him they had met Dawson on the plains and had been forced to disarm him because he had become so agitated at their sight they feared he might shoot somebody. That the Cheyenne also had taken Dawson's mule and most of his clothes may indicate that they had planned to rob him. But they agreed to hand over the items, which Fitzpatrick returned to the young man, who from then on became known as "Cheyenne."[8]

Such tales were told and retold during the 1840s, but the migrants faced little real threat from the plains tribes. "The dangers of interruption by the Indians is very small," Burnett noted in his 1843 letter to the *New York Tribune*, echoing thousands of other migrant letters written on the trail. So inconsequential was the Indian threat, in fact, that migrant guidebooks barely mentioned it. *The Prairie Traveler*, a best-selling guide by Army captain Randolph B. Marcy, contains plenty of information on Indian habits and customs, suggestions on how to deal with them under various circumstances, even instructions on organizing a night attack *on* an Indian camp, but no warnings about wagon trains being attacked. Theft of property and the robbing of stragglers, the guidebooks agreed, constituted the major Indian threat overlanders were likely to encounter.

IN MANY AREAS, the Indians actually were of great assistance to the migrants. Journals kept on the trail show that the Indians shared their knowledge of the local country and wildlife, cut and delivered grass, lent horses, helped wagons over rough terrain, and provided firewood, water, game, fish, and other foods to supplement the travelers' dreary diet of bacon, salt pork, flour, and cornmeal. Occasionally the Indians even carried migrant letters to settlements from where they could be forwarded to families back East. Some migrant parties hired, although they also sometimes kidnapped, Indian guides. Many more entrusted their families and worldly goods to Indian swimmers and ferrymen at dangerous river crossings.[9]

While some Indians aided the migrants without expectation of reward, many did so as entrepreneurs, expecting or demanding payment, usually in the form of a trade. Contrary to the image of the Indian being taken advantage of by whites, most of them, long accustomed to dealing with tough fur company agents, proved to be extremely shrewd in their dealings, which frequently surprised the migrants.

Knowing that they could make more money by negotiating separately with each member of the Reuben Shaw company, for example, three Lakota men in 1849 refused to accept a package deal to deliver letters for the party. Amos Steck, a member of another migrant party, noted in his journal that "except in negotiating for Whiskey they get as much as their Articles usually are worth—no other article than whiskey will purchase their ponies & then not a good one." Because they were accustomed to life on the plains, Indian ponies were much sought after by migrants. But the Indians seldom were willing to part with good animals. Migrant journals are full of stories of unsuccessful horse trades. They also show that, unlike fur traders, most migrants, concerned about the effects of alcohol on the Indians and a desire to keep liquor for their own use, were very reluctant to trade whiskey.[10]

A certain number of people in every culture always being ready to take advantage of strangers, a few Indians even overcharged for assistance and resorted to underhanded tactics in their dealings with migrants. On occasion they would sell a horse stolen from another migrant or lead wagons across a river, and then refuse to bring the owners over until they were paid more than the agreed-upon amount.

Practically from the start of the overland migration, the plains tribes were well aware of the many changes that the migrants were bringing to their country. To compensate for game the migrant wagons scared off and the grass their livestock destroyed, many Indians began to demand tribute for passage through their lands and levied tolls for the use of bridges. While the Indians saw such payments as only fair, overlanders tended to view them as blackmail. Tribute and tolls became very touchy matters. Summing up the feelings of many migrants, Isaac Lord wrote: "The whole is a gross imposition. . . . The 'idea' that an old Indian should lay claim to a tract of land as large as all the New England States, and levy black mail on all passers, is sufficiently absurd; but when it is done by the connivance of the U.S. government . . . language becomes useless, and men had better think."[11]

ALTHOUGH MIGRANTS commonly encountered Indians on the trail, they did not attach much importance to most such meetings in their diaries and journals. Probably in an effort to spice up their stories, however, letters and memoirs written after the journey pay much more attention to encounters with Indians. So, while only a handful of migrant journals and diaries contain entries about Indians attempting to trade for white women, many reminiscences, written years and decades after the fact, are laced with accounts of Indians attempting to trade a hundred and more horses for a single, usually fair-haired, migrant girl. On the rare occasion when a trade involving a person was proposed, it almost always was the other way around, with an Indian offering to trade his wife or a daughter to the migrants.[12]

As they grew older and came to realize that they were not going to be arrested or punished for past deeds, many Indians also embellished their stories. The Battle of the Little Big Horn would become especially fertile ground for tall tales. Rain In The Face, one of the most famous Lakota of the late nineteenth century, loved to tell stories, and the more gullible his audience, the better. At times he claimed to have personally killed Custer and cut out the heart of Custer's brother, Tom. Henry Longfellow even wrote a poem in which Rain is portrayed riding off with: "That brave heart, that beat no more,/Of the White Chief with yellow hair." But two months before his death, Rain confessed: "Many lies have been told about me. Some say that I killed the chief, and others say that I cut the heart out of his brother, Tom Custer, because he had caused me to be imprisoned. Why, in that fight the excitement was so great that we scarcely recognized our nearest friends."[13]

When Indians were mentioned at all in migrant journals and diaries, it usually was as a colorful highlight of the journey. Caroline Richardson wrote in 1852: "We were honored with a visit from about a dozen Indians this morning, while we were partaking of our break-fast. They are of the Chien [Cheyenne] tribe. Some had their heads adorned with skulls and brass rings about two inches in diameter." Julius Birge in 1866 thought the dress of the squaws "quite decol-lette," while Dr. C. M. Clark in 1860 was captivated by the pageantry: "Indians with travois pass. They consider themselves superior to palefaces, trudging along like squaws. Their taste evinced in the mat-ter of dress is peculiar. Many are seen wearing fancy colored shirts, gaudy vests, and old felt hats; and one had an umbrella which he car-ried spread above his head. They all wear trinkets such as coils of brass wire and bands of silver on their arms and fingers, together with a long string of circular pieces of silver, graduated in size, and attached to a leather strip, which is suspended from the black hair like a queue. Their clubs, lances and bows are often thickly studded with brass nails. Many wear looking glasses around their necks."

Other migrants, though, were less than charmed. The Reverend V. P. Crawford wrote in 1851: "The Indians seated themselves on the ground and commenced to pick lice from each others' heads and crack them between their teeth as though they were precious mor-sels. There was more filth than I expect to see among human beings." Ada Millington wrote in 1862 that she "thought the Indians very ugly." But she had to admit that "they are very friendly and want to shake hands with us, and say 'how, how.'"[14]

Racism also played a role in the way a scattering of migrants viewed the Indians. Among those was Jim Kinnery, a former slave-owner from Texas. Spying an Indian near the trail in 1845, Kinnery announced that he was going to make the man his personal slave and threatened to kill any member of his party who tried to stop him. He then rode up to the Indian, stunned him with a blow, handcuffed him, tied a rope around the man's neck, and attached it to the back of his wagon.

While his wife drove the wagon, Kinnery rode behind, whipping the Indian. He continued to beat and cow the Indian for a week, until he felt the man's spirit was broken. Then he put him to work, brag-ging that if the Indian tried to escape "he could follow him and kill him to show the other Indians the superiority of the whiteman. He said he had killed plenty of negroes and an Indian was no better than a negro." One windy night, the Indian disappeared, taking with him a number of Kinnery's personal belongings, including his one-hundred-dollar rifle, which caused the rest of Kinnery's party to quietly rejoice.[15]

THERE IS NO DOUBT that Indians from the start of the overland migration stole migrant horses, livestock, and other property, and occasionally robbed, harassed, and even killed stragglers. Most such encounters, though, were not organized affairs but the work of young men out to make a reputation or to acquire wealth. Neither were all of them the work of "wily savages." Diarist Isaac Pettijohn wrote of a somewhat less than adept horse thief in 1847: "One of the guards shot at an Indian last knight. . . . He was crawling up to steal a horse, pulling grass as he came so that the guard would take him for a calf. . . . He left in so great a hurry that he left his moccasins."[16]

In many instances "Indian raids" were in reality the work of renegade whites. The situation was so bad in some areas that Mormon leader Brigham Young, in an 1854 editorial in the *Deseret News*, warned his followers to be careful of "a numerous and well organized band of white highwaymen, painted and disguised as Indians," who stole travelers' stock "by wholesale" and committed murders. Some of the most vicious Indian raids reported during the overland migration were the work of whites, among them an attack on the Shepherd party in July 1859.

The Shepherd train was traveling through a canyon in southeastern Idaho when the attack occurred. It began with a sudden crossfire from the rocks and bushes along the trail. Four of the party's men were immediately killed, and another man and his wife severely wounded and left for dead. The attackers also broke the leg of a small child when they threw the youngster into the air. The raiders burned the party's wagons and stole thirty-five horses and mules, various other valuables, and about a thousand dollars in cash. Survivors recognized at least three white men disguised as Indians among the attackers.

One month later, nineteen migrants from Iowa, who included Nelson Miltimore, were attacked about twenty-five miles outside of Fort Hall, Idaho. According to sworn testimony by Miltimore, three men who had light brown hair, beards, and who spoke perfect English approached his company and "conversed pleasantly" before ordering an attack from both sides of the road. Eight migrants were killed, scalped, and butchered. The attackers also cut off both ears of one five-year-old girl, gouged out her eyes, and then cut off her legs at her knees and forced her to walk on the stumps until she died. In the West's most famous incident of whites posing as Indians, Mormon fanatics, fearing attack by the federal government, in 1857 massacred 120 migrants from Missouri and Arkansas who they imagined were agents of the government in the Mountain Meadows area of Utah.[17]

It was because newspapers favored the drama and color inherent in such stories, just as television today focuses on murders, fires, accidents, and disasters because they make good video, that deadly encounters between whites and Indians became a central tenet of the western myth. But usually the Indians were guilty of little more than begging. At least that was what the migrants considered their requests and demands for gifts, since the sharing of worldly goods was considered a virtue by the Lakota and other plains tribes. Many Indians also felt that they were owed something for allowing the migrants to pass through their land and because they scared off game.

From the beginning, too, many Indians allowed their desire for the abundance of Fort Laramie to rule them. They set up camp near the white enclave and sought to make their living off the white man by begging, running errands, selling game, trading pelts, or serving as guides. The women sold clothing and moccasins they made and, as one distressed officer's wife put it, "wares to which a Christian woman could no more than allude." Among many of their own people, the Indians who chose to reside near the fort became derisively known as "Laramie Loafers."[18]

Farsighted chiefs of the plains tribes regarded the loafers' village as an ominous portent for their peoples. They could see nothing good coming from such dependence on whites. Adding to the tension was the effect that growing migrant numbers was having on game along the trails. Joel Palmer, who headed west in 1845, recorded Lakota complaints during a dinner at Fort Laramie. "This country belongs to the red man," an unnamed chief told him, "but his white brethren travels through, shooting the game and scaring it away. Thus the Indian loses all that he depends upon to support his wives and children. The children of the red man cry for food, but there is no food.

But on the other hand, the Indian profits by the trade with the white man. He was glad to see us and meet us as friends. It was the custom when the pale faces passed through his country, to make presents to the Indians of powder, lead, &c. His tribe was very numerous, but most of the people had gone to the mountains to hunt. Before the white man came, the game was tame, and easily caught, with bow and arrow. Now the white man has frightened it, and the red man must go to the mountains. The red man needed long guns."[19]

Fed by a long national history that focused on violent encounters between whites and Indians; colorful, though usually fictitious, accounts about Indian depredations; attacks on migrants by whites masquerading as Indians; Indian anger over the effects of ever-increasing white encroachment on their lands; and the natural mis-understandings that occur when cultures clash, the frequency and seriousness of disputes between whites and Indians grew as the 1840s progressed. Unlike in the movies, however, it was the Indians who usually were attacked by the overlanders. Migrant journals show that overlanders killed more Indians than Indians killed migrants during the migration period. But in neither case were the numbers very high. That was true even during the Gold Rush years, when so many migrants crossed the northern plains that even white fur traders, trappers, and hunters became concerned about their effect on the buffalo herds from which they earned a living.

The first person to be killed during the overland migration was an Indian shot by migrants in 1841. It was the only death recorded on either side that year. Following that single death there is no record of an Indian or a migrant being killed for three years, until 1845, when four migrants and one Indian were killed. Those totals rose to twenty Indians and four migrants in 1846; two Indians and twenty-four migrants in 1847 (the shift in total was caused by the apparent annihilation of an entire wagon train of twenty-three migrants at Tule Lake, California); two migrants and two Indians in 1848; sixty Indians and thirty-three migrants in 1849; and seventy-six Indians and forty-eight migrants in 1850.

Although whites tended to lump all Indian attacks together, most depredations did not involve plains tribes. Violent encounters between whites and Indians were far more common in Utah and points west than on the plains. Throughout the 1840s, plains tribes remained more interested in fighting each other than in fighting overlanders. Lakota winter counts for the period report nothing about attacks on white migrants, but note numerous raids against other tribes, traditional enemies against whom success and failure long had been measured.[20]

The content of White Bull's count is typical of what the Lakota saw as important during the first decade of overland expansion. The winter of 1840 to 1841 is the time "They killed three Assinibons"; 1841 to 1842, the years "They brought back many spotted horses," a reference to a raid against the Crow; 1842 to 1843, the time "One Feather prayed and charged the enemy," a reference to One Feather's wish to avenge the death of relatives caused by the Crow. Then, from 1843 to 1844, "Buffalo head kept inside," a time when the Sans Arc made medicine to bring the buffalo; 1844 to 1845, "Pine tree fort winter camp," a reference to a stockade made of pine logs that the Miniconjou built to protect their camp; 1845 to 1846, "They camped for the winter in an ash grove where there was a lot of food"; 1846 to 1847, "They killed them from the rear." Sitting Bull, who was fourteen years old at the time, counted his first coup ("killed from the rear" is a reference to a returning Lakota raiding party in which three stragglers were killed by pursuing warriors). Also, from 1847 to 1848, "Two Herds was left behind for dead but later returned home safely," probably a reference to a warrior who was separated from other members of a raiding party; and 1848 to 1849, "Hole Creek froze to death," a reference to a hunter who was caught and died in a blizzard.

The only apparent reference to white migrants in White Bull's count is an oblique one that appears for 1849 to 1850, "A shortage of grass this year." Since that year marked the start of the California Gold Rush, when the number of overlanders passing through Fort Laramie suddenly ballooned from four thousand in 1848 to thirty thousand in 1849 and to more than fifty-five thousand in 1850, the notation would seem to indicate a time when migrant stock destroyed the grass for miles surrounding the Oregon and California trails.[21]

The status of Crazy Horse's family might be seen in Cloud Shield's winter count, which calls 1844 to 1845 the years when "Crazy Horse says his prayers and goes to war." Since Curly would only have been about five years old at the time, the reference apparently is to his father, Worm. And since there was no fighting with white migrants, the war the elder Crazy Horse went off to fight most likely was against another tribe.[22]

Other sources also reveal the 1840s as a period when the plains tribes were more interested in intertribal war than in fighting whites. George Hyde noted one such encounter in *Red Cloud's Folk* in 1847 when about four hundred Lakota warriors attacked a hunting camp of more than two hundred Pawnee, killing more than eighty. In his autobiography, Red Cloud also describes several raids on other tribes during the period, including one on the Pawnee in which he was seriously wounded by an arrow and nearly died. As the overland migration was beginning, Red Cloud found himself, too, at the center of one of the most far-reaching events of the period for the Oglala Lakota—the November 1841 killing of Bull Bear, the man who first led the Oglala to Fort Laramie.

AT THE START OF THE 1840S, Bull Bear and Old Smoke stood as the leaders of the two largest Oglala bands, the Bad Faces and the Walks As She Thinks.[23] Old Smoke, or Smoke, was a plump, good-natured fellow whose affable ways made him a favorite of the traders at Fort Laramie. Bull Bear is most often described as arrogant and a bully. He had been dead for "five or six years" when Parkman made the 1846 trip west, out of which came *The Oregon Trail*. His guide on that journey was trader Henry Chatillon, whose wife was Bull Bear's daughter, which may have influenced what Parkman wrote:

> Mahto Tatonka [Bull Bear], in his way, was a hero. No chief could vie with him in warlike renown, or in power over his people. He had a fearless spirit, and an impetuous and inflexible resolution. His will was law. He was politic and sagacious, and with true Indian craft, always befriended the whites, knowing that he might thus reap great advantages for himself and his adherents. When he had resolved on any course of conduct, he would pay to the warriors the compliment of calling them together to deliberate upon it, and when their debates were over, quietly state his own opinion, which no one ever disputed. It fared hard with those who incurred his displeasure. He would strike them or stab them on the spot; and this act, which, if attempted by any other chief would

have cost him his life, the awe inspired by his name enabled him to repeat again and again with impunity. In a community where, from immemorial time, no man has acknowledged any law but his own will, Mahto Tatonka raised himself to power little short of despotic.[24]

Among the Lakota angered by Bull Bear, according to Parkman, "Smoke in particular, together with all of his kinsmen, hated him cordially."[25] Since Bull Bear's people most often hunted around the headwaters of the North Platte River, and Old Smoke's people to the east, near the forks of the Platte River, the two rivals were kept apart much of the time. But the favoritism the traders showed Old Smoke angered Bull Bear. That anger was inflamed over the years by the numerous slights and altercations, and by whiskey.

While Old Smoke was sitting in his lodge one day, according to Parkman, Bull Bear approached and loudly challenged his rival to a fight. When the frightened Old Smoke, aware that he did not stand a chance against such a large and fierce opponent, refused to move, Bull Bear "proclaimed him a coward and an old woman." He then strode up to the entrance of the lodge and stabbed Old Smoke's best horse. But even that immense insult failed to bring out Old Smoke.

Bull Bear's "hour of reckoning" arrived sometime later, when Old Smoke's people, including Red Cloud, were in the middle of a trading session with fur company men. Bull Bear also was there, with some of his people. As usual, among the items being traded was whiskey. As Bull Bear lay in his lodge, a fight broke out between his people and Old Smoke's people.[26]

"The war-whoop was raised," Parkman wrote, "bullets and arrows began to fly, and the camp was in confusion. The chief sprang up, and rushing in a fury from the lodge, shouted to the combatants on both sides to cease. Instantly—for the attack was preconcerted—came the reports of two or three guns, and the twanging of a dozen bows, and the savage hero, mortally wounded, pitched forward headlong to the ground. . . . The tumult became general, and was not quelled until several had fallen on both sides."[27]

Red Cloud's account, which has been described as self-serving by some historians, differs from Parkman's account in several respects, starting with the cause of the fight. Red Cloud claimed the fatal dispute began when a young member of Old Smoke's band who was hated by Bull Bear stole a young woman from Bull Bear's band.

Lakota culture permitted a man to acquire a wife in such a manner as long as the bride's family did not object. When the parents of the girl involved complained, Bull Bear, who was related to the young woman, decided she should be returned and the young man punished.

Among the members of Old Smoke's band was a man named Trunk or Box, an uncle of Red Cloud. To avoid a confrontation with Trunk, according to Red Cloud, Bull Bear and his supporters invited him into their camp to share the whiskey some members of the camp had just obtained. Trunk accepted the offer but did not get as drunk as Bull Bear had planned. When Bull Bear and his party started for Old Smoke's village, Trunk followed, arriving there just in time to see Bull Bear's party kill the father of the young man who had stolen the girl. Trunk began shouting to his people: "Are you going to lay there and be killed? Where are all the young men? Where is Red Cloud? Red Cloud, are you going to disgrace your father's name?"

Aroused by Trunk, twenty-year-old Red Cloud and the other young men of Old Smoke's village hurried to meet the intruders. In the fight that ensued, Bull Bear was wounded in the leg and fell to the ground. As Bull Bear sat clutching his leg, Red Cloud, who would later gain a reputation as a merciless warrior, ran up to the chief and shot him in the head, exclaiming: "You are the cause of this." The young men of Old Smoke's band then raced to Bull Bear's village, where they took captive the women and children who had not fled.[28]

The death of Bull Bear and the capture of his band's women and children finally ended the dispute between his band and that of Old Smoke. After negotiating the return of their families, the remainder of Bull Bear's band moved to the South Platte River, where they held a council to determine who would be the new chief. Several names were proposed and discussed without drawing a decision. Then an old man grabbed a garter snake that had wandered into the area and stepped forward. Holding the snake by the head and the tail, he bit it in two and said: "This shall be our name, Ki-ya-ksa." The literal translation, according to Red Cloud, is "bitten in two," but the band became known as "Cut Off."[29]

Parkman learned of the effect of Bull Bear's death on the Lakota one day as the Oglala band he was staying with prepared for a buffalo hunt near Medicine Bow Mountain. Parkman asked Eagle Feather "if the village would move in the morning. He shook his head, and said that nobody could tell, for since old Mahto Tatonka [Bull Bear] had died, the people had been like children that did not know their own minds. They were no better than a body without a head."[30]

BY THE END OF SUMMER 1849, migrant cattle had devoured all the grass along the western trails in a swath from one to several miles wide, extending from jumping-off places in Missouri to the Continental Divide. Timber along the routes also had been cut for firewood and rafts, and buffalo killed, some for food, many more for sport, their bodies left to rot.

Frightened by the wagons and robbed of grass, the buffalo became skittish and difficult to hunt. They drifted out of the Platte River area north to the Powder River and south to the Republican, South Platte, and Arkansas rivers. Separation of the buffalo into a northern herd and a southern herd has been attributed to the completion of the Union Pacific Railroad in 1869, but actually began twenty years earlier, with wagon traffic on its way to the California goldfields. Overlander Isaac Foster wrote in 1849: "The valley of the Platte for 200 miles presents the aspect of the vicinity of a slaughter yard; dotted all over with skeltons of buffalo; such waste of the creatures that God has made for man seems wicked, but every migrant seems to wish to signalize himself by killing a buffalo."[31]

Along with frightening game and consuming grass and wood, the migrants also brought disease with them. Mortality tables are nonexistent, and some of the deaths can be attributed to accidents, but migrant Sarah Wisner, writing in 1866, calculated that 30,000 whites died on the trails west between 1842 and 1859. During the peak Gold Rush years of the early 1850s, according to Wisner, there was an average of one grave every 200 feet. Other writers use a more conservative total of 20,000 deaths along the entire 2,000 miles of the California Trail. Assuming a total migration of about 350,000, that means one out of every seventeen people who started the journey west died along the way.[32]

Among the diseases that claimed lives on the trails were measles, smallpox, tuberculosis, pneumonia, whooping cough, mumps, and, most feared of all, Asiatic cholera. Some wagon trains lost as many as two-thirds of their members to cholera. The toll was even worse among the Indians. George Bent, the son of Owl Woman, a Cheyenne, and Colonel William Bent, described the effects of the 1849 epidemic on the plains tribes:

> "Cramps" the Indians called it, and they died of it by the hundreds. On the Platte whole camps could be seen deserted with the tipis full of dead bodies, men, women and children. The Sioux and Cheyenne who were nearest to the road, were the hardest hit. . . . Our tribe suffered very heavy loss; half of the tribe died, some old people say. A war party of about one hundred Cheyennes had been down the Platte, hunting for Pawnees, and on their way home they stopped in an emigrant camp and saw white men dying of cholera in the wagons. When the Cheyennes saw these sick white men, they rushed out of the camp and started for home on the run, scattering as they went; but the terrible disease had them already in its grip, and many of the party died before reaching home, one of my Indian uncles and his wife dying among the first. The men in the war party belonged to different camps and when they joined these camps they brought the cholera with them and it was soon raging in all the villages. The people were soon in a panic. The big camps broke up into little bands and family groups, and each little party fled from the rest.[33]

Like the effects of whiskey on the Lakota, disease and the destruction of hunting grounds must have contributed to Curly's view of the white world. It is easy to imagine the young Oglala overhearing his parents' worried talk about the disappearance of the buffalo and the deaths of friends or relatives from white man's diseases, and where they might camp to escape the "cramps" raging around them. Such parental concerns are easily transmitted to young children, filling them with an anxiety that can color their entire lives and lead to rage, anger, fear, determination, murder, fantasy, resignation, hopelessness, or resistance.

During Curly's formative first decade, white expansion became so detrimental to the Lakotas that a number of traders and scouts at Fort Laramie expected real trouble between the plains tribes and migrants by 1849 and 1850. War probably would have erupted if it were not for the cholera outbreaks of those years, followed by epidemics of smallpox and measles that devastated many bands. It was becoming clear that something had to be done if peace was to prevail.

6

THE GREAT SMOKE

After a long night of dancing and feasting in most of the villages that lined the banks of the Platte River and its tributary Horse Creek in far western Nebraska, "every one, white and Indians, seemed to look for the morning, and every body was early afloat," wrote A. B. Chambers, editor of the *Missouri Republican.*

> From dawn until 9 o'clock, when the cannon fired and the flag hoisted, as a signal for the Council to assemble, parties of Indians were coming in from every direction. . . .
>
> When the cannon had given forth its thunder, the whole plains seemed to be covered with the moving masses of chiefs, warriors, men, women and children, some on horse-back, some on foot. The Chiefs and Braves who expected to go into Council . . . generally came on foot; then followed the young men mounted and on foot, then the squaws and children. Until the signal was given for the Council to assemble, the masses had remained at a distance from the temporary arbor prepared for the occasion. But then the whole body commenced moving to the common centre, a sight was presented of most thrilling interest. Each nation approached with its own peculiar song or demonstration, and such a combination of rude, wild and fantastic manners and dresses never was witnessed. It is not probable that an opportunity will again be presented of seeing so many tribes assembled together displaying all the peculiarities of features, dress, equipment, and horses. The manner of painting themselves and horses, and everything else, exhibiting their wild notions of elegance and propriety.[1]

No record exists to indicate that the approximately ten-year-old Curly was present at the Horse Creek Treaty Council of 1851. But it would seem likely, since it was such an important political and social event. The treaty that grew out of the council was one of the most important the United States government ever signed with the plains tribes. Chambers, who served as secretary for the government, estimated that the council attracted more than ten thousand Indians (other sources report eight thousand to twelve thousand) to the treaty grounds, about thirty-six miles east of Fort Laramie.[2]

The council was sought by the government to address long-simmering and growing complaints by both Indians and whites caused by the overland migration to California and Oregon. The division of the buffalo by the migrant trails into a northern herd and a southern herd, and the destruction of grasslands and game along the trails by the migrants, had forced the Lakota and other tribes to seek new hunting grounds. These factors, in turn, led to a rise in intertribal warfare. Even though migrants were not involved in such fighting, war parties riding across the plains were a frightening sight to them. When combined with a continuing increase in violent and disruptive encounters, real or imagined, between whites and Indians, and the effects of whiskey and white man's diseases on the tribes, the situation had created a crisis atmosphere on the plains by the late 1840s.

Based mainly on reports by Thomas Fitzpatrick, the former mountain man and guide of the first overland train who became Indian agent for the Upper Platte Agency in 1847, and Colonel David D. Mitchell, superintendent of Indian Affairs in St. Louis, U.S. Commissioner of Indian Affairs William Medill in his 1848 annual report suggested moving native inhabitants of the central plains to two secluded "colonies" located north and south of a belt of land "six geographic degrees" wide, extending from the western boundary of Missouri to the Pacific Coast. Such an action, Medill wrote, would create an ample opening "for our population that may incline to pass or expand in that direction; and thus prevent our colonized tribes from being injuriously pressed upon, if not swept away." Until that was possible, the report recommended compensating the Indians for the damage done by the migrants.[3]

As a first step in his plan, Medill in June 1849 sent a letter to the Secretary of the Interior proposing a council with the plains tribes and buying them off with "goods, stock, agricultural implements, &c, which would be more useful and far better for them than money." He noted that such items could be used to encourage the tribes to give up their hunting way of life for "agricultural pursuits in order that they may be prepared to sustain themselves when the buffalo shall have so far disappeared as no longer to afford them a certain or adequate means of subsistence." The Indians, he added, would be bound to remain in the country established for each tribe.[4]

Preoccupied by the Compromise of 1850, which sought to calm tensions between the North and the South by, among other means, admitting California to the Union as a free state and amending the Fugitive Slave Act to require Northerners to assist in the capture of runaway slaves, Congress did not act on Medill's proposal until it passed the Deficiency Appropriations Act on February 27, 1851. The act contained an appropriation of $100,000, half of what had been requested, "for Expenses of holding treaties with the wild tribes of the prairie, and for bringing delegates on to the seat of government."[5]

Shortly after he laid out the treaty plans, Medill was replaced as commissioner of Indian Affairs by Orlando Brown. A supporter of a treaty, Brown sent letters to Mitchell and Fitzpatrick instructing the two men to assemble the Indians and negotiate a treaty with them. "To impress the Indians of the Prairies with some just idea of our greatness and power, and to inspire them with a proper respect for the government," Brown further ordered Mitchell to bring a delegation of chiefs to Washington following the council.[6]

BY THE TIME Congress actually approved the Deficiency Appropriations Act, money and politics had resulted in the replacement of Brown as commissioner of Indian Affairs by Luke Lea, a corrupt supporter of the fur companies. At the same time, Fitzpatrick and Mitchell responded to their charge to arrange a treaty council by sending out what John J. Killoren in *Come, Black Robe*, his biography of the Jesuit missionary Father De Smet, calls "the Circular That Changed the West."[7]

Sent to "Indian Agents, Traders, &c.," the circular announced that Congress had authorized a treaty with tribes living south of the Missouri River and north of Texas. "The objects of the Government are just and humane," it proclaimed, "and intended entirely for the benefit and future welfare of the Indians." But it also made clear that such a treaty "will tend to greatly promote the safety and interests of the traders, as well as the Indians themselves."

The circular told traders and agents to invite the tribes to meet "en masse" on September 1, 1851, at Fort Laramie with all their women and children or send a delegation composed of men alone.

> The former, . . . however, would be preferred, as the presence of the women and children would be an additional guarantee for the good conduct of the parties present. It is hoped, among other beneficial arrangements (intended for the permanent good of the Indians), that we will be enabled to divide and subdivide the country into various geographical districts, in a manner entirely satisfactory to the parties concerned. This, if accomplished, will go far towards extinguishing the bloody wars which have raged from time immemorable—producing such a horrible waste of human life, and innocent blood.

For many Indians, though, the main attraction of the council was the promise that they would be "amply compensated for all the depredations of which they complain, on account of the destruction of game, timber, &c,. by the passing of white men through their country." The circular also told traders and agents that they could tell the Indians "that after ratification of the contemplated Treaty, each tribe will receive an annual present, in goods, from their Great Father—the amount to be contingent upon their faithful observance of their treaty stipulation. A suitable quantity of provisions will be provided."[8]

RESPONDING TO the urgings of traders and agents, the tribes gathered at Fort Laramie throughout August. So many Indians came that by the end of the month practically all game and grass had disappeared from the country around the fort. Then word arrived that the wagons bringing the annuities had gotten a late start and would not arrive in time for the opening of the council. Increasingly anxious about provisioning the throng, the commissioners decided to extend the council, distribute what supplies were available from the post sutler, and seek a new site for the talks.

On September 1 a company of dragoons sent to impress the tribes with the might of the United States assembled in the vicinity of Colonel Mitchell's tent and waited for the Indians. Once the two sides were gathered, tobacco was handed out and smoked "after lifting it east, west, north, south, and up to the Great Spirit." Then Mitchell told of the delay of the supply wagons and diplomatically asked that the tribes select a new site to meet, then distributed what beef, tobacco, and vermillion cloth was available at Fort Laramie.

After a prolonged debate among the Indians, it was agreed to follow the suggestion of the Brulé Lakota Blue Earth, called by the *Missouri Republican* Terra Blue, and move the council down the Platte River to the mouth of Horse Creek. As the council moved over the next few days, evidence of the need for a treaty appeared along the Platte in the form of a Mormon train of twenty-nine wagons on its way to Salt Lake City.[9]

IF THE IMAGES preserved by the *Missouri Republican*'s Chambers are any indication (there were no photographers or artists on hand to render the scene), the gathering on Horse Creek must have been one of overwhelming excitement for a ten-year-old boy such as Curly. According to Chambers, the treaty grounds were covered by Indians attired in their finest "toggory," displaying "quite as much sense and taste as his city prototype." The exceptions, ones that may have painted a stark contrast in Curly's mind, were the eastern tribes. Compared with the "proud, manly and high toned sons of the wilds," Chambers wrote, "the latter are dirty, beggarly and cowardly. . . . The latter have had more to do with the whites, have learnet many of their vices and few of their virtues. What contamination may do with the former remains to be seen."[10]

Soon after the council was assembled, Mitchell announced that the government would not negotiate separately with each band and directed the various tribes to select a "suitable man" to serve as "chief of the whole nation." As long as such a chief acted in a manner deemed proper by the government, Mitchell said, the Great Father would "support and sustain him in his place as Head Chief of the nation" and tribal members would be required to respect, obey, and support him in his office.[11]

Such a stand completely ignored the Lakota custom of freedom of choice and their willingness to follow a leader only so far as each person feared that leader or believed he deserved to be followed. Blue Earth tried to explain to Mitchell that the idea of a single chief for the Lakota nation was absurd. "We have decided differently from you, Father," he said, "about this chief for the nation." He told

Mitchell that it would be better if the Lakota had a principal chief for each band. If Mitchell would "make one or two chiefs for each band, it will be much better for you and the whites," Blue Earth said. "But, Father, we can't make one chief." The Yankton Sioux Painted Bear added: "Father, this is the third time I have met with the whites. We don't understand their manners, nor their words. We know it is all very good, and for our good, but we don't understand it all."[12]

Essentially ignoring the problem, Mitchell directed the tribes to convene private councils to select candidates for head chiefs and adjourned the council. Talks were to resume two days later, on September 10, but before they could commence, word arrived that the Crows were coming. Some of the tribes and bands at the council recently had sent war parties against the Crows, which caused some tense moments, but there was no trouble. Mitchell greeted the newcomers with open arms and had them smoke for peace.[13]

The first two days of the council were given to the approval of chiefs to represent the various tribes and discussions about territory. The Lakota again balked when the boundary among them, the Cheyenne, and the Arapaho was set as the Platte River. Although they did not seek ownership of the southern side of the river, they argued that they had always hunted on the southern side, as far as the Republican Fork of the Kansas and the waters of the Arkansas, and continued to claim that right. The Oglala Black Hawk told the commissioners on September 13:

> You have split the country, and I don't like it. What we live upon, we hunt for, and we hunt from the Platte to the Arkansas, and from here up to the Red But[t]e and the Sweet Water. The Cheyennes and Arapahos agree to live together and be one people; that is very well, but they want to hunt on this side of the river. Those lands once belonged to the Kiowas and the Crows, but we whipped those nations out of them and in this we did what the white men do when they want the lands of the Indians. We met the Kiowas and the Crows and whipped them, at the Kiowa Creek, just below where we now are. We met them and whipped them again, and the last time at Crow Creek. This last battle was fought by the Cheyennes, Arapahos and Ogallahlas combined, and the Ogallahlas claim their share of the country.

Mitchell responded in a way that must have totally confused many of the Lakota and left some of them wondering if all whites were as crazy as those at the council. After telling the Lakota that the government wanted to put a boundary around their country, Mitchell then said that the government, in fixing a boundary, had no intention of limiting their hunting outside of that boundary or prohibiting them from going into the territory of any other tribe as long as they remained at peace. What nation would allow another nation to enter and freely use its land without responding with war?[14]

By september 15 most of the work of the council had been concluded and time was approaching to vote on a treaty, except for one item. As Chambers noted: "The only difficulty that presented itself was the selection of a *Chief* for the Sioux nation." The situation had become so frustrating to the commissioners that Mitchell, in an extraordinary act of paternalism and interference in tribal affairs, informed the Lakota that

> if they could not select a chief among themselves, in whose support all the bands would unite, he would select one, but that he would not force them to take any one whom they did not approve; that, if the man he selected was not acceptable to a majority of the bands and the Sioux nation, he would choose another, and so on, until he found some one who would be acceptable to them all.

Before making a selection, Mitchell had his men count the Lakota lodges and required each band to select a certain number of candidates for head chief based on the number of lodges they had at the council. "This gave to some of the bands six or seven, and to others only three voices, but a fair representation according to numbers," Chambers wrote.

Twenty-four candidates for chief, who also would do the voting, were selected by Mitchell and directed to sit on the grass in a semicircle before the commissioners while their people spread out behind them. Mitchell then had two dozen sticks cut of equal length and passed out to the group. He informed the voters that he would select and place in the center of the circle a candidate for chief. If the other voters approved of his choice, they should give the candidate their stick. If they did not, they should keep their stick. According to Chambers, the voting procedure "was very fully explained to each band, and every one understood it." The accuracy of that statement is doubtful, though, since the Lakota had no experience in such voting and, as Painted Bear had noted, did not understand the white man's ways.

The Lakota's lack of experience with such voting may be further evident in the fact that they gave their support to the first candidate selected by Mitchell, a man who had not even been present during the most important negotiations. Chambers called him Frightening Bear, but he is better known as Conquering Bear. The *Missouri Republican* editor gushingly described him as between thirty and forty years of age and, indicative of the racist way whites viewed Native Americans, "as fine a formed person as was to be found among the Indians." According to Chambers, Conquering Bear's large family was well connected among the various Lakota bands and "although no chief, he is a brave of the highest reputation." Perhaps revealing the reason for Conquering Bear's choice by Mitchell, Chambers added that "among the whites, and nearly all of them knew him, he bears an unspotted reputation for honesty, courage and good behavior."

In a bit of salesmanship aimed to soothe his white readers, Chambers went on to describe Conquering Bear and his selection in terms that make him seem a populist leader in the mold of Andrew Jackson or Abraham Lincoln. At least his description fits the popular image of those two cagey politicians. "His face indicates intelligence, firmness and kindness, and his eyes are clear and piecing," Chambers wrote. "His dress, which was much inferior to those of his band associated with him, indicated indifference to his personal appearance. In form and manner, I certainly did not meet with his superior, if there was any one equal to him, among all the Indians assembled."

At Conquering Bear's selection, Chambers reported, using a well-established stereotype, the usually "stoical" Indians, so "indifferent to danger or surprise, that no occurrence can change his countenance or disturb the stolidity of his nature," could not control their joy. The squaws sent up such shouts of approval that they interfered with the business of the council, forcing a reluctant Conquering Bear himself to "indignantly" rebuke them before addressing Mitchell.

"I am a young man and have no experience," Conquering Bear said.

> I do not desire to be chief of the Dahcotahs. I have not attended Councils much, because there are older and better heads in our nation than I am. There are men who know the white man longer than I have, and they know better what to do, and understand what you and our Great

Father proposes for our good, better than I do. Father, I have not attended the councils for several suns. I have been hunting buffalo, and I would not have come here today if I had known that this would have happened. Father, I think you should have selected some older and wiser man than myself.

Mitchell explained that he had chosen Conquering Bear because he was known among both the Indians and whites for his "honesty, intelligence and courage" and because it was necessary to have one chief to speak for the entire Lakota nation. He then promised the support of the "Great Father."

"I am not afraid to die," Conquering Bear answered,

but to be chief of all the Dahcotah, I must be a Big Chief. If I am to be chief I must be a Big Chief, or in a few moons I will be sleeping [dead] on the prairies. I have a squaw and papooses that I do not wish to leave. If I am not a powerful chief, my opponents will be on my trail all the time. I do not fear them. I have to sleep [die] on the prairies some time, and it doesn't concern me what time it comes. If you, Father, and our Great Father, require that I shall be their chief, I will take the office. I will try to do right to the whites, and hope they will do so to my people. And, Father, if any of my people are determined to leave me on the prairie [kill me], I will have a large company of my enemies to accompany me to the Great Spirit. I know the Great Spirit will protect me, and give many spirits of my enemies to accompany me, if I have to sleep for doing what you and our Great Father ask. The Great Spirit, the sun and moon, and the earth, know the truth of what I speak.

Almost exactly three years later, Conquering Bear would find himself "sleeping" on the plains in an incident that would rock the Lakota nation. At the council, however, Mitchell reacted to his speech by telling the Lakota voters that they should hand Conquering Bear their sticks if they supported him. For more than an hour the puzzled Lakota and Dakota debated Mitchell's choice, their doubts evident by the fact that "it appeared exceedingly doubtful whether the Indians would approve the selection." Then a voter from the Yankton band rose, walked to the center of the semicircle, and handed Conquering Bear his stick. He eventually was followed by the others, and Conquering Bear was designated by Mitchell as chief of the Lakota nation.[15]

FORMAL SIGNING of the treaty, the first major attempt by Congress to directly interfere in the government of the plains tribes, occurred on September 17, 1851, after the document was read by Mitchell and repeated by several interpreters, which still caused problems, though Chambers downplayed them: "At the insistence of some of the Chiefs, portions of it were read several times, for their better understanding. Every effort was made, and successfully too, to give them the full and just import of each article."[16]

Under the treaty, the Indians agreed to cease hostilities among themselves and to make a lasting peace. To that end, the boundaries for the country of each tribe were set. The territory of the Lakota was to run from the mouth of the White Earth (White) River on the Missouri River northwest to the forks of the Platte River, then up the South Fork of the Platte to Red Butte and along the Black Hills to the headwaters of the Heart River, and then down the Heart back to the mouth of the White Earth River.

In signing the treaty, the Indians also recognized the rights of the United States to establish roads and military posts in their territories, and promised to make restitution for depredations committed against whites passing through their territories. In return, the government agreed to protect the Indians against depredations committed by whites and to pay annuities of $50,000 per year for fifty years. As former commissioner of Indian Affairs Medill had suggested, payment was to be made in "provisions, merchandise, domestic animals, and agricultural implements, in such proportions as may be deemed best adapted to their condition by the President of the United States."

Reporting on the treaty, Mitchell noted that the annuities distributed to the Indians had satisfied them for past damage to their lands and the buffalo by migrating whites. He then sought to justify the spending of $50,000 annually on annuities for fifty years by pointing out that the money would be distributed to "at least 50,000 Indians, especially we consider that we have taken, or are rapidly taking away from them all means of support, by what may be considered a partial occupancy of their soil. On the score of economy, to say nothing of justice or humanity, I believe that amount would be well expended."

Mitchell further saw no other way to change the Indian from a hunter to a farmer, and thought that the fifty-year period prescribed for payment in the treaty would be long enough "to give the experiment a fair trial, and solve the great problem whether or not an Indian can be made a civilized man."[17]

The treaty was submitted to the Senate for ratification by President Millard Fillmore on February 17, 1852. When the full Senate finally considered the treaty on May 24, it immediately ignored Mitchell's recommendations and struck out the fifty-year time provision. Thinking $2.5 million over fifty years was too much to pay for a treaty in which no land was ceded, and hoping the "civilizing" process would take effect sooner, Senate members attempted to substitute twenty-five years and then twenty years before unilaterally settling on "the term of ten years with the right to continue the same at the discretion of the President of the United States for a period not exceeding five years thereafter."[18]

EVEN AS the federal government was dividing the high plains among the tribes and promising to "protect" their interests and preserve their lands, the population of the nation continued to creep west. The 1840 census set the population of the United States at 17 million and its center sixteen miles south of Clarksburg, West Virginia. Spurred by the California Gold Rush and immigrant fares as low as $10 from Europe, the population by 1850 had grown to 23.2 million and its center drifted west to 23 miles southeast of Parkersburg, West Virginia, on the Ohio River, the nation's once-great, and distant, western river.

During the decade that followed the Great Smoke, President Millard Fillmore was replaced by Franklin Pierce and then James Buchanan. "Washington Crossing the Delaware" was painted by Emanuel Leutze; Herman Melville published *Moby Dick*; Nathaniel Hawthorne, *The Scarlet Letter*; Stephen Foster, "Old Folks at Home" and "My Old Kentucky Home"; Thoreau, *Walden*; Henry Wadsworth Longfellow, "The Song of Hiawatha"; Walt Whitman, "Leaves of Grass"; Dan Emmett, a resident of northern Ohio who had never seen the South, "Dixie"; and Harriet Beecher Stowe, *Uncle Tom's Cabin*. The *New York Tribune* also reprinted an editorial by John B. L. Soule, editor of the *Terre Haute (Ind.) Express*, titled "Go West, Young Man, Go West."

As tensions between the North and the South rose toward the boiling point, the Republican Party was formed; Matthew Perry sailed into Tokyo Harbor, opening Japan to Western trade; Theodore Roosevelt and Woodrow Wilson were born; the Kansas-Nebraska Act was passed, allowing all states and territories to choose whether they wished to be free or slave; a transcontinental railroad survey was authorized by Congress; senatorial candidate Abraham Lincoln gave a speech in which he used the phrase "a house divided cannot stand" and later debated Stephen Douglas on the issue of slavery; the U.S. Supreme Court in the Dred Scott decision ruled that Negroes were not citizens of the United States, so could not sue; and frenzied abolitionist John Brown seized the federal arsenal at Harpers Ferry, Virginia. The first demonstration of electric home lighting was conducted in Salem, Massachusetts; the first cable message was sent across the Atlantic; and Edwin Drake drilled the first well specifically for oil, in Titusville, Pennsylvania.

In the West, Nebraska and Kansas established their first territorial legislatures; California, Minnesota, and Oregon were admitted to the Union; Lawrence, Kansas, was sacked by "border ruffians" and proslavery Kansas men; the slogans "Bleeding Kansas" and "Pike's Peak or Bust" came into use; the first railroad bridge was built over the Mississippi, and a rail line was opened from Rock Island, Illinois, to Davenport, Iowa; the first overland mail service to the Pacific Coast was started; and the Comstock Lode was discovered in Nevada.[19]

7

BUFFALO AND WAR

Based on his age and custom, probably sometime after the signing of the Horse Creek Treaty, Curly probably would have passed two high-water marks on his path to Lakota manhood—his first buffalo hunt and his first war party.

For boys growing up in rural communities where the hunt remains alive today, their first deer or first elk is an event to be celebrated and recalled by family and friends for years to come. Among the mid-nineteenth-century Lakota, a boy's first buffalo was immeasurably more important. No culture in history was ever so dependent on a single species of wildlife as the plains tribes were on the buffalo. The Lakota's very existence was so tied so closely to the herds that in their creation myth they called themselves Oyate Pte (Buffalo People). Some of their most sacred ceremonies and legends also involved the buffalo.

In the sun dance, the most devoted Lakota warriors showed their desire to find the one, true way by willingly sacrificing and selflessly enduring suffering for their people when they allowed buffalo skulls to be attached to their bodies by rawhide thongs tied to skewers forced through the folds of the skin of their backs or chests. During ceremonies inside sweat lodges, warriors seeking favor from Wanka Tanka (The Great Mystery) sometimes sliced small sacrificial bits of skin off their arms or legs and deposited them under a sacred, life-giving buffalo skull placed at the entrance to the lodge.

In the White Buffalo Ceremony, the Lakota honored the memory of the White Buffalo Maiden who gave them the sacred pipe through which man became part of all things. It happened one day when the Lakota were in camp and sent two scouts to find buffalo. The scouts rode to the top of a hill and looked to the north, where something appeared in the distance. As the figure drew closer, one scout said: "That is a woman coming." Then the other had bad thoughts of her. The first scout told him: "This is a sacred woman; throw all bad thoughts aside."

As the woman neared the scouts, they saw that she was very beautiful. She had long hair hanging down and was wearing a beautiful buckskin coat. When she reached the scouts, she stopped and put down what she was carrying; covered it with sage; and, knowing of the bad thoughts that had entered one of the scouts' minds, said: "Probably you do not know me, but if you want to do as you think, come."

The scout who had the bad thoughts said to his friend: "That is what I told you, but you would not listen to me." He rode up to the woman and faced her as a cloud came down to cover them. Then the beautiful woman walked out of the cloud and stood alone as the cloud blew off to reveal a skeleton being eaten by worms, all that was left of the scout who had the bad thoughts.

As the other scout stared in horror, the woman said: "You shall go home and tell your nation that I am coming. Therefore in the center of your nation, they shall build a tipi and there I will come."

The scout left at once and returned to camp, where he told the people what had happened. The people became excited and quickly prepared a place for the woman. They built a tipi in the center of camp, and when she arrived, she laid down what she was carrying facing east and entered the tipi and began singing: "With visible breath I am walking. A voice I am sending as I walk. In a sacred manner I am walking. With visible tracks I am walking. In a sacred manner I am walking."

After her song, the woman presented the object she had laid on the ground to the chief. It was a pipe with a calf carved on one side and twelve eagle feathers tied to it with grass that never breaks. The woman told the chief: "Behold this, for you shall multiply with this and a good nation you shall be. You shall get nothing but good from this pipe, so I want it to be in the hands of a good man, and the good shall have the privilege of seeing it."

The woman was not really a woman, but a white buffalo. She told the Lakota that when there was no food, they should offer the pipe to the Great Spirit. She said they would know from the pipe when trouble was coming. It would grow long if hard times were coming and short if the times were to be good. Then she went back into her tipi and sang another song until a white buffalo came out of the tipi, kicked its hind legs high in the air, and hurried off, snorting across the plains.

The White Buffalo Ceremony honoring the White Buffalo Maiden would start after midnight. Participants would listen to the song of the White Buffalo Maiden, make offerings, burn sweet grass, and dine on meat and chokecherries in a special tipi in which a buffalo skull altar stood. Then they would smoke. "The old die, the new are born, and the nation of men lives on forever," the holy man leading the ceremony would pray. "The White Buffalo is the leader of the nation, and from the nation comes life-giving food."[1]

STANDING BEAR provides the only detailed, personal, prereservation account of a Lakota taking his first buffalo. Elements of his experience may have been shared by Curly. It began when a group of scouts reported seeing a herd of buffalo. The chief questioned them about the size of the herd, and then sent out a crier to alert the village. "Your knives must be sharpened, your arrows shall be sharpened," the crier announced. "Make ready, make haste, your horses make ready. We shall go forth with your arrows. Plenty of meat we shall make."

When everybody was ready, the *akicita*, the soldier bands, led the way, riding twenty abreast to ensure that nobody rode ahead to frighten the herd and ruin the hunt. Anybody who attempted to ride ahead of the soldier bands was beaten back.

Behind the soldier bands came the hunters, riding four or five abreast. From among the hunters, a hunt leader selected several of the best young men with good horses and brought them forward, telling them: "Good young warriors, my relatives, your work I know is good. What you do is good always, so today you shall feed the helpless and feed the old and feeble and perhaps there is a widow who has no support. You shall help them. Whatever you get you shall donate to the poor."

As they neared the herd, the hunters divided to surround it. Then the leader shouted: *"Hoka hey!"* This is a term similar to "Charge!," and the hunters raced forward.

"They were dressed as light as possible," Standing Bear wrote,

> had only a robe over them and after charging on the buffalo they fling the robe back and they are partly naked, as they fastened their robe around their waists. The quiver of arrows was on the left side of each warrior. When they got close to one they shot the buffalo behind the left shoulder. After getting the buffalo, they yelled, *"Oohee!"* (meaning that they had gotten one buffalo). Some of the arrows would go in up to the feather and some of them not striking bones went right straight through the buffalo's body. Everyone enjoyed this immensely.

Alongside the older men, the young hunter after his first buffalo would charge the herd, possibly picking out a yearling that would be easier to handle for a boy of about twelve years of age than a bull or even the cows the Indians preferred for their tender meat and smaller, easier-to-work hides. Over the hills and down the draws he would race until he was at the animal's side, something he had watched the older hunters do many times when he was tending their pack animals, and let loose his arrow.

"The arrow went in about a foot and probably . . . hit his heart and he began to sway back and forth while running and . . . the blood coming out of his mouth," recalled Standing Bear of his own first kill.

> I was overjoyed. I was supposed to say "Yuhoo," once, but I kept on saying it. They thought I was killing a whole herd, the way I yelled. . . . When he went down, I got off my horse and began butchering him myself, and I was very happy. All over the flat, as far as I could see, there were men butchering bison now, and the women and the old men who could not hunt were coming up to help. And all the women were making the tremolo of joy for what the warriors had given them.[2]

Roughly about the same time a boy killed his first buffalo, he took part in his first war party. But, as when he was very young and learning about the hunt, his activities on those first raids were very limited and held little danger. Mainly he acted as a servant to the adult warriors, staying behind to care for their horses and traveling equipment while they rode off to count coup and steal enemy horses. The warriors in turn generally made the youngster's life miserable, abusing him with their orders and making him the butt of their jokes.

But those first raiding parties also gave the Lakota boy an opportunity to exhibit some of the lessons he had learned from his parents, in the games he played with his friends, and from his own observation of adult warriors. As the day neared for Curly to join his first raiding party, Worm probably gave him advice similar to what his contemporary White Bull was given by his father:

> You have a good knife. Keep it sharp and do not lose it. I will make you some arrows, and I want you to keep them and also keep the ropes I gave you. When you go on the warpath, look out for the enemy and do something brave. Do not make me ashamed of you. Study everything you see, look it over carefully and try to understand it. Have good-will toward all your people. Tell no lies; the man who lies is a weakling. He is a coward. Keep an even temper, and *never* be stingy with food. In that way your name will become great.[3]

Sometimes boys were taken on their first war party by a relative, perhaps a trusted uncle. But it was considered better if he showed initiative by running away to join a raiding party with his friends.

Based largely on Black Elk's hearsay account, Hump, also known as High Backbone, has been portrayed as an older warrior who was Curly's mentor in war. Black Elk said: "The people told stories of when he [Crazy Horse] was a boy and used to be around with the older Hump all the time. Hump was not young anymore at the time, and he was a very great warrior, maybe the greatest we ever had until then."[4]

That Hump and Curly were close friends and Hump a great warrior are supported by several sources, among them White Bull's winter count. In that record of Lakota history, Hump's death during a raid against the Shoshone is considered so significant that it marks the winter of 1870–1871.

Black Elk's description of Hump as being much older than Curly, however, is not so certain. He Dog said Hump was "just about the same age as Crazy Horse and I."[5] Credence is added to He Dog's claim by the realities of time. Black Elk says Hump "was not young anymore" when he and Curly became friends. Exactly what "not young anymore" means is impossible to determine. But if Curly was born about 1840, and if his friendship with Hump was one of a boy and a mentor, as Black Elk indicates, it most likely did not take root until Curly neared adolescence in the early 1850s and became more involved in adult activities.

If Hump "was not young anymore," it might be assumed that he was somewhere near forty years of age, certainly "not young" for the mid-nineteenth century. If Hump was about forty years old at the start of the 1850s, he would have been close to sixty when he was killed in the winter of 1870–1871, rather old to be on a raiding party. Even if Hump was thirty years old when he and Curly became friends, he would have been close to fifty when he was killed, again rather old for a raiding party. Even if Hump was twenty-five when he became friends with Curly sometime near the start of the 1850s, he still would have been in his mid-forties when he was killed twenty years later, an age at which renowned warriors typically gave up the field to serve more as counselors.

The likelihood that Curly and Hump were closer in age than Black Elk claims also seems to be revealed in the way the two men argued on Hump's last raid. As related by He Dog, Hump's anger over Crazy Horse's reluctance to fight in the snow and mud they encountered sounds more like the comments of a hothead than a wise old warrior, a mentor who educated Crazy Horse in the art of war.[6]

In another bit of hearsay, Black Elk encouraged speculation about the relationship of Curly and Hump when he reported: "They say people used to wonder at the boy and the old man always being together; but I think Hump knew Crazy Horse would be a great man and wanted to teach him everything."[7] The remark hints at a possible sexual relationship between Curly and Hump. Such a relationship might be supported in some people's minds by the fact that Crazy Horse did not marry until he was about thirty-one years old, late for a first marriage by both Indian and white standards of the nineteenth century, and another subject of gossip among the Lakota.

Speculation about Crazy Horse's sexuality also might be fueled by the fact that he did not marry until after Hump had been killed and that among his friends as a boy was Woman's Dress, known in his youth as Pretty One. The son of Bad Face and grandson of Old Smoke, Woman's Dress was a well-known *winkte* or homosexual whose catty tales about Crazy Horse would play an important role in the war chief's life after he surrendered at Camp Robinson.

As a people, the Lakota were ambivalent about but relatively tolerant of homosexuality. Since winktes had dreamed the path they were to follow, and no Lakota would ever question another's dream, winktes generally were both feared and respected, a duality that led many to become shamans. Iron Shell reveals that fear when he recalled his father's comments:

> My father told me the way to go and what to do until I was married—among these things was to leave the wintkes alone. . . . These men are good shamans and go about calling one another sister. Each has his own tipi, for after men have had sexual relations with them, their parents put up a tipi for them. If a man goes to a winkte and treats him as a woman, something serious will befall him. When the winkte dies, and after you have died, you will regret your relationship, for you will suffer when you reach the land beyond. Here you will not live in the main circle, but away with the murderers suffering, for here the winktes will torture you.[8]

The respect the Lakota had for winktes is evident in Blue Whirlwind's comments:

> There is a belief that if a winkte is asked to name a child, the child will grow up without sickness. My grandson was given the name Iron Horse when he was three days old by a winkte, and I gave him a horse. Fathers will go to the winkte and flirt with him. Whatever the winkte says will become the secret name and this he will name the child. Winkte names are often unmentionable and therefore are not often used. Girls never had winkte names.[9]

Even though the bravest warriors were known to lie with winktes at times, often in hopes of seeking some power or wisdom, there is no evidence of Curly engaging in such activity. The talk that Black Elk said was engendered by Curly's relationship with Hump simply may have been idle gossip. The Lakota, like any people who live in small, insulated groups, loved to gossip. While there could have been something to the talk about Curly and Hump, it is just as likely that their close friendship was based on Curly's shyness. It is not unusual for a shy boy to form a deep friendship with another boy with whom he feels he can safely bare his soul. The fact that Curly cared so much about a woman that it nearly cost him his life in later years also would seem to negate speculation about a winkte relationship with Hump.

8

THE COW

TREATIES ARE in a way illusions, breakwaters of hope erected in efforts to alter an emotional tide that has ebbed and flowed for centuries, and even may be ingrained in human nature. They can bring relief for a few years—a few generations, if conditions are good—until a building torrent of emotion and history once again washes away the walls. So, restrained only for periods of time by treaties, the fighting, hatred, and atrocities in the Balkans that filled the front page of the *Chicago Times* in the weeks leading up to Crazy Horse's surrender in 1877 repeated themselves in World War I, World War II, and again in the early 1990s. And after the Horse Creek Treaty the Lakota went back to raiding the Pawnee, Crow, and Shoshone, with whom they had warred since venturing onto the plains, while the "Manifest Destiny" of white America pushed west in record numbers.

As the Senate in early 1852 debated the Horse Creek Treaty and voted to cut the annuities the treaty promised the plains tribes, the tide of migration rose to the highest mark of the overland period. The size of the onslaught is revealed in migrant journals. Ezra Meeker wrote from Council Bluffs in western Nebraska that wagons formed "an unbroken column fully 500 miles long." Alonzo Delano likened traffic on the western trails to the passage of Napoleon's army, calling it "the greatest crowd of adventurers since the invasion of Rome by Goths, such a deluge of mortals had not been witnessed, as was now pouring from the states . . . for the golden shores of California." And Mrs. Fink noted of the conjuncture of the Independence and St. Joe trails: "It seemed to me that I had never seen so many human beings before in all my life."[1]

Led by about 10,000 Mormons, the largest Mormon contingent ever to make the overland crossing to Utah, and encouraged by the provisions of the Horse Creek Treaty that promised safe passage through lands owned by the plains tribes, an estimated 60,000 whites made their way west in 1852. The migration that year surpassed by about 10,000 the estimated number of whites who headed west to California with the initial flush of gold fever in 1850. The total would fall to about 27,500 in 1853 and to 18,000 in 1854 as returning migrants, a sizable force on the overland trails, spread the word back East that California was not littered with gold.[2]

The pressure such numbers exerted on Indian lands was extraordinary. So many overlanders left St. Joseph, Missouri, on the same day in 1852 that their wagons had to travel twelve abreast. At times fathers became separated from sons in the endless throng and did not see each other again until they arrived in California. At Ash Hollow in western Nebraska, migrants sometimes had to circle that popular rest area well into the night in search of a campsite. The image of the lonely wagon train heroically making its way west is pure Hollywood myth. As migrant Franklin Langworthy reported from near South Pass, west of Fort Laramie, in 1850: "The road, from morning till night, is crowded like Pearl Street or Broadway."[3]

DESPITE WHAT was happening, incidents involving migrants and plains Indians remained relatively minor until 1853. That summer, between 1,000 and 1,200 Lakota and Cheyenne warriors and their families were camped about four miles outside of Fort Laramie, awaiting their annuties for the year. Curly and his family could have been among them, but there is no way of knowing whether they were present.

Alarmed by yet another year of heavy migration, with its subsequent destruction of game and grass, and the many new diseases it brought, Lakota and other plains tribes were becoming increasingly hostile to overlanders and the small garrison of about fifty soldiers stationed at Fort Laramie. When, on June 15, 1853, a soldier in a skiff used as a ferryboat refused to take a group of Miniconjou Lakota across the North Platte River, the Miniconjou took the vessel. A sergeant from the fort recovered it, but while he was crossing the river one of the Miniconjou fired a shot into the water near him.

When informed of what had happened, the post commander, First Lieutenant Richard B. Garnett, ordered Second Lieutenant Hugh B. Fleming to take twenty-three men and an interpreter and "proceed to the village and demand the individual who had shot at the sergeant, and in case he was not forth coming, to take two or three prisoners, by force, if necessary."[4]

On reaching the village, Fleming demanded that the man who had fired the shot be turned over to him. The Miniconjou refused. Fleming then marched into the center of the village, causing the Miniconjou to retreat into a ravine near the rear of their camp and begin firing at the troops. In the skirmish that ensued, three Miniconjou were killed, three wounded, and two taken prisoner.

Several days after the incident, a group from the band that had been involved appeared at the fort to talk. But the army felt the Indians needed to be disciplined and that its response had been proper. The Lakota did not retaliate, but the affair left a festering wound. When Indian agent Thomas Fitzpatrick arrived at the fort on September 10, 1853, to have the Lakota sign the revised Horse Creek Treaty with its reduced annuities and time limit, he found the Miniconjou in a bitter mood. In his report, he wrote: "They stoutly insisted upon the immediate removal of the post from amongst them, saying that, when first placed there, they were told it was for their protection, 'but now the soldiers of the great father are the first to make the ground bloody.' At length one or two of the head men went so far as to decline having anything more to do with treaties."[5]

Further trouble was averted when Lieutenant Garnett explained why he had taken the action he had, but the course was set. It always had been set in the minds of many whites, as is evident in Commissioner of Indian Affairs Lea's 1852 report, filed months before Fitzpatrick arrived at Fort Laramie to persuade the confused Lakota to sign the revised treaty. Although Lea was supposed to represent the interests of the Indians, his report was full of lengthy strictures on why "enlightened and Christian" whites were justified in taking Indian lands:

> Among the errors that abound respecting our Indian relations, there is one so injurious to our national reputation that it should not be disregarded. The opinion is extensively entertained that our whole course of conduct towards red men of this country has been marked by injustice

and inhumanity. An enlightened consideration of the subject will lead to a different conclusion.

When civilization and barbarism are brought in such relation that they cannot coexist together, it is right that the superiority of the former should be asserted and the latter compelled to give way. It is, therefore, no matter of regret or reproach that so large a portion of our territory has been wrested from its aboriginal inhabitants and made the happy abodes of an enlightened and Christian people. . . . Much of the injury of which the red man and his friends complain has been the inevitable consequence of his own perverse and vicious nature. In the long and varied conflict between the white man and the red—civilization and barbarism—the former has often been compelled to recede, and be destroyed, or to advance and destroy. . . . The embarrassments to which they [Indians] are subjected, in consequence of the onward pressure of whites, are gradually teaching them the important lesson that they must ere long change their mode of life, or cease to live at all. It is by industry or extinction that the problem of their destiny must be solved.[6]

Along that same vein, Thomas A. Twiss, Indian agent for the Upper Platte Agency, would observe a few years later in another official report:

This great wave of emigration to the prairie west is moving onward with greatly increased velocity. It is beyond human power to retard or control it, nor would it be wise to do so, even were it possible.

This process of development, this law of Anglo-Saxon progress, is a necessity and a consequence of, and flowing directly from, our free institutions, which, in their strength, purity, and beauty, tend to stimulate and bring forth the vast resources of agriculture, mineral and commercial wealth, within the boundaries of our great empire.

Hence, it is that the savage, the wild hunter tribes, must give way to the white man, who requires his prairie hunting grounds for the settlement and homes of millions of human beings, where now only a few thousand of rude barbarians derive a scanty, precarious, and insufficient subsistence; and where, by improved methods in agriculture, and an application of labor-saving machinery, these millions may be fed and clothed, and add, yearly, to our great staples and products of national and individual wealth.[7]

Manifest Destiny could not be stopped. The attitudes exhibited by Lea and Twiss found personification in countless whites who ventured into Indian country. Among those was Lieutenant John L. Grattan, who on the afternoon of August 19, 1854, set in motion a series of events that eventually would lead to the Little Big Horn; the deaths of Crazy Horse and Sitting Bull; Wounded Knee; and the final destruction of the free-living plains tribes.

AUGUST IS a heavy month on the high plains, a time of dust and heat so arid and oppressive that it sucks the breath from a person's lungs. The overwhelming color, practically undisturbed except for occasional lines or pockets of green cottonwood and willow marking the locations of rivers and spring seeps, is a dead brown. But breezes make the shade comfortable. So the plains Indians had learned to rest during the day when they did not need to hunt or perform other work and spend the cool evening hours socializing, sometimes dancing and feasting through the night.

It was on the dusty, lazy afternoon of August 18, 1854, that a cow, often described as a sore-footed old cow (some accounts also call it an ox), belonging to a party of mostly Scandinavian migrants who had converted to the Mormon faith, was killed by a Lakota. That is what is known for sure. Exactly how it happened, though, is so hidden by personal interest, perception, language, and time that it is impossible to determine.[8]

Most accounts claim the cow was killed by a Miniconjou named High Forehead after it either ran or wandered into the Brulé camp where he was visiting. High Forehead is said to have shot the cow because he, like the other roughly four thousand Lakotas who had been camped near the fort for several weeks waiting for their annual annuities, had grown impatient and hungry. As during the Horse Creek Treaty Council, the Indian pony herds had devoured the best grazing near the fort and had to be driven farther afield every day to find good grass. Game, too, had grown scarce, forcing hunters to ride into the Laramie Mountains to the west to feed their families.

Another account holds that the animal was a bag of skin and bones, its feet worn through to the flesh. It had been abandoned by the Mormons and shot by boys who found it dying along the trail and wanted its hide. Still another version of the incident claims that a Miniconjou, possibly High Forehead, angered by various things whites had done and wanting revenge, shot an arrow at a migrant, missed him, and then shot another arrow, killing his cow. The Mormons themselves, in the *Latter-Day Saints Journal History* under the date August 19, 1854, matter-of-factly report: "At Sarpy's Point, eight miles east of Laramie, while a company of Saints were passing a camp of Indians, about 1000 strong, a cow belonging to the company became frightened and ran into the Indian camp, where she was left; some of them killed and ate her."

No matter what led to the cow's killing, Conquering Bear and other Brulé leaders recognized the potential seriousness of the affair. Under the Horse Creek Treaty, the plains tribes were obligated to settle such disputes before they could receive their annuities for the year. As the head chief of the Lakota in the eyes of the whites, Conquering Bear headed for Fort Laramie (some accounts say he was ordered to the fort), where he found that the Mormons had reported the loss to Lieutenant Fleming, who had replaced Lieutenant Garnett as post commander. Fleming at first seemed to view the killing as a trivial matter, but the Mormons demanded a good price for the cow. Conquering Bear offered a horse from his herd in payment, a far more than fair exchange.

According to trader Frank Salaway, who was present, Fleming brushed aside Conquering Bear's offer and told him: "I want you to bring that man in here." Conquering Bear explained that he could not do so because the man did not belong to his band. The rules of Lakota hospitality precluded such an action. Visitors were to be accorded every respect. The Horse Creek Treaty also stated that in case of an offense against whites, the offending Indian's tribe, through its chief, should offer satisfaction. But none of that mattered to Fleming. He wanted the man brought to the fort. He had concluded that the killing of the Mormon cow was just the latest in a series of incidents involving migrant property that had occurred over the summer and that the Indians needed to be taught respect.

"If you want him why don't you go up there and arrest him?" Conquering Bear told Fleming. "That is what you soldiers are here for." The lieutenant grew angry at the remark. Conquering Bear was supposed to be chief of all the Sioux, but claimed no power. Fleming told Conquering Bear that his soldiers would come to the Brulé camp the next day. "All right," Conquering Bear answered. "I'll show you his lodge; I'll show you the man."

On his way back from the fort, Conquering Bear stopped at the Oglala camp and told them what had happened. Nobody could believe that the whites would make trouble over a cow, especially since they had been offered their choice of a pony and had done nothing about earlier thefts and killing of stock. It probably was during or shortly after Conquering Bear's visit that Curly, who was then about fourteen years old and may have been in the Oglala camp with his family, heard about the incident involving the cow through camp gossip.[9]

THAT NIGHT, Conquering Bear and the other Brulé leaders appear to have seriously counseled over the matter. In the morning it was decided to send the Oglala chief Man Afraid Of His Horses to the fort to talk with Fleming. The respected Man Afraid's visit was probably intended as a conciliatory move by the Lakota. In testimony recorded in early October 1854 during an inquiry into the incident, Man Afraid reported that he went to Fort Laramie with a visiting Crow to meet with the post commander. There he watched as twenty-five-year-old Second Lieutenant John L. Grattan roused troops from their barracks and prepared a cannon.[10]

Born in Vermont, Grattan had been appointed to the U.S. Military Academy from New Hampshire. Upon graduation from West Point in 1853, he was given a brevet or temporary commission on the plains because there were no openings for second lieutenants in the regular army. Usually described as brash and boisterous, Grattan hated the assignment and sought to relieve his boredom with drink. But he also was anxious to gain attention and prove himself worthy of a regular commission. When drunk, he often complained that the Indians were not treated tough enough and claimed he could ride through the entire Sioux nation with twenty men and a field piece. Yet he also could be reasonable and generous with individual Indians. He previously had convinced Fleming that he should be allowed to lead the next detail against the Indians.

In assigning Grattan to the detail, Fleming told him "to receive the offender, and in case of refusal to give him up, after ascertaining the disposition of the Indians, to act upon his own discretion, and to be careful not to hazard an engagement without certainity of success."[11]

As Man Afraid watched Grattan's preparations, interpreter Lucien Auguste, who hated the assignment and had been drinking, rode up and told him: "It is my place to do as the Captain tells me and I suppose the Sioux will want to kill me or think hard of me that they were going to get the Indian who had killed the cow." An officer then complained that Conquering Bear had been chief of the Sioux for three years and "had always done something foolish." Man Afraid listened, and then told Fleming he was leaving. Fleming said: "No, do not go. If you get there and tell the news, the Indian who killed the cow will run off."[12]

With the wind blowing hard and thunder in the background, the officers discussed the situation while Auguste rode up to Man Afraid and told him "that he believed that he had to die. At this time the young officer [Grattan] was playfully sticking at the interpreter with his sword, telling him to make haste. The interpreter said to me, 'I am ready but must have something to drink before I die.' They gave him a bottle and he drank." Salway also reported that Grattan was drunk. He said the enlisted men were nervous and one complained: "They are drunk and we will all get killed; it is a piece of foolishness anyway." Most other sources do not report Grattan as drunk. One has him destroying a bottle of whiskey belonging to Auguste.[13]

IT WAS BETWEEN two and three o'clock in the afternoon by the time Grattan had finally readied his troops and started from Fort Laramie. Of the seventy-one men stationed at the fort, thirty-two were out cutting wood. According to Fleming's report, Grattan had with him interpreter Auguste, twenty-seven privates, a sergeant, a corporal, and two field pieces—a twelve-pounder and a mountain howitzer. Grattan, Auguste, and a few other men were mounted; most of the others rode in a mule-drawn wagon. Contrary to Hollywood, most troops stationed on the plains during the Indian wars were infantry, not cavalry.

About an hour after the troops left the fort, they reached the American Fur Company trading post, also known as the Gratiot Houses for the trader who operated it, about five miles down the

Platte River from Fort Laramie. There Grattan ordered a halt and had his men load, but not cap, their muskets. According to a statement given by migrant guide Obridge Allen, who had decided to ride along with the troops, Grattan instructed the men "to obey only his orders or those of the sergeant; said he, 'When I give the order, you may fire as much as you damned please.' He told them he didn't believe a gun would be fired, but he 'hoped to God they would have a fight.'" Before reaching the trading post of James Bordeau about three miles farther downriver, Grattan ordered another halt and had the cannons loaded.

As the troops passed the Oglala camp, Grattan sent orders to the band "not to leave their camp; if they did he would crack it to them," according to Allen. A half mile later, Allen warned Grattan that the Oglala had begun driving in their pony herds, a standard preparation for battle among the Lakota. But Grattan ignored the warning and continued on to Bordeau's trading post, where the troops halted again. Bordeau was called out and asked to send for Conquering Bear.[14]

While Grattan and Bordeau waited for Conquering Bear, the drunken Auguste began waving his pistol, making war whoops and calling to the Lakota women. He would kill them and eat their hearts before sundown, he shouted, as he rode back and forth, giving his horse its second wind as the Indians did before a buffalo hunt or an attack on their enemies. Bordeau saw that Auguste's actions were resented by the Lakota and could provoke a fight. In the inquiry about the event, Bordeau would testify he told Grattan that Auguste "would make trouble and that if he would put him in my house I would settle the difficulty in thirty minutes. He said he would stop him. He told him several times to stop, but he would not mind him."[15]

A few minutes later, Conquering Bear arrived, accompanied by Man Afraid, Little Thunder, and Big Partisan. Grattan told them he had come for the man who had killed the cow. He was going to take him back to the fort. Man Afraid reported that Conquering Bear then turned to him and said: "You are a brave, what do you think of it?" Man Afraid replied: "You are a chief, what do you think?" Conquering Bear then explained to Grattan, as he had earlier to Fleming, that High Forehead was not a member of his band, but a guest in his village. Grattan then asked Man Afraid to go into the village and persuade High Forehead to give up.

Man Afraid left and returned to report that High Forehead had refused to surrender. He and the five Miniconjou with him were loading their guns. "Last year the soldiers killed three of us," High Forehead told Man Afraid, alluding to the ferryboat affair the previous summer. "And again this year, as we sat by the side of the road, an emigrant shot at us and hit a child in the head. The child still lives. Our chief, the Little Brave, is dead, and we want to die also." According to a letter written just over a week after the affair, Captain L. B. Dougherty wrote that High Forehead said: "I am alone. Last fall the settlers killed my two brothers. This spring my only relative died (an uncle). I have a gun with plenty of powder and balls, a bow and quiver full of arrows and the soldiers will have to kill and then take me."[16]

In another effort to defuse the situation, very generous offers were again made by the Lakota to pay for the cow with horses. Grattan also was urged to delay action until the Indian agent arrived. But the glory-seeking lieutenant ignored all suggestions. He ordered his men to cap their rifles and announced that he was going to march into the Brulé camp and take High Forehead. The traders and the Lakota shook their heads. Bordeau later testified that he told Grattan: "He was going into a very bad place and that he had better prepare himself well. He said he had two revolvers with twelve shots. I told him to take them out of his holsters and be ready."[17]

Conquering Bear, riding on the back of Auguste's horse, Man Afraid, and the others returned to the camp about three hundred yards away. Wisely, Allen, Bordeau, and the other traders who had followed the troops decided to remain behind.

THE BRULÉ CAMP was tucked within a bend of the Platte River, an area occupied by a ranch today and remembered only by a lonely granite marker along Wyoming Route 157 across the North Platte from U.S. Route 26. Conquering Bear's lodge stood on the bank of a dry creek, with the two Miniconjou lodges to the left. Grattan halted his men about sixty yards from the lodges and ordered the cannons primed and aimed at the lodges; then he dispersed his troops in a line on either side of the cannons.

For the next forty-five minutes the two sides continued to talk while High Forehead stood in the doorway to his lodge. Through a messenger, he informed Grattan that he would not surrender and was willing to die. He complained bitterly of the way whites had treated his friends and offered to fight Grattan to the death.

As tensions built, Conquering Bear and Man Afraid attempted to mediate. They urged High Forehead to give up and Grattan to postpone settling the affair. Conquering Bear offered a mule for the cow if Grattan would wait for the Indian agent. How well the two sides understood each other is impossible to say, since Auguste, who was doing the interpreting, was both drunk and distrusted by the Lakota. He also was looking to get even with the Indians for recently stealing two of his horses.

While the two sides continued to talk, young warriors, possibly including the teenage Curly, streamed down from the Oglala camp upriver. Here and there Lakotas shouted and raced their horses. Others crept quietly up the dry creekbed to the left of the soldiers as the frightened Brulé women gathered their children and began moving toward the North Platte. Soon hundreds of warriors were in position to do battle. Their movement was seen by the traders and other observers who had hung back, and may even have been noticed by Gattan, though he might have concluded that the way the Lakota were standing off in the distance indicated that they were scared.

Seeing everything that was happening, Man Afraid went to Bordeau and asked him to replace Auguste. "My friend, come on," Bordeau reported Man Afraid telling him. "The interpreter is going to get us into a fight and they are going to fight if you don't come." The frightened Bordeau, who had been preparing to defend his trading post, mounted Allen's horse and began to follow Man Afraid, but then stopped, complained that the stirrups were too long, and turned back. Man Afraid would return and get Bordeau to follow him, but by then it was too late.[18]

As Man Afraid and Bordeau rode toward the Brulé camp, Grattan broke off talks, moved back to his troops, and gave a command that the Lakota did not understand. Two or three shots were fired as Conquering Bear headed back to his own lodge and a Lakota fell wounded. Bordeau was near enough to hear Lakota leaders shouting to their warriors not to fire; perhaps the soldiers had satisfied their honor by wounding a good man and would leave. Bordeau wheeled on his horse and fled to his trading post as Grattan ordered his men to fire a volley. Conquering Bear fell wounded, and the Lakota hidden in the dry creekbed attacked.

Vastly outnumbered and surrounded, Grattan, Auguste, and all but one of the twenty-nine soldiers who had ridden out with them soon were dead. Badly wounded private John Cuddy survived by hiding in a stand of wild rose bushes near a spring. Swift Bear found Cuddy, brought him into camp the next day, and hid him until he could be returned to Fort Laramie. He died of his wounds on August 21, 1854.[19]

Long-simmering anger and resentment among the Lakota over their treatment by whites boiled over onto the bodies of the dead soldiers. The victorious Indians made the most of counting coup, and then hacked and otherwise mutilated the bodies. Grattan was found with twenty-four arrows in his body, including one that went completely through his head. He was identified by his watch.

FOLLOWING THE VICTORY, the Brulé wanted to attack Fort Laramie. But Bordeau, Man Afraid, Swift Bear, and other Lakota leaders successfully argued against taking the fight to the fort. The Lakota knew that Fort Laramie was only lightly defended. Bordeau maintained that the "Great Father" would see the soldiers had been partly at fault for what had happened and would forgive the Indians. But he would never forgive an attack on the fort. Little Thunder, who had replaced Conquering Bear as headman of the Brulé, and other Brulé leaders recognized the probable truth of Bordeau's remarks and were able to restrain their warriors.

In the face of threats against himself and his trading post, Bordeau allowed the Lakota to empty the shelves of his store and raid his stock. The next day, after a long night of counciling, threats, and general excitement, the Lakota concluded that they would never receive their annuities, rode to the American Fur Company post, now owned by the Chouteau company, and emptied it of goods.

Although the Grattan fight was a resounding victory for the Lakota, some historians feel it also revealed the weaknesses of the tribe. A white army would have followed up the victory with the destruction of Fort Laramie and a blockading of the Oregon and California trails. But that overlooks the way the Lakota viewed themselves. They considered themselves to be a people, not an army. Lakota warriors went home when they decided the fighting was over, a condition hardly conducive to a disciplined fighting force. Most Lakota simply wanted to be left alone to live their lives as their fathers and grandfathers had lived their lives. They also wanted to believe that they could coexist as a people with the whites flooding into their country. So they gave in to Bordeau's reasoning that the "Great Father" would forgive them because the soldiers, too, had done wrong.

In the end it was the Lakota women who decided what the tribe should do after the Grattan fight. Many of them already had fled the area with their children and were now wandering unprotected on the plains. It was the duty of all warriors to protect such helpless ones. After raiding the American Fur Company post on August 21, the Lakota left the North Platte Valley.

9

A Death and a Life

In the wake of the Grattan fight and the looting of the trading posts, most of the Lakota men followed their families across the North Platte River and up Rawhide Creek. Somewhere, probably north of Lusk, Wyoming, the Oglala and the Brulé stopped and divided. The Oglala continued north to hunt buffalo in northern Wyoming, while the Brulé, with the severely wounded Conquering Bear lashed to a travois, turned east down the Niobrara River, called Running Water by the Lakota, into northwestern Nebraska. Several days later, while the Brulé were camped along the Niobrara near the mouth of the Snake River, Conquering Bear died of his wounds.[1]

Although an Oglala, Curly is believed by some writers to have stayed with the Brulé and to have seen Conquering Bear on his deathbed. Shortly afterward, the story goes, the teenager wandered alone into the lake country of the Sand Hills, where he had the vision that would guide him for the remainder of his life.[2]

Since Curly's two stepmothers were Brulé, and since Lakota men frequently went with the family of their wife, or wives, in times of trouble, it is entirely possible that Worm and his family would have gone with the Brulé instead of the Oglala when the two tribes split. It also is possible that Curly was so traumatized by the Grattan fight and the suffering of Conquering Bear that he fled into the Sand Hills to seek relief and had his vision. However, something about the scenario seems a little too literary. As with so much of Crazy Horse's life, there is no sure way to separate fact from legend.

That Curly had a vision as a teenager is better documented than the time period of that vision. Actually, it was not unheard of for

Lakota boys as young as ten and twelve years of age to have visions. Among them were Sitting Bull and Rain In The Face. White Bull was eleven years old and Black Elk just nine years old when they had their visions. For the Lakota male, *hanble ceyapi*, or "crying for a vision," was considered important to success in life, though by no means a guarantee of success.

Before the quest, the vision seeker normally was taken into a sweat lodge by a medicine man for a purification ceremony to remove "all that makes him tired, or all that causes disease, or all that causes him to think wrong." The seeker then would go off alone on the plains to pray for a vision. His hair unbraided and clothed only in a breechcloth and buffalo robe as a sign of his humility, the seeker would force himself to stay awake and cry aloud for a vision. He made himself pitiful so that the Great Spirit would be moved to hear his prayers and guide him. Then he would return to the sweat lodge and tell his vision in a ritual speech that brought out the power of the vision.[3]

Some Lakota, though, were given a vision without such preparation or effort. Black Elk was eating in a friend's lodge when a voice called him, saying: "It is time; now they are calling you." The next day, he became sick. His legs, arms, and face swelled, and two men rode out of the clouds to lead him off to met his grandfathers.[4] White Bull's vision came while he was hunting swallows. In Lakota culture, the swallow was a sacred messenger of the Thunder Being. Suddenly White Bull fell to the ground and a man appeared in the west. He was riding a black horse painted with red lightning streaks. Men riding horses painted with lightning streaks were standard embodiments of Thunder Beings and appeared in the visions of many plains Indians.[5]

Lakota men who had a vision were invested with an aura that set them apart from others in their tribes. The powers granted by the vision also placed on them a sacred duty to use their gift for the benefit of their people. That duty might include fighting in battle, performing ceremonies, curing illnesses, and healing wounds. The vision was to be followed and interpreted throughout life. Not to follow the vision was to risk punishment from the Great Spirit.

Curly's vision, according to the best-known accounts, was more of a struggle than that of either Black Elk or White Bull. For two days

Curly fasted, keeping himself awake by placing sharp stones under his body and between his toes so he could not lie down and sleep, but no vision came to him. Disappointed, he gave up and started down the hill on which he had been waiting. As he reached his horse, hobbled near a lake, the dream finally came, possibly because, like Black Elk and White Bull, he fainted.

As with Black Elk and White Bull, too, a man appeared on horseback. He rode out of the lake, changing colors as he neared and floated above the ground. The man was dressed in plain leggings and a simple shirt. His face was without paint and he wore a single eagle feather in his long brown hair. Behind one ear was tied a small, brown stone. The man did not speak, but Curly heard him. He told the young Lakota never to wear a war bonnet or tie up his horse's tail, as was the Lakota custom, because a horse needed its tail to jump streams and brush away flies in the summer. The man told Curly that before going into battle he should rub dust over his hair and body. He said Curly would never be killed by a bullet or an enemy and should never take anything for himself.

As the man talked, floating above the lake, he brushed aside constant attacks from a shadowy enemy, riding straight through waves of arrows and bullets that disappeared. Several times the man and the horse were held back, possibly by his own people coming up behind him and holding his arms, but he freed himself and rode on. Then a storm arose. Lightning appeared on the man's cheeks and hailstones on his body. The storm passed, and the man's people gathered around him. They grabbed him and hung on to him as a hawk screamed overhead; then the dream faded.[6]

THE STORY OF CURLY'S VISION comes mainly from the white trader and interpreter Garnett, who claims to have heard it from Crazy Horse himself in 1868. Garnett's account is supported, at least in part, by the manner in which Crazy Horse prepared himself for battle. Chips said: "Crazy Horse never wore a war bonnet. He did not paint as the Indians usually do; but he made a zigzag streak from the top of his forehead downward and to one side of his nose at the base to the point of his chin. This was done with one finger. He striped his horse with a mould from the earth."[7] Crazy Horse's friend He Dog noted: "He never wore a war bonnet. A medicine man named Chips had given him power if he would wear in battle an eagle-bone whistle and one feather and a certain round stone with a hole in it under his left arm, suspended by a leather thong that went over his shoulder. The one central feather that is in the middle of the war-eagle's tail, that was the feather he wore in his hair." Crazy Horse's brother-in-law, Red Feather, also reported that the war chief wore a stone, though a "white stone," on a thong under his left arm when going into battle.[8]

Further support is lent to Garnett's account by the Cheyenne John Stands In Timber. He reports seeing a drawing that Crazy Horse made of his vision on sandstone along Reno Creek after the Battle of the Little Big Horn. Stands In Timber almost surely did not know of Garnett's story, which was privately collected and never published, so he could not have been parroting the trader's tale. At the same time, though, it must be noted that he did not see Crazy Horse make the carving himself. He heard about it thirdhand from a friend who himself had been told about it by his father. But Stands In Timber did see the carving. "I have been there and copied it," he says. "Whistling Elk's father was a witness that he [Crazy Horse] did it. There is a horse with a snake above it and lightning marks. Whistling Elk's father told him Crazy Horse had dreamed the horse was standing on a high pinnacle and he saw a snake above it and streaks of lightning moving over it."[9]

While Garnett's description is important, it should be viewed with at least some skepticism because it was recorded decades after Crazy Horse's death, at a time when he was passing farther and farther into legend. Since Black Elk's father, a cousin of Crazy Horse, admitted to his son that he did not know all of the war leader's vision, it would appear doubtful, too, that a white trader was privy to the complete vision. According to Black Elk:

> Curly dreamed and went into the world where there is nothing but the spirits of things. That is the real world that is behind this one, and everything we see here is something like a shadow from that world. He was on his horse in that world, and the horse and himself on it and the trees and the grass and the stones and everything were made of spirit, and nothing was hard, and everything seemed to float. . . . It was this vision that gave him his great power, for when he went into a fight, he had only to think of that world to be in it again, so that he could go through anything and not be hurt.[10]

Although Black Elk's comments need to be taken into consideration, they also must be viewed critically because he heard them secondhand from his father long after Crazy Horse's death. Chips, though, is another story, since he was both a longtime friend and a spiritual mentor of Crazy Horse; the person who interpreted the war leader's vision told him how to prepare for a fight and gave him the talismans that he carried into battle. He told Crazy Horse, too, that he would be killed with a knife while his arms were being held. Of Curly's vision, Chips says: "There is no truth in the story of the horseman coming out of the pond and telling Crazy Horse what to do."[11]

Adding to the confusion, Flying Hawk, a distant, younger cousin of Crazy Horse who claimed to have fought in nine battles with the war chief, relates a vision story that Crazy Horse once supposedly told him:

> I was sitting on a hill or a rise, and something touched me on the head; I felt for it and found it was bit of grass. I took it to look at; there was a trail nearby and I followed it; it led to water; I went into the water; there the trail ended and I sat down in the water; I was nearly out of breath; I started to rise out of the water, and when I came out I was born by my mother. When I was born I could know and see and understand for a time, but afterwards went back to it as a baby; then I grew up naturally— at the age of seven I began to learn, and when twelve began to fight enemies. That was the reason I always refused to wear any war-dress; only a bit of grass in the hair; that was why I always was successful in battles.[12]

There was nothing unique about Crazy Horse wearing a small stone on his left side and not wearing a war bonnet into battle. Many Indians carried stones for luck or as talismans. And war bonnets were cumbersome affairs better kept for ceremonial occasions than for wear on war parties, where free, quick movement could mean the difference between life and death.

In the most often repeated account of the vision, Curly is not very impressed by his dream and remains alone on the plains hoping for more. Finally he falls asleep. When he awakes, he finds Worm and Hump standing over him. They are angry because he had gone off alone while everybody in the village was concerned about the dying Conquering Bear. They tell him a Crow or a Pawnee raiding party could have found him. When Curly says he had gone in search of a vision, Worm explodes. His son had not properly prepared himself for such a sacred quest. He had not purified himself in the sweat lodge or councilled with a medicine man. He had no right to do such a thing. Chastened, Curly quietly follows his father and Hump back to their village without telling them what he had seen.[13]

In the wake of the Grattan fight and the impending death of Conquering Bear, certainly a father and close friend such as Hump would have worried about Curly disappearing alone onto the plains for three days. Worm also may have chided his teenage son for behaving in such a manner. But none of the primary sources on Crazy Horse's life report such an incident. Neither do they indicate that Worm chided his son for seeking a vision without the proper preparation. While it could have happened, especially if Worm was angry, there is nothing to support such an action. Since young Lakotas occasionally were overcome by visions, though, Worm just as likely could have been happy to learn of what had happened to his son. He could have seen it as a sign of future greatness.

Stories about the Grattan fight began appearing in newspapers about three weeks after the incident. The *Missouri Republican* carried a doctored army "express" or news release in its September 11, 1854, edition under the headline "Treacherous Slaughter of U. States Troops at Fort Laramie." The story reported:

> Following a period of mounting depredations by the Indians, a poor emigrant complained on August 18th that one of his oxen had been shot down by an Indian. The commandant had sent out a detachment of about thirty men, under Lieutenant Grattan, to apprehend the Indian offender. As head chief of the Sioux, the Bear "had expressed a willingness to give up the offender," and, along with the interpreter, accompanied the detail to the Indian encampment. The express indicated the need for reinforcement, for "the entire detachment had been massacred, and the head chief was reported among the Indians killed."

The story goes on to conclude that Grattan's troops were the "victims of a deliberately contrived plot on the part of the Indians." Within days, the newspaper proclaimed that "a state of war now exists between the United States and the powerful, warlike nation of the Sioux."

As the source for much of the commerce serving the plains and California, Saint Louis had a special interest in what had happened at Fort Laramie. "While the State of California is so dependent for stock of every description," the *Missouri Republican* noted, "we are dependent on them for a market—and this stock trade across the plains will now be suspended." The newspaper played up the story for months.[14]

Thanks to the telegraph, the story of the Grattan fight was carried by some eastern newspapers at almost the same time that it appeared in Saint Louis. "Troops Massacred by the Indians," the *New York Daily Tribune* proclaimed on September 11, 1854. "Indian Outrages," the *New York Daily Times* announced in a slightly more detailed story on September 12, 1854, the same day the *Pittsburgh Gazette*, possibly because of a mistake by its telegraph operator, reported that the fight occurred near "Fort Lawrence."

Based on the army "express," all of the stories, none of which were more than a few paragraphs in length, are very similar in detail and tone. They report that an Indian had slain a migrant's ox and that Conquering Bear had told Lieutenant Fleming to send a detachment to his camp and he would surrender the man. Lieutenant Fleming did as was requested, and when the detachment reached the camp it was attacked and annihilated in what "appeared to be a pre-concerted plan on the part of the Indians to waylay and murder the party."[15]

As might be expected, follow-up stories generally held the "treaty breaking" Lakota responsible for the incident, although some stories pointed the finger at "greedy traders," the "negligent Indian service," and "incompetently-led military."[16] The Washington correspondent for the *New York Daily Times* was among the first who called for revenge. After blasting Congress for its "niggardly and disgraceful neglect" of the army and the garrison at Fort Laramie, he wrote in the newspaper's September 14, 1854, edition:

> If the War Department had the troops at its command, the present would be an excellent opportunity to teach the treaty breaking Indians a lesson of the consequence of their bad faith, such as would nip in the bud the prolonged Indian war which now seems about to break out. But the service is absolutely without the means to do this; and as a consequence, doubtless, the savages will become utterly regardless of all their treaties, will laugh at our inability to enforce them, will destroy our property and cut the throats of our fellow citizens traversing the Plains *ad libitum*. The country should speak out on this subject, and demand of Congress an increase of the Army commensurate with the recent expansion of our borders.[17]

Seeing what was happening in the country, Father De Smet sadly wrote in an April 17, 1855, letter to superiors in Europe: "An unpardonable offense, it appears, had been committed in the eyes of our civilized people by the Indians." After outlining the incidents that lead to the Grattan fight, he noted: "Will you, in Europe, believe this tale of a cow? And yet such is the origin of a fresh war of extermination upon the Indians which is to be carried out in the course of the present year."

Historians consider the Grattan fight as the start of the plains Indian wars. But, as in the past, not all whites immediately sought war with the Indians because of the incident. Missouri senator Benton, who had been outspoken in promoting the nation's expansion west, even suggested in a speech before Congress that men with knowledge of the plains tribes "go to every hostile tribe and arrange every difficulty with them in the very first interview."[18] Instead of demonizing Conquering Bear, Benton honored him by reading into the *Congressional Record* a tribute to him written by *Missouri Republican* editor Chambers.

In that tribute, Chambers calls Conquering Bear "this Logan of the West," a reference to a Mingo Indian whose entire family was killed by white militiamen in western Pennsylvania during Lord Dunsmore's War in 1774. After a rampage in which he satiated his anger and pain by killing every white he encountered, Logan gave a speech that became known as "Logan's Lament" and that Thomas Jefferson favorably compared to the best oratory of ancient Rome.[19] Chambers wrote of Conquering Bear:

> We knew him well, and a better friend the white man never had. He was brave, and gentle, and kind—a wise ruler, a skillful warrior, and respected chieftain. Even in accepting his position, assigned to him some four years ago at the treaty of Laramie [Horse Creek], he only consented after much persuasion; and then remarked when he did so, that he gave his life to the Great Spirit. So far from any charge of treachery attaching to his conduct, his own fate is a sufficient proof of his fidelity; in recording it, we feel like inscribing a worthy memorial of one of the most high-toned and chivalric of all Indians we have known.[20]

10

BLUE WATER

Conquering bear died from his wounds in either late August or early September 1854. The exact date and location of his passing are unknown. After Conquering Bear's death, most of the Brulé headed for the tribe's fall hunting grounds. One story has Curly leading the tribe to a herd of buffalo by placing his ear to the ground and listening for hoofbeats. During the hunt, he supposedly made the first kill, and that evening the entire village, led by Hump, danced and sang the praises of the young teenager. There is nothing to refute the story, but neither is there anything to support it.[1]

Since war in the eyes of the Lakota did not call for the destruction or the continued pursuit of a defeated enemy, no serious plans were made by the Brulé to cut off migrant trails or to attack military posts after Conquering Bear's death. Only a small band of the chief's relatives and a few young men hungry to make a name for themselves sought revenge, and generally they contented themselves with stealing horses and livestock. But on November 13, 1854, they also attacked the Salt Lake mail-wagon train near Horse Creek. In that incident, five Brulé, including Curly's uncle Spotted Tail, killed three whites and supposedly carried off mail pouches containing twenty thousand dollars in gold. One source alleges that the money ended up in the pocket of trader James Bordeau, but that was never proved.[2]

Although most Brulés remained peaceful after the Grattan fight and the death of Conquering Bear, whites on the plains were understandably alarmed by what had happened, and rumors of Indian troubles raced up and down the Platte and Missouri rivers. On August 20, 1854, the day after the fight, Lieutenant Fleming, commander of Fort Laramie, sent an appeal for reinforcements to Fort Leavenworth, Kansas Territory. On September 30 he wrote again, warning his superiors: "Should a sufficient force be sent out immediately by the government to punish the offenders in an effectual manner, no hostility from other tribes may be expected. But should this not be done, then great sacrifice of life may be expected; as all surrounding tribes, stimulated by neglect of this bloody massacre, will join hand in hand and rush on to the slaughter."[3] Reinforcements in the form of 111 men under Lieutenant Colonel William Hoffman finally reached Fort Laramie on November 12, 1854.

On November 29 Colonel Hoffman wrote his superiors that a thousand lodges of Brulé, Miniconjou, and other Lakota were camped on the Running Water (Niobrara River) and that they would keep up the fight all winter, then in the spring attack troops on the plains. He recommended that three commands be sent against the Lakota—one from Fort Pierre on the Missouri River, one from Fort Kearny on the lower Platte River, and one from Fort Laramie. Hoffman maintained that three commands were necessary because the Lakota could elude a single command in the vastness of the plains.[4]

Alfred Vaughan, Indian agent on the upper Missouri, also wrote, from Fort Pierre on November 21, warning that the Brulé, Miniconjou, and their allies "openly bid defiance to the threats of the government, and go so far as to say that they do not fear the result should soldiers come to fight them." While returning from the Yellowstone River, he had met Hunkpapa and Blackfoot Lakota, who told him they did not want annuities but "preferred scalps and stealing horses." Vaughan concluded: "Something should be done to show the power of the government, and that speedily, otherwise there is no knowing the result. Every man's life in this country is in jeopardy."

Trader and former Indian agent John Dougherty added: "It is highly important that a decisive blow should be given them at the very onset. This would have the effect to deter all other neighboring tribes from joining in with the Sioux against us. . . . A prompt and decisive blow on the Sioux in effect would be worth to us, for years to come, millions of dollars and many strong armies."[5]

The letters of Colonel Hoffman, Vaughan, and Dougherty made their way up the chain of command to Secretary of War Jefferson Davis. He submitted them to President Franklin Pierce, who in turn presented them to Congress on January 16, 1855. President Pierce used the letters to renew his call to increase the size of the regular army. To combat the Indian threat, he urged Congress to employ volunteer troops. Unless, he said, "a force can be early brought into the field, adequate to the suppression of existing hostilities, the combination of predatory bands will be extended, and the difficulty of restoring order and security greatly magnified."[6]

Even before such warnings reached the East, though, General Winfield Scott, commander of the army, had decided that "a single punishment" should be delivered to the Lakota.[7] On October 26, 1854, the War Department sent a message to General William S. Harney, on leave in Paris, informing him that he was being placed in charge of an expedition against the Lakota. Colonel Harney returned to the United States on March 22, 1855. He arrived in St. Louis on April 1 and began working on plans to put Colonel Hoffman's recommendation for a three-arm movement against the Lakota into practice. From St. Louis, Harney traveled to Fort Leavenworth in mid-July and moved his troops to Fort Kearny on the Platte River, where he was joined by additional troops from Fort Riley. When he set out from Fort Kearny on August 24, 1855, he had with him more than six hundred men and was determined to teach the Lakota a lesson. Known for his puritanical severity, he reportedly announced: "By God, I'm for battle—no peace."[8]

WHILE THE U.S. GOVERNMENT geared for war, the Lakota continued life as if the Grattan fight simply had been a skirmish with another tribe. Through the spring and into the summer, small bands of Brulé and other Lakota continued to raid trading posts, steal stock, and harass migrants. Bordeau and other traders warned that the white army was coming to avenge the killing of Grattan, but the Lakota paid little heed. Instead of preparing to defend themselves, they went off on a buffalo hunt north of the Platte River. Then, in June 1855, a war party of about five hundred Lakota rode off to seek two traditional enemies, the Pawnee and the Omaha.

On the Loup Fork of the Platte River in south-central Nebraska, the war party divided; half of the warriors went down the Platte, in search of the Pawnee, and the other half east, after the Omaha. The Pawnee camp was empty when the Lakota reached it. Along Beaver

Creek, though, the second group found an Omaha village. In the ensuing fight Logan Fontenelle, the half-French chief of the Omaha, was killed.[9]

Various accounts mark the fight with the Omaha as the first time Curly killed a person. According to that story, Spotted Tail led the attack on the Omaha village. During the fight, Curly noticed a figure sneaking through the brush, shot an arrow at it, and saw it fall. When he reached the scene ready to take his first scalp, he found the figure to be a woman and froze in near horror. Even though Lakota custom did not view the killing of an enemy woman as wrong, but rather saw it as a disgrace for the warrior who had failed to defend her, Curly was so upset by what he had done that he vowed never again to kill a woman.[10]

There is no way to refute the tale, but support for it is sketchy. Since teenage boys frequently were taken on raids by their uncles, Curly may have been part of Spotted Tail's party. It is possible, too, that he swore never to slay another woman after the incident. But that part of the story simply could be an effort to paint Curly in a favorable light to match the legend of a great warrior fighting the good fight.

While there is no doubt that Spotted Tail was a leader of the Brulé war party, his biographer, George Hyde, does not specifically place him with the Brulé who attacked the Omaha village. If Curly was riding with Spotted Tail, that means there is nothing to place him at the scene of the Omaha fight.[11]

Of the Oglalas who knew Crazy Horse, only He Dog and White Bull address the incident. He Dog reports: "When we were seventeen or eighteen years old we separated. Crazy Horse went to the Rosebud [Brulé] band of Indians and stayed with them for about a year. Then he came home. After he had been back a while, I made inquiries about why he had left the Rosebud band. I was told he had come back because he had killed a Winnebago woman."[12] White Bull said that Crazy Horse fought the Skili, possibly the Skidi Pawnees, who lived near Omaha, and "struck a woman first."[13]

If, as seems likely, Curly was born in either 1839 or 1840, he would have been only fifteen or sixteen years of age at the time of the raid on the Omaha in 1855, not the seventeen or eighteen that He Dog reports. If Curly was seventeen or eighteen, that may mean he took his first life a year or two later and may not have taken part

According to one story, Brulé leader Spotted Tail led the attack on an Omaha village in which Crazy Horse killed a person for the first time.

in the raid on the Omaha. However, that discrepancy could be attributed to the passage of time. He Dog's remarks were recorded sixty-five years after the raid. His reason for Curly's return to the Oglala also could support the claim that he vowed not to kill another woman. It might be taken to mean that the future war leader was driven to seek refuge at home because of guilt, self-doubt, shame, or even teasing from other warriors who thought him too sensitive.

He Dog's description of the victim as a Winnebago woman does not necessarily refute the story. If the woman was a Winnebago, she could have been married to an Omaha or visiting the village. The two tribes were friendly. When the Winnebago were pushed out of Wisconsin in the 1860s, they sought refuge with the Omaha. The tribe eventually sold the Winnebago the land in eastern Nebraska that became their reservation.

IF THE BRULÉS and other Lakota showed little interest in the plans of the U.S. government, Thomas Twiss, newly appointed Indian agent for the Upper Platte Agency, was extremely concerned. A former officer in the regular army who believed wholeheartedly in Manifest Destiny, the superiority of the Anglo-Saxon race, and the inevitable demise of the Indians, Twiss nevertheless met with traders as soon as he reached Fort Laramie on August 10, 1855. He warned that the army was bent on revenge and sent out riders urging all Indians considered "friendly and peaceable" to come into Fort Laramie.[14]

Although some warriors talked about fighting the whites, when word reached the camps that Harney was on his way and would attack any Indians found north of the Platte River, most of the Lakota thought better of taking on the army. They dismantled their lodges and headed for Fort Laramie. Among those who sought refuge at the fort were Oglala under Man Afraid Of His Horses and Brulé under Stabber, who was among the chiefs Parkman met near Fort Laramie on his 1846 trip across the plains. During a visit to the Arkansas River, Stabber had seen U.S. troops preparing to invade Mexico. The numbers of troops and their weapons left a lasting impression on him. Learning that the army was coming to avenge Grattan, he immediately led his people into Fort Laramie and informed Twiss that he had driven off the family of Conquering Bear. Stabber probably told Twiss that he had driven off Conquering Bear's family to impress the agent with his desire for peace. What actually happened was that Stabber and Conquering Bear's brother, Red Leaf, had quarreled. Red Leaf wanted to avenge Conquering Bear's death, Stabber wanted peace, so the band divided.[15]

On August 20, 1855, Agent Twiss wrote the Secretary of the Interior that four or five bands were under his protection, including Lakota, Cheyenne, and Arapaho. To strengthen his case for protection of the Indians at the fort, he wrote: "The Band which murdered the Mail party is called the Wasazahas [a Brulé band], and was the [Conquering] Bear's Band before his death. I cannot ascertain where this band is, at present, hunting. I expect, however, that my Runners

will soon bring news of them." He concluded that "the Sioux difficulties have been magnified by false and malicious reports. There is not,
as I can find, within this Agency, a hostile Indian. On the contrary, all
are friendly."[16]

By September 8 about four hundred lodges of Lakota had gathered on the Laramie River thirty-five miles above Fort Laramie. About
seven hundred lodges were camped near the fort when the Grattan
fight took place. Only three bands remained north of the Platte River,
among them Little Thunder, who was camped on the Blue Water, a
small tributary of the Platte that emptied into the river near the confluence of its North and South forks.

THE LOCATION of the Battle of the Blue Water, also known as the Battle of Ash Hollow and Harney's Massacre, is even tougher to find
than the site of the Grattan fight. The battle took place on what is
now private property near Lewellen in far southwestern Nebraska.
There is no granite monument commemorating the fight, only a road
sign along U.S. Route 26 announcing Blue Creek, the present name
of the Blue Water.

Why Little Thunder chose to camp on the Blue Water when other
Lakota were hurrying to Fort Laramie has mystified many historians.
The camp was only six miles from Ash Hollow, a major resting place
for migrants on the Oregon Trail, and close enough for travelers on
the trail to see smoke from its fires. Little Thunder also was considered to be friendly to whites, though with him at the time were Spotted Tail, Red Leaf, and Iron Shell, three strong advocates of fighting.
He had been warned, too, by Bordeau that troops were coming up
the Platte.

According to the Lakota version of events leading up to the
attack, Little Thunder held a council, and the camp of forty-one
lodges decided to remain on the Blue Water, about two miles downstream of another camp of eleven lodges of Miniconjou, Oglala, and
Cheyenne. Together the two camps held about 250 people. The
council decided to stay because the women were drying meat from a
hunt. So unconcerned were they of the approaching danger that even
after a second warning arrived from Bordeau, Little Thunder and the

other Lakota leaders did not bother to send out scouts to assess the situation. The man who brought the warning was still in camp when it was attacked.[17]

Led by Joe Tesson, a trader familiar with Little Thunder's camp, Harney and his troops reached Ash Hollow late in the afternoon of September 2. As the exhausted troops, mostly infantry that had force-marched twenty miles without water, collapsed and refreshed themselves in the North Platte, Harney set about making plans for an attack. At 3:00 A.M. Lieutenant Colonel Phillip St. George Cooke and Tesson led the cavalry and mounted artillerymen on a twelve-mile-wide swing around the camp. Then, at 4:30 A.M., Harney began marching his infantry up the Blue Water toward the camp "with a view to attacking it openly in concert with the surprise contemplated through the cavalry."[18]

As the infantry approached the camp, the Brulé struck their lodges and retreated up the valley. Before they encountered the cavalry, though, they stopped and, according to Lakota accounts, Little Thunder, Spotted Tail, and Iron Shell rode out under a white flag to parley with Harney. The plan of the three leaders was to delay the troops with talk while the women and children fled. It was an ancient Lakota strategy, but Harney did not fall for it. Instead, he kept his infantry moving up the Blue Water. Seeing what was happening, Little Thunder, Spotted Tail, and Iron Shell panicked. They broke off talks and raced back to the camp under a barrage of fire.[19]

Several white officers and a correspondent for the *Missouri Republican* have left corroborating accounts of events leading up to the fight that differ from the Lakota version.[20] According to those journals and news stories, the Brulé leaders signaled for a parley, but it was ignored by Harney. "As we had come for war and not for peace, we paid no attention to them," the *Republican* reported.

In his journal, Lieutenant G. K. Warren wrote: "As soon as we could see the Indian camp, we discovered that they were moving off up the valley of the stream, and by the time we came opposite it, they had struck nearly all their lodges and gone. The hindermost kept about a mile in advance." When it became evident that the infantry was not going to catch up to the Lakota, Harney began to worry that they would escape. To gain time and learn something about the disposition of the Lakota, he sent out an interpreter, who was met by

Little Thunder; no mention is made of him being accompanied by any other Lakota. According to Warren, the chief said he would come in if the infantry halted its advance. "A halt took place on both sides," Warren wrote, "both sides being anxious spectators, but few knowing its nature, and none its results."[21]

Captain John Todd, another witness, also does not mention Spotted Tail or Iron Shell. He said Little Thunder "came down on horseback at full speed to meet him [Harney], and when within thirty or so feet stopped, and the 'talk' began. This lasted over thirty minutes, probably nearly an hour." According to Todd, Harney reproached Little Thunder for the death of Lieutenant Grattan and his troops, the attack on the mail train, and depredations against migrants. Little Thunder replied "that he could not control his young men, that he himself was friendly and finally that he did not want to fight." He offered his hand to Harney, who refused it. "The chief toward the close became quite uneasy, but the Genl. assured him that he had nothing to fear, as he would allow him to rejoin his people before he attacked. Finally, he told him to go and tell his young men that a battle had to settle their differences and to come out and fight, and if he, himself, did not want to be hurt to get out of the way as quickly as possible."[22]

A few minutes after Little Thunder had rejoined his people, according to Todd, the order to advance was given and he was asked by Harney if his troops could reach the retreating Lakota with their new, long-range rifles. Todd said they could, and the order to fire was given. "The words were barely out of his [Harney's] mouth," Todd wrote, "before the rattle of the rifles of my company was heard, and the Sioux Campaign initiated in earnest."[23]

ALTHOUGH THE CAVALRY was discovered before the end of the talk, Lieutenant Colonel Cooke did not order an advance until he heard Todd's infantry fire. The *Missouri Republican* correspondent described the scene: "The Indians ran, of course, to the hills and were in a fine position to repel an attack of Infantry when the Dragoons showed themselves, then . . . the fun commenced in reality. I never saw a more beautiful thing in my life. When the Infantry saw the Dragoons coming down in such beautiful style, they gave a yell, which resounded far and wide. The Indians threw away everything they had in the world. We suppose we killed about 70."[24]

Caught by the long-range rifle fire, the Lakotas retreated north. "About this time," Todd wrote, "a warrior dashed out from the crowd and, approaching us, rode down the line at full speed parallel to it, and distant about 300 yards. Poor fellow! What hope of escape for him, what chance to come off scatheless from the Hundred Minnies levelled upon him, as furiously he dashed along this fiery gauntlet, his scalp lock and streamers trailing in the wind, now hanging close upon the neck of his horse and now proudly erect, shouting his cry of defiance, down they go, this daring fellow and his horse, now up again, then dips beyond the crest and disappears."[25]

As the infantry's rifles took their toll, the cavalry appeared in front of the retreating Lakotas, forcing them toward a sand draw to the east, above which the troops had taken their position. "As they passed, from a high commanding point . . . ," Todd wrote, "we poured a plunging fire upon them with our long range rifles, knocking them out of their saddles, right and left. The party was large and compact and, as their people fell, others jumped from their horses and picking them up, replaced and carried them off. A few moments after, the cavalry came down, and our work ceased."[26]

Survivors of the deadly gauntlet scattered through the surrounding sand hills, pursued by the cavalry for a distance of up to eight miles before the troops were recalled. Of the roughly 250 Lakota in the two camps, Harney reported killing 86, wounding 6, and capturing 70 women and children. He lost 4 men killed; 4 seriously wounded; 3 slightly wounded; and 1 missing, presumed captured.

Little Thunder and Iron Shell escaped injury. Spotted Tail, however, suffered two wounds to the body and two saber cuts. According to Lakota accounts, Spotted Tail was one of the last warriors to flee. He either gave his horse to one of the escaping families or had it shot out from under him. On foot, he fought bravely and killed some of the soldiers. Spotted Tail's wife and a baby daughter were among those captured by the troops.[27]

IN A JOURNAL PASSAGE that contains none of the sporting tone of the *Missouri Republican* story but does sound as if he is observing wounded animals, Warren recorded the horror of the fight:

> The recall having sounded, I went with others in search of the wounded. The sight on top of the hill was heart-rendering, wounded women and children crying and moaning, horribly mangled by bullets, most of this had been occasioned by these creatures taking refuge in the holes in the rocks, and armed Indians sheltering themselves in the same places. These later fired upon our men, killing 2 men and wounding another of the artillery company. Our troops then fired in upon their retreat. Two Indians were killed in the hole, and two as they came out. Seven women were killed in the hole and 3 children, 2 of them in their mothers' arms. . . .
>
> One young woman was wounded in the left shoulder, the ball going in above and coming out below her arm. I put her on my horse. Another handsome young squaw was wounded just below her left knee, the same bullet hit her baby in the right knee. . . . I had a litter made, and put her and the child on it. I found another girl about 12 years old laying with her head down in a ravine and apparently dead. Observing her breath, I had a man take her in his arms. She was shot through both feet. I found a little boy shot thru the calves of his legs and thru his hams. I took him in my arms. He had enough strength left to hold me around the neck.[28]

Warren also reported seeing a girl shot through the right breast, a boy shot in the thigh, another shot in the arm, and an Oglala woman badly wounded in the shoulder by a cavalry man who had found her hiding in the grass after the fight and mistook her for a warrior. In his reminiscence, General Richard Drum told of finding a "little child naked, save for a scarf around his waist in which a little puppy was wrapped."[29]

Drum apparently saw the same "handsome young squaw" with the wounded baby as did Warren. Like migrants who recorded far more colorful encounters with Indians in their reminiscences than in journals, however, Drum apparently spices up his account by making the woman a white captive. "I found that she was undoubtedly a white woman . . . ," he wrote, "the woman had evidently been captured in her childhood and grown up among the Indians; for in every respect she was a thorough hostile, except in the display of her grief at the loss of her child—for it is well known that the Indian is rarely demonstrative in sorrow."[30]

Curly reportedly was living in the Little Thunder camp that summer, but was out hunting when the Blue Water fight occurred. According to that story, he returned to the camp in the afternoon and found a survivor, a Cheyenne named Yellow Woman, hiding with her dead infant. Yellow Woman was a niece of the medicine man Ice. Curly made a travois and carried her away to safety. Out of the incident grew his long association with the Cheyenne.[31]

While it is possible that Curly was in the Little Thunder camp, support for that view does not include the primary sources. It could just as likely be another part of his legend or the embellishment of a storyteller seeking drama.

OVER THE NEXT FEW DAYS, Harney had his men search and burn the Little Thunder camp and construct a stockade, Fort Grattan, at Ash Hollow. Among the items found in the camp was a drawing on Post Office stationery of the raid on the mail train. Harney enclosed some of the papers with his report on the engagement. "They were mostly taken, as their dates and marks will indicate, on the occasion of the massacre and plunder of the mail party, in November last," he noted. "There are also in the possession of officers and others, in camp, the scalps of two white females, and remnants of the clothing, etc., carried off by the Indians in the Grattan massacre; all of which, in my judgement, sufficiently characterize the people I have to deal with."[32]

Since Harney does not say he personally saw the scalps of the two white women or clothing from the Grattan fight, those parts of his report should be viewed skeptically. While the scalps and especially the clothing could have been in the Little Thunder camp, his remarks sound too much like those of migrants who passed on stories of Indian attacks and atrocities in letters home from Oregon and California or in reminiscences written years later, but rarely reported attacks or atrocities in diaries kept on the trail. They also might be seen as an attempt by Harney to put the actions of his troops, particularly because they had killed a number of women and children, in a better light and as a reflection of the general's puritanical severity that saw the Indians as naturally inferior to whites.

But Harney did not need to justify his actions, at least not at first. Word of his victory was enthusiastically received by his superiors in the army and by President Pierce, who hailed him as a hero. As

Harney prepared to march up the North Platte to Fort Laramie, his actions also received the approval of whites on the plains, among them William Chandless, a teamster whose freight train arrived at Ash Hollow on September 6, 1855, just three days after the battle. While camped with the troops, Chandless "heard plenty about the fight, infantry and dragoons each making out that they had borne the brunt of it." The troops also told him that before the battle Harney had made an obscenity-laced speech about the Indians to key the men for the fight.[33]

Chandless agreed that Harney's "policy was quite right. Shilly-shallying does not answer with the Indians." But he also foresaw trouble. In his journal, he wrote: "Northern newspapers are apt to set down old Harney, who is a Southerner, as a truculent barbarian, but he is certainly popular with his army." As news of the fight spread east, Harney eventually was condemned as a "Butcher" and a "Squaw Killer," a title that would follow him the rest of his life. Historians since have sought to present a more objective portrait of the general by pointing out that many of the women and children were killed before the troops had any knowledge of their presence and because they were hiding with warriors who were firing on the troops.

In light of the horror Drum, Todd, and Warren felt at the sight of dead and wounded women and children, and the way they and their men aided the surviving Lakota after the battle, it would seem that many of the troops did not know they were killing women and children. However, it is impossible to believe that the troops, certainly the officers who had planned the attack, had no idea there were families in the camp. They had reports from scouts about the camp, and it would have been only logical for Little Thunder to have mentioned the presence of women and children in his camp when parleying with Harney.

Harney's view of the Indians is evident, too, by the way he treated the Lakota dead. As Chandless left the army camp at Ash Hollow about five days after the battle and came opposite the mouth of the Blue Water, he saw that the Indian dead had been left unburied. "A good many wolves and ravens were still at work," he wrote in his journal, "though most of the bodies had been already picked clean."[34]

AFTER SENDING the captured Lakota women and children down the Platte River in wagons to Fort Kearny, Harney, on September 9, 1855, started up the North Platte for Fort Laramie. As he neared the post, a band of Indians raided his livestock, making off with about fifty horses and mules. Harney sent a troop of cavalry out after the raiders, but they returned empty-handed two days later. The incident angered the general and left him in a foul mood. When he reached Fort Laramie on September 15, he stopped Agent Twiss from distributing annuities to the Indians camped near the fort and ordered their leaders to meet with him on September 22. At that meeting Harney told the Indians "that the only conditions on which they could expect peace were, the prompt delivery of the murderers of the Mail party in November last, the restoration of all stole animals, and a pledge on their part to keep the road through their Country open and Safe for travel."

Having little choice, the Indian leaders acceded to the demands. Although Harney did not believe that the tribes would keep their promise of peace, he considered "it just, to give them an opportunity to prove their desire for peace by their acts." He also felt the promise would allow him to march north unimpeded to Fort Pierre and was warranted by "the fact that I had already inflicted a severe chastisement upon them in killing some 100 of their people, and taking over 70 of them prisoner. . . . Should the Indians fail to comply with these conditions the delay will at least allow me to mature my plans and bring more troops into the field next Spring."[35]

Whether or not Curly had been part of the Little Thunder camp when the Blue Water fight occurred and afterward rescued a Cheyenne woman, he certainly would have heard about what had happened. As Chandless learned on his way to Salt Lake: "The news of this battle spread like wildfire over the prairies, and many tribes, even beyond the mountains, questioned us as to the rifles that killed at half a mile."[36] Curly's uncle Spotted Tail also lay wounded in a camp in the Nebraska Sand Hills, his wife and one child among the prisoners Harney had sent to Fort Kearny.

The effect on Curly can only be imagined, but it would seem safe to say that his attitude of resistance to the whites grew. Never in living memory had such a large Sioux camp suffered such a defeat. The Lakota named Harney the "Hornet" and very carefully sought to avoid his sting. Starting for Fort Pierre on September 29, 1855, Harney

marched directly through the heart of Brulé country. He passed the
headwaters of the Niobrara River, where the previous November a
large camp of Lakota had argued over fighting the whites; entered the
wintering grounds of the Wazhazha band, Conquering Bear's people,
on the White River; and continued to the Bad River, arriving at Fort
Pierre without encountering a single Lakota. The only sign of resistance came from the Hunkpapa camped on the Missouri River.
Except for traders, most of them had never seen white men and were
feeling brave. Harney made plans to attack the Hunkpapa, but then
decided it was too late in the year and his supplies too short, and settled in for the winter.[37]

11

CRAZY HORSE

BY THE TIME OF the Blue Water fight in September 1855, the old days of self-reliance were gone for the Lakota. The plains tribes had become so dependent on the white man's goods that many were at a loss as to how they would live when Harney stopped the flow of annuities and traders fled their posts for the safety of military forts. They also were fearful that the Hornet's troops would do to their villages what they had done to Little Thunder's people.

General Harney's demand that the warriors who had attacked the Salt Lake mail train in November 1854 surrender was another blow to the Lakota, particularly since traders had passed along the word that Harney intended to send them to a distant fort in Kansas to be hanged. In other times the proud Lakota would have paid no heed to such a demand. But now tribal leaders were deeply concerned. Harney had warned he would be back in the spring of 1856 if the warriors did not give themselves up. Councils were held, and those who had been involved in the mail raid were begged to surrender for the good of their people.

Exhibiting incredible courage, Spotted Tail, Red Leaf, and Long Chin rode into Fort Laramie on October 18, 1855, little more than two weeks after Harney issued his demand. Believing they were going to be killed, the three approached the fort singing their death songs. When they dismounted, a troop of infantry escorted them to the guardhouse, where they were held awaiting the appearance of two boys who also had been part of the raiding party. On October 28 Agent Twiss reported that the two boys had not surrendered because one was too sick to travel and the other was far off in a Miniconjou camp on the Little Missouri River.

Eventually, two young warriors, Standing Elk and Red Plume, surrendered in place of the boys and were sent down the Platte to Fort Leavenworth to join Spotted Tail, Red Leaf, and Long Chin. The three warriors had earlier made the trip under heavy guard in an army ambulance. They reached the post on December 11, 1855, after an uncertain and frightening journey through the land of their enemies the Pawnee and Omaha.[1]

Below Fort Kearny the road turned southeast away from the Platte River into unknown country for the Brulé. It was a land swarming with endless numbers of whites heading west and towns of large, permanent houses. In the new country the prisoners saw Kaws surrounded and forced to live on a reservation near Shawnee and Delaware who had been removed from their homes across the Mississippi River. Instead of following the buffalo herds, they lived in houses and raised crops like white people. Many of the Indian men had even taken to dressing like the whites.

The trip to Fort Leavenworth was a stunning revelation for the captive Brulé. For years they had talked about and argued over how to deal with the whites coming into their country. How little they really knew, though, now was evident. They never could have imagined the numbers or the power that they saw all around them. Only a year earlier, they had been eager to fight the whites. They had believed the death of Grattan and his troops had taught the whites a powerful lesson that would force them to leave the land of the Lakota. But now they could see how little the defeat of Grattan and even the Blue Water fight meant to a people as numerous as the stars. It was frightening.

Spotted Tail in particular never forgot what he saw during his captivity. Harney had every intention of hanging him and the others who had taken part in the mail train raid. But political considerations, a need to keep peace on the plains at as little cost as possible to the federal government, led President Pierce to pardon the raiders on January 16, 1856. And so, when Spotted Tail returned to his people, it was as an advocate of peace. He could see no other way. The knowledge he gained during his time as a captive would lead him to play an important role in the surrender of his nephew Crazy Horse two decades later.

AFTER ESTABLISHING winter quarters at Fort Pierre in late October 1855, Harney sent word to the Lakota that a council would be held at the fort in March 1856. All tribes wishing peace were to attend the council. The Hornet, the message implied, would again unleash his stinger if the Lakota did not meet all demands of the government.

Confused, frightened, and suffering extreme hardship from the embargo that had cut off the flow of white goods, the various Lakota tribes and bands sent delegations to the peace council, where they quickly acceded to all of Harney's demands. They even agreed to accept the "paper chiefs" Harney appointed as their leaders. It was a different world from that of the Great Smoke at Fort Laramie fewer than five years earlier, when Conquering Bear was selected as a chief of the Lakota only after great debate and a vote by the tribes—no matter how little the participants understood the procedure.

On March 8, 1956, Harney wrote the secretary of war proclaiming the success of the council and describing the condition of the Lakota:

> The character of the Indian is undergoing great modifications—The gradual decrease of their supplies of food—their poverty of means to eke out an existence with the disease and imposition which had been put upon them on all sides, have forced upon the minds of these people the irresistible conclusions, that to live hereafter, they must work. They now desire to do so, and have already in some instances commenced, but they have not been able to succeed—and they feel that they are obliged to depend upon the government for future aid and assistance, to enable them to live.[2]

Harney urged that the federal government help them "in raising corn and other simple grains and vegetables" by giving them "hoes and seed" and plowing their land until they learned to do so themselves. He noted that should the government agree to help the Lakota, they had pledged to follow the path laid out for them. "It is not yet too late for us to requinte in some degree," he noted, "this unfortunate race, for their many sufferings—consequent to the domain of our people on the soil of the Continent."

General Harney also laid out a plan for controlling the Lakota in the future. It was based on a system of chiefs, subchiefs, and warriors, and designed to keep the tribe weak by pitting members against each other. Under it, each chief appointed by Harney was to be allowed a certain number of warriors to carry out the general's wishes. Each warrior was to be given a uniform and while in the service of the chief receive rations. Harney believed that young men would be eager to seek such positions. "The dress should be durable and gaudy," he wrote, "particularly the head dress (they are fond of feathers). The uniform of the different Bands should be different, and the same should place in the different grades of Chiefs, sub-Chiefs and soldiers—By gradually causing the interests of a portion of the nation to depend upon the wishes of the Government the remainder will be easily controlled."[3]

To complete his plan, Harney urged that a large force of troops be kept on the plains through the summer to convince the Lakota "of the ability and intention of the Government to enforce obedience to its Commands, whenever occasion shall require it." He also blamed "all the difficulties which I have had with the Sioux of the Missouri" on the large amounts of ammunition brought to the plains by traders and questioned whether "such persons deserve to trade with the Indians."[4]

The Hornet may have quickly conquered the Lakota. But he was far less successful with the frontier bureaucrats and their political supporters back in Washington. Feeling as though his authority was being usurped by the general, Upper Platte agent Twiss attempted to block the Lakota camped at Fort Laramie from attending Harney's peace council. When Harney ordered him "to have nothing to do with the Sioux," and then later the Cheyenne and Arapaho, Twiss hurried to Washington, where he obtained the backing of Commissioner of Indian Affairs George Manypenny.[5] Aware of the extreme reluctance of Congress to spend any money on the Indians, Manypenny was able to block the Senate from ratifying Harney's treaty.

At the same time, though, Congress showed no reluctance to spend money on roads through Indian country. Although the tribes who signed the Horse Creek Treaty agreed to allow the construction of roads through their land, none of them was prepared for the road-building projects coming their way through Kansas and Nebraska. Between 1854 and 1858 Congress appropriated almost $1.5 million for roads. Following Harney's victory at the Blue Water, Congress also established an agency for the construction of western roads and ordered the Office of Indian Affairs to direct its agents to use their influence with the Indian leaders to eliminate any resistance to road projects.[6] Accommodation and peaceful coexistence with the Indians began to give way to a goal of territorial development, in the path of which stood the Lakota.[7]

HARNEY MAY HAVE BELIEVED he had arrived at a successful formula for peace after the Fort Pierre council in early March 1856, but just a month later a series of events began that would keep the flames of war burning on the plains. According to the Cheyenne George Bent, it started when a group of four young Cheyenne found four stray horses and took the animals back to their camp near the Platte River Bridge at what is now Casper, Wyoming. "Of course," Bent reported, "a white man at once laid claim to the whole four." The Cheyenne took three of the horses to the bridge and offered to give them up, but "the fourth animal they said the white man had not described correctly and they did not believe he had ever seen the horse before."[8]

White accounts have the young lieutenant in charge of the troops guarding the bridge receiving a report about a small band of Cheyenne possessing four stray horses that belonged to whites. The officer demanded the animals and promised a reward for them. Although nobody was claiming the horses had been stolen, the Cheyenne surrendered three of them. The fourth they claimed had been found much earlier and in a different location than the others. But the officer did not care. He ordered three of the Cheyenne arrested.[9]

"In those days," Bent wrote, "Indians did not understand being arrested. They never took full-grown men prisoners but always killed them in the fight and had it done with; so when the soldiers attempted to arrest any Indians, the Indians, of course, believed that the troops intended to disarm them and then kill them; so whenever such an attempt was made the Indians usually fought for their lives."[10]

According to Bent, the lieutenant ordered the arrest of all four of the Cheyenne. White reports, however, have the officer ordering the arrest of only three of the Indians. Whatever the number, when the soldiers moved forward, the young Cheyenne tried to escape. White accounts have two of the Indians attempting to flee, one succeeding, the other being killed. The third, who had not tried to flee, died while being held prisoner. Bent reports two of the Cheyenne being captured, one being shot, and the fourth, Little Wolf, a noted runner, getting away. In the course of fleeing, white reports have the Cheyenne killing an old trapper. Bent does not report the killing and has Little Wolf only escaping to the Cheyenne camp. "When he got to the Cheyenne camp with this news," Bent writes, "the people were thrown into a panic and fled at once, abandoning everything, for they believed that the Grattan affair was to be repeated. And they were not far wrong, for no sooner had they left their camp than the troops marched up."[11]

When the soldiers reached the abandoned camp, according to Bent, they looted whatever they wanted and then burned what was left. The incident caused the Northern Cheyenne to flee south and join the Southern Cheyenne between the Platte and Arkansas rivers. Aware of what had happened to Little Thunder, they made no raids and kept out of the way of troops. But it was too late; the whites already had decided the Cheyenne were hostile.

When two Cheyenne from a raiding party of seventy or eighty warriors who were prowling the Platte River in search of Pawnee approached a mail wagon in August 1856 to ask for tobacco, the driver, who had heard the Cheyenne were hostile, panicked. He fired at the warriors, one of whom shot an arrow back, slightly wounding the driver, who raced off at top speed, even though the Cheyenne made no attempt to follow.

As soon as he reached Fort Kearny, the driver told his version of the incident, and a troop of cavalry was sent out in pursuit of the Cheyenne. They followed their trail down the Platte to Grand Island, where they found the Indians camped the following afternoon. Without warning, the troops attacked, killing six warriors and capturing twenty-two horses, two mules, and assorted other supplies and equipment. Once the young warriors at the main Cheyenne camp found out what had happened, they could not be restrained. Raiding parties headed up the Platte. They attacked several wagon trains, killing at least eleven whites and capturing three others. Among those killed was Almon Babbit, the Utah Territory's delegate to Congress.[12]

ON OCTOBER 15, 1856, forty-two Cheyenne leaders met with Agent Twiss at Fort Laramie. They had come to the fort to report that they had regained control of the young men who had been raiding along the Oregon and California trails. The chiefs wanted peace, but it was too late. In one of his final official acts as secretary of war, the soon-to-be president of the Confederacy, Jefferson Davis, declared that a campaign would be conducted against the Cheyenne in the spring of 1857. The Cheyenne must be "severely punished," he said. "No trifling of partial punishment will suffice."[13]

True to Davis's word, Colonel Edwin V. Sumner left Fort Leavenworth in the spring of 1857 with a force of 400 cavalry and infantry in search of "hostile" Cheyenne. On July 29 he found and attacked a village of about three hundred Cheyenne on the Solomon Fork of the Kansas River, roughly sixty miles south of Fort Kearny. The Cheyenne fled after a short skirmish in which two soldiers and nine Indians were killed and many more wounded. The troops pursued but did not overtake the Cheyenne. The troops had to content themselves with looting and destroying 171 lodges. Reporting on the engagement, Sumner noted that no women or children had been hurt during the fight. When Harney heard of the remark, he replied in a way that calls into question the view some historians have of his killing of women and children on the Blue Water as mainly incidental. He pointed out that only four days after the fight on the Solomon about 150 of the same Cheyenne attacked a migrant party only twenty-eight miles from Fort Kearny. "They not only had no fear for their families from Colonel Sumner's Command," Harney complained, "but that his action was not attended by any moral consequences."[14]

In the contemporary mind, total war on an enemy population is most closely associated with World War II and such events as the London Blitz, the fire bombings of Tokyo and Dresden, the siege of Stalingrad, the sacking of Manila, the rape of Nanking, and the atomic bombings of Hiroshima and Nagasaki. Individuals with more of an interest in history might look back farther, to Germany's unrestricted submarine warfare during World War I, the rape of Belgium, or General William Sherman's march to the sea during the Civil War. A decade before Sherman put the torch to the South, though, total war was a fact for Indians living on the Great Plains.

Spurred by the Grattan and Blue Water fights, Army officers on the plains soon began vying for laurels as Indian-fighters. At the same time, white settlements pressed west into Kansas, Iowa, Nebraska, and the Dakotas. The Missouri River country was settled as far up as Sioux City, Iowa, in 1856. When Indians refused to give up their lands, popular sentiment was stirred against them. Whites began to abuse and harass border tribes such as the Kaw, Pawnee, and Omaha. Many frontier whites wanted to remove the tribes to Indian Territory, in what is now Oklahoma. When the Office of Indian Affairs opposed such a move, they attempted to have the tribes confined to reservations and deprive them of the annual buffalo hunts they were guaranteed by treaties.

While not directly affected by events along the lower Missouri River, the Lakota were very much aware of what was happening to tribes on the eastern edge of their country. When gold was discovered in Colorado in the late 1850s, more than a hundred thousand miners were added to the stream of hopeful migrants heading to the region and disappointed travelers heading back east from Oregon and California. Not content to follow the main trails along the Platte, the horde spread up the Republican River and various branches of the Kansas River into the hunting grounds of the Lakota, Cheyenne, and Arapaho. These whites even set up stage lines that ran through the hunting grounds of those tribes.

What had happened to Conquering Bear, Little Thunder, and the Cheyenne at the Platte River Bridge also taught the Lakota the ways of the whites coming into their country. They began to feel that the only way to save themselves was to resist the whites, especially after the Yankton Sioux signed a treaty ceding their lands on the Missouri. The western Lakota bitterly complained that the Yankton long ago had come up the Missouri begging land from them and now had traded it to the whites.[15]

To DEAL WITH the growing threat, Lakota leaders sent out a pipe, a traditional way of summoning the people, calling for a great council at Bear Butte. The tribes gathered together at the sacred mountain north of the Black Hills in the summer of 1857. When the lodges were pitched, the Lakota were pleased and excited at the strength they saw in their numbers. All of the northern Lakota were represented at the council. The names of such southern Lakota leaders as Spotted Tail and Little Thunder, however, are not mentioned in connection with the council. The hunting grounds of those tribes already were infested with whites. A number of them also had seen the military power and the numbers of the whites and concluded that it would be impossible to defeat them.

At the council, Lakota leaders are said to have pledged themselves to resist all further encroachment on their land. Shortly afterward a hunting band of Miniconjou encountered an army survey
party under Lieutenant Gouverneur K. Warren on the western edge
of the Black Hills. According to Warren's report on the incident, the
Lakota protested against his party proceeding farther into their country and frightening the buffalo they were hunting. Some of the
Lakota wanted to kill all of the members of the party. But, according
to Warren, "the lesson taught them by General Harney in 1855 made
them fear they would meet with retribution, and this I endeavored to
impress upon them."[16]

Warren understood and even sympathized with the Lakota's concern about disturbing the buffalo. He wrote: "Their feelings toward
us under the circumstances were not unlike what we would feel
toward a person who should insist upon setting fire to our barns."
The Lakota complained that the treaty with Harney allowed the
whites to make roads along the Platte and the White rivers between
Fort Laramie and Fort Pierre, and to travel up the Missouri River by
boat, but guaranteed that no white people should travel anywhere
else in their country. They argued that Warren's party had no right to
enter their country looking for places to build roads and forts. And
even if the Warren party was not doing so, the army still was gaining
knowledge of the country that it could use in the event of war. Having already given up all the country they could spare to the whites,
the Lakota said, the Black Hills must be left alone. Warren wrote: "I
was necessarily compelled to admit to myself the truth and force of
these objections."

Despite such complaints, enough of the Miniconjou remained
friendly that Warren camped near them. The situation grew more
tense when a large party of Hunkpapa and Blackfoot Lakota joined
the Miniconjou. Warren agreed to wait three days to meet Bear's Rib,
who had been appointed head chief by Harney. When Bear's Rib did
not appear, Warren struck camp and headed east through the Black
Hills, where Bear's Rib found him two days later. The chief warned
the party that it would be destroyed if it kept on. Warren, however,
chose to ignore the warning and told Bear's Rib that he planned to
continue north, to Bear Butte.

After a day of talks, Bear's Rib agreed to accompany Warren's
party part of the way through the Black Hills, and then return to his
people and use his influence to keep the party from being attacked.

"In return for this," Warren wrote, "he wished me to say to the president and to the white people that they could not be allowed to come into our country; that if the treaty presents were to purchase such a right then they did not want them. All they asked of the white people was to be left to themselves and let alone."

Bear's Rib also told Warren that the Lakota did not want his annuities if they were intended as payment to stop his people from fighting the Crow. As far back as 1800, the Lakota and the Crow clashed over the Powder River country west of the Black Hills. Much of the Powder River and all of the Big Horn Mountains beyond had been given to the Crow by the Horse Creek Treaty of 1851. The Hunkpapa and some other Lakota had objected to the treaty because they desired Crow land. Now, as white settlements moved closer, the Hunkpapa became adamant about continuing their war against the Crow.

Pressed on the east and south by the Lakota, and on the north by the Blackfeet, the Crow began to move closer to the whites. Many eventually would become scouts for the army in its fight against the Lakota. Custer's favorite scout, who died with him at the Little Big Horn, was the Crow Bloody Knife.

In defense of his people's desire to continue their old ways of war against the Crow, Bear's Rib also noted that

> General Harney had told them not to go to war, yet he was all the time going to war himself. Bear's Rib knew that when General Harney left the Dakota country he had gone to the war in Florida, and that he was at that time in command of the army sent against the Mormons. He said, moreover, that the annuities scarcely paid for going after them, and if they were not distributed at the time of their visits to the trading posts on the Missouri to dispose of their robes, they did not want them.

Although the Lakota may have been feeling powerful in the wake of the Bear Butte council, the way Lieutenant Warren was treated shows that their power was an illusion and they remained hopelessly divided when it came to resisting the whites. Most of them continued to be more interested in fighting traditional enemies such as the Crow than in taking on the white army that had destroyed Little Thunder's camp. After Bear's Rib's departure, Warren continued his mission without seeing another Lakota. Two years later, in 1859, Captain W. F. Reynolds led another military survey party through the heart of the Lakota homeland without a single confrontation.

THE DESIRE OF Bear's Rib and many other Lakota to be left alone by the whites to live in the old ways is further evident in both Spotted Tail's behavior after his return from captivity and in the way in which Curly became Crazy Horse. While speaking in favor of peace with the whites and avoiding conflict with such a powerful invader, Spotted Tail took part in many raids on the Pawnee and other old enemies of the Brulé. While Crazy Horse is best known for his fierce resistance to the whites, he earned his adult name in a fight with traditional enemies of his people.

As with most of Crazy Horse's life, there are conflicting and confusing accounts about when, how, and against exactly whom Curly exhibited the bravery that led his father to pass on the family name of Crazy Horse. According to He Dog, the fight leading to the change occurred when Curly was about eighteen years old. Chips reports, however, that it took place when Curly was twenty-one years old. Since Crazy Horse most likely was born in either 1839 or 1840, the epochal encounter in He Dog's telling would have occurred in 1857 or 1858, and in Chips's telling in 1860 or 1861.

He Dog's account would seem closer to fact because he and Crazy Horse were made shirt-wearers or war chiefs together in about 1865. According to He Dog: "It was many years after our first battles before we were made chiefs. A man had to distinguish himself in many fights and in peace as well before he could be chosen a chief." The four or five years that would have passed between Chips's account of the fight and the naming of Crazy Horse as a shirt-wearer does not seem long enough to fit that description. He Dog's telling also must be given additional weight because being made a shirt-wearer was such a monumental event in the life of both the individual chosen for the honor and the tribe. It is unlikely that he would have been far off on when such an event occurred, even in an interview given when he was elderly.

Chips and He Dog also provide conflicting accounts of the fight itself. According to Chips, it involved the "Crows and Rees and others whose language they [Oglala] could not understand." He Dog reports the fight was with the Arapaho. But that could mean "others whose language they could not understand." In Chips's telling, the fight produced Curly's first coup. It came when "a Shoshone lay dead on the field in a position that none would approach to strike the body. Crazy

Horse's horse became unmanageable and carried his rider wildly about and up within reach of the Shoshone body and Crazy Horse struck and counted coup, and from the crazy conduct of the horse the rider was dubbed Crazy Horse."[17]

Although there is no way of knowing the truth, Chips's account appears a bit too colorful, as if it were devised to entertain the interviewer, especially since it is known that Crazy Horse was a family name passed from father to son, and not something that grew out of an action or habit. He Dog's more matter-of-fact telling seems closer to the reality. He said the fight was "with the Arapahoes, who were up on a high hill covered with big rocks and near a river. Although he was just a boy, he charged them several times alone and came back wounded but with two Arapaho scalps. His father—whose name was Crazy Horse—made a feast and gave his son his own name. After that the father was no longer called by the name he had given away but was called by the nickname Worm."[18]

Whatever the circumstances surrounding Curly's name change to Crazy Horse, by the end of the 1850s the young Oglala was on his way to fulfilling his ambition of becoming one of the Lakota's greatest warriors.

12

THE WARRIOR

THROUGH THE LATE 1850s and early 1860s, Crazy Horse's reputation as a warrior grew and brought him fame among his people. Thunder Tail, who appears to have fought with Crazy Horse, notes that back in camp after one early fight: "He sat among all the bravest of the young men. They talked very much about him." After other fights from the same period, Thunder Tail said, the "Crazy Horse name was very much talked" and "Crazy Horse was very popular."[1] Eagle Elk, a distant cousin of the war chief, reports that Crazy Horse's fame started after a battle with the Pawnee in which "he took the lead, although he was just a very young boy. He was making a dash to coup an enemy. From that time he was talked about."[2]

Since the vast majority of all fights in which Crazy Horse fought were raids involving other preliterate plains tribes, the handful of records that survive make it impossible to determine when most took place. Accounts recorded long after the fact from the aged memories of participants make it difficult to even separate many fights. But the stories that remain are enough to provide at least a glimpse of the young warrior in action and explain why he became one of the Lakota's greatest warriors.

Crazy Horse's reputation spread because those early fights produced some remarkable feats of personal courage so highly prized by the Lakota. He also was incredibly lucky. Chips tells of a fight with the Shoshone in which Crazy Horse's horse was shot out from under him, but instead of running he "sprang forward to the enemy and counted coo [coup]."[3] White Bull may have been talking about the same fight when he said: "Crazy Horse in a fight with the grass house people (who lived where the Shoshone do now) had his horse shot out from under him. Crazy Horse started on foot, an enemy tried to head him off, and Crazy Horse killed the man, took his horse, and came home."[4]

Short Buffalo, youngest brother of He Dog, reports a fight during which "Crazy Horse charged the Crows, his horse was shot under him, and he was surrounded by the enemy. The Oglalas tried to help him but could not get near him. A man named Spotted Deer made a last effort to reach him. He broke through the enemy and Crazy Horse got onto his pony behind him and they made a charge for the open. They both made it back to the Sioux lines, riding double and closely pursued."[5]

That particular fight, according to Short Buffalo, occurred "The Time Yellow Shirt was Killed by the Crows." The Bad Heart Bull manuscript, which Short Buffalo helped interpret, contains drawings showing "Yellow Robe" or "Yellow Blanket" being killed by the Crows.[6] Yellow Shirt appears to be the same person; the difference in names probably is attributable to interpreters. If that is the case, the fight took place in 1858, making it one of the only early fights in which Crazy Horse took part for which there is a record. Since Crazy Horse already appears to have gained something of a reputation as a warrior, the fight also seems to support He Dog's contention that Curly's name change to Crazy Horse occurred in either 1857 to 1858, not the 1860 or 1861 reported by Chips.

THUNDER TAIL tells of two fights with the Crows that apparently took place while Crazy Horse was a young man. One of the fights was on Arrow Creek, a tributary of the Yellowstone River in Montana. The Bad Heart Bull manuscript records a fight with the Crow on Arrow Creek in 1856 or 1858, but there is no way to know if it is the same fight.

According to Thunder Tail, one fight started when a Crow was shot in front of his lodge. Crazy Horse "rode near. But though there was much shooting he went fearlessly and rode in at really close quarters. It turned out his horse was killed, yet on foot without fear he fought, killed, and scalped and left the place. There was much shooting, but he was not wounded."[7] On the way home from that fight, the Lakota raiders were pursued and attacked by the Crow.

While the Lakota were herding the horses they had stolen a group of Crow began shooting at them. "We withstood ten of them who took refuge on a hill," Thunder Tail said. "Then, again, Crazy Horse and Bear Stops together attacked them. They went up close, which helped. Crazy Horse first put himself in their midst and went to swinging his club. So, he sifted out the Crow and they sent him on his way, trying to kill him."

Soon afterward, Thunder Tail continued, "there was war, war brought among their camps. Then a great battle ensued and they came to get us. Crazy Horse's horse was shot." According to Red Feather, younger brother of Crazy Horse's wife, Black Shawl: "The enemy killed his saddle horse under him eight times, but they never hurt him badly."[8] A drawing of an apparently saddened Crazy Horse looking over his shoulder as he walks away from a horse with two bullet wounds in its chest appears in the Bad Heart Bull manuscript.

Thunder Tail claims that Crazy Horse was with his two younger brothers during the battle. Thunder Tail is the only source who reports Crazy Horse having two brothers, so that is a mistake. In the fight the two brothers dismounted:

> Two Crows intercepted them and so they came back. Crazy Horse came forward and really gave them a chase, helping the two younger brothers, and they put the enemy to flight. One of the Crows he shot, seized, killed, and scalped. The Crows then cried badly and fled. From then on Crazy Horse's name was very much talked. They were encamped on the Rosebud River when they got home. They people were very happy and Crazy Horse was very popular.

Short Buffalo tells of a fight with the Shoshone from the period. The Lakota were outnumbered and retreating. Crazy Horse and his younger brother Little Hawk were guarding the rear of a war party that had just raided a Shoshone camp. "After a lot of fighting, Crazy Horse's pony gave out. Crazy Horse turned it loose and the younger brother, who did not want to leave him, turned his own pony loose. Two of the enemy, mounted, appeared before them for single combat. Crazy Horse said to his brother, 'Take care of yourself—I'll do the fancy stunt.' Crazy Horse got the best of the first Shoshone; the other one ran away. He got the horses of the two Shoshones and they caught up with their party. They had saved themselves and their party and got the two horses and the scalp of the Shoshone who was killed."[9]

Although it is contrary to all other sources, a story by Flying Hawk also should be related, since it supposedly was told to him by Crazy Horse himself. It makes the fight with the Shoshone in which Crazy Horse escaped with his brother the war chief's first fight. "The Shoshones were chasing the Sioux," Flying Hawk reports Crazy Horse telling him. "I, with my younger brother riding double; two Shoshones came for us; we started to meet them; I killed one of them, took his horse; we jumped on him, my brother and I double, and escaped."[10]

Fly Hawk's story must be viewed skeptically because other sources point to Crazy Horse's raid on the Omaha in which he killed a woman as his first fight. Also, no other source mentions the presence of Little Hawk at Crazy Horse's side in his first fight with the Shoshone, the fight that is generally said to have resulted in his name change. If, as is most likely, that fight occurred in 1857 or 1858, Little Hawk, who was born in 1846, would have been only eleven or twelve years old at the time. Although Lakota boys of that age did accompany raiding parties, they normally were kept in the rear, out of harm's way. Of course, Little Hawk was known for being rash and rambunctious, so he could have charged ahead to join his brother. There simply is no way to know the truth.

As a warrior, according to He Dog: "Crazy Horse always led his men himself when they went into battle, and he kept well in front of them. He headed many charges and was many times wounded in battle, but never seriously." He Dog dismissed with a chuckle various stories about how Crazy Horse at different times threw away his rifle and charged his enemies with only a war club or a riding quirt. Such an action was a way in which many Indians sought to commit suicide. "Crazy Horse always stuck close to his rifle," He Dog said. "He always stuck close to his rifle. He always tried to kill as many as possible of the enemy without losing his own men.

"All the time I was in fights with Crazy Horse in critical moments of the fight," he continued, "Crazy Horse would always jump off his horse to fire. He is only Indian I ever knew who did that often. He wanted to be sure that he hit what he aimed at. That is the kind of fighter he was. He didn't like to start a battle unless he had it all planned out in his head and knew he was going to win. He always used judgement and played safe."[11]

Red Feather said Crazy Horse wore a little white stone with a hole through it under his left arm; the stone was given to him by Chips. Red Feather said Crazy Horse was wounded twice when he first began to fight, but never after he got the stone.[12] Several other sources also report that he was wounded in battle, but never seriously.

Eagle Elk, a distant cousin who claimed to have fought with Crazy Horse in many fights, described the war chief's preparation for battle:

> His hair was braided down on both sides. That was how he wore his hair all the time. He always wore a strand of braided buckskin—at the lower end was something like medicine tied up in the buckskin. He had an eagle wing whistle tied on. He had it with him all the time. Just before the start of battle, when they were ready to go into it, he got off his pony and got a little dirt from a molehill and put it between the ears of his horse and then on the hips of the horse and then he took some and got in front of the horse and throws it toward the tail, and then he got around behind the horse and threw some over toward his head. Then he went up to the horse and brushed it off and rubbed it on. Then he rubbed a little on his hand and over his head. Then he took a spotted eagle feather and put it upside down on the back of his head instead of standing up, as most did. He wore moccasins. He generally wore just a shirt and breech cloth, taking off his leggings.[13]

Chips said that Crazy Horse "did not paint [for battle] as the Indians usually do; but made a zigzag streak from the top of his forehead downward and to the side of his nose at the base to the point of his chin."[14] White Bull, who fought with Crazy Horse from 1865 to 1876, added some confusion about the paint when he said: "Before entering a fight, Crazy Horse painted his face with white spots by dipping the ends of his fingers into the paint and lightly touching his face here and there. Some warriors painted their faces like that to show they had been brave in some fight in a snow storm or when snow was on the ground, but Crazy Horse used that paint for his protection in battle."[15]

A somewhat puzzled Eagle Elk also described both the war chief's bravery and modesty. "He does not attack [an] enemy and strike coup as many times as he can," he said. "He does not count many coups. He is in front and attack[s an] enemy. If he shoot[s] down an enemy, he does not count coup. He drop[s] behind and let[s] the other count three of the four coup counts. He takes the last coup. I do not understand why he did that. I often wondered why he did that. He had such a reputation that he did not have to get more of that."[16]

According to Eagle Elk, Crazy Horse's generosity, and perhaps his view of himself as something of an outsider, led him to create a group known as The Last Child Society. It was comprised of about forty warriors who always fought with him. The group was called The Last Child Society because the members all were the last child in their families. He chose the last child, Eagle Elk said, because "the last one is not considered very much as the others in the Indian family. If they did great deeds or something very brave, then they would have greater honor than the first child. They were always making themselves greater."[17]

Crazy Horse's generosity and bravery can be seen, too, in Eagle Elk's description of a fight with the Utes. One of the Utes had a nice horse and was a good shot. According to Eagle Elk: "He came forward and no one could go up against him. Then Crazy Horse went for him and shot down the Ute. He rode right up to him. The Ute fell and Crazy Horse called for his younger brother to come and get his first coup."[18]

THE MOST DETAILED description of Crazy Horse during a fight with another tribe is provided by Eagle Elk. It occurred during a sun dance near what is now Crow Agency on the Little Big Horn. While preparations for the sun dance were under way, a group of warriors decided they would rather go out and steal ponies. Led by Crazy Horse, the raiders headed for the Missouri River country. A short distance above the mouth of the Little Missouri River they found a herd of buffalo grazing on the other side. Like Catlin and others, Eagle Elk contradicts claims that the old plains Indians killed only the buffalo they needed and used all of the animal, when he reports that the raiders crossed the shallow Little Missouri "to kill as many [buffalo] as we could and the idea was to get hides and build boats." The boats were needed to cross the Missouri River, on the other side of which was known to be a war party of Arapaho, Crow, Flathead, Nez Perce, and Absorika.

Once across the river, Crazy Horse, Eagle Elk, and three dozen other warriors circled ahead of the enemy raiders to set up a trap at a butte. "We sent out two scouts and they came back and told us to lose no time in attacking because part of the tribe was moving away from the rest and had just begun to set up their camp," Eagle Elk said.

> The scouts said as long as they are just small parties coming up here we had better attack now instead of waiting until the next come. . . . So we went sneaking around and made a charge against the camp and got away with over 100 ponies. . . .
>
> After we took the ponies, we struck for our own country and travelled quite a long time. When we thought we were away from the enemy far enough, we stopped to rest. We did not cross the river. All at once the enemies were coming, but we did not know it. They attacked by surprise and took about half of the horses that were grazing. Nearly all of us had to run on foot. Kicking Bear had a horse; he led the horse and ran on foot. Crazy Horse turned around and called to me, "Be brave. Fight even if we all get killed. Fight them." He dropped behind to do the fighting and let the others get away.

Eagle Elk and two others joined Crazy Horse and began firing as fast as they could at the attackers. Crazy Horse at the time was armed with a Springfield rifle that he called an "open and shoot." Then four other Lakota dropped back to help. "Everybody be of courage and let's fight them," Crazy Horse yelled. "It would not do to see the enemy kill all of us. Fight them until some get away alive. There has to be someone left to tell the tale."

The defenders retreated up a hill into a woods where some of the horses they had stolen were being held. When they reached the shelter of the trees, they found that Low Dog and Charging Cat were missing. Then Eagle Elk was cut off. Crazy Horse and two other warriors continued to fight while the horses were rounded up. Kicking Bear wanted to go out and find the two missing men. When no one volunteered to follow him, he called down the hill for the missing men to show themselves or make a sign if they were wounded so he could help them. The brush at the foot of a tree near a small stream at the bottom of the hill began to move, and Low Dog stepped out. Then a few moments later Charging Cat emerged from the brush. Kicking Bear and Two Hides raced their horses down the hill and picked up the two men. Neither was wounded.

As soon as all of the men were back together, the raiders fled. They traveled all night and into the next morning without being followed; then Crazy Horse ordered a halt in a deep canyon with a stream and a thick stand of pines. "We stop here," he said. "You all take a good sleep. If the enemy comes again, we are not running away, but we will go into this place and stay here and fight them. You must all go into this place to sleep. Remember if they surprise us again, we are not going to run, but we go into this place and fight them."

While the others were preparing a camp, Eagle Elk and White Metal decided they were going to kill a buffalo. It had been a long time since the raiders had eaten, and they were all very hungry. Crazy Horse told them: "All right, go ahead and kill a buffalo and have it ready. When the others are awake, we will come over there and have some meat." Then he took up guard duty while the others slept.

When the men awoke, they joined Eagle Elk and White Metal for a buffalo feast, then started for home. At the Missouri River they found their hide boats and crossed to the other side. Once they crossed the river, they traveled back the way they had come until they reached the Little Big Horn. Although they had more than a hundred enemy ponies with them, the people in the village paid little attention, since they did not bring back any scalps or count any coups. Hoping to save face, some members of the party began making plans for another raid against the Crow. A medicine man named Yellow Horse warned them of a vision he had in which One Horn, Charger, and five other Lakota were killed. Hearing of the vision, Crazy Horse declined to join the raiders when they went out. As Yellow Horse predicted, One Horn and Charger were killed.[19]

13

Nations Divided

In the spring of 1858, a dozen white men and thirty Cherokees from Georgia arrived at Bent's Fort, a Cheyenne trading post on the Arkansas River in southeastern Colorado. They had made the long journey west in search of gold. After a short stay at the fort, they continued west, prospecting their way through the Colorado foothills and into the Rocky Mountains. The group found gold in several locations, but never in paying quantities. In the fall, all but seven of the white men gave up the search and returned east.

The gold the men found was only enough to fill several goose quills with gold dust. None of the men earned enough to even pay his board for a single week. But when they showed the goose quills at settlements along the way, people lost all control. Word quickly spread of gold in Colorado. Thousands of men in Kansas, Nebraska, Missouri, and Iowa began making plans to head for the mountains in the spring. Despite the fact that it was fall, several parties set out immediately upon hearing the news and reached the mountains before winter.

Like the California Gold Rush a decade earlier, the ensuing Colorado Gold Rush proved a bust for all but a very few fortunate individuals, mainly shopkeepers, gamblers, and swindlers. Even as the real rush was starting in the spring of 1859, thousands of gold seekers were returning home without their fortunes, but plenty of tales of hardships. "Pike's Peak or Bust" became "Kill Byers and Oakes." W. N. Byers, founder of the *Rocky Mountain News*, and D. C. Oakes were the authors of two popular guidebooks to the goldfields. Sixty ragged, angry men returning on foot along the Platte River Road are said to have turned back fifty thousand men, who headed back east calling for the blood of Byers and Oakes.

Again, as overlanders did heading for California and Oregon in the 1840s, the miners abandoned everything imaginable along the Platte Road. Picks, shovels, slough pans, packs, clothing, provisions, carts, and wagons were left everywhere. Even some merchants, discouraged by stories of returning miners, dumped their entire stock of goods along the trail and turned back with empty wagons. Nobody will ever know how many gold seekers turned back before they reached Colorado, but a hundred thousand crossed the plains to the Rockies in 1859, while thousands of others abandoned their dreams of wealth in California for new dreams of riches in Colorado, which became a separate territory in 1861.

The Indians viewed the wild odyssey with amazement. They could not understand the madness of the white man for the yellow metal. That amazement turned to alarm for the Cheyenne and the Arapaho when the Leavenworth & Pike's Peak Express stage line started daily service through the heart of their hunting grounds. Their alarm increased when the buffalo were frightened off, the last of the timber along the rivers was cut, and some of the white men stayed and laid out towns with names such as El Paso, Montana, Auraria, and Denver, named for James W. Denver, governor of Kansas Territory. Those new settlers also saw the Indians whose land they now occupied as obstacles to be removed. The newcomers began talking about forcing the Indians onto reservations, where they could choose between farming and starvation.[1]

HAVING MOVED TO the abundant hunting grounds of the Powder River in eastern Wyoming and Montana, Crazy Horse and other Oglala Lakota were not directly affected by the Colorado Gold Rush. Undoubtedly, though, Crazy Horse was well aware of what was happening to the Cheyenne and their old hunting grounds south of the Platte. But the Lakota culture of independence made it impossible to organize a united front with the Cheyenne or even other Lakota to stem the flood of whites. Most Lakota simply were too busy hunting, making war on old enemies, and with the life of their own villages to grasp the larger picture. They also did not want to halt the flow of white goods they had come to enjoy. As ethnologist Lewis Henry Morgan found on a spring 1862 trip up the Missouri River: "They [the Sioux], in common with the Assiniboins, Minnetares, Crows, and Blackfeet, hate the whites and say they would clear their country of them if the white man had not become necessary to them. They want his guns, powder, and ball, coffee, blankets, and camp furniture, which have now become indispensable, and they therefore submit to his presence among them."[2]

Whites, of course, had no problem with the long view or planning. Soon after the new settlers secured a foothold in Colorado Territory, they began talking about moving the Indians onto reservations. They sent a delegation to Washington to make the federal government believe that the Cheyenne and Arapaho wanted to settle on small reservations and start farming. The delegation found receptive ears among politicians preoccupied with the approaching conflict between the states and ready for a quick fix. Congress accepted the view of the Westerners. It appropriated thirty-five thousand dollars to hold councils with upper Arkansas River tribes to induce them to give up their land.[3]

Commissioner of Indian Affairs A. C. Greenwood traveled to Bent's Fort in early September 1860 to hold a council with the Cheyenne and the Arapaho. The Indians, however, had not been informed of the meeting, and only a handful of Arapaho were on hand at the fort. Nevertheless, Greenwood produced a treaty that he handed over to Albert Boone, grandson of Daniel Boone and special agent to the upper Arkansas tribes. Greenwood then returned to Washington.

As owner of the town site of Boonesville east of Pueblo, Colorado, Boone had a direct business interest in seeing the upper Arkansas tribes removed to reservations. Over the late fall and winter of 1860 he gathered together at Fort Wise on the upper Arkansas a number of Arapaho and a handful of Cheyenne. After holding a council, Boone got them to sign the Treaty of Fort Wise on February 18, 1861. Under that treaty the Cheyenne and the Arapaho agreed to give up the lands assigned them by the Horse Creek Treaty and accept a reservation along the upper Arkansas. To get them to give up their hunting ways and communal life and to promote the whites' "settled habits of industry and enterprise," the land was to be allotted to individual tribal members. The treaty also provided annuities of $450,000 over fifteen years, to be spent at the discretion of the secretary of the interior for agricultural development and schools.[4]

Many of the Cheyenne and Arapaho, particularly those who hunted with the Lakota on the Solomon and Republican rivers to the north, denounced the treaty and the chiefs who had signed it. The government, though, ignored the complaints. Boone hired white men to dig irrigation ditches, plow the land, and plant crops. The reservation system had come to the free-living tribes of the high plains.

AT ABOUT THE SAME TIME that fortune hunters were flooding into Colorado and the Treaty of Fort Wise was being handed to the Cheyenne and the Arapaho, the federal government was taking the first steps toward forcing the Lakota onto reservations. On October 28, 1859, Upper Platte Agency head Twiss wrote to the Office of Indian Affairs seeking funds to purchase gifts for Lakota leaders who lived south of the Platte River. Twiss saw the gifts as a way to gain the favor of southern Lakota chiefs and eventually obtain their support for a treaty in which they would relinquish their lands.

Abraham Lincoln's election in 1860 brought a temporary halt to Twiss's plan. To help pay off his political debts, Lincoln swept clean the Office of Indian Affairs, replacing old agents with loyal Republicans. At the Upper Platte Agency, John Loree was courted by John Evans, governor of Colorado Territory, who was eager to settle Indians on reservations. In 1862 Evans and Loree joined forces in an unsuccessful attempt to seek a treaty with the Lakota who hunted along the Kansas River similar to the Fort Wise Treaty with the Cheyenne and the Arapaho.[5]

Meanwhile, the army sent an expedition under Captain William Reynolds to explore the Yellowstone River country. The purpose of the expedition was to gather information on the region's climate, topography, flora, and fauna to determine possible locations for military bases and to mark out a wagon trail connecting the Platte River trails with the basins of the Yellowstone and Missouri rivers. The route Reynolds took from the Big Horn Mountains in southeastern Montana through eastern Wyoming to the Platte River cut through the heart of Lakota country.[6] Trouble was coming. Then, on April 12,

1861, just three months after the Treaty of Fort Wise, Confederate shore batteries in Charleston, South Carolina, opened fire on the Union garrison in Fort Sumter.

THE OUTBREAK OF the Civil War made little impression on the Lakota. They noticed regular army troops marching out of their country, leaving behind only skeleton garrisons to guard their forts, and heard tales of great battles between the whites. But that was all in another country very far away and did not concern them. What happened in Minnesota in August 1862, however, was another matter.

After years of being cheated by traders, under heavy pressure from white settlers and government agents who wanted their land, Christian missionaries who wanted their souls, and reformers who wanted to turn them into farmers, the Santee Dakota Sioux of Minnesota rebelled. It started on August 4, 1862, when a group of warriors seeking food for their hungry people broke into stores at an agency along the Minnesota River. Then, thirteen days later, on August 17, a white woman was killed by a Dakota warrior in a dispute over a chicken, and another family of settlers was slaughtered. The next day, Santee warriors attacked a local agency. Among the people killed in the fight was trader Andrew Jackson Myra, who at a council once told a group of starving Santees that they could eat grass or their own dung. His body was found with the mouth stuffed with grass.

Over the next few days, Santee warriors attacked the local garrison at Fort Ridgley and a number of settlements, killing more than fifty whites and sending thousands more fleeing from the Minnesota River valley. The fighting immediately captured the attention of frontier whites, who generally viewed the Indians as beasts standing in the way of their progress. Colonel Richard Dodge, in a classic example of demonizing or dehumanizing enemies and members of another culture, summed up the frontier view in his 1882 memoir *Thirty-three Years Among Our Wild Indians* when he wrote that the Indian "is a savage, beast of prey, unsoftened by any touch of pity or mercy."[7]

Saint Cloud Democrat editor Jane Grey Swisshelm, who today is hailed as an abolitionist and pioneer for women's rights, chastised Minnesota authorities for not moving fast enough to quell the rebellion and wrote: "Every Sioux found on our soil deserves a permanent homestead six feet by two. Shoot the hyenas. Exterminate the wild beasts. And make peace with the devil and all his hosts sooner than these red jawed tigers whose fangs are dripping with the blood of innocents." Minnesota governor Alexander Ramsey noted that the "Sioux Indians of Minnesota must be exterminated or driven forever beyond the borders of the state."

For weeks the fighting continued, resulting in the near total destruction of the town of New Ulm and the deaths of hundreds of whites and Dakota. Amid continued calls to exterminate the Sioux, General John Pope, who had just been soundly defeated by the Confederates at the Second Battle of Bull Run, decided to take out his humiliation on the Santee. Under the veil of darkness, he surrounded and captured the main village of the rebellious Santee. The men were chained together and taken to a trading post, where they were tried at the rate of one every ten minutes.

In the end 392 Santee men were tried and 303 sentenced to death. More than 1,700 Santee women, old men, and children were herded together and removed from their land in a column almost three miles long. As they made their way through the country, they were continually abused and attacked by whites they encountered along the way. One enraged white woman snatched a nursing Santee child from its mother's breast and flung it to the ground. The child died a few hours later.

With the white death toll having passed the 500 mark, Lincoln was under heavy pressure to order the execution of all the captured Santee. He asked for someone else to assume the burden but was told he was the only one who could take such an action. Lincoln then assigned two clerks to review the trial proceedings of the 303 men sentenced to death. He asked the clerks to first select men who had molested white women. When they found only 2, Lincoln had them look again for individuals who had killed civilians. The number rose to 38.

On the day after Christmas 1862, just six days before Lincoln issued the Emancipation Proclamation, the 38 condemned Santee, whose death warrants were personally signed by the "great emancipator" himself, were hanged together in Mankato, Minnesota, from a single gallows while they sang their death songs and called out their names. It was the largest mass execution in the history of the United States. The men were buried on a sandbar in the Minnesota River.

That evening, physicians from as far away as Chicago dug up the bodies and carried them off to be used in medical experiments.

Not quite two months later, on February 16, 1863, Congress issued an order dispossessing the Santee of all their land and treaty rights. Then, on March 4, all members of the tribe were banished from Minnesota. A month later, Santee men who had been captured or surrendered were sent to prison in Davenport, Iowa. Two months later, the last of the Santee, more than thirteen hundred individuals, were shipped from Mankato by steamboat and barge to a new reservation called Crow Creek on the Missouri River in Dakota Territory.

Back in Minnesota, the state legislature increased the bounty on Indian scalps to two hundred dollars, which launched an open season on any Indian found in Minnesota and border areas. Little Crow, who had been a leader of the Santee during the revolt, was among the victims. He was shot while picking berries with his son near Hutchinson, Minnesota. The farmer who shot him was awarded a seventy-five-dollar bounty by the state of Minnesota and five hundred dollars more when it was learned that the Indian was Little Crow. The scalp and remains of Little Crow were put on public display by the state. He was finally laid to rest in 1971.[8]

NEWS OF THE Minnesota uprising spread panic all along the frontier. Settlers in Kansas, Iowa, and other border areas fled their homesteads for the nearest towns and banded together into militia units that began harassing the friendly tribes around them. Politicians and newspapers in border states and territories demanded that Washington send troops. Unable to ignore such widespread alarm and clamor, the government sent contingents of volunteer troops, mostly Westerners who despised Indians, to posts along the Missouri, Arkansas, and Platte rivers, where they languished in boredom and drunkenness that left them longing for any excuse to start a fight with the Indians. As Red Cloud noted: "The white soldiers always want to make a war."[9]

Accounts from the period are full of incidents of troops attacking Indians for amusement. Lieutenant Eugene Ware tells of Kansas troops at Camp Cottonwood along the lower Platte River casually amusing themselves by using a group of peaceful Lakota camped on an island in the river for target practice.[10] Lieutenant Casper Collins tells of members of the 11th Ohio Volunteer Cavalry stationed on the North Platte River listening enviously to tales of Indian fights told by local frontiersmen. Most of the soldiers soon discarded their uniforms for dashing buckskin outfits and Indian ponies they hoped to use in a fight. They were only held in check by their commanding officer, Lieutenant Colonel William O. Collins, who saw his job as maintaining peace on the plains.

But few plains officers were as astute or as conscientious as Colonel Collins. Colonel J. M. Chivington of the First Colorado Cavalry was a wholehearted believer in the Indian as a wild beast to be moved out of the way of Christian progress or exterminated. Before the end of the Civil War, Chivington's beliefs would result in one of the most ruthless massacres and accompanying atrocities in the history of the United States. Another officer, General James Craig, simply knew nothing about the Indians and chose to remain ignorant. In July 1862 he reported that a group of small raids on the Sweetwater River near Fort Laramie was the work of Indians camped four hundred miles away in Kansas. Major General S. R. Curtis, who imagined himself an authority on the Indians, had the Santee from Minnesota massing to attack Camp Cottonwood on the Platte River. Expecting an attack, he rushed a regiment to the scene even though nobody knew anything about the Santee, who were then near starvation after their defeat in Minnesota.

Perhaps the most inept example of militia leadership, however, belongs to Brigadier General Robert Mitchell, a goodhearted, easygoing man who knew nothing about Indians and readily admitted so. General Mitchell once reported that "Snakes, Winnibigoshish, and Minnesota Sioux" were raiding west of Fort Laramie. Winnibigoshish was the name of a lake.[11]

HAVING TAKEN IN Santee refugees from Minnesota and seen the changes in the soldiers at Fort Laramie, the Lakota were acutely aware of what was happening around them. But generally they did nothing. Living far from the whites in the remote Powder River country, Crazy Horse and most other Oglala Lakota spent the early 1860s hunting buffalo and making war on the Crow. The Powder River country between the Black Hills and the Big Horn Mountains was one of the last unspoiled hunting grounds left to the Lakota. Its grasslands held large buffalo herds, while the valleys of the Powder, Yellowstone, Tongue, Rosebud, and Little Missouri teemed with deer and other smaller game.

The situation was quite different, however, for the Lakota living south of the Platte River. More than a decade of heavy travel by white migrants on the overland trails had caused the buffalo to divide into small herds and disperse. By 1862, too, parties of white buffalo hunters were at work slaughtering the animals for market. Easterners had discovered the fine warming qualities of carriage robes made from buffalo hides.

Stage routes that followed the overland trails, the South Fork to Denver, and the Arkansas to Denver and Santa Fe also left tribes and bands living south of the Platte surrounded by whites. Along the Platte River, stage stations were built every twenty to twenty-five miles, and huge freight trains were seldom out of sight. When bands living between the Platte and the Arkansas became concerned about white encroachment and spoke up, many learned for the first time that a paper signed by some of their chiefs in 1860 gave most of their lands to the whites pressing in from all sides.

Aware of what had happened in Minnesota and in past confrontations with whites since the Grattan fight and General Harney's attack on Little Thunder's village in the mid-1850s, most Indian leaders were opposed to war with the invaders. They believed such an action would only hasten their demise. The situation became extremely delicate. Then, in 1863, John M. Bozeman began laying out a trail that roughly followed the path of Captain Reynolds's Yellowstone expedition from Fort Laramie north through the Powder River country to the newly discovered goldfields of Montana.

The opening of the Bozeman Trail marked a new era in relations between the government and the Lakota, especially the Oglala living in the Powder River country. In Washington, D.C., political and military leaders who had paid relatively scant attention to the distant plains tribes began to hotly debate western Indian policy, while Lakota leaders discussed ways to deal with this serious new encroachment on their lands. The alternatives on both sides included war.[12]

14

LOVE AND WAR

BLACK BUFFALO WOMAN was a niece of the renowned Red Cloud
and very beautiful. She caught the eye of Crazy Horse while the two
were children. Once, after they reached courting age, she allowed
herself to be wrapped inside a robe with Crazy Horse. Since Lakota
society seldom allowed teenage boys and girls to do anything together, and required girls to be chaperoned by older women, standing together under a buffalo robe or a blanket, heads buried close
together, was the only way young people could find privacy. Crazy
Horse stood under the robe with Black Buffalo Woman for so long
that an old women stepped forward and tore the robe aside. The
laughter of his friends that followed greatly embarrassed the shy
young man. But Crazy Horse could not get Black Buffalo Woman out
of his mind. He returned again to sit quietly by her side, content only
to be near her.

Although Crazy Horse's bravery rapidly was earning him wide
recognition as a warrior, Black Buffalo Woman's raven-haired beauty
and the standing of her family made him only one of a dozen young
suitors waiting outside her lodge. Then one day in the early summer
of 1862, Red Cloud sent word that he would lead a war party against
the Crow. Crazy Horse and his brother, Little Hawk, Hump, Black
Twin, Young Man Afraid Of His Horses, Lone Bear, No Water, and
their followers were chosen to accompany Red Cloud. On the way to
Crow country they stopped to eat and smoke and to talk of the fight
to come. Suddenly No Water grabbed his face and began complaining
about a toothache. Since No Water's medicine came from the two
fierce, canine teeth of the grizzly bear, he took the pain as a warning.

Red Cloud, chief of the Oglala Sioux, became the best-known
Lakota leader among the whites.

Members of the war party knew of a warrior whose medicine was
the forepaw of a raccoon. The man had gone into a fight with a pain
in his hand and was killed. No Water said he must turn back. The
others agreed and went on without him.

For two weeks the warriors were gone. When they returned, it
was with the scalp of an old Crow chief and many stories of coups.
They had struck a big Crow hunting party and driven it far back past
the Powder and the Tongue, and even the Little Big Horn. Then on
the way back to the village Woman's Dress appeared. A grandson of

Chief Old Smoke and nephew of Red Cloud, Woman's Dress was known as Pretty One for his habit of dress. He grabbed Crazy Horse by the arm, led him away from the others, and told him that Black Buffalo Woman had married No Water.

News of what had happened caused Crazy Horse to take to his mother's lodge. For two or three days he stayed inside the lodge, no one daring to disturb him, and then emerged to pack his horse and head back alone for Crow country. Crazy Horse did not return to the village again until the end of the summer. He never told anyone what happened while he was gone, but when he entered the village he threw two Crow scalps to the dogs. They were the only scalps he had taken in five years. He blamed Red Cloud for what had happened, thus starting the great rivalry that grew between the two men. Crazy Horse believed that Red Cloud had conspired with No Water to leave the war party and return to the village to court and marry Black Buffalo Woman.[1]

SUCH IS THE STORY that has been told about Crazy Horse and Black Buffalo Woman, and the roots of Crazy Horse's rivalry with Red Cloud. The existing record, though, is not nearly so colorful or detailed. What is available, in fact, bears little resemblance to the tale.

That Crazy Horse fell in love with Black Buffalo Woman and that she was a niece of Red Cloud there is no doubt. Both He Dog and Chips provide evidence of that involvement. There is no primary support, however, for that love having grown out of a childhood connection. In fact, according to He Dog, it was not until a few years after Crazy Horse was made a shirt wearer, a war leader of the Lakota, when Black Buffalo Woman already was married to No Water and the mother of three children, that he began paying attention to her. Crazy Horse and He Dog were made shirt wearers together in about 1865. That would place the start of Crazy Horse's involvement with Black Buffalo Woman in the late 1860s, when he was nearing thirty years of age, and not the summer of 1862, when he was in his early twenties.

Of course, Crazy Horse could have been infatuated with Black Buffalo Woman for years before finally doing something about it. But even though he was a quiet man, it seems likely he would have confided something about his attraction to Black Buffalo Woman to a close friend such as He Dog.[2]

Likewise, there is nothing in the record to support the toothache incident with No Water. Neither is there a mention of a conspiracy between No Water and Red Cloud to steal Black Buffalo Woman from Crazy Horse.

The story of Crazy Horse's early love for Black Buffalo Woman also is called into question by the fact that she married No Water while Crazy Horse was away with a war party. It would seem doubtful that Black Buffalo Woman would have so easily given up on such a rising young warrior as Crazy Horse if there was anything serious between them at the time. That Crazy Horse was rapidly rising in esteem by his early twenties is supported by the fact that he was made a shirt wearer while only in his midtwenties, an early age for such a high honor.

Black Buffalo Woman herself is a shadowy figure. She has been described as a great beauty with many suitors. That certainly is possible. But there is no evidence to support such an assessment. Primary sources do not provide a description. Actually, she was so obscure a person that sources usually refer to her only as the wife of No Water. He Dog even had to be asked to reveal her name.

Further bringing into question the romantic image of Crazy Horse and Black Buffalo Woman is He Dog's statement that he and Crazy Horse "courted the girls together." That would seem to indicate that Crazy Horse was interested in other girls besides Black Buffalo Woman and did not pine for her. If Crazy Horse courted the girls, though, why he allowed his early twenties, the traditional marriage age among the Lakota, to pass without taking a wife is a mystery.[3] Perhaps he did not marry at the usual age because of his ambition "to get to the highest rank." In Lakota society women were considered inherently dangerous, corrupting influences that could harm or even destroy a man simply by touching his medicine or his equipment. Other cultures have shared such a view, but Lakota men so feared the power of women that menstruating females routinely were segregated in their own lodge until their menstrual period ended.

While nobody knows for sure what made Lakota men so fearful of their women, some anthropologists think it may have grown out of the belief that love and sexual intercourse physically weakened a man, a very dangerous situation in a culture where men might be called on to defend their village at any time. Lakota men used to speak proudly of mastering their sexual urges—another possible indication that Crazy Horse's late marriage might be considered a reflection of the ambition that drove him to become a great warrior, a defender of his people, something that very soon would become more important than ever for the Lakota.[4]

PRESSED THE HARDEST by whites, the Cheyenne and Arapaho who lived south of the Platte in the summer of 1863 launched a series of sporadic raids against wagon trains, telegraph offices, stage stations, and other symbols of white intrusion. The Cheyenne particularly were angry about the Treaty of Fort Wise. They complained that the men who had signed the treaty did not know they were giving away the tribe's land and had been bribed to make their mark. They maintained that the treaty was worthless. But whites claimed it was a "solemn obligation" and that the Cheyenne who did not support it were hostiles.[5]

Raids such as those launched by the Cheyenne and the Arapaho in the past usually had been attributed to young men anxious to make a reputation. With some exceptions, tribal leaders generally were allowed to handle the problem and make restitution. The Minnesota uprising and the rumors of coming Indian attacks that swept the plains in its wake, though, left frontier whites with little patience. Many began to agitate for more troops to protect them. The government responded by sending as many troops as Civil War conditions permitted, among them "galvanized Yanks," former Confederate prisoners and deserters who saw fighting Indians in the West as a way to avoid the deadly fate that awaited them east of the Mississippi River.

Moves west by Confederate troops added to the paranoia of pro-Union white settlers in the region. Confederate strategists saw the goldfields of Colorado and other wealth of the West as a way to support their war effort. The capture of large amounts of land also was viewed as a way to gain support and possibly diplomatic recognition from the European powers. Recognition would enable the South to borrow money and buy military supplies on credit. If their troops could make it all the way to the West Coast, the Confederacy might even gain access to deep-water ports that were beyond the capability of the Union Navy to blockade.

To carry out those plans, though, the Confederacy needed men. Even through few Union troops occupied the frontier forts, forces still would be needed to control key cities and outposts. Since the South had no men to spare, their leaders came up with the idea of enlisting Indians. They reasoned that the Indians already so disliked the whites among them that they easily could be persuaded to fight them. In return for their support, the Confederates promised to return to the Indians all of the land from Kansas City to California once the war ended. About four thousand Indians eventually were recruited by the Confederates, and several thousand more were informally armed. Among the Indians who joined the Confederate side were a number of Lakota.[6]

To counter such threats, the government furnished military escorts for travelers west of Fort Kearny; built Fort McPherson on the South Platte River; sent a cavalry troop to reinforce Fort Laramie; and ordered General Alfred Sully, who had put down the Minnesota uprising, to move west and attack Lakota camps on the Little Missouri, thus forcing the Indians south into the Black Hills.[7] The attack so angered the Lakota that during the winter of 1863–1864 they sent a war pipe down to the Southern Cheyenne and Arapaho. Still hoping for peace, leaders of the two tribes refused to smoke the pipe. But "a miserable white man who had been loafing around the Arapaho camp, living on the Indians and keeping an Arapaho 'wife,'" went to Denver and told Governor John Evans that he had seen the Arapaho holding secret councils, smoking the war pipe, and preparing for war in the spring.[8]

In March 1864, after meeting with Cheyenne and Arapaho on the Arkansas River, agent S. G. Colley sent a report to Evans assuring him that the two tribes had refused to smoke the war pipe and remained friendly. But the governor already had made up his mind that the tribes intended to start a war. Then, on April 3, 1864, Cheyenne reportedly drove off a herd of about 175 oxen belonging to government freighters on Sand Creek east of Denver. The Cheyenne George Bent, who had talked to many of the men who were present on Sand Creek, denied the story, claiming that "the Indians had no use for oxen; there were plenty of buffalo on the range that winter, and the Indians never would eat 'tame meat' when they could get buffalo."[9] Other Cheyenne sources report that the oxen had stampeded.[10]

Shortly after the Sand Creek incident, a troop of Colorado militia that had been ordered east to fight the Confederates attacked a party of young Cheyenne along the South Platte River. The Cheyenne were on their way north to fight the Crow. Little Chief, who was present, described what happened:

> We saw fifteen or twenty soldiers riding toward us at a gallop with pistols in their hands. We all jumped on our ponies, which we were leading, and turned to face soldiers with our bows and pistols ready. Bull Telling Tales and Wolf Coming Out still stood on the ground in front of the rest of us, holding their ponies with one hand and their weapons in their other hand. Without any talk the soldiers rode up to us and began shooting. The officer, who was in front of his men, rode straight at Bull Telling Tales with a pistol in his hand. Bull Telling Tales dropped his pony's bridle and jumped at this officer with his bow and arrow in his hands. The next time I looked in that direction the officer was lying on the ground. Bull Telling Tales had shot him right through the heart with an arrow. As soon as this officer fell the soldiers all stampeded. We did not chase them as we were not at war with the whites and did not wish to kill any more of them, after they had stopped trying to kill us.[11]

In response to those two incidents, Major General Samuel Curtis ordered Colonel John M. Chivington of the Colorado Volunteers to pursue the Cheyenne. Chivington was a religious zealot and an Indian-hater with political ambitions that only could be enhanced in the minds of most Westerners by a victory over the Indians. His appearance on the scene set the stage for serious trouble.

THROUGH THE SPRING and summer of 1864, friction between whites and the Cheyenne, Arapaho, and Lakota living south of the Platte River escalated into a series of bloody encounters. One involved the family of Ward Hungate, foreman of the Isaac P. Van Wormer ranch southeast of Denver. On the morning of June 11, Hungate and Edgar Miller were out repairing fences when they spotted a cloud of black smoke rising from the area of the ranch house. While Miller rode off for help, Hungate raced back to the house, where his wife and two daughters were staying.

When Miller returned with help, he found Hungate lying on the road with numerous arrows protruding from his head and body. Riding on to the ranch, the men then found the bodies of Mrs. Hungate and the couple's two young daughters stuffed into the well. According to accounts at the time, Mrs. Hungate had been repeatedly raped, burned, and slashed with a knife. The two girls, who have been reported as one and four years of age, and four and seven years of age, had their throats slashed to the point where their heads were nearly severed from their bodies, and their abdomens ripped open and entrails pulled out. All three had been scalped.[12]

How true the details of the story are is debatable. Following twenty years of abuse and misunderstanding on both sides, conflicts involving whites and Indians by the mid-1860s had become much more vicious than at the start of the overland migration in the 1840s. Photographs exist of whites shot full of arrows, and there are plenty of accounts of white bodies being mutilated by Indians, so the Hungates could very well have been found in the state that was reported. That they were tortured while alive and Mrs. Hungate repeatedly raped are more doubtful. Torture, except self-torture in the form of such activities as the sun dance, was not a part of plains Indian culture. It was much more a practice of eastern tribes.

Rape also was not a part of Indian culture, either western or eastern, but more a figment of white imagination or perhaps projection. From colonial days stories had circulated about white women being raped by Indians with very little, if any, evidence to support them. Without forensic evidence, the rape portion of the Hungate story must be questioned, particularly since Mrs. Hungate reportedly had been burned. That she was found nude proves nothing, since the Indians often took the clothes of those they killed.[13]

Whether the Hungate incident occurred the way it was reported, however, does not matter. It was what the people of Colorado believed. When the bodies of the family were hauled into Denver in the back of a wagon, a large, angry mob formed and marched to the territorial house to demand revenge. With the mob outside, Governor Evans summoned Colonel Chivington and demanded to know how such a thing could have happened so close to Denver. Chivington responded by ordering Lieutenant Clark Dunn to "track down the

Indians who did this." Most accounts also have Chivington telling his men "not to encumber themselves with prisoners."[14]

Although the troops were hot for revenge, they searched all summer for the hostiles without luck. Their utter failure led to some desperate tactics. On October 22, 1864, Colonel R. R. Livingston had a detachment of cavalry set fire to the plains at short intervals on the southern side of the Platte River for two hundred miles. Livingston believed that the fire would burn out the hostiles, but Indians living south of the Platte never saw or heard of the fires.[15]

DURING THE FALL OF 1864 the plains began to calm down. As was their custom, the Indians lost interest in fighting as winter approached and turned to hunting buffalo in preparation for the lean months ahead. Roads west reopened and signs appeared that many Indians wanted peace. But the whites' sense of superiority over the "savages" demanded revenge.

Among the Cheyenne leaders who wanted peace were Black Kettle and White Antelope. Both men had been to Washington and had seen the power of the whites. Through the summer and fall they worked to control their young men, and when matters quieted down they seized the opportunity to lead their people nearer to Fort Lyon, Colorado. They went to Fort Lyon because that was where many peaceful Cheyenne and Arapaho were gathering. Some sources say they had been promised protection by the troops at the fort, but historians argue that point. Nevertheless, the Indians who set up camp, about a hundred lodges of Cheyenne and ten lodges of Arapaho, along a tight bend of Sand Creek southeast of Denver, appear to have felt safe until they awoke early on the morning of November 29, 1864, and found themselves surrounded by more than seven hundred army troops and militiamen under the command of Colonel Chivington.

The Cheyenne warrior George Bent was in bed when he heard shouts and people running through the camp. He jumped up and ran out of his lodge to see troops advancing at a trot up Sand Creek, with others in place to the east and across the stream to the west. "More soldiers could be seen making for the Indian pony herds to the south of the camps," Bent said.

> In the camps themselves all was confusion and noise—men, women, and children rushing out of their lodges partly dressed; women and children screaming at [the] sight of troops; men running back into their lodges for their arms, other men, already armed, or with lassos and bridles in their hands, running for the herds to attempt to get some of the ponies before the troops could reach the animals and drive them off. I looked toward the chief's lodge and saw Black Kettle had a large American flag tied to the end of a long lodge pole and was standing in front of his lodge, holding the pole. . . .[16]

Little Bear was out looking for his family's pony herd when he saw his friend Kingfisher running back toward the camp shouting that white men were driving off the pony herds. Then a long line of "little black objects" appeared to the south. Little Bear turned and ran back to camp, where he found panicked people running in every direction and Black Kettle with an American flag. Although both Bent and Little Bear reported seeing a flag, troopers later testified that they did not see a banner.

For the next seven hours the surrounded villagers fought from banks and holes along Sand Creek. The fight continued until just after two o'clock in the afternoon, by which time all of the Indians either had been killed, wounded, captured, or had escaped across the plains. Early reports by soldiers placed the death toll of the Indians at more than 500. Later accounts set it between 300 and 500. Bent said 137 Cheyenne and Arapaho were killed. Whatever the toll, accounts generally agree that about two-thirds of the Indians killed were women and children. Bent said that only 28 of the dead were warriors. Chivington lost 9 men. Another 38 soldiers were wounded.[17]

As terrible as were the Indian losses, it was what happened afterward that horrified the nation, at least a large portion of the nation living east of the Mississippi River. Whites living in the West took a different view. As Captain Ware would note in his book *The Indian War of 1864:* "Among the humanitarians of Boston it was called the 'Chivington Massacre,' but there was never anything more deserved than that massacre. The only difficulty was that there were about fifteen hundred Indian warriors that didn't get killed."[18]

Battlefield atrocities are as old at the human race and never will go away. As a sign of triumph, anger, madness, frustration, superiority, hatred, or perversity, victors of every culture have tortured or killed captives and mutilated the bodies of dead enemies. Only occasionally does the timing or viciousness of the atrocities cause much of an uproar among the victors. Sand Creek was one such incident.

ABOUT THREE WEEKS AFTER the Sand Creek massacre, the Colorado militiamen, led by a regimental band and Colonel Chivington holding a captive eagle on a pole, paraded through Denver to the cheers of the populace. "As the 'bold sojer boys' passed along, the sidewalks and corner stands were thronged with citizens saluting their old friends," the *Rocky Mountain News* noted.[19] Within seventy-two hours of the troops' return, though, doubts about what had happened on the plains began to surface. They started with the final paragraph in Chivington's report, when he wrote that he was considering filing charges against Captain Silas S. Soule for "saying he thanked God that he had killed no Indians and like expressions."[20]

Such a comment was startling because Soule had fought with Chivington during the Civil War, had been decorated for bravery, and was one of the colonel's most trusted aides and a personal friend. Then, within days, several other men began to talk, telling anyone who would listen that Indian women and children had been cruelly slaughtered during the attack and old men shot down while waving white flags of surrender. They reported seeing drunk soldiers laughing as they shot cowering, unarmed Indians.

As many conservative Americans leaped to defend Lieutenant William Calley and attack his accusers after the My Lai Massacre in Vietnam by citing atrocities committed by the Viet Cong, so citizens of Denver rose to the angry defense of Chivington. They pointed to deaths caused by the Indians and called Soule and the others who were speaking out cowards who had no right to be known as soldiers. Then Chivington filed formal charges against Soule and five other men. The charges described Soule as "a coward and a deserter in time of battle, who had abandoned his leadership post, disobeyed lawful orders of his superiors, refused to fight when the battle got underway, and—in fact—threw down his weapon and ran from the scene of the battle."[21]

Chivington ordered the six men placed under arrest and incarcerated in the Denver jail. His action caused Soule's wife to write officials in Washington. On December 23, 1864, Secretary of War Edwin Stanton responded by ordering Soule and the others released from jail pending a formal military inquiry into events surrounding the fight at Sand Creek. Five days later, Soule was gunned down on a Denver street. He was shot in the back by a man hiding in an alley. No one was ever charged in the murder. In the meantime, a hundred Cheyenne scalps were trotted out for display during a performance at the Apollo Theater in Denver. The scalps were "applauded rapturously," according to one writer.

In the congressional inquiry that followed Soule's death, details of the atrocities committed at Sand Creek emerged. Defenders of Chivington and the Colorado militia attempted to justify what had happened by claiming that scalps and bloody clothing belonging to whites were found in the Cheyenne camp. But their words were mostly lost in the uproar. One militiaman testified that he had seen the bodies of several Cheyenne children who had been slashed with sabers and one who had his ear cut off. An officer with a group of New Mexico volunteers said he heard a Colorado militiaman brag that he had a squaw's heart on a stick. Another witness reported seeing a lieutenant kill three Cheyenne women and five children.[22]

Robert Bent, a brother of George, told investigators:

I saw five squaws hiding under a bank. When the troops came up to them they ran out and showed their persons to let the soldiers know they were squaws. They begged for mercy, but the soldiers shot them all. I saw a squaw lying on the bank, whose leg had been broken by a shell. A soldier came up to her with a drawn saber. She raised her arm to protect herself when he struck, breaking her arm; she rolled over and raised her other arm when he struck again, breaking it. Then he left without killing her.

Some thirty or forty squaws and children were hiding in a hole for protection. [They] sent out a little girl about six years old with a white flag on a stick. She was shot and killed and all the [others] in the hole were killed.

I saw one squaw cut open with an unborn child lying by her side. I saw the body of White Antelope with his privates cut off, and I heard a soldier say he was going to make a tobacco pouch out of them. I saw one squaw whose privates had been cut out. I saw a little girl who had been hid in the sand. Two soldiers drew their pistols and shot her, then pulled her out of the sand by the arm. I saw quite a number of infants in arms killed along with their mothers.[23]

Whether Chivington actually ordered his men to kill women and children remains a matter of debate, but there can be no doubt that his attitude allowed for such an occurrence. At a political rally in Denver two months before Sand Creek, he told his audience: "We are under specific orders; we are to take no prisoners. We are to punish the Indians. As for their women and children, 'nits make lice,' as they say. A surviving squaw will have babies who grow up to be even more bloodthirsty braves, whom our children would have to deal with. Our orders are clear. There are to be no future generation of Roman Noses [a Cheyenne leader] harassing white men."[24]

Corporal Amos Miksch testified that on the morning after the battle he saw a boy still alive in a trench filled with dead Indians. He watched a major take out his pistol and blow off the top of the boy's head. He also saw soldiers cutting off fingers and ears to get at jewelry, taking scalps, and abusing corpses. "Next morning," he said, "after they were dead and stiff, these men pulled out the bodies of the squaws and pulled them open in an indecent manner."[25]

Major Scott Anthony reported three militiamen using a child of about three years of age for target practice, while Lieutenant James Connor testified that he did not see an Indian body that had not been scalped or mutilated "in the most horrible manner—men, women and children's private parts cut out, &c; I heard one man say he had cut out a woman's private parts and had them for exhibition. . . . I also heard of numerous instances in which men had cut out the private parts of females and stretched them over the saddle-bows and wore them over their hats while riding in the ranks."[26] Such testimony continued for fifty-nine days before the defense took the stand.

15

SHIRT-WEARER

Many nearly naked, their hands and feet frozen, survivors of the Sand Creek Massacre made their way south to a Cheyenne camp on the South Fork of the Smoky Hill River along the Colorado/Kansas line. Horrified and angered by the pitiful condition of survivors and the stories they told, the Cheyenne on Smoky Hill realized they could no longer trust the whites and held a council during which they decided to take the highly unusual step of going to war in the winter. A war pipe was sent to the Lakota camped on the Solomon River. The Lakota smoked the pipe and then joined with the Cheyenne and the Northern Arapaho in a camp of about eight hundred lodges on Cherry Creek, a tributary of the Republican River to the north. There, on about New Year's Day 1865, a decision was made to attack Julesburg, an important stage and telegraph town, and nearby Fort Sedgwick, a one-company army post on the South Platte River in northeastern Colorado.

A force of about a thousand Cheyenne, Lakota, and Arapaho warriors reached the Julesburg area on the evening of January 6, 1865. Posting guards to keep the young men from sneaking off to raid the town on their own and alert the whites, the force camped in the sand hills south of Julesburg and laid plans for an attack. Big Crow was selected to lead a Cheyenne decoy party to Julesburg and nearby Camp Rankin, renamed Fort Sedgwick on September 27, 1865. The idea was to draw the soldiers out of the fort and up a gully, where they could be attacked by the main force of Indians hidden in the hills.

At daylight, Big Crow and his men rode out of the gully and wildly charged a group of soldiers who had been spotted outside the fort. The soldiers fell back into the stockade and began firing at the Indians. Then a bugle blew and a few minutes later post commander Captain Nicholas O'Brien rode out of the fort with a force of thirty-eight men. A somewhat resigned George Bent described what followed:

> Big Crow and his men retreated back toward the hills, drawing the soldiers after them. They came nearer and nearer and it began to look like they would ride right into the trap; but, as usual, the Indians would not wait for the right moment, and some young men suddenly broke away from the main force and charged out of the hills toward the soldiers. The rest of the thousand followed them, as there was no longer any use in hiding.[1]

As the Indians swarmed out of the hills, Captain O'Brien ordered a retreat. Big Crow and his men turned and charged the soldiers. They were soon joined by a large party of warriors coming up from the rear. In the fight that followed at least fourteen soldiers and four civilians were killed. In a rare scene true to Western movies, the Indians then circled the stockade, yelling and shooting at the troops inside, until they tired of the game and rode off to plunder Julesburg. Throughout the day they carried off load after load of flour, bacon, corn, sugar, and anything else that caught their fancy. The pack ponies were so overloaded that it took three days to get the plunder back to the camp.

Back at Cherry Creek, there was great rejoicing. A blow had been struck in revenge, and the warriors had brought back more plunder than most of the Indians ever dreamed existed. Bent said: "That night the young men and young women held scalp dances in all of the camps, for all the soldiers who had been killed at Julesburg had been scalped by the warriors, and the young people kept up the dances and drumming until after daylight."[2] At the same time, the chiefs of the camp were meeting in council and deciding to make a great raid along the Platte River, then move north to join the Lakota and the Cheyenne living around the Black Hills and the Powder River.

WITH WAR PARTIES leading the way, the village of seven hundred to a thousand lodges broke camp on January 26, 1865, and headed north.

It reached the South Platte River two days later and began attacking ranches, stage stations, and wagon trains. Whites were killed wherever they were found. Soldiers who had been sent to protect settlers and travelers along the Platte hid inside their forts, too frightened to attack the huge village with so many warriors. When the village crossed the Platte about twenty-three miles west of Julesburg and pitched camp, the lodges stretched for nearly four miles along the river. The glare of their fires could be seen far up the valley and the pounding of their drums heard for miles as they danced and feasted through the night.

For six days the Indians remained at the camp. On February 2, 1865, the village finally started for the North Platte while a party of a thousand warriors went down the South Platte to attack Camp Rankin. Again, the chiefs sent out a decoy party to lure the troops into a trap. But the officers had learned a hard lesson during the first attack a month earlier and kept their troops inside the fort. Seeing little to gain by continuing the attack, the Indians moved off to loot Julesburg for a second time, and then burn it.

Several writers name Crazy Horse as one of the Lakota who took part in the second attack on Julesburg. Although his ambitions as a warrior could have taken him south with other young men to fight the whites, primary sources provide no solid evidence to support his involvement at Julesburg. At the time of the attack, Crazy Horse and He Dog were members of Man Afraid Of His Horses's band, which was peaceful toward the whites and living an isolated existence in the Powder River country.[3] Hyde writes in *Red Cloud's Folk* that the bands along the Powder seem to have been unaffected by what was happening to their southern relatives and allies until a large group of hostiles from the south joined them in early March 1865, a month after the second attack on Julesburg. Even then, the Powder River bands went about their usual business, as if there were no war with the whites.[4]

The only possible primary support for Crazy Horse's involvement at Julesburg might be that when Man Afraid Of His Horses's band subdivided, he went with the southern half. He Dog does not say exactly when that occurred or how far south the band moved. But the split was before Crazy Horse became a shirt-wearer, since he was nominated for that honor by the southern division of the band. Crazy Horse was made a shirt-wearer in about 1865, probably in the summer; consequently he could have been at Julesburg if the division he was living with was camped far enough south to quickly learn about Sand Creek and Julesburg.

However, it appears more likely that Crazy Horse was living somewhere in the Powder River country and may not have heard about the Julesburg raid until after the fact. That seems the case because He Dog reports that he and Crazy Horse were living around the White Mountains [Big Horn Mountains] west of the Powder River at about the time they were made shirt-wearers. Until July 1865, the Powder River bands were far more interested in fighting traditional enemies such as the Crow and Shoshone than whites. According to He Dog, he and Crazy Horse were made shirt-wearers after returning from a war trip west of the Big Horn Mountains, which was Shoshone country, a possible sign that Crazy Horse during the first half of 1865 was more interested in fighting traditional Lakota enemies than the new white enemy.[5]

Among the white soldiers on the northern plains at the time was Lieutenant Caspar Collins. He was a member of the 11th Ohio Volunteer Cavalry, which had been raised to fight Confederates, but was sent west after the Minnesota uprising in 1862. The 11th Ohio and Fort Laramie were both under the command of Collins's father, Colonel William O. Collins.

An inquisitive twenty-one-year old, the younger Collins frequently rode off on his own to explore the plains and visit Indian villages, where he got to know the inhabitants as people rather than savages. He eventually made friends with a number of Lakota. Some writers report that Collins and Crazy Horse became close friends and that Crazy Horse taught him the ways of the Lakota. It is a quaint, romantic image. Unfortunately, however, there is nothing in the record left either by Crazy Horse's friends or by Collins himself to support such an involvement.[6]

THE SHIRT-WEARERS whom Crazy Horse joined probably in 1865 were the voices of the Wicasa Itacans, which was a sort of executive committee charged with implementing the decisions of the larger tribal council. The number of shirt-wearers could vary from tribe to tribe. The Brulé, for instance, had two shirt-wearers, though they each could choose two associates, while the Oglala had four. They were called on to decide matters of tribal concern both great and small, from reconciling quarrels between individuals and families to negotiating diplomatic agreements with other nations. They also were responsible for finding bountiful hunting grounds and good camp sites. The welfare of the people was their primary obligation, one that they earned only after distinguishing themselves in many fights, as well as in peace.

Shirt-wearers earned their name from the fact that members of the group at their investiture were presented with either a blue and yellow or a red and green painted shirt fringed with hairlocks as a sign of their position. Some shirt-wearers also wore a yellow shirt. The colors of the shirts symbolized the powers of the natural world— blue for sky, red for sun, yellow for rock, and green for the Earth. The fringe of the hairlocks represented the people of the tribe for whom members of the group ultimately were responsible.[7]

Crazy Horse, He Dog, Young Man Afraid Of His Horses, and Sword were selected together by the Oglala as shirt-wearers. He Dog and Crazy Horse learned that they had been chosen when they returned from a war trip across the Big Horn Mountains. "The people came out of the camp to meet us and escort us back and at a big ceremony presented us with two spears, the gift of the whole tribe, which we met together," He Dog said. "These spears were each three or four hundred years old and were given by the older generation to those in the younger generation who had best lived the life of a warrior."[8]

The scout and interpreter Garnett was thirteen years old at the time and present in the Oglala camp when Crazy Horse and the others were installed as shirt-wearers. Horsemen circled the camp, collected the four warriors, placed them on horses, and led them to the council lodge at the center of the village. At the lodge, Crazy Horse and the others were taken from their mounts and placed on robes spread on the ground.

"The old men or leaders of the nation were seated at one end of the house in a half circle," Garnett said. "In front of these and facing them were the young warriors of the tribe. On either side the Indian women were ranged, and standing back of the young warriors promiscuously were a throng of children and all others. A feast of beef and dog flesh had been prepared for this important event and the women were waiting for the moment when they should address themselves to the important duty of serving the feast. An old man, probably the chief of the nation, arose and addressed the four young men seated within the circle . . . the speaker told them that they had been selected as head warriors of their people; that their duty was to govern the people in camp and on the march; to see that order was preserved; that violence was not committed; that all families and persons had their rights, and that none imposed on the others."[9]

With his appointment as a shirt-wearer, Crazy Horse finally fulfilled his ambition to reach the top of Lakota society. He was about twenty-five years of age and officially recognized as one of the greatest warriors in a culture that conferred its highest honors on warriors. But at the same time the forces of another, much more powerful, society were about to turn their attention toward the plains tribes.

NELSON MILES, Philip Sheridan, William Tecumseh Sherman, and George Armstrong Custer were the spearheads of the new forces about to focus on the plains. Schooled at Gettysburg, Vicksburg, Bull Run, Atlanta, and other battlefields of the Civil War, they would bring to bear the might of the industrial world on the Lakota. As the Civil War was the first modern, total war in which an entire population, not just an army, became the enemy, the plains Indian wars that followed were some of the first conflicts in which the might of an industrialized nation was directed toward the suppression of a native people. During the age of imperialism, it would be repeated countless times in Asia and Africa.

The United States, which would force many plains Indians onto reservations by the end of the 1860s, had a population of almost 33.5 million in 1860, about 8.5 million more than in 1850. By comparison, the Lakota population stood at roughly 25,000. The population center of the United States also had shifted farther west, from the Parkersburg, West Virginia, area to the Chillicothe, Ohio, area.

Along with providing an example for future conflicts, the 1860s gave birth to many weapons and tactics that would be used in those conflicts. The Civil War period saw Oliver F. Winchester produce the first repeating rifle, Richard Gatling patent the first machine gun, the Union enact the first draft law, and the Confederate Navy conduct the first successful submarine attack. To recognize bravery, Congress authorized the Medal of Honor, while President Lincoln proclaimed the first Thanksgiving Day and the nation sought to honor its war dead with the first national Decoration Day (Memorial Day).

Culturally, the decade witnessed the arrival of roller skating, cigarettes, summer camp, paperback books, Horatio Alger's first rags-to-riches stories, Mark Twain's "The Celebrated Jumping Frog of Calaveras County," Charles Darwin's *The Origin of Species*, and Lewis Carroll's *Alice's Adventures in Wonderland*. In sports, the first Belmont Stakes was run and the first professional baseball team, the Cincinnati Red Stockings, was formed.

Also during the decade, Congress passed the first Civil Rights Act, Internal Revenue Act, and Homestead Act, and levied the first income tax to support the Union war effort; a cable was laid aross the Atlantic Ocean, and the Ku Klux Klan was formed. "In God We Trust" was added to the nation's money, and Alaska was purchased from Russia for $7.2 million. Former presidents Martin Van Buren, James Buchanan, and Franklin Pierce died, and the first caricature of Uncle Sam appeared.

Though Crazy Horse continued to live free in the Powder River country and around the Black Hills, the extent to which white culture had enveloped his people can be seen in the chartering of the University of Kansas and the University of Nebraska, the appearance of newspapers in Wyoming and Montana, and the sending of the first coast-to-coast telegram. During the 1860s, Nevada, Dakota, Montana, Idaho, and Arizona also were formed into territories, and West Virginia, Nevada, and Nebraska were admitted to the Union as states.

As the Civil War set the tone for all wars to follow, the period after the fighting stopped gave birth to the modern corporate world. Driven by a pent-up desire of people to get on with their lives and unrestrained by government regulations, the years after the war became the most fertile in American history for schemers and dreamers, fast-talking hucksters and swindlers. A mania for invention and money overcame the nation. Wealthy young businessmen with names such as Rockefeller, Carnegie, Mellon, and Frick fed envy among veterans who wanted to emulate their good fortune.[10]

That cutting loose naturally turned west. Railroad expansion gained momentum, culminating in the driving of a golden spike marking the completion of the transcontinental railroad at Promontory,

Utah, in 1869. The new line ran through the heart of Nebraska and southern Wyoming, and spawned an accompanying growth in land deals and mining development. White Americans rushed to exploit natural resources that could be economically brought to market for the first time. And standing in the way once again were the Lakota. Although he would later deny ever making such a remark, General Sheridan captured the feelings of many white Americans after the Civil War when he said: "The only good Indian is a dead Indian."[11]

16

PLATTE BRIDGE

GENERAL ROBERT E. LEE's surrender of the Army of Northern Virginia at Appomattox Courthouse, Virginia, on April 9, 1865, theoretically freed large numbers of battle-hardened troops to be sent west against the Lakota and the Cheyenne, who in the wake of the Sand Creek Massacre had taken to attacking white settlements and travelers along the Platte River. Plans were laid by the War Department to send at least five columns of cavalry into the Powder River country and to erect forts along the Powder and Yellowstone rivers. Although such moves would have resulted in the conquest of the Lakota and the Cheyenne living in the region, the Indians showed no concern. Under the leadership of Man Afraid Of His Horses, an advocate of peace with the whites, the Powder River bands went about their usual business of hunting and raiding traditional enemies. So unaware were they of the force about to be directed against them that White Bull's winter count describes the winter of 1864–1865 as the one in which "The Miniconjou Killed Four Crows." For three weeks afterward the scalps of the men were danced, almost without pause, through all the Lakota and Cheyenne camps.[1]

In May the bands moved from the Powder to the Tongue River to hunt and raid the Crow. On the Tongue, the war chiefs finally held councils to consider action against the whites. Red Cloud and Young Man Afraid Of His Horses, the son of the old chief, are known to have been present at the councils. The Cheyenne George Bent is the primary source for what happened on the Tongue and the Powder. He does not report Crazy Horse at any of the councils. As a member of Red Cloud's band and a noted warrior who was about to be named a shirt-wearer, Crazy Horse had the standing to take part in the talks, but his reserved personality is known to have kept him from speaking up at councils, so he would have been easy to overlook.

One night, after the councils had been going on for some time, the chiefs decided that the ponies had grown fat enough on the good grass of the Tongue and that raiding parties soon would set out for the Platte. They told the warriors to remember everything they saw along the Platte and to look for the best place to carry out a great raid in June.

At about the same time that the raiding parties were being sent out, the Oglala Two Face decided to surrender and join other Lakota friendly to the whites who were living around Fort Laramie—the Laramie loafers, as they were derisively known by the free-living Lakota. As a sign of their goodwill, Two Face purchased from other Lakota a white woman, Mrs. Eubanks, and her daughter, who had been taken captive during the raids of 1864. He planned to take her and her child to Fort Laramie, probably both in hopes of a reward and as a sign to the whites of his friendship.

Near the Platte, Two Face ran into a troop of Indians who had been made police by the whites at Fort Laramie. Learning that Black Foot, another Oglala who was friendly to the whites, also was in the area, the Indian police rounded up both bands and took them to the fort. Two Face and Black Foot were turned over to Colonel Thomas Moonlight, commander of the fort and a drunk who hated Indians. When Mrs. Eubanks became hysterical in describing her captivity, claiming she had been repeatedly raped by the Indians, the drunken colonel ordered the arrest of Two Face and Black Foot. The pair were beaten by soldiers and shortly afterward taken out and hanged in artillery trace chains. Their bodies were left hanging until the weight of the balls at the end of the chains pulled off their legs.

Although the Laramie loafers were stunned by what happened, they had become so dependent on the whites and fearful of their power that they did nothing. Then orders came in to transport the people of Two Face and Black Foot to Fort Kearny, on the lower Platte River. Fort Kearny was in the country of the Pawnee, bitter enemies of the Lakota. To enter their country would have been considered a death sentence by most Lakota. But General G. M. Dodge, new commander of the military department of the Platte, paid no attention to the protest of the Lakota. On June 11, 1865, an extremely apprehensive group of 1,500 to 2,000 Lakota started down the Platte.

With them were 135 men of the 7th Iowa Cavalry, a troop of Indian police, and 25 to 50 whites, most of them men with Lakota wives.

On the evening of June 13 the column reached Horse Creek and camped on the 1851 council grounds. Their guards camped on the other side of the stream. That night some of the Lakota who did not trust their leaders held a secret council and decided to take action. For some unknown reason, the soldiers had not disarmed them at the start of the move. The rebellious Lakota planned to ambush the soldiers when they came for them the next morning. The plan was to allow the troops to enter in the center of camp and then attack and kill all of them. As often happened, though, the young men could not wait and started firing at the soldiers before they were all of the way into camp. In the fight that followed, one officer and four enlisted men were killed and seven soldiers were wounded. Four leaders of the loafers also were killed by the rebellious Lakota. The only Lakota to die at the hands of the soldiers was a prisoner being held in chains in the soldiers' camp. Reports failed to explain how the prisoner died.

The fugitive Lakota hurried across the Platte and fled north, toward the Black Hills. As soon as they were gone, a message was sent by the guard troops to Colonel Thomas Moonlight at Camp Mitchell, about twenty miles upriver from Horse Creek. Colonel Moonlight immediately set out with three troops of cavalry in pursuit of the Indians. The fugitives learned that they were being followed from a war party they encountered and, after hurrying their women and children father north, fell back to watch the soldiers. When, five days after the fight, Colonel Moonlight had his men camp on Dead Man's Fork near the Wyoming/Nebraska line, the Lakota sent down a raiding party of two hundred warriors to steal their horses.

In late morning the raiding party struck. "The soldiers were eating breakfast," Bent recalled, "when all at once the two hundred warriors swept over the bluffs and down into the narrow valley, yelling and shooting and waving their shields and lances to frighten the herd. The loose animals stampeded at once, and many of those which were picketed and hobbled in the camp broke free and joined the rush. Following close after the running animals, the warriors swept by the camp, turned the herd, and drove it over the bluffs."[2] Colonel Moonlight and his men were left to walk home eighty miles through the Sand Hills, wearing cavalry boots and carrying their saddles.

AT ROUGHLY THE SAME TIME as the loafers' rebellion, the free-living Lakota and the Cheyenne in the Powder River country, who almost surely would have included Crazy Horse, though again no primary records are available, began laying plans for a large-scale raid on the whites. Tribal leaders ordered a halt to small raids and appointed warriors to patrol the camps and keep young men from sneaking off on raids of their own. To ensure success, the Lakota held a sun dance and the Cheyenne a medicine lodge ceremony, while the camps, an estimated one thousand lodges, moved closer to the Crazy Woman's Fork of the Powder.

"Everyone was busy preparing for war," George Bent recalled,

> all the charms worn in battle were being repaired, new eagle feathers were out in the war bonnets and on the shields, war shirts were put into perfect condition. . . . It was believed that if a man went into battle without his charms, war bonnet, etc., in perfect condition, he would be sure to get killed. All this repair work had to be done with the aid of the medicine men, who knew the proper ceremonies, and these men had to be given feasts and presents by the warriors who asked their assistance.[3]

When the ceremonies were over and all of the equipment in order, the warriors paraded through the camps singing their war songs. The raid was one of the last occasions on record in which such a large number of warriors, about three thousand, prepared themselves for battle in the old ways. Bent reports seeing Red Cloud and Man Afraid Of His Horses wearing their scalp shirts in the parade. (The name Man Afraid Of His Horses does not mean that its owner was afraid of his horses, rather that his enemies were afraid even of his horses. It might better be translated as They Are Afraid Even Of His Horses.) Although no primary record exists, the number of men involved and the presence of such prominent Lakota warriors as Red Cloud and Man Afraid Of His Horses makes it almost certain that an ambitious warrior such as Crazy Horse would have been on hand.

The Platte Bridge across the North Platte River at what is now Casper, Wyoming, was selected as the objective of the great raid. Built in 1859, the bridge was heavily used by migrants, freight lines, and the military. At its southern end was an army post, a stockade, an

Reconstruction of a segment of the Platte River Bridge, now part of the Fort Casper Historic Site in Wyoming.

abandoned stage station, and an office of the Overland Telegraph Company. By taking the bridge, the Lakota and the Cheyenne would cut the communication lines of the whites and destroy a powerful symbol of white intrusion.

When the raiding party reached the bridge, a party of ten scouts was sent out to draw the soldiers across the river and into the open, while the main body of warriors hid behind the bluffs north of the post. It was a classic plains Indian tactic. Some writers have made Crazy Horse a member of the decoy party. While that is possible, nothing in the available record supports his participation as a decoy.

As the scouts approached the bridge, a troop of soldiers with a cannon rode out of the post and across the river. The scouts retreated toward the bluffs, drawing the soldiers closer to the main body of warriors. While still some distance away, the soldiers stopped and fired their cannon at the scouts. The sound of the cannon unleashed a frenzy among the warriors behind the bluffs. The warriors assigned to keep order tried to control the men, beating them back with lances and quirts, but the excitement was too great, and some of the warriors broke through and raced to the top of the bluffs, where they could see the scouts circling in front of the soldiers, drawing them farther and farther into the trap.

Knowing that the soldiers would quickly retreat if they saw what was waiting for them, the chiefs induced most of the anxious warriors to keep out of sight behind the bluffs. But it was too late. Although the scouts tried everything they could think of to tempt the soldiers into the trap, the white troops realized something was wrong and halted a safe distance from the bluffs. When it proved impossible to lure them any closer, the scouts rode off behind the bluffs to join the other warriors.

In the early-morning darkness, after long discussions among the chiefs, another party of scouts were sent out to lure the soldiers. Then, shortly after dawn, the warriors gathered and formed into three groups, two small and one large. One of the small groups headed down Casper Creek, while the other hid behind the hills north of the bridge. The third, largest group headed for the bluffs northwest of the bridge. At about nine o'clock that morning a troop of cavalry rode across the Platte Bridge and turned west to meet a supply train. When the warriors saw the soldiers, they rode to the top of the bluffs. Even though the Indians were clearly visible against the skyline, the troops continued their advance without any indication of alarm. They passed the bluff where the second small war party was stationed, effectively cutting themselves off from the bridge and the soldiers on the other side of the North Platte. Seeing the vulnerable position of the troops, some of the warriors wanted to attack immediately, but the leaders convinced them to wait. Slowly the troops continued on until they were opposite the bluff where the main body of warriors was hidden. "And then all at once we saw a couple of thousand mounted warriors swarm over the tops of the hills and sweep down into the valley," recalled Bent, who was part of the group behind the first bluff.

The sudden charge of so many warriors threw the troops into a panic. They broke ranks and raced back for the bridge. It was each man for himself. Then the warriors still behind the hill rushed down to cut off their retreat, and the third group, from along the creek, headed for the bridge. At the sound of the fighting, a company of infantry also rushed across the bridge, and a cannon was brought out and swung into position. But the Lakota and the Cheyenne were out of rifle range, and the firing did little damage. The second group of warriors closed in on the retreating troops. Bent related what happened next:

> As we rushed in among them, the air was thick with dust and powder smoke; you could not see a dozen yards, and the shots and yells deafened the ears. As we went into the troops, I saw an officer [Lieutenant Casper Collins] on a big bay horse rush past me through the dense clouds of dust and smoke. His horse was running away with him and broke right through the Indians. The Lieutenant had an arrow sticking in his forehead and his face was streaming with blood. . . . He dropped right in the midst of the warriors, one of whom caught his horse. I saw soldiers falling on every side. A few broke through and reached the infantry at the bridge; the infantry then ran back across the bridge and the cannon opened fire again. I do not think that more than four or five of the troopers succeeded in escaping. The road for a mile or more was dotted with dead bodies, and at the point where our party struck the troops the bodies of the men and the dead horses lay in groups.[4]

Whether due to excitement, a faulty memory, the confusion of someone caught in the middle of a battle, or a desire to make the Indian victory greater than it was in reality, Bent wildly overestimated the casualties among the troops. The record shows that only Lieutenant Collins and four of his men died. Although vastly outnumbered and cornered, most of the soldiers were able to ride straight through the Lakota and the Cheyenne back to the safety of the bridge. Historian George Hyde speculates that the troops were able to accomplish such a feat because only a relatively small number of Indians were able to get between them and the bridge, and because most of the Lakota and Cheyenne were poorly armed with lances and bows and could not face the losses that would occur if they got too close to the well-armed troops.[5]

After the troops made it back to the post, according to Bent, some warriors attempted to cross the bridge but were driven back by the cannon. A few warriors swam their ponies across the river, charged the troops, and drove them back to the stockade. Under continuous cannon fire, most of the warriors retreated back behind the hills from where they had come. Then word arrived that about two dozen soldiers were coming from the west. It was the supply train that Lieutenant Collins had gone out to escort into the post. The warriors immediately headed off to find the troops already under attack

about five miles away. The troops held out for about a half hour.
Only one teamster managed to swim the river and escape.

After the second fight, the Lakota and the Cheyenne returned to
their camp to celebrate. Then the next morning the camps broke up.
Most of the people headed back to the Powder River country, while
other, small groups rode off to raid the road heading west. Some writers have Crazy Horse, as well as Young Man Afraid Of His Horses and
Red Cloud, stopping in the middle of the fight when they saw Lieutenant Collins approaching. The thick dust and smoke that covered
the battlefield and made it impossible to see more than a few yards,
though, makes that claim seem ridiculous. Those writers sound even
sillier when they have the Indians parting before Collins's retreating
force, the lieutenant calling out a greeting to Crazy Horse and the
others, and the Lakota in turn shouting warnings about the Cheyenne behind Collins. Such a scene might play well in a movie, but
there is absolutely no evidence to support any of it.[6]

SHORTLY AFTER the Lakota and the Cheyenne returned to their camps,
General Patrick E. Connor, who had been appointed military commander of the Platte district after the attack on Julesburg, started his
columns north toward the Powder River after the Indians. Although
the end of the Civil War freed troops for use against the plains tribes,
the volunteer cavalry regiments sent west were in no hurry to go.
Tired of fighting, many of them marched off at a snail's pace, hoping
their mustering-out orders would arrive before they reached their
destinations. When the orders did reach them, many of the troops
immediately turned around. One Kansas regiment that had reached
the vicinity of Fort Laramie mutinied when ordered to march against
the Indians. Troops loyal to Connor surrounded the rebellious camp
and forced the Kansas troops to go on the Powder River expedition.
But they could not force them to fight. The troops returned to Fort
Laramie without ever finding the Lakota and the Cheyenne.

General Connor himself marched to the head of the Powder,
where he built a military post. Pawnee scouts discovered the Lakota
and Cheyenne camps and had several fights with their longtime enemies. But Connor ignored their reports and turned his attention to
a camp of Arapaho on the Tongue River. He attacked the Arapaho

even though there is no evidence that they had been involved in the Platte Bridge fight. The troops caught the Arapaho by surprise and ran off their pony herd, but the Indians fought back and recovered most of the horses. General Connor then marched down the Tongue to rendezvous with two columns led by Colonel Nelson Cole and Colonel Samuel Walker.

So bumbling were Connor and the others in their pursuit of the Lakota and the Cheyenne that the Indians did not even know the troops were moving through their country. The first warning that whites were along the Powder came when a hunting party in mid-August 1865 spotted a road-building crew and a wagon train of Montana gold seekers led by James Sawyer. The Indians kept the wagon train corraled near Pumpkin Butte for four days but never launched a serious attack. Then Sawyer indicated that he wanted to talk. During the parlay that followed, it was mentioned that General Connor planned to build a fort on the Powder, something he already had done. Sawyer then bought off the Indians with a wagonload of goods. The party was attacked a second time by Cheyenne who did not receive any goods. After two days, though, the Indians tired of fighting and moved off.

For several days after the fight, the wagon train wandered along the Powder until it found General Connor's post near the head of the river. There Sawyer secured an escort of cavalry and headed for the Tongue. Near the Big Horn Mountains the train ran into a party of Arapaho who were angry over Connor's attack on their camp. They launched a serious attack on the train, but one of the whites managed to break out and reach Connor's camp. The general dispatched a troop of cavalry, forcing the Indians to withdraw.

The wagon train incident shows that as late as mid-August 1865 the Lakota and the Cheyenne had no idea that the whites wanted to open the Powder River country. General Connor's advance up the Powder also indicates that they had learned little about the fighting ways of the whites since the Grattan fight and General Harney's retaliatory attack on Little Thunder's camp a decade earlier. As if they were fighting the Crow or the Pawnee, most Lakota and Cheyenne seemed to think that they could go back to hunting and living in the old ways after the attack on Julesburg and the Platte Bridge. By the beginning of September, though, three columns of troops were moving toward the Powder River. General Connor was marching down

the Tongue with a thousand troops, while Colonel Nelson and
Colonel Walker were moving in from the east with an additional two
thousand men.

The plan was to catch the Indians in a pincer movement between
the two regiments. But most of the troops had no desire to fight.
Colonel Walker's men were the Kansas troops who rebelled near Fort
Laramie. They dolefully marched into the Powder River country
between the Indians who had fought at the Platte Bridge and Sitting
Bull's Hunkpapa on the Little Missouri River. At about the time of
the Platte Bridge fight, Sitting Bull had led an expedition against Fort
Rice on the upper Missouri River. That attack did not go as well as
the one at the Platte Bridge because the troops could not be drawn
out of the fort. When Cole and Walker's troops were discovered, the
frustrated Hunkpapa, along with some Miniconjou, Sans Arc, and
Black Foot Lakota, attacked them on September 1, 1865.

Although they had two thousand troops, Colonel Cole and
Colonel Walker made no effort to take the offensive. For four days
Lakota warriors harassed the column, running off its horses and
mules, and delaying its line of march up the Powder. When the troops
finally moved beyond the Missouri, they were discovered by other
Lakota and Cheyenne who had been camped near the mouth of the
Little Powder River, who immediately sent out small war parties to
harass the troops. Then, on about September 5, a party of about two
thousand warriors attacked. The poorly armed Indians, however,
failed to break through the line of troops and succeeded only in
stealing about eighty horses from a unit trapped in a canyon. When
other attacks failed to produce more horses, the Cheyenne gave up
and headed for the Black Hills to hunt buffalo.

Three days later, the inept Cole and Walker almost stumbled into
the large Lakota camp on the Little Powder. About two thousand
warriors attacked the troops, forcing them to corral their horses and
occupying them for several hours while the women took down the
lodges and fled with the children and old people. Then a cold rain
began to fall and continued for a day and a half. The storm killed
414 of Cole and Walker's horses and mules, forcing the troops to
burn wagons and supplies before moving on.

On September 10, 1865, another large group of warriors appeared
to encircle the troops on their march. A lack of guns, however, kept
the warriors from doing much damage. Colonel Cole's officers later

estimated that the Indians had only four or five good muskets among them.

The day after the attack, Cole and Walker's men began slaughtering their horses and mules for food. Under continued harassment by the Indians, disaster seemed imminent for the troops until a messenger arrived with news that General Connor's column was only sixty miles away on the Tongue and that the new post the general had established on the Powder was even closer. Encouraged by the news, the troops mustered their strength and marched on to the post, ending the Powder River Expedition of 1865. Except for the capture of some Arapaho ponies, the expedition did nothing but drain the U.S. Treasury. The cost of transporting supplies into the isolated region alone was estimated at $2 million per month, about $32 million in late 1990s dollars. Meanwhile, the Indian camps were full of horses, mules, rifles, and pistols bearing the U.S. mark. Crazy Horse's role in the Powder River expedition is not documented, but it is impossible to imagine that a young warrior of his standing would not have been involved in at least a part of it.

17

ONE HUNDRED
WHITE MEN KILLED

Following the Sand Creek massacre, the fiasco and expense of the Powder River Expedition of 1865 drew cries of outrage from the white public. Pushed by churches whose desire to "save the savages" caused them to demand an end to such military actions and a fair approach to dealing with the Indians, Congress reacted in typical fashion and created a committee under Massachusetts senator James Doolittle, a critic of the military's role in Indian affairs. Their pockets shrunken by recent cuts in easily skimmed Indian appropriations, even some Indian-hating western politicians suddenly developed a Christian desire to promote the cause of peace and improve the welfare of the Indians with additional federal funds.

Caught by the current of public opinion, Congress also created the Northwest Treaty Commission under Newton Edmunds, governor of Dakota Territory, to negotiate peace treaties with tribes living along the upper Missouri River. Incredibly, the commission then selected Major General Samuel R. Curtis, who had ordered Colonel Chivington on the expedition that resulted in the Sand Creek Massacre, to lead the peace council. Curtis in turn allowed Indian delegates to be picked for the council from loafer bands. Lakota hostile to the white invasion were given no role in the council.

With the stage thus set, a gift-laden peace commission in October 1865 traveled up the Missouri to Fort Sully, near the mouth of the Cheyenne River. Guided by instructions from Secretary of the Interior James Harlan, the council's goal was to end violent confrontations between the plains tribes and the ever-advancing tide of whites by having the tribes give up their wandering life and settle on reservations. Under Harlan's plan, western tribes were to be assigned remote tracts of land far from roads and settlements. Realizing that "a sudden transition from a savage and nomadic life to the more quiet and confining pursuits of civilization is not to be expected," Harlan stipulated that reservation lands should be suitable for agricultural purposes. He also insisted that the government furnish the Indians with assistance to make the transition from hunters to farmers. To those Westerners and western newspapers opposed to the plan and calling for the extermination of the Indians, Harlan noted:

> The nation cannot adopt the policy of exterminating them. Our self-respect, our Christian faith, and a common dependence on an all-wise Creator and benefactor forbid it. Other nations will judge our character by our treatment of the feeble tribes to whom we sustain the relation of guardian. Morally and legally there is no distinction between destroying them and rendering it impossible for them to escape annihilation by withholding from them adequate means of support.[1]

Traders Kit Carson and William Bent echoed Harlan's concerns in an October 1865 report to General John Pope, commander of the army's Division of the Missouri. "Civilization now presses them on all sides," they wrote, "their ancient homes forcibly abandoned, their old hunting ground destroyed by the requirements of industrious agricultural life. . . . By dispossessing them of their country, we assume their stewardship, and the manner in which this duty is performed will add a glorious record to American history, or a damning blot and reproach for all times."[2]

Between October 10 and October 28, 1865, the peace commission signed nine treaties with the various Lakota tribes, or rather selected representatives of those tribes. In the treaties, the signers agreed to "obligate and bind themselves individually and collectively, not only to cease all hostilities against the persons and property of . . . [U.S.] citizens, but to use their influence, and, if requisite, physical force, to prevent other bands of the Dakota or Sioux, or other adjacent tribes, from making hostile demonstrations against the Government or people of the United States."[3]

Lakota signers also promised to end attacks on other tribes, promote peace in the region, submit disputes with other tribes to arbitration by the president of the United States, and stay clear of overland roads. In return, the tribes were to receive sums ranging from six thousand dollars to ten thousand dollars annually. In addition, the treaty contained provisions to assign individual parcels of land to any Indian who wanted to settle down and farm. After minor changes by the Senate—something that treaty rules permitted it to do without consulting the Lakota—the nine treaties were unanimously ratified on March 6, 1866.

Although the Fort Sully treaties might seem like just another effort to rob Indians of their lands, they marked an important turning point in the white world's relations with the Lakota. The treaties formally acknowledged that the settling of the Great Plains by whites was inevitable and that the government had a responsibility to save the Indians from extinction by moving them onto reservations and teaching them the white man's ways. Being a free-living Indian no longer was a viable option.

AT ABOUT THE SAME TIME that peace treaties were being signed on the upper Missouri, Crazy Horse and the other Lakota living in the Powder River country were pushing their victories over Colonel Cole and Colonel Walker by sending out raiding parties to attack the Platte River roads. Noticing what was happening, authorities back East realized that the new peace treaties would mean nothing without the support of the Powder River bands. A copy of the treaty signed by the Lakota loafers was sent to Colonel Henry E. Maynadier at Fort Laramie with instructions to have it signed by the leaders of the hostile bands.

So feared were the Powder River Lakota, though, that no one from the fort would carry the treaty into their country. Finally, Big Mouth and a contingent of loafers were persuaded to deliver the treaty to the hostile camps. For nearly three months, he and the others roamed up and down the Powder without finding a single Indian. Then, in mid-January 1866, Swift Bear approached Fort Laramie with a message that the Oglala were talking about coming in. Even though the winter was a hard one in which many of their horses died and they were often hungry, nothing more was heard about the Powder River bands until early March 1866, when Spotted Tail sent word that his daughter had died and he wished to bury her on a hill above Fort Laramie.

Sensing an opportunity to talk, Colonel Maynadier quickly gave his permission for the burial. Spotted Tail, who since seeing the power of the United States during his imprisonment after the Blue Water massacre remained friendly to the whites, spoke with bitterness of the many wrongs that had driven him and other Lakota who wanted peace into the hostile camps. For four years, he said, his people had been mistreated by the whites, especially the volunteer troops who had come into his country during the Civil War. The situation had become unbearable.

To facilitate the signing of a peace treaty by the Powder River bands, E. B. Taylor of the Indian office traveled to Fort Laramie. Promising plenty of gifts, Taylor sent messengers up the Powder calling for a peace council. Attracted by the gifts, especially arms and ammunition, Red Cloud and Man Afraid Of His Horses, possibly with Crazy Horse, finally came down in full force to Fort Laramie in June 1866.[4]

Instead of acquiescing to the wishes of the whites, Red Cloud, Man Afraid Of His Horses, and the other free-living Lakota demanded that every part of the treaty be carefully explained to them. As soon as the clause referring to construction of roads through the Powder River hunting grounds was read, they balked. Never would they sign such an agreement. Determined to return to Washington with a signed treaty, Taylor then attempted to trick Red Cloud and the others by telling them that the treaty did not permit new roads through their country. The roads mentioned really were a single road, the Bozeman Trail to Montana, which already existed. Before any decision could be made, though, a large troop of infantry accompanied by wagons was seen marching up the North Platte River. When the troops camped on June 16, 1866, Brulé chief Standing Elk, who was friendly with the whites, went to visit the camp and talk with the commanding officer, Colonel Henry Carrington. During that talk, Standing Elk learned that the troops were marching to the Powder River to build forts and guard the Bozeman Trail.

Returning to Fort Laramie, Standing Elk informed Red Cloud and the others of what he had learned. At the council that followed, the leaders of the Powder River bands reacted angrily. Young Man Afraid Of His Horses declared that if the troops went into the Powder River country "In two moons the command would not have a hoof left." Red Cloud said: "Great Father sends us presents and wants new road. But White Chief goes with soldiers to steal road before Indian says yes or no."[5] Backed by an approving chorus, Red Cloud accused Taylor and the peace commission of treating the Lakota leaders like children, "pretending to negotiate for a country which they had already taken by conquest."[6] He denounced the callous treatment of his people by the white man and how they had been forced north into an ever smaller area until now Lakota women and children were faced with starvation. He urged his people to fight rather than starve, and warned that the Lakota would attack any whites who intruded into their country.

Aroused by Red Cloud's rhetoric, the council grew disorderly, causing Taylor to end it. Riding back to Fort Laramie, a troubled Colonel Carrington was reassured by Colonel Maynadier that "Indians always have those tantrums." Maynadier said: "Red Cloud was no chief when he first came here, but as the old warriors said that he was at the head of the young men whom they call Bad Faces . . . the commission [appointed] him a chief as they did Spotted Tail . . . to make him our friend."[7] Maynadier's remarks indicate how little he understood of the Lakota living around him. Red Cloud and Spotted Tail were leaders of their people long before the peace council. After the failure of the council Red Cloud became the unquestioned leader of the Oglala.

Listening to Maynadier, Carrington felt there still was some hope that Red Cloud could be won over to the white view. But Jim Bridger knew better. He told Carrington there was little chance of winning over Red Cloud. He had seen Indians heading north away from the fort with kegs of powder tied to their ponies. That evening, Red Cloud and his followers dismantled their camp and headed back up the Powder. The ambitious Taylor hushed up the incident. He reported to his superiors instead that everything had gone well. He gave them the impression that most of the Powder River chiefs had signed the treaty and that Red Cloud and Man Afraid Of His Horses were inconsequential leaders whose signatures on the treaty did not matter.

THE DECISION TO build forts and roads in the Powder River country was approved by the military months before any attempt was made to sign a treaty with the free-living Lakota. Colonel Carrington had received his orders to march to the Powder River in April 1866.

None other than General Sherman had made a trip to Fort Kearny on the Platte to discuss the plan. Despite the fact that the Powder River bands had humiliated General Connor's force of three thousand cavalry less than a year earlier, Colonel Carrington was ordered into the region with only seven hundred infantry, including band members.

Some historians believe it was the desire of white America for peace with the plains tribes and a bedrock belief that all Indians wanted to become "civilized" and live as whites that allowed Carrington to march into the Lakota stronghold with only seven hundred men. Armed with Taylor's report and anxious to please voters who wanted peace, government leaders chose to believe that the trouble along the Powder River was caused by a small group of malcontents. They refused to think that any Indians might want to continue to live as they had in the past when they were being offered all of the advantages of "civilization."

Colonel Carrington reached General Connor's old post, now called Fort Reno, at the head of the Powder River on June 28, 1866. There he found waiting for him several wagon trains of gold seekers on their way to Montana. Two days later, the Lakota made their presence known when seven warriors ran off the post sutler's herd. Pursued by cavalry, the raiders had to abandon a packhorse loaded with gifts that had not been distributed at the Laramie peace council. Then, on July 10, 1866, Carrington marched forty miles down the Powder from Fort Reno to the forks of Big Piney and Little Piney creeks. There he began construction of Fort Phil Kearny, named in honor of a Union general killed by Confederates at Chantilly, Virginia, in 1862.

A day after Carrington's arrival at the forks of the Piney, Cheyenne in the area sent a messenger to ask if he wanted war or peace. When the colonel said he wanted peace, a party of friendly Cheyenne under Black Horse came in to talk on July 16, 1866. Black Horse told Carrington that he had been camped near the Lakota and that Red Cloud was gathering forces to fight the white soldiers if they did not return to Fort Reno. Black Horse said the Lakota were having a sun dance and that when it was over they wanted the Cheyenne to help them stop the whites from moving down the Powder. Red Cloud's War began at five o'clock the next morning, July 17, 1866, when several warriors infiltrated Carrington's picket line and stampeded about 175 of the command's horses and mules.

AT THE FIRST ALARM, Captain Henry Haymond flung a saddle on his horse, ordered a detachment to follow, and raced off with his orderly after the raiders. Haymond held to the high ground while waiting for his troops to catch up. The suddenness of the raid and the excited nature of the remaining horses, though, kept the troops from forming into a unit. Instead, they rode off in groups of twos, threes, fours, and fives, which left them strung out along the trail. Seeing what was happening, bands of Lakota warriors dropped back and attacked the scattered troops. Captain Haymond managed to rally his men and send messengers for reinforcements.

On receiving Captain Haymond's message, Colonel Carrington dispatched fifty cavalry men and two companies of infantry under Lieutenant William Bisbee. After a running fight that lasted for fifteen miles, Bisbee and his troops were able to recover only four of the stolen animals at a cost of two men killed and three men wounded.

Falling back to the Bozeman Trail, the troops sighted wagons belonging to French Pete Gazzous, a trader. The wagons had their covers torn off and goods strewn around. When the troops reached the scene, they found six dead men, all of whom had been mutilated. Lieutenant Bisbee reported that signs indicated that French Pete's "unlawful load of whiskey had led to this destruction, despite his squaw wife who was spared."[8] The troops found her and the five Gazzous children hidden in some nearby brush.

Back at Fort Phil Kearny, Mrs. Gazzous told Colonel Carrington that Black Horse and other Cheyenne chiefs had stopped at their camp the previous evening after leaving the fort. They talked and traded for several hours, until Red Cloud and a party of Lakota warriors appeared. Red Cloud asked Black Horse what Carrington had told him, whether he and his troops were going to leave the Powder River country. Black Horse replied that Carrington was not going back, but planned to continue north, building more forts. Red Cloud then asked what gifts Carrington had given Black Horse and the others. Black Horse replied that they had been given "all we wanted to eat," adding that Carrington had promised gifts for all the Indians of the Tongue River valley if they went to Fort Laramie to sign the treaty that had so angered Red Cloud and the Powder River Lakota.

"White man lies and steals," Red Cloud answered. "My lodges were many, but now they are few. The white man wants all. The white man must fight, and the Indian will die where his fathers died."[9]

Angered by Black Horse's compromising attitude, Red Cloud and the other Lakota warriors unslung their bows and "soldiered" the timid Cheyenne, attempting to shame them into fighting the whites by beating them across their backs and faces with their bows while shouting: "Coup! Coup!" After the Lakota left, Black Horse told French Pete that he was going to the mountains with his people and warned the trader to return to Fort Phil Kearny or the Lakota would kill him. Colonel Carrington listened to Black Horse's story, then ordered Captain Haymond to move his four companies closer to the fort site.

EXACTLY A WEEK after the horse raid on Fort Phil Kearny, on July 24, 1866, Red Cloud made real his threat to stop travel on the Bozeman Trail by simultaneously attacking three wagon trains heading for Montana. When Carrington sent out relief parties, the Lakota also attacked them. Trooper S. S. Peters described the scene on Crazy Woman Creek: "The entire detachment was in this dry bed urging the teams through the sand, when to our complete astonishment a volley of arrows and rifle-shots were poured into us. The shots were accompanied with a chorus of savage yells, and the timber land and brush above and about us was fairly alive with Indians."[10]

Such attacks continued through the remainder of July and into August. Colonel Carrington's troops could not ride a mile from Fort Phil Kearny without getting into a fight. In August, Carrington attempted to contact Red Cloud and other leaders of the free-living Lakota with the idea of talking peace. Mountain men Bridger, Bill Williams, and Jim Beckwourth sought the help of the Crow in contacting the Powder River Lakota. Having lost a portion of their hunting grounds to the Lakota, the Crow and the Cheyenne who had been shamed by Red Cloud's warriors offered to help Carrington fight the Lakota. The Crow also told Bridger and the others that the Lakota had offered to return part of their hunting grounds if they would join them in fighting the whites. Some of the young Crow favored joining the Lakota, but the alliance never materialized.

From the Crow and the shamed Cheyenne it was learned, too, that the Lakota had allied themselves with some Northern Cheyenne and the Arapaho whose camp was attacked by General Connor in the fall of 1865. They warned that the Lakota were planning two big fights at "Pine Woods" near Fort Phil Kearny and "Big Horn" near Fort C. F. Smith on the Big Horn River in southern Montana. The attacks were planned for the late in the year, after the autumn buffalo hunts were over.

No details survive on Crazy Horse's role in the events of July and August 1866. But his well-known love of the free life, his ambitions as a warrior, and his determination to resist white intrusion into his country would make it all but certain that he would have been in the middle of the fighting. His name does not appear in the record, however, until December 21, 1866, in what would become known among whites as the Fetterman Massacre.

LIKE LIEUTENANT GRATTAN, whose arrogance led to the destruction of his command by the Lakota near Fort Laramie a dozen years earlier, Captain William Fetterman was an extremely ambitious officer. During the Civil War he earned numerous commendations for bravery and played an important role in the siege of Atlanta. For his actions in that battle he was cited for "conspicuous gallantry and bravery" and "great gallantry and spirit" in the face of repeated enemy attacks.[11] By the end of the war he was a breveted lieutenant colonel. But like Grattan, Fetterman knew nothing about Indian warfare and was openly contemptuous of their fighting abilities. He bragged of "taking Red Cloud's scalp"[12] and often was heard boasting that "A single company of regulars could whip a thousand Indians. A full regiment could whip the entire array of hostile tribes." And "With eighty men I could ride through the Sioux nation."[13]

Fetterman arrived at Fort Phil Kearny on November 3, 1866. Two days later he approached Colonel Carrington with a plan for luring the Indians into a night ambush. He proposed hiding a detachment of troops in a cottonwood stand along Big Pine Creek opposite the fort. Between the detachment and the fort he would hobble a herd of mules to lure the Indians into the trap.

Despite plenty of misgivings, Carrington gave Fetterman permission to try the plan, but warned him not to expose his men to danger by a mass charge. The Lakota, he told the captain, did not fight like the Confederates. Fetterman took note of the remark and laid his trap. All night long the hobbled mules grazed between the fort and the stream while the detachment waited in the cottonwoods. Finally, at dawn a disgusted Fetterman returned to the fort. It was then that the Lakota struck. Riding down on the opposite side of the fort from the stream, they stampeded a small herd of cattle belonging to a trader and were gone again.

After the failed ambush, life at Fort Phil Kearny returned to normal until November 21, 1866, when the Lakota attacked a beef train on its way to the fort from Fort Reno. Soldiers guarding the wagon train fought off the attack, but the Lakota escaped. The next day, Fetterman rode out with an escort troop that was to accompany the wagon train to Fort Phil Kearny. At Piney Island, Fetterman and Lieutenant Bisbee, who had ridden ahead of the escort, stopped to water their horses. "Suddenly from behind a huge log fifty yards away came yells and shots from ambushed redskins," Bisbee recalled.

> Taking immediate shelter under the bank of the creek for better observation and to await reinforcements from the train guard in rear, we plainly discovered larger parties of Indians in the timber waiting our further approach. One lone "buck" only came into the open, plainly a decoy tempting us to a trap. It was not accepted, but in temptation to see what the young brave was really made of I charged him. Zip, zip, came several shots from concealed Indians in the woods to which he escaped in haste.[14]

The Lakota were gone by the time a relief party arrived on the scene. Four days later, on November 25, 1866, Carrington received a letter from General Philip St. George Cooke ordering him to prepare a winter offensive against the Powder River bands. Carrington wrote back informing the general that he was short of the arms and men needed for such a campaign. But he would follow orders and lead an expedition in search of the Lakota as soon as the weather confined them to their camps. That same day, the Lakota raided the fort's beef herd, making off with sixteen head of cattle. An extremely angry Carrington personally took charge of the pursuit troops. The force, including Fetterman, never overtook a single Lakota, but it recovered eight steers and found five others dead and partially slaughtered.

About two weeks later, on December 6, 1866, the Lakota struck again. This time a large party of warriors attacked a wood train four miles west of the fort. Once more Carrington reacted by ordering out every available man. In below-freezing temperatures, the mounted troops pursued the Indians over and through the hills around the fort. During the chase, Lieutenant Horatio Bingham dashed ahead with a handful of men. Once he was out of sight, a party of about one hundred Lakota swarmed out from the base of a hill to attack the main body of troops and cut off Bingham. Then suddenly a dozen warriors who had been hiding in a small valley appeared in Bingham's rear. Bingham was among the first to die: "He fell off his horse, shot in the head," Private John Guthrie reported.[15] Bingham's body was found with more than fifty arrows in it. A sergeant with him also died, and another sergeant and four privates were wounded.

Although troop losses were minimal, the foolish actions of Bingham told Red Cloud and his fellow chiefs who watched from the hills above that they could defeat the Fort Phil Kearny soldiers. That belief was bolstered later in the week when Yellow Eagle told what he saw on the field. The Lakota leaders decided that on the first good day after the next full moon they would lay a trap with more than a thousand warriors. They would send another decoy party to lure as many men as possible out of the fort, kill them, and then burn the fort. It was an old trick, one the Lakota had used many times and that was well known to experienced Indian fighters. But Fetterman quickly forgot the lesson. A mere fifteen days later, his ambition and disdain for Indians would lead him into the U.S. Army's first fight with the plains tribes from which there would be no white survivors—the winter of One Hundred White Men Killed. It would launch a national debate among whites that would last until overshadowed by the actions of another rash officer who would lead his troops ten years later along the Little Big Horn River into the army's second defeat by plains Indians from which there were no white survivors.[16]

FOR TWO WEEKS following the December 6 fight, the Lakota and their Cheyenne friends kept their distance from Fort Phil Kearny except for small scouting parties who appeared almost daily on the hills above the fort. Then tribal leaders decided to launch a big decoy attack on December 19, 1866. A war party of more than a thousand Miniconjou and Oglala Lakota and Cheyenne was formed and started up the Tongue toward the fort. Leading the Oglala was Crazy Horse. According to White Bull, Crazy Horse "rode with his friends Long Man and He Dog, leading his brother's pony, which he had borrowed, a bald-faced bay with white stockings, very fast."[17]

Crazy Horse's leadership of the Oglala in the Fetterman Fight could be taken as an indication that by the winter of 1866 he had moved beyond being a shirt-wearer to become head war chief of his people. That he became head war chief of the Oglala there is no doubt, but there also is no way to know exactly when that happened. He Dog reports only that it occurred after he and Crazy Horse had been made shirt-wearers, probably in the summer of 1865. "Later on," he says, "the older, more responsible men of the tribe conferred another kind of chieftainship on Crazy Horse. He was made war chief of the whole Oglala tribe. A similar office was conferred on Sitting Bull by the Hunkpapa tribe. This was still early, a long, long time before the Custer fight."[18]

When the warriors reached a point about ten miles northwest of the fort, they halted and made camp. During the council that followed, a decision was made to lure the troops out of the fort and into the rough country to the north. The plan called for a decoy party to lure the soldiers in Fort Phil Kearny into a fight by attacking the fort's wood train. The decoys would then lead the relief party to the forks of Peno Creek five miles from the fort. Between the forks stood Lodge Trail Ridge, a long, narrow, very steep hill over which the hated Bozeman Trail ran. The main body of warriors would hide around the ridge until the soldiers were drawn into the trap, and then rise up to attack. But the troops did not take the bait this time.

As soon as the picket stationed above the fort signaled an attack on the wood train, Colonel Carrington ordered his most cautious officer, Captain James Powell, out with explicit orders: "Heed the lessons of the 6th. Do not pursue Indians across Lodge Trail Ridge."[19] Powell did as he was ordered. When he reached the beleaguered woodcutters, the decoys rode off. Instead of pursuing them, he ordered his men to guard the wood train and then escort it back to the fort. Neither side suffered or inflicted any casualties. At a military court inquiry into the Fetterman Massacre in the spring of 1867, Carrington testified that Captain Powell "did his work—pressed the Indians toward Lodge Trail Ridge, but having peremptory orders did not cross it, he returned with the train, reporting the Indians in large force, and that if he had crossed the ridge he never would have come back with his command."[20]

SNOW ON THE NIGHT OF December 19 forced the Lakota and Cheyenne to spend the following day in camp. Then the weather turned mild; the snow melted except for those areas the sun did not touch. Medicine men said this time the soldiers would ride into the trap, and Lakota and Cheyenne leaders decided to try again. They selected a handful of the most daring young warriors to serve as decoys and sent them out before daybreak on December 21. The main body of warriors followed at sunrise. Many writers have Crazy Horse leading the decoy party, but that is difficult to support from primary sources. As the leader of the Oglala warriors it seems more likely that he would have stayed back with the main force.

At about eleven o'clock that morning, the lookout at Fort Phil Kearny signaled "many Indians," and orders were given to prepare a detachment to protect the woodcutters working in the pine forest to the west. Pleased with Captain Powell's handling of the decoy attack two days earlier, Colonel Carrington ordered him to lead the relief party. When Fetterman appeared, though, he reminded Carrington that he outranked Powell and demanded command of the relief detachment. Carrington acquiesced, but told Fetterman: "Support the wood train. Relieve it and report to me. Do not engage or pursue Indians at its expense. Under no circumstances pursue over the ridge, that is, Lodge Trail Ridge."[21]

For the main body of warriors hidden around Lodge Trail Ridge, the opening of the fight of One Hundred White Men Killed began with the faint sound of firing off in the distance. The shooting lasted only a few minutes. Then there was silence and more firing, this time a little closer. Finally, a third burst of shots sounded only a short distance off, and the decoys appeared riding back and forth across Lodge Trail Ridge, shooting as if they were desperate to hold off the soldiers chasing them and save someone left behind. In the coulees and draws around Lodge Trail Ridge, the warriors waited, readying their weapons and pinching the nostrils of their ponies to keep them from whinnying and warning the soldiers' horses.

Across Big Piney Creek and up the side of Lodge Trail Ridge to the Bozeman Trail the soldiers came in two columns of eighty-one men, about half of them infantry and half of them cavalry. Led by the cavalry, the troops slowly advanced across the top of the ridge until they reached the flat at the forks of Peno Creek. Then the decoys forded the small stream and divided, riding off in opposite directions for a short distance before turning and crossing each other's paths. It was the signal to attack. Up out of their hiding places all around the ridge rode the Lakota and the Cheyenne, the Miniconjou striking the soldiers first.

Caught by surprise, the infantry halted, fired at the attackers, and then retreated to a group of large rocks along the slope. From behind the rocks, the troops unleashed a barrage of fire against the attacking Lakota and Cheyenne, who were armed mainly with bows and lances. Eats Meat was shot down while riding through the infantry at the same time the cavalry fell back and took up a position about a hundred yards above the infantry.

From the north and east Crazy Horse's Oglala and the Cheyenne swept around the infantry, while the Miniconjou circled to the south and west. For a short time the cavalry played little role in the fighting. "The Indians kept riding around," recalled White Bull, "hanging on the sides of their horses, loosing arrows at the infantry, and there were so many of them that the fight with the infantry did not last long. But it lasted long enough to kill and wound a number of Indians and their horses."[22] Three of the about forty infantrymen made it up the slope to the cavalry.

The infantry destroyed, the cavalry began fighting its way back along Lodge Trail Ridge toward the fort. Holding close together, half hidden by powder smoke, they kept up a steady fire, holding off warriors who tried to count coup with their bows and lances. The hail of arrows became so thick that some of the Lakota and Cheyenne were hit. Then the cavalry reached the highest point of the long ridge and released their horses. The action caused many of the Lakota and

Cheyenne to stop fighting and race off after the animals, while the cavalry fell back behind a line of rocks.

Lodge Trail Ridge, in the area where the cavalry made their stand, is only about forty feet wide and falls away steeply in every direction except the south. The closeness of the terrain and the slippery nature of the grass after the previous day's snow made horses useless to both sides. On foot, the Lakota and the Cheyenne fought their way up the slopes under a tremendous fire. The infantry had been armed with the muzzle-loading muskets; the cavalry was better armed, with faster-firing breech-loading carbines. The fighting became intense. As the Lakota and the Cheyenne neared the top of the ridge, Long Fox rose and shouted. The Indians rushed the top of the ridge. In the hand-to-hand fighting that followed, all of the cavalry were killed. It was near noon. Roughly forty minutes had passed since the Lakota and the Cheyenne had sprung their trap.

The body of the arrogant and disdainful Fetterman was found with a bullet hole surrounded by powder burns in his temple. Having often had said he would never be taken alive by the Indians, Fetterman apparently had committed suicide, though some sources have him and Captain F. H. Brown, who had made a similar pledge, shooting each other.[23]

At about the time the firing ceased, a relief column led by Captain Tenedor Eyck reached the hill above the battlefield. Eyck found the Peno Valley full of Indians. As the Indians stripped and mutilated the bodies of the dead soldiers, they taunted the relief column to come after them. But Captain Eyck stood his ground until the Indians were finished and drifted back to their camp on the Tongue. All eighty-one members of Fetterman's force were dead. The Lakota had lost eleven men, the Cheyenne had lost two, and the Arapaho one.

Four days later, Christmas Day on the white calendar, the Indians held a great victory dance. That same night, John "Portugee" Phillips, a civilian miner who had been at Fort Phil Kearny, arrived at Fort Laramie in the middle of a full-dress ball. Phillips had ridden 236 miles through a raging blizzard in fewer than four days to relay the news, which had been circulating among the Laramie loafers for forty-eight hours.

18

WAGON BOX FIGHT

Colonel carrington was relieved of command of Fort Phil Kearny as soon as news of the Fetterman Fight reached army headquarters. His successor, Colonel H. W. Wessels, was then ordered to launch a winter campaign against the Powder River bands. But Wessels's force was small and composed mainly of infantry. When the weather turned bad, the plan was abandoned and the winter passed quietly on the northern plains.

Meanwhile, the finger-pointing began among the whites. Military leaders blamed the disaster on the Indian office. They claimed that Superintendent Taylor was inept in negotiating the Fort Laramie Treaty of 1866, and that the Indian office's policy of appeasement and its willingness to supply the plains tribes with guns and ammunition made the defeat possible. The Indian office, in turn, blamed the army's desire for a military solution to the Indian "problem" for Fetterman's destruction. In response to the outcry, a commission headed by General Sanborn and General Sully was created in February 1867 to investigate the Fetterman disaster and other Indian troubles of 1866, and to negotiate peace with the plains tribes.

Among the things the aftermath of the Fetterman Fight made abundantly clear was the polarization of the white East and the white West when it came to the plains tribes. Having already driven most Native Americans across the Mississippi River, many Easterners followed a tradition dating back at least to the early nineteenth century of viewing the "last of the Mohicans" as a quaint, picturesque bit of America's past. The plains Indians to them were poor, unfortunate creatures who needed to be preserved like specimens in a zoo. Westerners derisively referred to those soft Easterners as "humanitarians."

To the Westerners, the free-living bands of the Powder River country were standing in the way of progress, hindering the inevitable march of Christian civilization. Fetterman's defeat in the West brought thunderous cries for the extermination of the native peoples of the plains. Extermination would be good for business. The Indians were blocking the creation of fortunes in cattle, mining, farming, and railroads.

The staunchly individualistic and independent Westerner, carving the Great Plains into cities and ranches, bringing civilization to an untamed land, is one of the great American myths. It has made fortunes for writers such as Zane Grey and actors such as John Wayne and Clint Eastwood. But in reality, by the end of the Civil War most "independent" Westerners were existing on government welfare. In an 1866 report to General Ulysses Grant, General Sherman complained: "All the people west of the Missouri river look to the army as their legitimate field of profit and support." Because of that dependence, Grant warned Sherman that "little confidence be placed in the suggestions of citizens who have made their homes in the territories, in selecting points to be occupied by troops. My experience is, and no doubt it is borne out by your own, that these people act entirely from selfish and interested motives."[1]

Following his committee's report on the Fetterman Fight, General Sanborn concluded: "The war policy is not urged by general public sentiment of the country, but furiously urged by ranchmen on the plains, army contractors, and some army officers who in this matter at the present time seem to be ruled and controlled by the ranchmen and contractors." Commissioner of Indian Affairs Dennis Cooley supported the views of Sanborn and Sherman in his report for 1867, noting that rumors of a horrible massacre that had been circulated in the West were the results of "the rapacity and rascality of frontier settlers, whose interests are to bring war and supply our armies at exorbitant prices." General N. B. Buford, a member of the Sanborn/Sully commission, noted of roads leading past Fort Laramie: "Nine-tenths of all business that is being done on the route is paid for by the government. At least two-thirds of the entire business of the Union Pacific railroad is for carrying troops and army supplies. Its employees are all for war."[2]

ON JUNE 12, 1867, the Sanborn/Sully commission met with Man
Afraid Of His Horses, Iron Shell, Red Cloud, and other Lakota leaders. Whether Crazy Horse was present is impossible to say, since he
was not then known to the whites and rarely spoke at councils. Man
Afraid Of His Horses and the other chiefs told the commission that
their people had abandoned the war and wanted to come in and join
the loafers. But the chiefs also anxiously were inquiring about
ammunition. By 1867, the Powder River bands were short of ammunition for the few firearms they possessed and desperately trying to
obtain powder and lead from traders along the Platte River. So bad
was their need that they had even taken to trying to trade with the
hated Crow.[3]

At the same time that General Sanborn was at Fort Laramie,
General Sully was on the Missouri River searching for chiefs from
the Powder River bands who could be bribed into signing a treaty.
He promised an abundance of guns, powder, lead, blankets, axes,
knives, and household goods to any chief who "touched the pen."
Those who refused to sign would receive nothing. A number of loafers and unimportant Lakota, many of whom had signed the treaty of
1866, came forward to sign a new treaty. But they only wanted the
gifts. Leaders of the free-living bands refused even to talk to the
commission.

When Sully learned of a large "hostile" camp near the Black
Hills, he sent out a party to call in the chiefs. Iron Shell and a few
other Lakota leaders responded by riding in with their own demands
for peace: All whites except traders must leave the Powder River, the
forts must be abandoned, and the Bozeman Trail given up. Only then
would they talk peace. General Sully bluntly informed Iron Shell and
the others that the troops and forts would remain until the Indians
stopped fighting. He then allowed three loafer chiefs representing
twenty-eight lodges to sign a treaty and announced that peace had
been achieved.

Even before the Sanborn/Sully commission was formed, though,
federal officials had decided that all Indians living on the central
plains had to be removed. In his 1866 annual report, General Sherman had proposed restricting the Lakota to an area north of the
Platte River between the Missouri River and the Bozeman Trail, and
the Cheyenne and the Arapaho to the land south of the Arkansas
River. His plan left open to the whites a wide belt of land between

the Platte and the Arkansas, over which the bulk of travel to the far West occurred. Everybody agreed that construction of the transcontinental railroad could not be stopped. As Commissioner of Indian Affairs Lewis Bogy noted, to complete the railroad "the removal of the Indians from this strip of country is, therefore, an absolute necessity. . . . The time has come when these Indians must abandon this portion of country."[4]

The only real question that remained was how to remove the Indians. General Grant insisted that removal not conflict with any treaty obligations. Commissioner Bogy felt that the Indians could be removed more cheaply by diplomatic means than by war. He suggested that the tribes be bought off for the "few years which, in all probability, they will yet exist."[5] On the other side, General Sherman, who had called for the extermination of the plains tribes as soon as he learned of the Fetterman Fight, thought that the military might of the United States should be used to immediately end the problem.

Supported by western newspapers and politicians, Sherman by the start of 1867 completed plans for a three-pronged military expedition against the plains tribes. General Alfred Terry would direct operations along the upper Missouri and northern plains. General Christopher Augur would eliminate Indian problems for railroad builders south of the Platte River and miners along the Bozeman Trail. And General Winfield Hancock, a hero of the Battle of Gettysburg, would handle the Lakota and the Cheyenne along the route to Denver. Accompanying Hancock was another hero of Gettysburg, Lieutenant Colonel George Armstrong Custer, known to the Indians as "Long Hair" for his long, flowing, reddish locks.

Hancock's assignment in the spring of 1867 called for him to intimidate Indians living in Kansas by a show of force. Knowing what had happened at other times when large bodies of troops had approached camps of their people, the Lakota and the Cheyenne became very nervous when they saw Hancock's troops, and abandoned their lodges and fled the area. Unfamiliar with the plains tribes, Hancock regarded their fleeing as proof of their hostility. He ordered the camp burned. The Lakota and the Cheyenne in turn regarded the general's actions as a sign that he had a "bad heart."[6] They began conducting raids. Hancock saw the raids as confirmation of his original assumption and turned loose Custer and his 7th Cavalry. The Lakota and the Cheyenne in turn regarded Hancock's action as final proof that he had always planned to attack them. Easily eluding the troops, they stepped up their raiding.

At about the time that Hancock was moving into Kansas, Man Afraid Of His Horses and Red Cloud rode into Fort Laramie to trade for arms and ammunition. When they failed to obtain what they needed, their followers quarreled and split. Most of the people who left the bands were southern Oglala led by Little Wound and Pawnee Killer, who had fled to the Powder River country in March 1865 after being driven into hostility by the Sand Creek Massacre and other assaults by General Curtis. They were camped on the Platte near Fort McPherson when Custer arrived. Having heard about the burning of the Lakota camp by Hancock, the camp became nervous at Custer's appearance. Saying they were going to hunt buffalo, they took down their lodges and headed for the Republican Fork.

Instead of simply allowing the camp to leave, though, the glory-seeking Custer convinced General Sherman, who was at Fort McPherson, that Pawnee Killer was a troublemaker who needed watching. Sherman ordered Custer to follow the band. Although the Lakota found it easy enough to avoid Long Hair, Custer's persistence became an annoyance and frightened off the buffalo. Pawnee Killer finally decided to confront the problem. Gathering together his warriors, he attacked Custer's troops. Although the army trooops were outmaneuvered, their superior firepower allowed them to escape. The war party then discovered a troop of twenty soldiers coming from Fort McPherson with orders for Custer. They attacked and wiped out the troop. A new war was under way.

ONCE AGAIN taking the offense, Red Cloud, Crazy Horse, and other leaders of the Powder River bands pressed their campaign to force the whites out of Lakota country throughout the spring of 1867. Fort Phil Kearny, Fort C. F. Smith, and Fort Reno were so closely blockaded that troops often had to fight to obtain wood and water. Attacks on wagon trains along the Bozeman Trail became so frequent that on May 21 General Augur, who had been appointed commander of the Department of the Platte after the Fetterman Fight, admitted to Sherman that there would be no more travel on the trail that year except for army supply trains. More alarming to the government, though, were raids along the Platte because of the threat they posed to the Union Pacific Railroad. Completion of the first transcontinental railroad was the nation's top priority in the West.

But back East there was little sentiment for a major Indian war. The national focus was aimed at reconstruction of the South through military means. Radical Republicans in Congress who wanted troops to police the former Confederate states felt the West could wait. A large number of Easterners, including many influential individuals with connections in Congress, also had been critical of the government's handling of Indian affairs since the Sand Creek massacre. Well into the summer, rumors of peace were eagerly devoured by the eastern public.

On the northern plains, though, the issue among the Lakota and the Cheyenne was not peace, but rather which post to attack along the Bozeman Trail. During the Lakota's big sun dance in June or July, a great debate occurred. Sensing the symbolic significance of another victory at the site of the Fetterman Fight, Red Cloud argued for an assault on Fort Phil Kearny. Feeling that Fort C. F. Smith was more vulnerable to a successful attack, Cheyenne leaders Two Moons and Dull Knife pushed for an assault on that northern post. Finally, in typically divided fashion, the two tribes agreed to take the fight to both forts: the Lakota would move on Fort Phil Kearny, and the Cheyenne on Fort Smith.

ON AUGUST 1, 1867, a band of about five hundred Cheyenne and Arapaho, accompanied by a few Lakota, descended on a party of six haycutters and nineteen soldiers three miles northeast of Fort Smith. Desperate to save themselves, the whites fled to a nearby corral where they kept their horses and mules at night. The bottom rails of the corral were on the ground and provided good protection against the mounted warriors, who began circling the makeshift fortification.

Confronted with stubborn resistance, after several hours of fighting, the war party set fire to the grass around the corral in hopes of flushing out the defenders. When that failed, they launched an attack on foot through the smoke. Equipped with new, rapid-firing Springfield breech-loading rifles, however, the troops were able to maintain a heavy fire and repel the assault, finally forcing the war party to withdraw. The haying party suffered three dead and three wounded. Indian casualties also are believed to have been light.

While the Cheyenne and the Arapaho were preparing to attack Fort Smith, a large body of Lakota left their camps along the Tongue and Rosebud rivers for Fort Phil Kearny. Among the leaders of the force, which most likely numbered about a thousand warriors, were Red Cloud, Crazy Horse, and Hump. Their target was a woodcutting party south of Little Piney Creek about five miles from the fort.[7]

Few details exist as to Crazy Horse's role in the Wagon Box Fight, which takes its name from a makeshift corral made of fourteen wagons from which the wheels had been removed and canvas stripped away, but there is plenty of information on the action that day. According to White Bull and Captain James Powell, commander of the white troops, it began at nine in the morning, though some participants claim it started two hours earlier. It opened with seven Lakota decoys charging in single file toward Little Piney Creek. At the appearance of the decoys, Sergeant Sam Gibson brought his new Springfield breech-loading rifle to rest on a rock, adjusted the sights to seven hundred yards, and fired. His bullet struck the horse of the lead rider, bringing it down and forcing the rider to jump up on the horse of another decoy.

At the sound of the shot, the young men in the main body of warriors swarmed out of their hiding places in the hills north of Big Piney Creek. They circled the wagon box corral, made off with the work party's horses and mules, and attacked the side camp south of Little Piney, where four civilian woodcutters had been working under the guard of four soldiers. Leading the assault on the side camp was Crazy Horse with Red Bear, With Horn, Eagle Thunder, and Painted Brown. They forced the men to retreat toward the mountains and set fire to the group's wagons. Woodcutter J. I. Minnick recalled that one of the biggest Indians grabbed the camp's whiskey jug and was promptly shot by another woodcutter. The death of the big Indian "and the loss of the 'firewater' seemed to make the other Indians quite angry and eager for revenge," Minnick said.[8]

After Crazy Horse and the other Lakota destroyed the side camp, they turned toward the wagon box corral. As in the Hayfield Fight, almost all of the troops in the corral were armed with Springfield breechloaders. Remembering what had happened to Fetterman, about half of the defenders also removed their shoes. Gibson recalled that they

> tied the laces together and made two loops of the laces—one loop to go over our right foot and the smaller loop to fit on the Trigger of our Rifle so that if the Indians ever got inside the Corral we were going to stand up and after putting the small loop on the trigger, we would place the muzzle of the Rifle underneath our Chins and blow our own heads off before we would be captured by Red Cloud's Cut Throat Sioux Indians.[9]

Inside the corral were two officers, twenty-four enlisted men, and six civilians. To go with their Springfield breechloaders, however, they had seven thousand rounds of ammunition. The wagon bodies also provided excellent protection from the Lakotas' arrows and lances. Entrenched in such a manner, the defenders were able to keep up such a furious fire that the corral was hidden in smoke most of the time. The Lakota sustained so many casualties that their leaders ordered a halt to mounted charges. "Finding that they could not enter the corral, they retired to a hill about six hundred yards distant and there stripped for more determined fighting," Captain Powell noted in his report.[10]

On foot, the Lakota moved into a ravine that ran about a hundred yards to the east and north of the corral. From there they kept up sniping attacks and threatening movements until they were ready to launch a second assault. Once in position, an estimated seven hundred warriors advanced on foot from the north and the west, while a second body, of mounted warriors, readied to charge from the south. As the attackers advanced, several soldiers ran out from the corral and tore down tents that were obstructing their view. With a clear field of fire, the defenders inside the corral unleashed such a relentless barrage that their rifle barrels began to overheat.

At about noon, scouts spotted a relief column coming from Fort Phil Kearny. The Lakota responded by mounting another charge against the corral. Like the others, though, it was repelled. The attackers withdrew to the ravine, from which they continued a desultory fire until about one in the afternoon, when the sound of the relief column's mountain howitzer convinced them to give up the fight. Losses inside the wagon box corral included three men killed and two wounded. Four other whites died at the side camp. Nobody knows how many Lakota were killed or wounded. The totals run from an unlikely low of two to an absurd high of fifteen hundred. In his report on the fight, Captain Powell estimated that "there were not less than sixty Indians killed on the spot and one hundred and twenty severely wounded." Other defenders believe Powell's estimate to be low. The Oglala Fire Thunder stated that there were "dead warriors and horses piled all around the boxes and scattered over the plain."[11]

What is known about Lakota casualties for sure is that some of the soldiers returned to Fort Kearny with Indian scalps and one head, which post surgeon Samuel Horton subsequently sent off to Washington, D.C., for study.

19

VICTORY

E<small>AGER TO MEND</small> its tarnished image after the Fetterman Fight, the army immediately declared the Wagon Box Fight a victory. They cited Indian losses and the prompt dispersal of the war party as proof. Although the poorly armed Lakota suffered heavier losses than the white defenders, the Lakota did not consider the encounter a defeat because they captured large numbers of horses and mules. Their scattering after the fight was a natural occurrence to prepare for the fall buffalo hunt, as they had scattered into winter camps after their victory over Fetterman. The Lakota also continued raiding travelers along the Bozeman Trail after the Wagon Box Fight, harassed Fort Reno, and attacked a Union Pacific freight train, hardly the actions of a defeated enemy.[1]

Concern about the raids was enough to prompt the army to establish Fort Fetterman, about eighty miles northwest of Fort Laramie, and lead to threats from the Union Pacific to suspend operations until the attacks were stopped. But except for some elements of the army and western settlers, most whites continued to want peace with the plains tribes. Still feeling guilty about the Sand Creek Massacre, many pious and educated whites sought peace because they saw it as the humane thing to do; others continued to support peace for political and economic reasons. Peace would allow the government to focus its attention on reconstruction of the South and the completion of the transcontinental railroad.

The Indian Peace Commission formed by Congress on June 20, 1867, reflected the general mood of the country when it met in St. Louis on August 7 and declared its desire to make two treaties. One treaty would be with the northern, Powder River Lakota and their allies, the other with tribes on the southern plains. The plan was to meet with the northern tribes at Fort Laramie on September 13 and with the southern tribes a month later at Fort Larned, Kansas.

In pursuit of peace, the commission traveled up the Missouri River for talks with tribes in that area. They returned south to Omaha on September 11, late for the meeting with the Powder River bands at Fort Laramie. General Sherman telegraphed Fort Laramie to find out if the commission should rush to make the meeting. Instead, he learned that Red Cloud and his people would not be present by mid-September. They proposed rescheduling the council for early November, although people familiar with the region's weather pointed out that snow probably would make travel by the Lakota unrealistic at that time of year.

Anxious to show some progress, the commission traveled on September 18 to the North Platte, where they met with Spotted Tail and other Brulé leaders. During the meeting, Sherman informed the Brulé that construction of railroads west through Kansas and Nebraska was not an issue for debate. "We are building costly roads of iron with steam locomotives," he said. "You cannot stop these anymore than you can stop the sun or the moon."[2] Largely because the Union Pacific promised a new way into the goldfields of Montana and beyond, however, Sherman told the Lakota that the government was willing to negotiate the issue of the Bozeman Trail at the Fort Laramie meeting in November. Then he informed the Brulé that their options were limited. They must accept the reservations assigned them by the commission or be exterminated.

In mid-October the peace commission gathered at Medicine Lodge Creek, seventy miles south of Fort Larned, Kansas, and presented the Cheyenne, Comanche, Kiowa, Arapaho, and Kiowa Apache with reservations in what is today southwestern Oklahoma. Lavishly praising itself for concluding a peace treaty with the southern tribes, the commission returned to St. Louis and prepared for its second trip to Fort Laramie. But on reaching North Platte, where they anticipated a large gathering of Lakota leaders, the commissioners were disappointed to find only the Brulé chief Swift Bear. Their disappointment grew when they arrived at Fort Laramie and found only a group of friendly Crow waiting to greet them. Red Cloud had sent word that he would not come in to talk until Fort Phil Kearny and

Fort Smith were abandoned. The Powder River country was the last good hunting grounds left to his people.

On their return east, the commissioners stopped again at North Platte on the chance that more Indians had come in to talk. When they found only a few, they continued on to Washington, D.C., where they conducted their final meetings of 1867 on December 11–12. The two most important items on the agenda were the issue of abandoning the Bozeman Trail and the creation of two huge reservations out of the way of the main white travel routes. No decision was made on the Bozeman Trail, but the commissioners were unanimous in their selection of the two reservations. The first, for the southern tribes, was to be bounded on the north by Kansas, on the east by Arkansas and Missouri, on the south by Texas, and on the west by either the 100th or the 101st meridian.

The second reservation, for the more troublesome northern tribes, was to be bounded on the north by the 46th parallel, on the east by the Missouri River, on the south by Nebraska, and on the west by the 104th meridian. To tempt the northern tribes to follow the plan, the commission report suggested some temporary accommodations: "If the hostile Sioux cannot be induced to remove from the Powder River, a hunting privilege may be extended to them for a time, while the nucleus of settlement may be forming on the Missouri, the White Earth, or Cheyenne River. To prevent war, if insisted on by the Sioux, the western boundary, might be extended to the 106th or even 107th meridian for the present."[3]

Although most leaders of the plains tribes did not fully understand what the commission had done and some remained committed to resisting the whites, they now were restricted to reservations. The commission's desire to please Congress and accommodate the whites' greed for land also had resulted in the territory for the northern reservation being reduced to one-third of what had been recommended by the Sully/Sanborn commission formed in the wake of the Fetterman Fight.

WITH THE EXTENSION of the Union Pacific into western Montana, peace with Red Cloud increasingly came to be seen as the most practical and economical way to accomplish the nation's goals. Grant wrote

Sherman on March 2, 1868, telling him to close Fort Kearny, Fort Reno, and Fort Fetterman. Fort Smith was added the following day and the order implemented after the removal of Fort Fetterman, which Grant had mistakenly included on the list. Encouraged by Grant's actions, the peace commission returned to Fort Laramie on April 7 and sent riders north to inform Red Cloud, who had become the best-known Lakota leader among the whites, that they desired another treaty council.

No record exists of Crazy Horse's reaction to the peace offer, but the burning of the hated forts and the closing of the Bozeman Trail must have pleased him. Establishment of the Great Sioux Reservation, however, was another story. The reservation was to run from the Big Horn Mountains east to the Missouri River and from the 46th parallel south to the Dakota/Nebraska line. The eastern portion was to be for a reservation and the western portion was to be unceded Indian territory. In addition, the treaty called for the Lakota to be granted hunting rights along the Republican River and above the North Platte River, and supplied with rations and annuities for thirty years.

Through the spring of 1868 the peace commission met with the northern tribes at Fort Laramie. It signed treaties with the Crow, Cheyenne, Arapaho, and various Lakota tribes. But Red Cloud and the Powder River bands refused to meet with the commission until the forts along the Bozeman Trail were demolished. Furious and humiliated by the snub, the commissioners returned east, leaving the commander of Fort Laramie with the treaty and instructions to obtain Red Cloud's agreement as soon as possible.

Closing of the forts, which were the main stumbling blocks to a treaty, proved to be more difficult than had been imagined. Prospective buyers of post supplies were afraid to go to Fort Smith, where the sale was to be held. Eventually the government found a freight firm willing to purchase some of the supplies. What was left was given to the Crow or abandoned. Fort Smith finally was closed on July 29, 1868. The next day, members of the Powder River bands swept down on the deserted post and set it on fire. Fort Reno and Fort Kearny were abandoned and torched a few days later.

Now confident of a treaty with the northern bands, white peace forces labored through August in preparation for a council with Red Cloud. Their plans came to a halt when Red Cloud sent word that he would not appear at Fort Laramie until after the fall buffalo hunt.

Whites involved in the peace plan began to doubt that Red Cloud would ever come in, and fears about a new war grew. On August 29, troops were warned to take extra precautions against an attack because of the unsettled situation.

The new delay also angered General Sherman. When the peace commission gathered in Chicago on October 9, he pushed through several measures designed to get tough with the Powder River bands. One resolution dissolved the commission, which despite its problems had tried to achieve a fair peace. Another resolution transferred the Office of Indian Affairs from the Department of the Interior to the Department of War, which favored a military answer to problems involving the plains tribes. Most ominous of all, though, Sherman wanted an end to the tribes' "domestic dependent nations" status, capable of negotiating treaties with the U.S. government. Instead, they were to be treated as individuals subject to the same laws as white citizens, but with none of their rights.

Sherman's attitude toward the plains tribes was made clear that same day in a letter to General Sheridan. "Go ahead in your own way and I will back you with my whole authority," he wrote.

> I will say nothing and do nothing to restrain our troops from doing what they deem proper on the spot, and will allow no vague general charges of cruelty and inhumanity to tie their hands, but will use all the powers confided to me to the end that these Indians, the enemies of our race and of our civilization, shall not again be able to begin and carry out their barbarous warfare on any kind of pretext they may choose to allege.[4]

Congress provided Sherman with the means to carry out his views when it stipulated that all funds appropriated for implementation of recent Indian treaties be distributed under the general's direction. Sherman responded by authorizing his commanders to act as agents for Indians not on reservations. Colonel A. J. Slemmer used Sherman's order to act as agent for the Powder River bands. He then barred J. P. Cooper, the Indian office's special agent to the Sioux, from dealing with the Powder River bands. Slemmer also told Cooper that when Red Cloud came in to sign the treaty that had been left behind at Fort Laramie, he and his people would not be permitted to linger. Although Fort Laramie had been at the center of Lakota trade since the 1840s, Fort Randall, on the Missouri River, was to be the new trading and annuities center for the Lakota.

AFTER WEEKS OF rumor-filled waiting, word finally reached Fort Laramie in late October 1868 that the Powder River bands had completed their fall buffalo hunt and Red Cloud was ready to talk. Surprised by the news, Major William Dye, who had replaced Slemmer as post commander, telegraphed General Augur on November 2 for instructions. Augur reminded Dye that the peace commission had been dissolved and told him to direct Red Cloud to General Harney, perpetrator of the Blue Water Massacre, at Fort Randall.

At midmorning on November 4, Red Cloud arrived at Fort Laramie with about 125 other chiefs and warriors. The record does not show Crazy Horse among the delegation. But as a shirt-wearer and one of the leaders of the Powder River bands in the Fetterman Fight and the Wagon Box Fight, however, it would only seem logical that he would have been somewhere on the scene.

From the moment he appeared at Fort Laramie, Red Cloud, by promptly making himself the center of attention, made it clear that he was the person the whites would have to satisfy if they expected peace. During introductions, when the other chiefs rose and extended their hands as a sign of friendship, Red Cloud remained seated and offered only the tips of his fingers. He then told Major Dye that any talks they held would mean little because no members of the peace commission or anybody else of sufficient authority were present. Dye responded diplomatically by informing Red Cloud that many of his fellow Lakota already had signed the treaty and that he was authorized to represent the commission.

Over the next three days, Red Cloud engaged in a series of maneuvers that kept Dye and the other white negotiators off balance. Red Cloud peppered them with questions about everything imaginable and had Dye go through every item in the treaty. Red Cloud said his people had no interest in the farming provisions of the treaty, demanded lead and powder, and announced that his people would never go to Fort Randall to receive their annuities from General Harney. Through great patience and persistence, though, Dye finally was

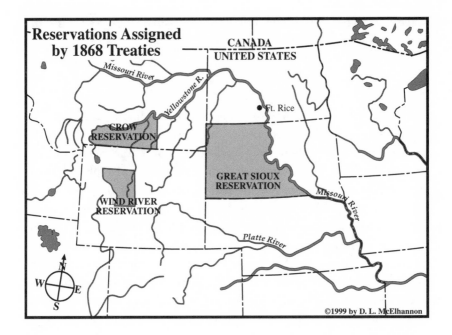

able to get Red Cloud to sign the treaty. Red Cloud concluded the council with a long speech in which he announced that the Lakota were not ready to move onto reservations or trade at Fort Randall. They would resume trade with the whites at Fort Laramie. He also made it clear that he would have a difficult time getting some of his young warriors to follow the treaty.

But Red Cloud either did not understand the ramifications of what he had done or, as some of the more militant members of the Powder River bands feared, he was equivocating. Long known for his political skills, Red Cloud already may have accepted the fact that the Lakota could never defeat the whites and had begun maneuvering to gain power within a new world, for the treaty was squarely aimed at changing the Lakota from hunters to farmers. It contained extensive provisions for seeds and farming implements, the construction of warehouses and other buildings, a land book to record individual land allotments, compulsory education in schools operated by whites, and the annual issuing of clothing. In exchange the Lakota agreed to make the reservation their home and allow the United States to pass laws governing them.

FOLLOWING THEIR SIGNING of the Fort Laramie Treaty of 1868, the Powder River Lakota once again dispersed and were not seen for months. Meanwhile, the Senate ratified the treaty on February 16, 1869, and the military continued its efforts to move the Lakota to Fort Randall, on the Missouri River. Resistance to the move among most Lakota, however, was strong. They felt that Fort Randall was too far to the east, the country around it devoid of game, and they disliked the idea of being under the control of General Harney. The military succeeded only in moving the "Laramie loafers" closer to Fort Randall and Spotted Tail's Brulé to the White River, about a hundred miles from the fort. So formidable was the resistance of other Lakota that Major Eugene Carr in 1869 led an expedition to drive Lakota and Cheyenne bands out of their old hunting grounds along the Republican River.

The question of the whereabouts of the Powder River bands finally was answered on March 22, 1869, when Red Cloud appeared outside Fort Laramie with a force of about a thousand warriors. Again, there is no evidence to indicate Crazy Horse's presence among the warriors. But given his standing as a warrior and his other exploits with the Powder River bands, it is difficult to imagine that he would not have accompanied Red Cloud.

While the sight of so many Lakota warriors must have caused consternation among the occupants of Fort Laramie, Red Cloud and the other Lakota leaders had not come to make war. The previous winter had been a hard one, game was scarce, and they needed food for their people. Post commander Dye again urged Red Cloud and the others to go to Fort Randall and offered supplies for the trip. The Lakota took the supplies, but then headed west across the Big Horns into central Wyoming and the Wind River country of the Shoshone.[5]

Even before Red Cloud and the others had eaten their first meal made with Dye's supplies, though, rumors of gold in the Big Horn Mountains of Wyoming and Montana, and the Black Hills of Dakota Territory, were beginning to spread, bringing with them an influx of fortune hunters into Lakota country. By the winter of 1869–1870, citizens of Cheyenne, Wyoming, had organized the Big Horn Mining Association to send an expedition in search of gold into territory granted the Lakota by the Fort Laramie Treaty. Dakota territorial governor Andrew Faulk soon was suggesting that the Great Sioux Reservation established by the treaty be moved away from the Black Hills and the Powder River, and north of the 45th parallel to the Yellowstone and Little Missouri valleys. The world promised the Lakota was already headed for change.

20

LOVE AND DEATH

R ED CLOUD and his followers may have headed for the Wind River to avenge the death of the chief's son in a raid against the Shoshone a year earlier. Whether Crazy Horse took part in that raid is unknown. But he might have led small raids against the Crow that same year and in the fall was involved in a disastrous fight with the Shoshone along the Wind River that led to the death of Hump. For the most part, though, the Powder River bands spent 1869 hunting while tensions with white fortune seekers grew and the federal government stepped up efforts to move all Lakota north, to the Missouri River.

Hoping to prevent the looming crisis from exploding into war, the government in early 1870 invited Red Cloud to visit Washington to discuss the Fort Laramie Treaty with the "Great White Father."[1] In April 1870 Red Cloud sent word to Fort Fetterman that he accepted the government's invitation. Despite the resistance of some members of his administration, among them General Sherman, who believed that Red Cloud and his followers should be told "plainly and emphatically"[2] to report to their reservation, President Grant agreed to receive Red Cloud and a dozen other Lakota leaders selected by the chief, including Man Afraid Of His Horses and Spotted Tail.

As a sign of his sincerity, Grant also ordered the army to stop gold seekers from entering the Big Horn Mountains. Finally, on May 16, Red Cloud arrived at Fort Fetterman to prepare for his journey to Washington. The man who in the eyes of the whites symbolized Lakota resistance was sent off on his journey by a crowd of about five hundred enthusiastic Indians. Whether Crazy Horse was present is impossible to determine. Because of his well-known resistance to the whites, it is likely he was out on the plains somewhere hunting or raiding the Crow, but curiosity just as easily could have led him to Fort Fetterman to witness Red Cloud's departure and its effect on his people.

ALTHOUGH INDIANS had been traveling to Washington for talks with the government almost since the city was laid out, few of their visits drew the publicity of Red Cloud's first trip. The visit was carefully orchestrated to both impress the Lakota leaders with the wealth and might of the United States and to enhance Red Cloud's image as the ultimate leader of the Lakota. Whites needed to believe that there was a head chief who could speak for the Lakota and sign treaties they would follow. A reporter for the *New York Times* picked up the bombast when he wrote on June 1, 1870, that Red Cloud was "undoubtedly the most celebrated warrior now living on the American Continent . . . a man of brains, a good ruler, an eloquent speaker, an able general and fair diplomat. . . . The friendship of Red Cloud is of more importance to the whites than that of any ten chiefs on the plains."[3]

Except for Man Afraid Of His Horses, who became ill at Fort Fetterman and stayed behind, Red Cloud and the other members of the Lakota delegation boarded a Union Pacific train at Pine Bluffs, about forty miles east of Cheyenne, Wyoming, and arrived in Washington on June 1, where they met Spotted Tail and his Brulé delegation.

On June 3, at his first meeting with government officials in Washington, including Commissioner of Indian Affairs Ely S. Parker, a Seneca, and Secretary of the Interior Joseph Cox, Red Cloud made three demands. He wanted more rations for the women and children in his band, ammunition so his people could hunt, and a telegram sent to his people informing them that he had arrived in Washington. The telegram was promptly sent, but Parker and Cox lacked the authority to deal with the first two demands. Following the meeting, Red Cloud, Spotted Tail, and the others were taken to observe a session of the Senate, which most of the delegates showed little interest in. They also refused to enter the big buildings shown them on a tour of the city.

The next day, June 4, the Lakota were taken to see the U.S. arsenal and navy yard. During the visit, the delegation saw practically every type of weapon in the arsenal. Red Cloud used his eagle feather fan to measure the diameter of a fifteen-inch coastal gun and examined with great interest the huge grains of powder used in the weapon, which was then fired down the Potomac River. At the navy yard the delegation also was treated to a parade by a regiment of marines and shown the ironclad ships at anchor in the river.

But if Red Cloud was impressed by the might of the United States, he did not reveal it when a council was held on June 8. Instead, he was all business, informing the whites that he had come to Washington to prevent a new war and to procure for his people the right to trade on the Platte River. When the issue of moving to the Missouri was brought up, he replied: "I have said three times that I would not go to the Missouri, and now I say it here for the fourth time."[4] He added that no roads should be built through the Powder River country and that Fort Fetterman must be moved and the Oglala given the right to trade at Fort Laramie.

The following day the Lakota delegation was taken to meet President Grant, who listened to their demands, then suggested that the Oglala move to the Missouri and start farming. Red Cloud and the others did not like what they heard, but listened politely. That night they were taken to an elaborate state banquet in the White House. Spotted Tail took the occasion to remark on the great difference in the quality of food eaten by the whites and that sent to his people.

Two days later, on June 10, the council reached a crisis. Hoping to bully the Lakota into moving to a reservation on the Missouri, Secretary of the Interior Cox brought out a copy of the Fort Laramie Treaty to prove that the Oglala had no right to trade at Fort Laramie or live in the area. Red Cloud responded by angrily denouncing the treaty. He claimed the paper had not been read to the Lakota leaders when they signed it and that he had been coaxed into signing it by an interpreter who had told him it was the only way to keep white soldiers away from the Powder River. He further said he had been told the treaty allowed the Lakota to continue to trade at Fort Laramie. The other chiefs backed up Red Cloud, and the delegation left the council in a black mood, demanding to be taken home at once.[5]

Newspapers began to predict a new Indian war if Red Cloud were to return to the Powder River in his current mood. At that point, the white peace crusaders stepped in with a scheme to force the government's hand. They took Red Cloud to New York, where he spoke to a mass meeting of peace supporters. Red Cloud began his talk by raising both arms to the sky, and then sweeping them downward to the earth and praying. The audience was instantly impressed. The *New York Times* noted on June 17, 1870, that "his earnest manner, his impassioned gestures, the eloquence of his hands, and the magnetism which he evidently exercises over an audience, produced a vast effect on the dense throng which listened to him yesterday. 'You have children, and so have we. We want to rear our children well, and ask you to help us in doing so.' It seems to us that this is not an unreasonable request even though it does come from a 'savage.'"[6] The *New York Tribune* gushed: "The remarkable triumph of Red Cloud yesterday in the great speech he delivered . . . was one of the most striking incidents in the history of the aboriginal race. . . . His opening invocation to the Almighty Spirit was solemn, earnest, and highly dramatic; and as he went on to recount the wrongs of his people and to demand justice for them, in words that were at once simple, strong, and heartfelt, the audience was greatly impressed."[7]

As could be expected, western newspapers took an entirely different view of Red Cloud's speech. They found nothing of worth in it and decried whites who attended it as "humanitarian greenhorns" and "Quakers." Eastern newspapers countered by pointing out that the chances of war with the Lakota, which a number of western newspapers and military leaders had claimed was unavoidable, had vanished. Secretary of the Interior Cox was pressured to send a delegation of peace advocates with a trainload of gifts to Fort Laramie and with the authority to sign an agreement with the Powder River bands.

FROM NEW YORK, the Lakota delegation headed home by way of Buffalo, Chicago, and Omaha, where they remained for several days to select horses, saddles, and other gifts that the government had made available. They reached their original departure point of Pine Bluff on June 24 and immediately started for Fort Laramie. From the fort they headed for Rawhide Creek, about forty miles to the northeast, where they were greeted by about a thousand lodges of Lakota and Cheyenne confident that Red Cloud had obtained permission for them to trade at Fort Laramie.

Riding with Red Cloud was General John Smith, who sent a report urging that the Lakota and the Cheyenne be permitted to trade at Fort Laramie. If they were stopped from trading, he warned, a plan to establish an agency for the Oglala on the Big Cheyenne River, about eighty miles to the north of Fort Laramie, would fail. The Big Cheyenne was considered a viable alternative to the Missouri River because the Oglala had wintered in the area many times in the past. Red Cloud also was promised the right to choose his own agent and trader.

In line with General Smith's request, the government gave in and allowed the Lakota and the Cheyenne to trade at Fort Laramie. After they finished trading, the bands headed north to the Powder River, where they held a sun dance and organized a great war party that attacked the Crow and drove them into the mountains. Following the attack on the Crow, Red Cloud spent the remainder of the summer of 1870 traveling to camps along the Powder explaining what he had been told in the East and exactly what was contained in the Fort Laramie Treaty. It was the first time most of the Lakota and the Cheyenne learned of the content of the treaty. Then trader John Richards came out from Fort Laramie with word that the government was sending two men from Washington to hold a council and cement the agreement that would give the Oglala an agency on the Cheyenne River. Richards also promised many fine gifts. Some Lakota complained that they did not want their leaders signing any more papers. Others wanted to know if the gifts would include guns and powder, while many more were simply satisfied with the promise of gifts and more food.

F. R. Brunot and Robert Campbell were the two negotiators promised by Richards. They arrived at Fort Laramie on September 21 and had to wait for Red Cloud until October 5. At the fort the following day a council was held at which Red Cloud complained about the old California Trail, which still ran for a few miles along the northern bank of the Platte River in Lakota territory. He acknowledged that the road was a small matter not worth a war, but claimed it demeaned him in the eyes of his people. Brunot and Campbell attempted to deflect the complaint by pointing out that they had brought many fine presents.

Even more controversial, though, was the location of the proposed Oglala agency. Red Cloud had gone east with instructions from his people to obtain an agency near Fort Laramie. Brunot and Campbell, however, had explicit instructions not to consent to an agency near the fort. They suggested instead Rawhide Butte, which the Lakota refused. Red Cloud explained that a camp at the site had once been struck by lightning, a very evil omen, and that the Lakota warriors would never agree to an agency away from Fort Laramie. After hours of arguing, Man Afraid Of His Horses finally said: "There is too much talk. Give us our presents and let this other matter lie where it is."[8] Brunot and Campbell suggested that the chiefs talk over the matter during the winter and return in the spring with a decision. Then, two days later, they turned over the trainload of gifts they brought with them.

Red Cloud's trip to Washington had managed to forestall the war Westerners had been predicting. But it also set a precedent among whites of humoring Red Cloud that would help to create a rivalry with Crazy Horse. That remained in the future, though. During the spring and early summer of 1870, it was love that occupied Crazy Horse.

IT WAS ABOUT TEN DAYS after the battle When They Chased the Crow Back to Camp in 1870 that Black Buffalo Woman finally gave in to Crazy Horse's attention. She placed her children with friends and rode off with him and a small group of warriors on a raid against the Crow.[9] Lakota custom allowed a woman to divorce her husband at any time. She could do it by moving in with relatives or with another man or by simply placing the husband's belongings outside their lodge. Although some compensation might be required to smooth over hurt feelings, the rejected husband was expected to accept his wife's decision for the good of the tribe. No Water did not.

Although No Water was away from camp when Crazy Horse and Black Buffalo Woman eloped, it did not take him long to guess what had happened. For some time he had been well aware of Crazy Horse's interest in his wife. Hurriedly he gathered up his children, borrowed a pistol from Bad Heart Bull, put together a war party, and headed after the lovers. He found them on the second night camped with several bands along the Powder River.

"My friend, I have come!" No Water shouted as he rushed into the lodge where Crazy Horse and Black Buffalo Woman were sitting by the fire. Crazy Horse leaped to his feet and reached for his knife, while Black Buffalo Woman scurried out from under the back of the lodge. No Water fired, hitting Crazy Horse just below the left nostril. The bullet followed the line of the war chief's teeth, fracturing his jaw and causing him to tumble forward into the fire. No Water then ran from the tent to announce that he had killed Crazy Horse and fled the camp. He departed so fast that he left behind his mule.[10]

IN THE CONFUSION that followed the shooting, Crazy Horse's friends allowed No Water to escape. When they found out what had happened, they killed No Water's mule in revenge and then took Crazy Horse to the camp of his uncle, Spotted Crow, to be nursed. Meanwhile, No Water's friends made a sweat lodge to purify him of what they believed was Crazy Horse's murder. No Water then sought refuge with his brother, Holy Bald Eagle, or the Black Twin, as he was known, for his dark complexion. When Crazy Horse's friends demanded that No Water be turned over to them for punishment, Holy Bald Eagle told his brother, "[I]f they want to fight us we will fight."[11]

For a time it appeared as if a lot of blood would flow. But then cooler heads prevailed. Spotted Crow; Ashes, another uncle of Crazy Horse; Bad Heart Bull; and He Dog worked behind the scenes to keep the peace. "After a while the thing began to quiet down," He Dog recalled.

> No Water owned a very fine roan horse and a fine bay horse; he sent these and another good horse to atone for the injury he had done. Spotted Crow, Sitting Eagle, and Canoeing brought No Water's wife to Bad Heart Bull's tent and left her there on condition that she should not be punished for what she had done. This condition was demanded by Crazy Horse. Bad Heart Bull arranged for her to go back to her husband in peace.[12]

Because of the incident, Crazy Horse was stripped of his position as a shirt-wearer. No longer did he exemplify the ideal of a Lakota warrior. The affair and the shooting were such a scandal that the institution of shirt-wearer itself deteriorated. Nobody was ever given Crazy Horse's shirt. "Everything seemed to stop right there," He Dog said. "Everything began to fall to pieces. After that it seemed as if anybody who wanted to could wear the shirt—it meant nothing."[13]

But still the trouble did not end. One day after he had recovered from his wound, Crazy Horse joined several bands camped near the mouth of the Big Horn River. No Water appeared in the camp while Crazy Horse was off hunting buffalo on the other side of the Yellowstone River. When No Water saw Crazy Horse returning from the hunt, he jumped on a horse owned by Moccasin Top and took off across the plains. Puzzled to find Moccasin Top in camp, Crazy Horse asked who had ridden off on his horse. Moccasin Top told him it was No Water.

"I wish I had known it!" Crazy Horse told him. "I would certainly have given him a bullet in return for that one he gave me."

Crazy Horse then stripped off his pack, jumped on his horse, and headed off after No Water. He chased him to the Yellowstone, giving up only after No Water plunged his horse into the river and swam it across. Afterward, No Water traveled south to join the loafer Indians at the Red Cloud Agency.[14]

AT ABOUT THE TIME that Crazy Horse was wounded, yet another tragedy struck. His younger half brother Little Hawk, born in about 1844, was killed while on a war expedition south of the Platte River. All that is known of Little Hawk is that he was impulsive. Some Lakota later claimed that he would have been an even greater warrior than Crazy Horse had he lived. But that just may be rose-tinted thinking. He Dog judged him "too rash" and too "reckless" to be a great warrior.

Short Buffalo provides the only primary account of Crazy Horse and Little Hawk in action. It occurred in a fight with the Shoshone in northwestern Nebraska. The Lakota were outnumbered and on the run. "Crazy Horse and his younger brother were guarding the rear of their war party," Short Buffalo said.

> After a lot of fighting, Crazy Horse's pony gave out. Crazy Horse turned it loose and the younger brother, who did not want to leave him, turned

his own pony loose. Two of the enemy, mounted, appeared before them for a single combat. Crazy Horse said to his brother, "Take care of your-self—I'll do the fancy stunt." Crazy Horse got the best of the first Shoshone; the other ran away. He got the horses of the two Shoshones and they caught up with their party. They had saved themselves and their party and got the two horses and the scalp of the Shoshone who was killed.[15]

After he recovered from his wound, and while Red Cloud was in Washington, Crazy Horse rode south, gathered up his brother's remains, and buried them.[16] But still his bad luck did not end.

In the fall of 1870, Crazy Horse and Hump led a war party across the Big Horns into Shoshone country. Along the Wind River they en-countered a drizzling rain that turned to ankle-deep snow. With their horses slipping and sliding, Crazy Horse wondered if they should give up their plans for a fight and return to Cone Creek. "He [Crazy Horse] didn't like to start a battle unless he had it all planned out in his head and knew he was going to win," He Dog said. "He always used judgment and played safe."

When Hump learned of his friend's remark, however, he reacted in a way that does not meld with the image of the wise old warrior that some writers have created for him. Like Little Hawk, He Dog saw Hump as reckless. "This is the second fight that he has called off in this same place!" Hump complained when he heard of Crazy Horse's remark. "This time there is going to be a fight." He then con-fronted his friend. "The last time you called off a fight here," he said, "when we got back to camp they laughed at us. You and I have our good name to think about. If you don't care about it you can go back. But I am going to stay here and fight."

"All right, we fight, if you feel that way about it," Crazy Horse answered. "But I think we're going to get a good licking. You have a good gun and I have a good gun, but look at our men! None of them have good guns, and most of them have only bows and arrows. It's a bad place for a fight and a bad day for it, and the enemy are twelve against our one."

In the fight that followed, the Shoshone soon had the Lakota on the run. Only Crazy Horse, Hump, and Good Weasel kept up the fight. "It was a running fight, with more running than fight—only these three would fight at all," He Dog said. "Crazy Horse charged one side of the Shoshones and High Back Bone [Hump] the other.

When they came back, High Back Bone's horse was stumbling. He said, 'We're up against it now; my horse has a wound in the leg.'"

Crazy Horse answered: "I know it. We were up against it from the start." With that they both again charged the Shoshone. When Crazy Horse retreated, he found only Good Weasel left. Hump had fallen from his horse and been killed by the Shoshone. Seeing what had happened, Crazy Horse and Good Weasel gave up the fight.[17] Four days later, according to Red Feather, who was part of the war party, Crazy Horse returned to the scene of the fight to bury his friend: "He didn't find anything but the skull and a few bones. High Back Bone had been eaten by the coyotes already. There weren't any Shoshones around. When the Shoshones found out whom they had killed, they beat it."[18]

21

AGENCY INDIANS

As CRAZY HORSE GRAPPLED with love and death through the summer and fall of 1870, white America was approaching the end of its first century by quickening the pace of its march west and shedding its agrarian past in favor of a new industrialism that promised boundless wealth for all. By 1870 the population of the United States had grown to 39.8 million and the population center had moved west, from about Chillicothe, Ohio, to near Cincinnati, Ohio. The Lakota population continued to hold steady, at roughly 25,000 individuals.

During the final few years of Crazy Horse's life, *Harper's Weekly* also published the first political cartoons featuring the Democratic donkey and the Republican elephant. The National League and the baseball glove were born. The Fifteenth Amendment to the Constitution, barring the United States or any state from depriving a citizen of the right to vote because of race, color, or previous condition of servitude, was adopted. The National Rifle Association and the Woman's Christian Temperance Union were established.

The first half of the decade in addition saw the emergence of John D. Rockefeller's Standard Oil Company, the invention of barbed wire, and the first runnings of the Preakness and the Kentucky Derby. In New York City, construction of the Brooklyn Bridge began, and Central Park was completed. Robert E. Lee died. Thomas Edison invented the phonograph, and Mark Twain published *The Adventures of Tom Sawyer*. During the period, too, Yellowstone National Park was created and Colorado was admitted to the Union as a state. In politics, Grant and Hayes served as presidents, and Congress, on March 3, 1871, passed the Indian Appropriation Act, which made all Indians national wards and nullified all treaties with them.

DURING HIS VISIT to Washington, Red Cloud never gave any indication that he was impressed by the power of the white man. However, he must have recognized that his people faced a far more formidable foe than the Crow and the Pawnee, since within a few weeks of his return he traveled to the Powder River country to organize a council. His aim was to convince his fellow Oglala, as well as their Cheyenne and Arapaho allies, that the Fort Laramie Treaty was of benefit to them. With game becoming more and more scarce, and the buffalo herds under heavy pressure from professional hide hunters, he suggested that they move to an agency where they would be given plenty to eat and kept supplied with the trade goods promised by the treaty.

But most Oglala either were indifferent or opposed to Red Cloud's efforts. Some even resented his description of the power and wealth he had seen on his journey. "Red Cloud saw too much," one Lakota leader insisted.[1] Many Oglala reacted by returning to the old ways of hunting and warring on the Crow. Anxious to stabilize the situation and establish an Oglala agency headed by Red Cloud, the government in August 1870 responded by sending Board of Indian Commission members Felix Brunot and Robert Campbell, who was one of the founders of Fort Laramie, west to talk with Lakota leaders.

As he had in the past, Red Cloud kept the two commissioners waiting for several weeks. When he finally appeared in late September, an estimated seven thousand Lakota were camped around Fort Laramie. Crazy Horse may have been off with Hump at the time on their tragic raid against the Shoshone. If Crazy Horse was not raiding, it seems unlikely that he would have missed such a gathering of his people. Although he was known as an introvert, he was not antisocial, and such large gatherings were as much social affairs as councils. That he did not avoid large gatherings is supported by his presence in the large village on the Little Big Horn that Custer would attack six years later.

When the conference finally opened, Red Cloud reiterated his demand for an agency on the North Platte River near Fort Laramie and inquired about gifts for his people, especially ammunition for hunting. Brunot and Campbell were prepared for those demands and as usual declined the request. But they were caught off guard when Red Cloud complained that the government had suspended the fifty-year annuity payments promised the Lakota by the Horse Creek Treaty of 1851. He also maintained that the government had violated treaty agreements by allowing whites from Fort Laramie to use the migrant road above the North Platte.

Brunot and Campbell surprised Oglala leaders when they responded to Red Cloud's demands by backing down on the government's long-standing insistence that the tribe accept an agency on the Missouri River. They suggested the establishment of an agency near Rawhide Buttes, about forty miles north of Fort Laramie, and attempted to sweeten their offer by promising teachers to train Oglala children how to farm. The latter offer made Red Cloud so angry, he became adamant about having an agency on the North Platte. Although he agreed that the buffalo were in decline, he insisted there would be enough for his people to continue their hunting ways if whites were kept out of Lakota country. As long as the buffalo remained, he would not permit Oglala children to undertake such a demeaning activity as farming. The Lakota were hunters and warriors.

For three days the talks continued, with little results. Then the commissioners called a private conference with Red Cloud, Man Afraid Of His Horses, American Horse, and Red Dog to discuss an agency at Rawhide Buttes. When Red Cloud continued to stall on a decision about Rawhide Buttes, Brunot became angry and took a hard stand. He insisted that the Lakota would have to go to the Missouri for their rations unless Red Cloud agreed to an agency at Rawhide Buttes. Red Cloud responded by departing Fort Laramie for the Powder River country. By mid-December, though, many of his people began drifting back to Fort Laramie in search of food and warm clothing. By mid-February 1871 almost three thousand Lakota, Cheyenne, and Arapaho were at the fort, and by mid-May more than six thousand. The situation became so serious that the army was given a hundred thousand dollars to feed and clothe the horde.

Having told Red Cloud in October that his people would have to go to the Missouri to receive rations, Brunot did not like the government's decision to feed the Indians at Fort Laramie. John M. Wham, who had been appointed as Red Cloud's agent, agreed. But Wham and Fort Laramie commandant Colonel John Smith also felt that Red Cloud's people should be given a temporary agency near the fort. Called to Washington to discuss the problem, Colonel Smith recommended sending Brunot back to Fort Laramie to choose a site for an agency. Brunot reluctantly agreed and returned to the fort on June 9, 1871. At the conference that followed he pressed Red Cloud to choose a location. Red Cloud responded by demanding that his people be compensated for land taken by the Union Pacific to build the transcontinental railroad. When Brunot, Smith, and Wham would not accede to that demand, he asked if a decision could be delayed until he traveled north and consulted with Black Twin. They agreed, but warned Red Cloud that he must return to Fort Laramie within fifteen days or they would negotiate with the Lakota who remained at the fort.

When Red Cloud failed to return within the time limit, Wham and Smith—Brunot had by then returned east—convened talks with the Lakota at the fort. Generally they were more agreeable than Red Cloud, but still refused to relocate from the Platte because of the drought conditions that characterized much of the northern plains during the summer months. They argued for an agency on the North Platte about eighteen miles below Fort Laramie. On June 30, 1871, Wham and Smith telegraphed Commissioner of Indian Affairs Parker, endorsing the plan. Hoping to avoid possible trouble, Wham also suggested that rations be issued to the more than seven thousand Indians who also were camped around the fort. Parker at first balked, but a week later changed his mind and approved both the site plan and the issuing of rations.

The site finally selected for an Oglala agency was thirty-two miles downriver of Fort Laramie, on the northern bank of the North Platte about a mile west of the Wyoming/Nebraska line. Wham was so pleased with the settlement that he even recommended that the Lakota be supplied with the arms and ammunition they so often requested. His recommendation was denied.

AMONG THE FEW OGLALA who remained along the Powder River after the establishment of Red Cloud's Agency in the summer of 1871 was Crazy Horse. The winter population of the Powder River band at the time was roughly fifty lodges, and the summer population, inflated by Lakota who left their agencies to hunt, about two hundred lodges. The band camped for a time with Sitting Bull on the Yellowstone River near the mouth of Rosebud Creek, and then joined with the Miniconjou and the Sans Arc to hold a sun dance and organize a war

The second Red Cloud Agency near Camp Robinson.

party to attack the Shoshone and avenge the death of Hump. When the raiding party, possibly under the leadership of Crazy Horse, failed to find the Shoshone, it headed for the North Platte, where it killed some whites and made off with large numbers of horses and mules.[2]

It was probably during one of his forays north from the Powder River in 1870 or 1871 that Crazy Horse met Sitting Bull. What the two most famous plains Indians might have said during that meeting has been lost to time. Some writers imagine that the two immediately became fast friends because of their shared ambitions as warriors and made a mutual vow to resist any change in their way of life.[3] But that is nothing more than speculation. Crazy Horse's aversion to speaking at councils probably made their relationship a private affair for which no record exists. What seems clearer is that by the start of the 1870s, both men were seen by their people as symbols of resistance to the whites who were destroying the buffalo and encroaching on their land in ever-increasing numbers.

Sometime during 1871, Crazy Horse also married Black Shawl. Like his first wife, Black Buffalo Woman, very little is known about Black Shawl. Primary sources report only that she married Crazy Horse six years before his death and stayed with him to the end of his life.[4] Of the marriage, Black Shawl's brother Red Feather said: "All I can say about that is, that both Crazy Horse and my sister stayed single much longer than is usual among our people." Crazy Horse probably was thirty-one or thirty-two years of age when he married Black Shawl.

Nellie Laravie, Crazy Horse's third wife.

Red Feather reports, too, that the couple had one daughter, They Are Afraid Of Her, who looked like Crazy Horse. Why she was given the name They Are Afraid Of Her is unknown, but it may have had something to do with her father's reputation as a warrior and his desire to pass on something of that to her. Red Feather said she died when three years of age. He Dog said she died when she was two years old. Some secondary sources report that she died of cholera, but there is nothing in the primary sources to support that claim.

And Lakota winter counts do not indicate a cholera epidemic when They Are Afraid Of Her died in 1873 or 1874.

A number of writers have depicted Crazy Horse as an extremely devoted father who often gathered children around him to tell stories. While there is nothing in the primary record to dispute that fact, there also is little or nothing to support it. That he would have been devastated by the loss of his only child, however, is understandable. After his death, the *New York Sun* reported that the death of They Are Afraid Of Her led Crazy Horse to found the Last Child Society, a warrior society whose members were selected from the last-born males of Lakota families, but that actually happened earlier.[5]

Although Crazy Horse's personality often led him to behave in a manner many of his people thought was "queer," descriptions of his behavior following the death of his daughter need to be considered with at least an eye toward the primary source—Frank Grouard. A half-white, half-Polynesian scout and interpreter, Grouard got to know Crazy Horse while living with the Lakota. But Grouard, called The Grabber by the Indians, was well known for bending a story to suit his purposes.

According to Grouard, They Are Afraid Of Her was about four years old when she died in a village located between the Little Big Horn River and Rosebud Creek. Crazy Horse was off leading a war party against the Crow at the time and did not learn of her death until he returned. By then the village had moved about seventy miles, to the Tongue River. When Crazy Horse was told of his daughter's death "his grief was pathic," Grouard said. Although large parties of warring Crow lay between him and his daughter's death scaffold, he was determined to visit the site and asked Grouard to accompany him. At least that is what Grouard said.

For two days, Crazy Horse and Grouard supposedly rode until they reached the death scaffold. Crazy Horse then asked Grouard to make a camp and rode off alone to the scaffold. He crawled up on the platform and stayed there mourning for three days and nights. On the morning of the fourth day, Crazy Horse awoke Grouard at sunrise and told him it was time to depart. During the entire three-day period, not a morsel of dried meat or a drop of water passed his lips. Back at the village, Crazy Horse never told a soul where he had been or what he had done.[6]

ALTHOUGH THE LAKOTA who were camped at Fort Laramie agreed to move to the new Red Cloud Agency, tensions between the Indians and the government remained high. Suspicious that the government wanted to drive them north so whites could take over the Black Hills, the Lakota made Agent Wham and his employees near-prisoners in the agency stockade. Every time Wham was seen leaving the stockade on horseback, he was surrounded by warriors who forced him to return. Then, in late July 1871, news arrived that a wagon train was at Fort Laramie preparing to head north to Spotted Tail's Agency, which had been established on the White River. Even though the wagon train was carrying goods for Spotted Tail's people, Red Cloud's people did not want it crossing Lakota land. To avoid war, the government gave in and allowed for the distribution of Spotted Tail's supplies at Red Cloud's Agency.

Under heavy criticism for his solicitous approach toward the Oglala and his handling of events at Red Cloud's Agency, Wham was replaced as agent for the Oglala by J. W. Daniels on October 31, 1871. An Indian agent from Minnesota, Daniels arrived with a plan to relocate the agency to the White River in northwestern Nebraska, far from white travel routes along the Platte. But first Daniels had to contend with the deteriorating conditions at the agency.

With the fur trade dead and buffalo for the robe trade growing scarce, whiskey quickly became the main item of trade at the agency. Whites would carry it across the Platte to trade for clothing, blankets, flour, bacon, and other goods supplied to the Oglala by the government. Drunkenness was rampant among residents of the agency. Daniels sought to change the situation with the help of Red Dog, whose trust he gained when he had the agency carpenter build a coffin for the chief's son. Working together, the two men, and other supporters of the agency plan, gradually improved the atmosphere at the Red Cloud Agency. The winter of 1871–1872 passed more or less quietly, until Red Cloud appeared at Fort Laramie in March 1872.

Unhappy that the decision to move to the agency was made without him, Red Cloud criticized the location and demanded that his rations be delivered to Fort Laramie. The government refused. When Red Cloud finally visited the agency on March 21, he tried to pressure Daniels into sending his rations to Rawhide Creek. After lengthy negotiations Daniels gave in to the demand with the understanding that Red Cloud would choose a new site for an agency on the White River. Aware of Red Cloud's talent for stalling, he gave the chief two weeks to make a decision. Pressed by his own people, Red Cloud agreed to a move during an April 10 meeting with Daniels, Colonel Smith, and General E. O. C. Ord, the new commandant of the Department of the Platte.

In typical fashion, Red Cloud then tried to stall the move by seeking permission for the Oglala to use their own people to haul their annuities to the new location. Tired of all the delays and bickering, Colonel Smith denied the request. Then he put the Oglala on the defensive by bringing up a recent raid near Fort Fetterman in which several horses and mules were stolen, and the robbery and murder of a rancher near the Red Cloud Agency. Red Cloud admitted to Lakota participation in the incidents, but refused to accept responsibility because no one from his band had been involved. He also agreed that the incidents showed the problems that could arise when an agency was located too close to the whites.

The truth of Colonel Smith's remarks notwithstanding, they still angered the Oglala and delayed action on a new agency site for about a month. During that time Daniels took Red Dog and a few other supporters of a move north to the White River. There they found a suitable location for an agency near where the Little White Clay River emptied into the White. Even though Red Cloud did not make the trip, he approved of the location and would even claim during the visit to Washington that followed to have selected it. While Red Cloud was in Washington, President Grant also suggested that the Lakota might be better off as agency Indians if they moved to what is now Oklahoma. He noted that the White River was in Nebraska and that citizens of the state might one day demand the removal of the Lakota to another location.

Ignoring Grant's remarks, Red Cloud remained enthusiastic about the White River site. "I shall not go to war any more with whites," he declared. "I shall do as my Great Father says and make my people listen." He told his people: "Make no trouble for our Great Father. His heart is good. Be friends to him and he will provide for you."[7] His words, however, had little impact on Crazy Horse and other members of the Powder River band, or on some of the Lakota at the agency. In August 1872 a group of young Lakota warriors swam their ponies across the Platte to graze on the southern bank of the river, an area closed to them. When troops from Fort Laramie arrived on the scene to force the Lakota back across the river, the warriors became incensed and threatened to kill the soldiers and other whites at the Red Cloud Agency. Bloodshed was avoided only when Red Cloud appeared and used his powers of persuasion to convince the warriors to move their ponies back across the river.

More trouble occurred on September 11, 1872, when Red Cloud reversed himself and, perhaps hoping to regain some of his esteem among opponents of relocation, announced that he was now opposed to moving his agency to the White. He argued that the Treaty of Fort Laramie did not require the Lakota to move from the Platte Valley for another thirty years. It was an argument that fell mainly on deaf ears but sparked new hostilities at the agency. In October a group of young warriors, intoxicated on whiskey supplied them by white traders, threatened to kill Agent Daniels and his staff. For twenty-four hours Red Cloud and a few other Lakota leaders struggled to restrain the drunken young men until troops from Fort Laramie arrived on the scene.

Even though Red Cloud had announced his opposition to an agency on the White, shortly after the incident with the drunken warriors he and a group of followers moved to Hat Creek, only a few miles from the site that had been selected for a new agency. Red Cloud's action renewed the debate over relocation, but by November 1, 1872, almost all of the Lakota at the old agency had moved north and were preparing to winter along the White. Agent Daniels quickly decided to make Red Cloud's move official by distributing supplies at the new location.[8]

While happy to receive supplies at the White River site, Red Cloud would continue to object to the move through 1873. Other Lakota also would rebel against the relocation, but it was too late. The final nail was struck on January 14, 1874, when agent J. J. Saville, who had replaced Daniels, requested the establishment of a military post at the agency. Still clinging to the idea of forcing the Oglala to move even farther north, to the Missouri River, the War Department refused to send troops until April. Army officials changed their minds, though, when a member of the agency staff and two troopers were killed in separate incidents shortly afterward. On February 18, 1874, General Ord dispatched a force from Fort Laramie to keep peace at the agency. That spring they began building Camp Robinson near the Red Cloud Agency. The new facility was named for Lieutenant Levi Robinson, one of the two soldiers killed by Lakota earlier that month.[9]

ALTHOUGH CRAZY HORSE often is depicted as wanting nothing to do with whites or agencies, there is evidence that he was at least familiar with the affairs at the Red Cloud Agency. When Red Cloud returned from his second trip to Washington, in the summer of 1872, Crazy Horse's friend Little Big Man was at the agency with a large number of warriors from the Powder River band. That they would not have kept Crazy Horse, who was said to be hovering nearby, making small raids along the Platte River roads, abreast of what was happening at the agency and with the whites they encountered, seems absurd.[10]

On August 14, 1872, Crazy Horse and Sitting Bull also took part in the first attack by the Lakota on troops escorting the Northern Pacific Railroad survey crew. The attack occurred two days after a large sun dance was held along the big bend of the Yellowstone River in southeastern Montana. It began when word arrived that four hundred soldiers were approaching the mouth of Arrow Creek. A war party of five hundred warriors rode all night and toward dawn halted near the soldiers' camp, which was on the northern bank of the Yellowstone, opposite the mouth of Arrow Creek. The attack was to begin at daybreak. But once again the young men could not wait. Many slipped through the line of akicita and in the darkness overran the tents of the civilian surveyors. The soldiers, under the command of Major E. M. Baker, counterattacked, driving the young warriors out of the brush and timber near the camp and up to bluffs where the main war party had gathered.

From the heights, the war party laid a withering fire into the camp. Then Long Holy, who was eager to show off his power with a group of seven young warriors who were his followers, shouted to the other Lakota: "Now I am going to make these men holy [bulletproof]. We are going to make four circles toward the white soldiers, and each time we shall ride a little nearer to the enemy. When we make the fourth circle, we are going to charge, and all of you must charge with us."[11]

After putting on their war paint and rubbing their bodies and their horses with spit made from a sacred root given them by Long Holy, the seven young men, among them Sitting Bull's nephew White Bull, rode out with Long Holy to attack the soldiers. They circled closer and closer through a ceaseless fire until four of them were hit. Then, on their third circle, Sitting Bull suddenly rushed out between the young men and the soldiers. "Wait! Stop! Turn back!" he shouted. "Too many young men are being wounded! That's enough!"

Indignant at Sitting Bull's interference, Long Holy said: "I brought these men here to fight. But of course, if they want to quit, they can."[12] Sitting Bull paid no attention. He continued shouting for the young men to stop until he convinced them to return to the bluffs.

For a time after Sitting Bull halted the young men's exhibition, the Lakota lay on the bluff exchanging fire with the troops. Occasionally one or more of the young warriors would race out into the open, and then back to the bluffs. Among those warriors who rode into the open appears to have been Crazy Horse. White Bull said the young men greatly admired him and he "seemed very brave and lucky that day."[13] Crazy Horse's daring also apparently stirred Sitting Bull into action. He decided it was time that he did something to remind members of the war party who was the greatest warrior among them.

Laying down his gun and quiver, Sitting Bull took his pipe bag, walked out toward the line of soldiers, and sat down on the open plain about a hundred yards in front of the Lakota line. Then he calmly took out his pipe, struck a fire with flint and steel, and began to smoke. Looking back at the Lakota line, he called for any warrior who wished to smoke to join him. White Bull, Gets The Best Of Them, and two Cheyenne answered his call by walking out, sitting down, and passing the pipe. "Our hearts beat rapidly, and we smoked as fast as we could," White Bull recalled. "All around us the bullets were kicking up dust, and we could hear bullets whining overhead. But Sitting Bull was not afraid. He just sat there quietly, looking around as if he were at home in his tent, and smoked peacefully."[14]

While they sat smoking, Two Crow rode out to make a circle in front of the troops. As he passed close to the smokers, his horse was hit and fell headlong, kicking up dust into the faces of Sitting Bull and the others. Still, Sitting Bull continued to smoke until the pipe

Sitting Bull.

was empty. Then he took from his pipe bag a sharp stick that he used to clean the pipe before returning it to the pouch. Finally he rose and, as White Bull and the others raced past him, walked back to the Lakota line. Once back among his warriors, Sitting Bull gathered up his weapons, mounted his horse, and called for an end to the fight. It was about noon.

Feeling his own bravery challenged, however, Crazy Horse was not ready to stop. He turned to White Bull and said: "Let's make one more circle toward the soldier line." He then told White Bull to go first. But

White Bull had had enough. He answered: "Go first yourself, I'll follow."[15] Crazy Horse then raced away with White Bull close behind. The two warriors rode past the soldiers without being hit, but as they turned back toward their line, the troops unleashed a barrage that killed Crazy Horse's pony. The war chief was unharmed, but hardly lived up to Sitting Bull's example as he ran back to the Lakota line.

22

CHIEF OF ALL THE THIEVES

THE BATTLE OF ARROW CREEK had barely ended when a messenger arrived in the Lakota camp with word of more soldiers approaching from the east. The messenger had been sent by the Hunkpapa Lakota Gall, who with about two dozen warriors had discovered Colonel David Stanley's expedition out of Fort Rice on the Missouri River. Stanley was to link up with Major Baker and assist with the Northern Pacific survey. Primary sources do not place Crazy Horse at the scene when word arrived about Stanley. But his presence at Arrow Creek means he could have been in the area and ridden off with Sitting Bull to fight the soldiers.

Gall attacked Stanley's troops two days after the Arrow Creek fight. He struck near daybreak on August 16, 1872, while the soldiers were still asleep in a camp along O'Fallon Creek, a tributary of the Yellowstone River in east-central Montana. Screaming wildly and firing their weapons, the Lakota rode out of the timber and through the center of the camp. They tried to make off with the troop's stock herd, but were thwarted and soon broke off the fight.

Down O'Fallon Creek and up the Yellowstone, Gall and his men shadowed the troops until they reached the mouth of the Powder River. There he struck again. The second attack began when the warriors caught one of the party's engineers wandering alone in the hills above the river. They chased the engineer back into the valley, where the troops rode to his rescue. After a brief exchange of fire, the war party withdrew to the western bank of the Powder. A short time later, Gall appeared on the bank, laid down his rifle, and shouted that he wanted to talk with the soldier chief. Stanley replied by laying down his pistol and walking to the edge of the river. He offered to meet

Gall on a sandbar in the middle of the Powder, but Gall refused and demanded to know what the soldiers were doing in his country. Stanley told him they were there to build a railroad. Gall asked how much they intended to pay the Lakota. When Stanley could not provide an answer, he threatened to bring all of the bands together for a "big fight."[1]

Noticing warriors gathering in the trees behind Gall, Stanley broke off the talk and started back for his own lines. He had gone only a few steps when the Lakota opened fire. The soldiers answered with their own barrage, hitting two of the warriors.

Soon after the exchange between Gall and Stanley, Sitting Bull arrived with a large group of warriors. The party did not attack, but followed the troops on their return march down the Yellowstone and up O'Fallon Creek. On the evening of August 22, Sitting Bull rode out to threaten and harangue the troops, then the next morning, as the soldiers were breaking camp, attacked with a large force of warriors. Stanley answered the attack by sending two companies to dislodge the Lakota from the bluffs where they were hiding. In the midst of the fight, Sitting Bull launched into a long speech, declaring that if the railroad came through "there would be no more Indians"[2] and warning that he had sent for all the tribes to come and wipe out the soldiers and the railroad men. The troops, meanwhile, continued to work their way up the bluff until they forced the Lakota from their firing positions.

Unable to summon enough warriors to make good on their threats, Gall and Sitting Bull trailed the Stanley expedition east across the Little Missouri and down the Heart River. They managed to kill two officers and Stanley's black servant along the way.

The withdrawal of Major Baker's force after the Arrow Creek fight and Stanley's troops after encounters along O'Fallon Creek and the Powder River left some Lakota thinking that they had won important victories and stopped the railroad from crossing their country. What stopped the Northern Pacific, though, was the Panic of 1873 and bankruptcy. What the fights with Baker and Stanley actually showed the army was that the Lakota were no match for dug-in troops with long-range rifles. The fights also promoted General Sherman to again warn that the transcontinental railroad was a national enterprise that would not be stopped by the Lakota. He backed up his warning by sending additional forces to the upper Missouri River. Among them was the 7th Cavalry, under Lieutenant Colonel Custer.

BEFORE WALL STREET MANIPULATIONS halted the advance of the Northern Pacific, the railroad had reached the Missouri River. There it gave birth to Bismarck, North Dakota and Fort Abraham Lincoln. The fort was the new home of the 7th Cavalry, whose members joined with those of Colonel Stanley on June 20, 1873, at Fort Rice for another survey expedition west.

Possibly because the withdrawal of Baker and Stanley the previous summer had left them feeling strong and relaxed, the Lakota once again did not spot the survey expedition until it was well within their country in early August. When they finally became aware of the expedition, it already was on the Yellowstone nearing the mouth of the Tongue River on a line of march that was heading directly toward a village of about four hundred lodges. Among the warriors in the camp was Sitting Bull. Some secondary sources also place Crazy Horse at the scene and even go so far as to describe Custer as taking a nap when Crazy Horse saw him for the first time.[3] But there is nothing in the primary record to even vaguely support such a claim. If anything, the fact that the village was made up of Hunkpapa and Miniconjou suggests that Crazy Horse's Oglala were off somewhere else.

In the fight that followed discovery of the expedition on August 4, the Lakota turned to an old tactic that by then was well known to seasoned Indian-fighters. They sent out a decoy party of about a hundred warriors to lure the two cavalry companies scouting the way into an ambush. Custer was in command of the advance party, though, and would not allow himself to be drawn into the trap. He followed the decoys to a point, and then withdrew into a stand of timber from which his men held off the war party until Stanley arrived with help.

Fearful that the reinforced troops might attack the village, the Lakota retreated to the strands of some unusual music. The scout Grouard, who was with the Lakota at the time, said: "The soldiers expected to fight and we were making preparations to protect the women and children if they should attack. I could distinctly hear the

band playing. It was years since I had heard a band. They were playing Custer's favorite battle tune. That was 'Garry Owen.'"[4]

Even though Custer pushed his men on a forced thirty-six-hour
march, the Lakota were able to avoid the troops in their race up the
Yellowstone. Near the mouth of the Big Horn River, the Lakota piled
their belongings into boats made of buffalo hide and, despite the fact
that the river was running high, successfully swam their ponies
across the river. When Custer arrived at the location on August 10,
he tried to follow the Lakota, but his men could not ford the river.
Then the next day, after recruiting more Miniconjou, Oglala, Sans
Arc, and Cheyenne who were camped on the Big Horn, Sitting Bull
returned with a large party of warriors. The presence of Oglala makes
it likely that Crazy Horse would have been part of this second war
party, though there are no records to support that assumption.

From hiding places in the timber on the southern bank, the Lakota opened fire on the cavalry. Custer's men returned the fire, and
the exchange dragged on for most of the day. When parties of warriors crossed the river above and below the troops, mounted cavalry
advanced and drove them back while the band played "Garry Owen."
Then Stanley arrived, set up a field piece, and began firing exploding
shells into the timber, bringing to an end the Battle of the Yellowstone, possibly the first encounter between Crazy Horse and Custer.

STANLEY AND CUSTER were not the only whites to lead expeditions
into Lakota country in the early 1870s. Formed in Bozeman, Montana, in January 1874, the Yellowstone Wagon Road Association set
out on February 13 with the aim of opening a road to the head of
navigation on the Yellowstone and prospecting for gold between Rosebud Creek and the Powder River. The expedition consisted of about
150 mostly seasoned frontiersmen. Aware that they would be bla-
tantly trespassing in a region closed to whites by treaty, the expedition went heavily armed with repeating rifles and two cannons
supplied by Montana governor Benjamin Potts out of the territorial
arsenal.[5]

Sitting Bull's Hunkpapa spotted the expedition as it cut across
country from the Yellowstone to the lower Rosebud. A small party of
warriors struck the advanced guard on March 26, but was chased off

by reinforcements. Another small party, concealed in a ravine, fired at members of the expedition who rode out of camp to look at the country on March 30. The whites returned the fire and fled back to camp. "Shortly after," according to Addison Quivey, a member of the expedition, "one of our pickets, seeing an Indian a short distance from his post, who seemed desirous of talking with him, started out to interview the 'red brother,' when he was attacked by four others, who were concealed in the brush. He turned his horse to run, but received four wounds, and was even struck on the head with their whip-stocks, but he held to his horse, and finally escaped, aided by some of our party, who heard the firing and went to his assistance."[6]

The Lakota left the expedition alone until the early morning of April 4, 1874, when a party of several hundred warriors struck the whites along Rosebud Creek about thirty-two miles upstream of the mouth. Led by Sitting Bull, the warriors kept up a sniping fire through the night, killing several of the expedition's horses. Then, at daylight, one of the warriors rode out into the open in an apparent bid to show his bravery. He was not as fortunate, however, as was Sitting Bull at Arrow Creek. The whites quickly cut down his horse and sent him hobbling, wounded, back to his lines. Under the cover of heavy small-arms and artillery fire, two parties of whites then charged the Lakota, killing and scalping seven of them and sending the remainder fleeing.

Three more times during April, the Lakota attempted to destroy the interlopers. They attacked the expedition along Rosebud Creek at the mouth of Greenleaf Creek, at the head of Reno Creek, and on Lodge Grass Creek. As in the first fight, though, they were driven off each time by the better-armed whites. Some secondary sources report that Crazy Horse took part in the last two fights.[7] Since he often was reported in the area by various friends that is very possible, but there is no way to verify the claim for certain.

During the three fights, the Lakota managed to kill only one of the whites. Expedition members killed and scalped eight Lakota and found signs of numerous others being wounded or killed and carried off. Hoping to kill even more, the expedition after the first fight left its campsite strewn with pemmican, biscuits, and beans laced with strychnine. The Lakota, however, were suspicious and did not eat the tainted food. But they were caught by another trap. In a camp along the Little Big Horn, expedition members faked a grave that they rigged with a howitzer shell blanketed with nails, bolts, and other pieces of scrap metal. When the Lakota arrived on the scene, High Bear began digging up the grave. As he worked, someone among the warriors warned that the whites might have put something on the body that could harm them. They began to move back from the grave just as High Bear found the lanyard rigged to the shell and pulled it. The grave exploded, throwing High Bear into the air and blinding many of the warriors with dust. Although the bomb badly shook up the Lakota, nobody was killed.[8]

EVEN BEFORE the Yellowstone Wagon Road Association set out to find gold in Lakota country, western newspapers, politicians, and settlers were demanding access to the wealth they believed lay hidden and unused in the Black Hills.[9] It was a clamor that grew louder and more intense as the Panic of 1873 deepened into a depression.

Rising some four thousand feet above the brown plains, the Black Hills, Paha Sapa, were long esteemed by the Lakota as the center of the earth. Its sheltered valleys and thickly timbered slopes provided plenty of game, fine poles for tipis, and shelter and firewood during bitter winters. Many Lakota also saw the hills as a mystical place of spirits. Normally, the Lakota only entered the Black Hills in family groups or small bands. Rarely did they go there alone or in large numbers or stay for very long. "The Black Hills were full of fish, animals, and lots of water . . ." Standing Bear said. "Indians would rove all around, but when they were in need of something, they could just go in there and get it."[10]

French traders François and Joseph de la Verendrye generally are credited as being the first white men to see the Black Hills. They left Fort de la Reine south of Lake Manitoba on April 29, 1742, in search of a route to the Pacific Ocean. On August 11 they arrived at a "Mountain of the Horse Indians," what many historians believe was Bear Butte, and on November 9 traveled southwest toward the Hills. If they did not enter the Black Hills, there is general agreement that they at least passed near them at some point in their journey.[11]

The Black Hills as a source of gold may have started with the next purported white visitor, English trader Jonathan Carver, who claimed to have made a seven-thousand-mile trip through the west in 1766–1768. From that trip, Carver brought back tales of "Shining Mountains" that sparkled and glowed when the sun shone upon them. The mountains very possibly could have been the Black Hills, since Professor A. B. Donaldson described the hills in a similar vein when he visited them in 1874.

Such visits by white traders and trappers continued through the late eighteenth century, until by the time the Lewis and Clark Expedition reached the area in 1804, they carried with them a fairly accurate map showing the location of the Black Hills. Even the gold later "discovered" with much bluster and fanfare appears to have been known by the start of the nineteenth century. In a letter to the lieutenant governor of Louisiana dated May 28, 1804, Regis Loisel mentions that nuggets of gold might be found in the Black Hills north of the Niobara River.

By the 1870s, the wealth of the hills was so widely known that a certain view had solidified. It can be seen in a September 3, 1874, editorial in the *Yankton Press and Dakotaian*. The paper complained about marauding bands of Indians making war on whites in the summer and living off the federal government in the winter. Then it blasted the Fort Laramie Treaty for giving the Black Hills to the Lakota, calling it an "abominable compact" and a barrier to "improvement and development" of one of the richest and most fertile regions of America. "What should be done with these Indian dogs in our manger?" it asks.

> They will not dig the gold or let others do it. . . . They are too lazy and too much like mere animals to cultivate the fertile soil, mine the coal, develop the salt mines, bore the petroleum wells, or wash the gold. Having all these things in their hands, they prefer to live as paupers, thieves and beggars; fighting, torturing, hunting, gorging, yelling and dancing all night to the beating of old tin kettles. . . . Anyone who knows how utterly they depend on the government for subsistence will see that if they have to be supported at all, they might far better occupy small reservations and be within military reach, than have the exclusive control of a tract of country as large as the whole State of Pennsylvania or New York, which they can neither improve or utilize.[12]

Succumbing to the pressure, General Alfred Terry, with the approval of his superiors General Sherman and General Sheridan, on June 8, 1874, authorized Colonel Custer to lead an expedition into

the Black Hills. The purpose of the expedition was "to make a recon-
naissance of the country about which dreamy stories have been
told."[13] Equipped with 110 wagons, 3 Gatling guns, a 3-inch Parrott
rifle, and a 16-member mounted band, the expedition of about 1,000
men left Fort Abraham Lincoln on July 1, 1874.

The Custer expedition lasted about two months. It entered the
Black Hills along Castle Creek, where it encountered Indians for the
first time on the morning of July 26. They were a band of twenty-
seven Oglala led by One Stab that had come to the hills from the Red
Cloud and Spotted Tail agencies. Perhaps frightened by the expedition's Arikara scouts, the Oglala attempted to flee the area. Needing
the Lakota as guides through the unknown country, Custer dispatched the Arikara to stop them. In the ensuing confusion, a scout
shot one of the Oglala. Custer then informed One Stab, who was in
the expedition's camp, "that he would be kept as a hostage until we
were out of the Hills, and must show us a good road."[14] According to
the Arikara, One Stab was tied to an iron picket pin and his feet were
hobbled. "The Dakota captive cried in the night and by signs said
that his children would cut their hair as for his death since he was as
good as dead."[15]

News of One Stab's capture and the presence of the whites in the
Black Hills quickly spread through the Red Cloud and Spotted Tail
agencies, then the camps of more hostile Lakota. The news stirred a
great deal of anger among the Lakota, but nothing in the way of
action. Custer had proven that stories of the Black Hills teeming with
Indians were a myth. The expedition also found little gold, so little
that neither the date of its discovery nor its discoverer were recorded,
and the men barely paid it any notice in their journals and letters.
But that fact was quickly lost on the nation's press.

NEWS OF "CUSTER'S GOLD" left the Black Hills on August 3, 1874, in
the saddlebags of Lonesome Charley Reynolds. The army scout was
directed by Custer to proceed to Fort Laramie with a report to Sheridan and letters from the men. At the fort he was to post the mail and
send a number of dispatches by telegraph. If a telegram could not be
sent from Fort Laramie, he was to ride on to the nearest station, and
then return to Fort Abraham Lincoln to await further orders.

Custer's report to Sheridan was a lengthy affair that addressed the issue of gold only in its final few lines. After noting that some members of the expedition believed that gold could be found in paying quantities, he wrote rather cautiously:

> I have upon my table 40 or 50 small particles of pure gold, in size averaging that of a small pin head, and most of it obtained today from one panful of earth. As we have never remained longer at our camp than one day, it will be readily understood that there is no opportunity to make a satisfactory examination in regard to deposits of valuable minerals. Veins of lead and strong indications of the existence of silver have been found. Until further examination is made regarding the richness of gold, no opinion should be formed.[16]

Reynolds, who was known for his reliability and soft-spoken manner, performed his duties as directed and then rode on to Sioux City, where he was immediately accosted by news-starved citizens of the town. He gave the *Sioux City Journal* a mildly enthusiastic report of the gold situation, noting that he had not personally picked up any nuggets nor knew whether anybody else had found nuggets. But, he added, he had seen gold worth two or three cents a pan washed from surface dirt.

As with television, talk radio, and certain publications today, however, the newspapers of the mid-1870s were not particularly interested in the facts. They wanted drama. Instead of approaching the story cautiously, as had Reynolds and Custer, they chose to focus on dispatches sent by two journalists, Nathan Knappen of the *Bismarck Tribune* and William Eleroy Curtis of the *Chicago Inter-Ocean*, who were accompanying the Black Hills Expedition. Knappen was a tough-talking Westerner who was in favor of finding gold in the hills and against coddling the Indians. Curtis was an inexperienced, excitable journalist of just twenty-three.

Knappen set the tone for newspaper stories to follow in the August 12, 1874, edition of the *Bismarck Tribune* when he wrote: "Here, in Custer's Valley, rich gold and silver mines have been discovered, both placer and quartz diggings; and this immense section bids fair to become the El Dorado of America."[17] Following the *Tribune*'s lead, the *Yankton Press and Dakotaian* proclaimed on August 13: "STRUCK IT AT LAST! Rich Mines of Gold and Silver Reported Found by Custer. PREPARE FOR LIVELY TIMES! Gold Expected to

Within days of the news breaking in 1874 of gold in the Black Hills, mining parties were formed to move into the area.

Fall 10 per Cent—Spades and Picks Rising.—The National Debt to be Paid When Custer Returns."[18] Curtis's editors were so taken with his report that they gave him the entire front page, starting with the headline "Gold! The Land of Promise—Stirring News from the Black Hills." In the story, Curtis reports that "all the camp is aglow with the gold fever."[19]

Lost in the uproar was the more moderating voice of another journalist with the expedition, Samuel Barrows of the *New York Tribune*. While noting that gold had been discovered, Barrows cautioned that there was no way to determine the extent or the value of the goldfield. He warned that the region was owned by the Sioux, "who have sworn to repel any intrusion by the white man," and concluded: "Those who seek the Hills only for gold must be prepared to take their chances. Let the over-confident study the history of Pike's Peak. The Black Hills, too, are not without ready-made monuments for the martyrs who may perish in their peaks."[20]

But Barrows's voice was one crying in the wilderness. Within days of the news breaking, mining parties were being formed with plans to enter the Black Hills. Acting Secretary of the Interior B. R. Cowan wrote Dakota territorial governor J. L. Pennington, making it clear that the opening of the hills to settlement rested with Congress, and until it took action, his department would do everything possible to prevent violations of the Fort Laramie Treaty. General Sheridan was even prepared to use force to keep miners out of the Hills. In a telegram to General Terry, he noted:

> Should the companies now organizing at Sioux City and Yankton trespass on the Sioux Indian Reservation, you are hereby directed to use the force at your command to burn the wagon trains, destroy the outfits and arrest the leaders, confining them at the nearest military post in the Indian country. Should they succeed in reaching the interior you are directed to send such force of cavalry in pursuit as will accomplish the purpose above named.[21]

The citizens of Yankton reacted by condemning Sheridan's directive and forming the Black Hills Pioneers to explore the region. Then, in October, a group of miners left Sioux City for the Black Hills. Once again the race was on. Soon the trail Custer took into the Black Hills became known to the Lakota as "Thieves' Road" and Long Hair as "Chief of All the Thieves."

23

PAHA SAPA

THE WINTER OF 1874–1875 was long and terribly cold on the northern plains. Starting in September, members of the Powder River bands began arriving at the Red Cloud and Spotted Tail agencies. By October they were there in numbers and angry over Custer's invasion of the Black Hills. Talk arose about sending a war party after the first miners, but soon died because of the presence of troops near the agencies. Then agent J. J. Saville decided to erect a flagpole inside the stockard at the Red Cloud Agency.

On October 22, 1874, Saville had his men cut a tall lodge pole pine in the Hills above the White River and haul it into the agency. Whether Saville simply wanted to fly the flag over the agency or use it to signal the troops at Camp Robinson in the event of trouble is not known. The Lakota, though, viewed the flag as a provocation. They saw it as a threatening symbol of the white troops. But Saville ignored their complaints and ordered the flagpole raised.

The following day, October 23, a large group of armed and painted Lakota from the free-living bands entered the agency stockard and sullenly sat on the ground, watching the whites work. When Agent Saville was told of their presence, he walked to the door of his office to assess the situation. Suddenly the Lakota leaped up and rushed forward to attack the flagpole with axes and tomahawks. Saville ordered them to stop, but they ignored him. Then the agent ran back to his office, where Red Cloud and Red Dog were sitting, and appealed for their help. Either because the two chiefs were afraid or did not want to help, they refused to move. Saville reacted by sending a rider to Camp Robinson for troops. Somehow, the warriors learned that troops had been sent for and quickly left the stockard, scattering among several camps in the area.

When word arrived of trouble at the agency, Lieutenant Emmet Crawford was sent from Camp Robinson with twenty-six soldiers. As the troops started along the White River, a mass of warriors from the northern bands gathered at the agency and set out to meet the soldiers. Firing their guns and yelling wildly, they rushed the troops, circling and bumping the horses of the soldiers with their own ponies. The incident had all the potential of another Grattan fight until Young Man Afraid Of His Horses and a party of warriors from the agency broke through the circle of young men and began beating them back with their war clubs and riding quirts. They then led the troops into the stockard, which the young warriors attempted to burn until Old Man Afraid Of His Horses and Red Cloud appeared to harangue the crowd and quiet the young men.

Angered about what had happened, the agency Lakota turned on the warriors who had been involved in the incident and told them they would not broker any trouble at the agency. Stunned, angered, and confused by the agency bands siding with the whites, members of the northern bands that evening packed their belongings and left the Red Cloud Agency for the badlands to the north.

Hardly had the flagpole incident ended than agent Saville stirred more trouble by announcing that he had orders from Washington to withhold the distribution of annuities until a census of the agency had been conducted. The agency Indians counciled for an entire week on the issue, until November 4, when Red Cloud informed Saville before all the chiefs that a census would not be permitted, and that if he tried to conduct one, there would be trouble.

Saville responded by contacting the troops at Camp Robinson. Badly outnumbered, the commander delayed responding to the agent. Then Young Man Afraid Of His Horses and Sword, a nephew of Red Cloud, called a council at which some of the Lakota decided to move closer to the agency and be counted. Once the decision was made, one band after another moved toward the agency, except for members of the northern bands who were still mixed in with the agency Indians. They instead fled across the White River toward the badlands to join their kin who had gone there after the flagpole incident.

The census that finally took place showed 9,339 Lakota at the Red Cloud Agency. To that number were added 800 to 900 Kiyuksa Oglala Lakota who were hunting south of the Platte River, 1,202 Cheyenne, and 1,092 Arapaho. On November 10, 1874, the agency Indians were given their annuities and went back to their old camp sites. Clearer than ever, though, the two incidents showed how accustomed most Lakota had become to agency life and dependency on the whites. The old ways were fast dying. When trouble now loomed, most Lakota shied away and preferred not to face it. The dismay that Crazy Horse must have felt when word of what happened at the Red Cloud Agency reached him can only be imagined.[1]

FRICTION BETWEEN the free-living Lakota and whites arose again in July 1875, when Fellows D. Pease, a trader and former agent to the Crow, led forty-five men down the Yellowstone from Bozeman to establish a trading post. Near the mouth of the Big Horn, almost on the site of Custer's fight with Sitting Bull in 1873, Pease erected several log cabins that he planned to use to trade with the Lakota and the Crow. As usual, though, the two old enemies were more interested in fighting each other than in trading. Supported by Nez Perce from Idaho, the Crow fought the Lakota in a two-day battle across the Yellowstone at the same time that Pease was building his post. The fight occurred just five miles downstream of the post. Although the Crow won, they retreated to the north, where the Lakota followed.

As at the Red Cloud Agency, the appearance of the U.S. flag above Pease's trading post was viewed as an insult and a threat by the Lakota. Throughout the remainder of the summer and well into the winter of 1875–1876 they held the post under close surveillance, killing six of Pease's men and wounding eight others in a series of incidents.[2]

Despite such encounters, clashes between Lakota and whites during 1875 were largely verbal. Montana territorial governor Potts and troops stationed in Lakota country warned of Indian attacks that never materialized. The Lakota failed to carry out on threats by Sitting Bull to come together and kill any whites entering their country.

Stories from the period suggest that Crazy Horse sneaked off by himself to kill dozens of prospectors who dared enter Paha Sapa in the wake of Custer's expedition. While it is quite possible that Crazy Horse did kill some miners, gold seekers who defied the government's ban on entering the Black Hills encountered few problems with Indians. The movement of most Lakota to the Red Cloud and Spotted Tail agencies also nearly halted the depredations that had been occurring for years along the Platte River.

DURING 1875, the federal government began pressuring the Lakota to sell the Black Hills. Those efforts produced a major split among the Lakota and left the tribes divided into three major factions. The largest faction, led by Red Cloud and Spotted Tail, and made up primarily of agency Indians, believed the Black Hills were lost and favored getting the best price possible for them. The second faction, led by Young Man Afraid Of His Horses, wanted to work for an accommodation with the whites that would allow the Lakota to live as much as possible in the old ways. They felt that selling the Black Hills would be disastrous for the Lakota way of life. Caught in the middle, they neither wanted to fight the whites nor sell the Black Hills.

Like Young Man Afraid Of His Horses' followers, the third faction also opposed selling the Black Hills. Led by Crazy Horse and Sitting Bull, though, they were prepared to fight. The group was made up mainly of members of the free-living Lakota of the Powder River and Yellowstone country but included some agency Indians. Among the Lakota ready to fight were those who felt that Paha Sapa was sacred and should not be sold at any price, and young men who found agency life boring and who were spoiling for a fight to earn honors.

Seeing Red Cloud and Spotted Tail as their best chances for success, government officials in the spring of 1875 invited a delegation of thirteen Lakota from the Red Cloud Agency and six from the Spotted Tail Agency to Washington to discuss the Black Hills. Having enjoyed the attention he received during his 1870 trip, Red Cloud was anxious to go to Washington. But he also was well aware that nothing he agreed to would mean a thing without the support of the northern bands. To gain that support he sought to have Crazy Horse, Black Twin, and Young Man Afraid Of His Horses made part of the delegation. All three leaders refused the invitation. Crazy Horse and

Black Twin even refused to come to the Red Cloud Agency to discuss the issue.

Newspapers throughout the country hailed the Washington meeting as a great opportunity to persuade the Lakota to cede the Black Hills. Despite the government's insistence that the Black Hills belonged to the Lakota, gold seekers by the spring of 1875 were heading for them in ever-increasing numbers. But while the government wanted to discuss purchase of the Black Hills, Red Cloud was more interested in airing his complaints about Agent Saville. When President Grant, who was preoccupied by the scandals then plaguing his administration, announced at a White House meeting that discussions would be handled by the secretary of the interior and the commissioner of Indian affairs, the Lakota delegation viewed the move as an insult, and the summit quickly turned into a fiasco. So little was accomplished that even the *New York Herald*, which was friendly to the Lakota, complained that the summit should bring to "an end the foolish practice of [bringing] Indian embassies to negotiate with the government."[3]

When Red Cloud, Spotted Tail, and the others returned to the plains in June 1875, they found the Black Hills at the center of a media blitz and an issue of great contention among the Lakota. Hoping to attract business to their towns, newspapers in places such as Yankton, Sioux City, Cheyenne, and Sidney ran stories about miners preparing to defy the government and move into the hills. The Sioux Commission, headed by Episcopal bishop William Hare and formed to report on conditions at the Lakota agencies, tried to stem the illegal gold rush by insisting that the Black Hills were not the new El Dorado portrayed by the newspapers. But like the people who rushed to California in 1849 and to Colorado a decade later, most whites were attuned only to the fantasy of striking it rich.

Angered by the whites entering the Black Hills, the Lakota reacted to the invasion by destroying the goods of a merchant who was traveling there to establish a store. The incident brought an outcry from newspapers and western politicians, even though the Fort Laramie Treaty gave the Lakota the right to drive intruders from their land. The army responded with halfhearted efforts to keep the miners out of the hills. General George Crook, who succeeded General Ord as commander of the Department of the Platte in July, reacted like most military personnel when he encountered a group of twelve hundred miners during a tour of the Black Hills. He ordered them out, and then did nothing to ensure that his orders were followed. Among miners who were evicted by the army, most immediately turned around and headed back to their claims.

The government gave an indication of where it really stood, too, by sending another expedition into the Black Hills in May 1875. Led by Professor Walter P. Jenney of the New York School of Mines, the new expedition included a staff of well-equipped scientists and experienced miners who were to conduct a complete survey of the country and determine the wealth of its goldfields. Upon his return from the Washington conference, Spotted Tail rode to the Black Hills with his agent to judge their value. He wanted to see the miners and the gold everybody was talking about. With the help of his agent, who wanted the Lakota to receive the best price possible because it would increase his own profits, Spotted Tail decided that Paha Sapa was worth $7 million, plus annuities for the Lakota for seven generations.[4]

Seeking to settle the potentially dangerous situation growing around the Black Hills, federal officials decided to follow a suggestion made by Red Cloud and send a commission to address the problem. On June 18, 1875, a commission was appointed under Iowa senator William Allison, a friend of President Grant's. In September members of the Allison Commission arrived at the Red Cloud Agency to discuss the sale of the Black Hills. To placate Red Cloud and Spotted Tail, who were jealous of each other and locked in a struggle for leadership of the agency Lakota, the commission met on a site eight miles east of the Red Cloud Agency at a remote spot along the White River dominated by a lone tree.

REPRESENTATIVES OF ALL SEVEN of the Lakota tribes were present for the council, as were the eastern Dakota Yankton and Santee, the northern Cheyenne, and the Arapaho. Because the Fort Laramie Treaty required the consent of three-quarters of all Lakota adult males before any revision could be made in the treaty, the Allison Commission wanted as many Lakota as possible at the council. It did not, however, expect the fifteen thousand to twenty thousand Indians who arrived for the talks. A *New York Tribune* correspondent put the total at twenty-five thousand but admitted that was a rough estimate.

The delegation of Sioux to the council that led to the treaty by which the Black Hills were surrendered to the U.S. government.

"Such a gathering has never been seen west of the Missouri," he wrote, "perhaps the same numbers, but not so varied a representation." He further estimated that about five thousand of the Indians had "never attended a council with the whites."[5] Whatever the exact total, it was an impressive gathering and clearly showed the value that the Lakota, Dakota, Cheyenne, and Arapaho placed on the Black Hills.

A story about the council in the September 21, 1875, edition of the *Tribune* just as clearly revealed the way in which the majority of whites looked at both the Black Hills and the Powder River country to the west. While lamenting the way whites had broken past treaties with the Indians, the article noted: "We are buying in one sense what we already possess; we are purchasing land within our own territory, made ours by the deeds of the Pilgrim Fathers and beyond discussion. We are buying the right of way across our own cow lot."

Typically, Crazy Horse declined to participate in the council. Loaded down with tobacco and other goods meant to sweeten the offer, Grouard and a group of Lakota were sent out to convince the war leader and other members of the Powder River bands to come in to discuss a treaty for the Black Hills. The group found Crazy Horse camped with about two thousand lodges on the Tongue River near where Dayton, Wyoming, now stands. If Grouard can be believed, Crazy Horse's passive response to the offer would seem to indicate a certain resignation on his part. Perhaps he had concluded that the world of the Lakota was lost if so many of his people were willing to sell Paha Sapa and that the only thing left to him was to continue to live in the old ways as long as possible. Grouard recalled:

> They received us in a very hostile manner. They were just on the point of going on the warpath. I went out to Crazy Horse's lodge as soon as I got in and told him what we had come for. His father went out and harangued the camp and told them it was best to listen to what we had to say. Crazy Horse told me himself that all who wanted to go in and make this treaty could go, but he said, "I don't want to go." He said whatever the headmen of the tribe concluded to do after hearing our plan, they could and would do.[6]

The next day Crazy Horse went with Grouard to see Sitting Bull. Grouard had had a falling out with Sitting Bull two years earlier after he told the chief that he was going on a horse-stealing raid and instead went to Fort Peck to trade. The lie so angered Sitting Bull, who had treated Grouard like a son, that he vowed to kill the scout, who fled his camp in the fall of 1873 to live with the Oglala. Historians generally believe that Grouard took Crazy Horse with him to the meeting with Sitting Bull because he was frightened of the Hunkpapa leader. But time had cooled Sitting Bull's anger. He only demanded to know why Grouard had come to his camp. When Grouard told him about the Black Hills Treaty, Sitting Bull answered: "You will hear what I have to say at the council."[7]

In the morning, the men formed in a great circle in the center of the camp. Grouard estimated that about a thousand warriors were present. Big Breast was the first to speak. He talked for a long time, telling Grouard and the others that he would not go to the Red Cloud Agency and that he did not want to sell Paha Sapa. But, he added, "All those that are in favor of selling their land from their children, let them go."[8]

After Big Breast finished, Sitting Bull rose and reiterated his friend's remarks. He pointed out that he had never been to an agency and would not go to one to discuss selling Paha Sapa. Instead, he told Grouard to go back and tell the whites at the Red Cloud Agency that "he declared open war and would fight them wherever he met them from that time on."[9] Then Little Hawk stood and spoke for Crazy Horse, saying, "My friends, the other tribes have concluded not to go in, and I will have to say the same thing."[10]

During the council about a hundred members of the Powder River bands and the agency Lakota who had come to convince them to meet with the Allison Commission spoke. Grouard recalled:

> They told us that all who wanted to go would probably move across the Tongue River . . . that we could take them and go back, but that the majority of them would stay there and fight it out. That night they came very near massacring the whole party. I know Crazy Horse saved us. He said that he supposed that when anybody came in amongst them they would feed him, water him, and give him a smoke. He called the parties together who were the leaders of the proposed massacre, called them by name, and told them it would have to be stopped. He said: "My friends, whoever attempts to murder these people will have to fight me, too."[11]

Crazy Horse's threat cooled the situation, but Grouard and the others in his party knew better than to over stay. They left the camp a day earlier than planned and crossed the Tongue, where they found a larger camp than they expected waiting to go to the Red Cloud Agency.

AFTER GREETING THE LAKOTA at the opening of the council on September 20, 1875, commission chairman Allison outlined the purpose of his visit: "We have now to ask you if you are willing to give our people the right to mine in the Black Hills, as long as gold or other valuable metals are found, for a fair and just sum. If you are willing, we will make a bargain with you for this right. When the gold and other valuable minerals are taken away, the country will again be yours to dispose of in any manner you wish." The "Great Father," he added, only desired peace with the Lakota and their relatives and friends.[12]

Soon after Allison concluded his speech, Red Cloud informed the commission that because of the presence of so many tribes the Indians would need seven days to discuss the issue. The majority of Indian delegates then rose and departed the council grounds. In the talks that followed, two opposing groups emerged. The larger group, made up mainly of agency Indians, wanted to lease Paha Sapa to the whites. The smaller group, comprised mostly of young warriors, opposed leasing the hills for any price and wanted to fight. The two sides were so adamant in their stands that by September 26 at least half of the delegates were convinced that no agreement could be reached and left the council grounds.

Over the next three days the delegates who remained delivered a series of carefully rehearsed speeches that were a mixture of complaints and demands so extraordinary the commission judged it useless to continue the talks. Red Dog demanded supplies for seven generations to come. Several others rose to demand guns, ammunition, horses, cattle, oxen, wagons, clothing, knives, tobacco, and food, "a great deal more than we get now," Little Bear said.[13] Spotted Tail announced that the Indians expected seven million dollars to allow mining in Paha Sapa and wanted an agreement in writing that included a plan schedule. Crow Feather said he wished the president would not be stingy with his money so as not to grant the Lakota wishes. He also made it clear that he was unimpressed by the power of the government and told the commission he never called anybody "Great Father" but Wanka Tanka, the Great Mystery. Little Big Man, only recently arrived from the north, added in a threatening tone: "My heart is bad and I have come from Sitting Bull to kill a white man."[14]

Three days after the opening of the council, Little Big Man provided the most memorable moment of the conference. Based on accounts recorded at later dates, some all the way into the 1920s, historians generally describe Little Big Man on September 23 as leading a mock charge of two hundred stripped, painted, whooping, and rifle-firing warriors toward the commission tent. Riding full speed into the opening between the Indian delegates and the commission, they report him roaring that he had come to kill the white men who were stealing Lakota lands.

Writing from the scene, however, the *New York Tribune* correspondent was not nearly as dramatic. In a story dated September 24 and headlined "A Plot to Massacre the Black Hills Commission," he describes the incident as occurring shortly after one o'clock in the afternoon, when "it was discovered that almost 200 of the worst Indians, well armed and mounted on their best horses, had crossed White Earth River in [the] rear of the cavalry, and had slipped to

Little Big Man.

their right flank, until nearly the whole line of the cavalry was well covered by the Indians' rifles, one or two Indians with Winchester rifles to each man." Aware of what was happening, Young Man Afraid Of His Horses "quietly ordered his own soldiers to clear the undergrowth of all Indians behind the troops and the Commission. His lieutenant at once moved, and over two hundred Indians by actual count were made to march to the front."

Following the removal of the Indians from the rear of the troops and commission tent, Young Man Afraid Of His Horses' men took up protective positions around the whites with orders to kill any Indian who aimed a weapon at the commission. Of Little Big Man, the correspondent wrote that he and "his gang from the North, who were all present, each well-mounted, and naked save a robe, were also constantly covered by the rifles of friendly Indians." Whether Little Big Man charged the commission, the *Tribune* does not report. The mock charge that has so often been reported still could have occurred, but it is difficult to believe that a journalist at the scene would have missed an opportunity to write about it if the incident was as dramatic as later reported.

In an interview with one of Young Man Afraid Of His Horses' men immediately following the incident, the *Tribune* writer was told that the Indians involved mostly were young Cheyenne, Arapaho, and Oglala who did not want the delegates to consider any plan for selling or leasing the hills. They had promised to make trouble during a private council at which Young Man Afraid Of His Horses had replied "that he would kill every man who dared to fire at a white man or the Indians." At that council Little Big Man "also threatened to shoot down any chief who should speak in favor of disposing of the Black Hills, and he so told Spotted Tail, who did not speak."

The commissioners on September 27 unanimously rejected an Indian demand of $3.5 million per year for an indefinite period of time for the right to mine in Paha Sapa. They countered with an offer of $100,000 per year. The offer included a stipulation that allowed the president to terminate the agreement at any time with a two-year notice. If the Indians would sell Paha Sapa, the commissioners added, the president would deposit $6 million in a special account that could be used to finance their annual subsistence and to pay educational expenses. The Indians countered with several proposals of their own, running as high as $70 million, which may have been a mistake by the translator.[15] The council concluded, according to the *Tribune*, with an offer by the commission to purchase the right to mine Paha Sapa for $400,000 annually. The proposal gave the government the right to terminate such an agreement at any time on a year's notice. It also included an offer of $50,000 annually for the Big Horn country and $50,000 to be used immediately for the purchase of gifts for the tribes. The Indians were left to consider the offer over the winter.

How divided the Indians remained on the issue of Paha Sapa was made evident again on the final day of the council when, according to the *Tribune*, Lone Horn of the Miniconjou "disturbed the council by riding up and delivering from his saddle a violent speech against the Brulés and Ogalallas for trying to sell his country." Spotted Tail and Little Wound then rose to air final complaints about their agents. "The council closed with 'Hows' and handshakes," the *Tribune* noted.

But if the Indians who had attended the council thought they would have time to consider the commission's offer and come to some sort of consensus about Paha Sapa, they were badly mistaken. Frustrated and angry over its inability to lease or purchase the Black Hills, the Allison Commission on its return to Washington urged Congress to simply affix a fair value on the Black Hills and notify the Lakota of its decision. The commission further noted that the four years of rations and annuities guaranteed the Lakota by the Fort Laramie Treaty had expired and if the Indians balked at the offer all issues would be cut off. Nevertheless, the commission concluded, no agreement appeared likely until the army had taught the Lakota a lesson.

BY THE TIME the Black Hills Council ended, leaving the Lakota and other tribes involved confused, resentful, and arguing among themselves, at least a thousand miners had staked claims in Paha Sapa. They also had established a mining association for mutual aid and protection, and within a few months would discover most of the important placer deposits. Generally, efforts by the army to keep miners out of the hills were halfhearted. After comparing their meager wages to the possible riches surrounding them, many soldiers actually deserted to become miners. Even those miners who were apprehended by the army and taken under guard to Fort Laramie for a hearing invariably were released without punishment.

As reports of illegal mining activity increased, Secretary of War Belknap concluded that the young warriors who had opposed leasing or selling the Black Hills soon would take up arms to protect their unceded lands. Then, in mid-October, Agent Saville reported that many Oglala warriors had left the Red Cloud Agency and were headed north for the Powder River country. Since the young men had left their families behind at the agency, Saville believed that they were not heading north to join with the war faction, but only wanted to hunt the buffalo that had been sighted crossing the Yellowstone and slowly moving toward the Tongue. General Sherman and General Sheridan, however, disagreed. They felt that the Oglala from the agency did plan to join the war faction and decided the fate of the reservation system depended on the ability of the army to destroy the Lakota's military strength.

President Grant himself did not view protection of Indian reservations as a proper duty for the army. Following a meeting on November 3, 1875, with Belknap, Sherman, Crook, and Secretary of the Interior Zachariah Chandler, Grant decided that miners still would be forbidden to enter the Great Sioux Reservation, but that troops would be removed from the Black Hills and that the army would offer no further opposition to the miners. Grant saw the policy, which was never publicly announced, as a way to avoid criticism from Indian-sympathizers in the East, while at the same time placating western interests that hungered for Indian land. To Easterners, he could point to the fact the miners were forbidden by law from entering Sioux lands, while Westerners could readily see that the army had no intention of enforcing the law.

The secret policy was put into effect on November 17, 1875, when Captain Edwin Pollock and his troops were ordered to leave Camp Collins, a central holding area for miners who had been arrested and that had been built on the site of Custer City, which was laid out on August 10, 1875. With Pollock and his troops out of the way, miners were free to pour into Paha Sapa. By mid-January 1876, close to fifteen thousand miners were digging in and around the Black Hills. Camp Collins became Custer City, with a population of about a thousand. It was followed through the end of 1875 and into the spring of 1876 by Hill City, Sheridan, Rapid City, Pactola, Hayward, Rockerville, Deadwood, and other mining towns. Commissioner of Indian Affairs Edward Smith responded to Grant's decision and the reality of the situation on December 6, 1875, by ordering agents for the Lakota, Cheyenne, and Arapaho to inform all bands that they must report to their respective agencies by January 31, 1876. Those who failed to report would be considered hostile and dealt with accordingly by the army.

As the deadline neared, Agent James Hastings, who had been appointed to replace Saville after the latter had been accused of corruption and resigned, was ordered by Commissioner Smith to halt

By mid-January 1876, close to 15,000 miners were digging
in and around the Black Hills. Camp Collins had become
Custer City, with a population of 1,000.

the sale of all arms and ammunition to the Oglala. Hastings balked,
insisting that sensational articles on the Indians that had appeared in
western newspapers were not accurate and that the Lakota were
"perfectly quiet and have evinced no disposition to be otherwise."[16]
Banning the sale of arms and ammunition, he insisted, would only
anger the young men by making it more difficult for them to kill the
live cattle that were delivered to the Red Cloud Agency as part of the
Oglala food rations. He suggested that licensed traders be permitted
to sell arms and ammunition in limited quantities to the Oglala. The
proposal was quickly rejected by the Indian office.

A surprise came in late January, when Crazy Horse and Black
Twin were reported moving toward the Red Cloud Agency with three
thousand to four thousand followers. Hastings was so delighted by
the news that two of the most prominent leaders of the war faction
appeared to be coming in that he telegraphed Commissioner Smith
with the good news. Deep snow and freezing temperatures, however,
slowed the march. Scouts sent word that Crazy Horse and Black Twin
were camped near Bear Butte, while Sitting Bull was heading for the
Yellowstone. But Hastings's excitement was short-lived. By the end of
February more than a thousand Lakota had complied with Smith's
order and come in to the Red Cloud Agency. Crazy Horse and Black
Twin, however, were not among them.

24

GREASY GRASS

Unaware of President Grant's decision and the military forces being arrayed against them, out in the Powder River country Crazy Horse and other members of the free-living bands from late 1875 through early 1876 went about their usual routine of hunting, trading, visiting, storytelling, and occasional raiding of the Crow. On the Yellowstone opposite the mouth of the Big Horn, the Sans Arc, Miniconjou, and Cheyenne kept up the pressure on the white traders and hunters in hated Fort Pease. In February the beleaguered occupants of the fort sent word for help to Bozeman. A relief column of cavalry reached the fort on March 4, 1876, to find only nineteen of the original forty-six occupants cowering inside the stockade. The column returned to Bozeman with the men, but as a portent of the world to come left its flag defiantly flying on the fort's flagpole.

Following the demise of Fort Pease, the free-living bands scattered in small camps along the Powder and its eastern tributaries. By the time of the fort's closing, too, most of the bands had learned through riders sent out from the agencies of the government's ultimatum to come in or be attacked. According to Short Buffalo, the riders attempted to coax in the Powder River Lakota by telling them that the trouble over the Black Hills was to be settled. They counciled with the bands of Crazy Horse, He Dog, Holy Bald Eagle, and Big Road at the forks of the Tongue where Sheridan, Wyoming, now stands. "All the hostiles agreed," Short Buffalo said, "that since it was late and they had to shoot for tipis [i.e., shoot buffalo] they would come in to the agency the following spring."[1]

Since the bands had no plans for war against the whites, news of the government's stand and the deadline attached to it left their leaders puzzled. They looked on the ultimatum not as an order but rather as an invitation similar to what they had received for the Black Hills council. As had happened when the riders spoke with Crazy Horse and the others, they typically responded by sending word back that they had no ill feelings toward the whites, but were busy hunting. They would come in to trade their buffalo robes early in the spring, at which time they would then discuss their future.[2]

The army's answer to the confusion and the reluctance of the Powder River bands to stop hunting was delivered on March 17, 1876. It came when Grouard led six troops of cavalry under Colonel Joseph Reynolds to what he believed was the village of Crazy Horse. The camp was along the Powder a few miles north of the Wyoming border and contained about 735 people, among them about 210 warriors.

Near daybreak, when the cavalry was in position around the camp, the temperature was forty to fifty degrees Fahrenheit below zero and the Powder shrouded in a thick ice fog. "When I got within twenty yards of the camp, I yelled to Crazy Horse," Grouard said. "I recalled what he had told me during my endeavors to secure the Black Hills treaty—that he would rather fight than make a treaty—and told him that now was the time to come out and get the fighting he wanted, as troops were all around his camp!"[3]

But before an answer could come, the cavalry charged. Naked or just scantily clad, men, women, and children frantically struggled to free themselves from sleeping robes and tipis tied up tight against the cold. While the women, children, and old men scattered for the snowy hills, the warriors grabbed their weapons and raced for their horses, only to find that soldiers already had seized half the herd. Caught by surprise and greatly outnumbered by the much better-armed troops, the warriors retreated to the breaks on the western edge of the village. From there they kept up a steady fire as the troops tried to burn their possessions. Shortly after noon, the fight ended, with the camp in flames. The troops suffered four dead and six wounded. One Lakota and one Cheyenne warrior were killed, several others were wounded, and an old, blind woman was taken captive after being wounded. She was later left at the camp, "as nobody wanted her."[4] That night, the incompetence of Reynolds allowed the Lakota and the Cheyenne to trail the retreating column and steal back nearly all of their horses, which the colonel had decided did not require a guard.

Although Grouard's account claimed the village Reynolds attacked was that of Crazy Horse, later it was revealed to have been a Cheyenne camp under Two Moons in which a few Lakota were living. According to Short Buffalo, members of the village, which included He Dog, were traveling to join Crazy Horse a few miles down the Powder when they were attacked. Survivors of the attack retreated west to the mouth of Otter Creek on the Tongue River in search of friends. Finding none, they turned back east toward the Powder, where they found Crazy Horse's camp near Pumpkin Creek.

Comprised of no more than thirty lodges, Crazy Horse's camp did not have the resources to meet the needs of Two Moons's band. They gave what they could, and then, alarmed at what they heard, struck their lodges and joined the refugees. "This is it," Crazy Horse said. "The Grandfather's young men have been trained to the warpath. For the last few years (I have heard) he has been trying to get them to stop fighting and give up their guns and horses and follow the plow. But these white soldiers would rather shoot than work. The Grandfather cannot control his young men, and you see the results."[5]

Freezing and hungry, the people of Two Moons and Crazy Horse pushed on sixty miles down the Powder to the camp of Sitting Bull at Chalk Butte. There they were welcomed with pots of meat, warm clothing, robes, blankets, cooking utensils, even horses and tipis. "Oh, what good hearts they had!" Wooden Leg recalled. "I never can forget the generosity of Sitting Bull's Uncpapa [Hunkpapa] Sioux on that day."[6]

Reynolds's attack on Two Moons's camp had stunned the Powder River bands. Despite the government's ultimatum, they had never expected the army to attack. They thought they were at peace with the whites. If it had not been for Reynolds, Short Buffalo said, "we would have come in to the agency that spring, and there would have been no Sioux war."[7] Short Buffalo made his comments fifty-four years after the fact, which probably added a softening element. Nevertheless, by the spring of 1876 most Lakota realized that their old way of life was rapidly passing and concluded that they must accept white ways.

As Short Buffalo noted, Reynolds's attack "was the turning point of the situation" for the free-living bands.[8] It aroused them and brought talk of revenge. Chiefs previously favoring peace began to encourage their young men to raid trading posts to obtain the arms and ammunition for war against the whites. In Sitting Bull's camp, the chiefs gathered to decide on a course of action. "At this great council, such as I have only seen once, all agreed to stay together and fight," Two Moons said.[9] Meanwhile, Lieutenant John Gregory Bourke, an aide to General Crook, observed in his diary: "We are now on the eve of the bitterest Indian war the Government has ever been called upon to wage."[10]

DESPITE THE IMAGE of bloodthirsty Indian hordes promoted by westerners, in the spring of 1876 the number of Lakota and Cheyenne who were part of the free-living bands that rarely, if ever, visited an agency did not exceed 3,400 people, of whom maybe 1,000 were warriors. With more than 150 lodges, Sitting Bull's Hunkpapa were the most numerous, followed by about 100 lodges of Cheyenne, 70 of Oglala, 55 of Miniconjou, 55 of Sans Arc, a few Brulé, a few Blackfeet, and a scattering of other Lakota and Dakota, including survivors of the Great Sioux Uprising of 1862 in Minnesota. The major unknown for both the free-living bands and the army was how many agency Indians would join Crazy Horse and Sitting Bull along the Yellowstone and Powder once the spring grasses were high enough to feed their pony herds.[11]

Throughout April and May, members of the free-living bands who had scattered into small camps during the winter gathered. By mid-April the bands had about 360 lodges, by mid-May about 430 lodges, and by early June about 460 lodges housing roughly 3,000 people, among them possibly 800 warriors. In search of buffalo, the bands during the spring moved west across the Powder and the Tongue to lower Rosebud Creek. Along the way they picked up a few agency Indians who had come north to hunt. Since it was not until late May that the grass had grown green enough to allow normal travel, however, as late as mid-June the number of agency Indians who had joined the free-living bands was tiny.

Shortly before the move to the Rosebud, word arrived through a small band of probably Yankton Dakota of soldiers approaching from the northeast. The troops were those of Colonel Custer. On the Rose-

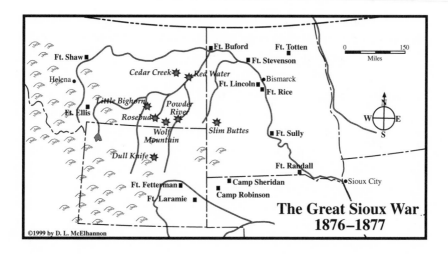

The Great Sioux War 1876–1877

©1999 by D. L. McElhannon

bud, Short Buffalo said, the Lakota soon were joined by Cheyenne from the south who reported soldiers with "a lot of Crows and Shoshonis" massing at Fort Laramie and "coming north to capture all the Sioux."[12] The two columns were part of a three-pronged movement designed to trap the free-living Lakota and Cheyenne on the buffalo range of southeastern Montana. It called for troops under Custer and General Terry to move on the Indians from the east, while General Crook's forces approached from the south and Colonel John Gibbon's command moved east down the Yellowstone from Bozeman.

Despite what had happened to Two Moons's people and the many boasts of revenge made after the Powder River attack, members of the free-living bands avoided contact with the army until the night of May 2, when about fifty warriors made off with horses belonging to the Crow scouts of Gibbon's command. The ponies had been picketed on an island in the Yellowstone opposite the mouth of the Big Horn. Then, at the beginning of June, a Cheyenne hunting party spotted soldiers on the headwaters of the Tongue and rode back to alert the camp on the Rosebud. Planning to steal the soldiers' horses, another party of Cheyenne, probably numbering no more than a dozen men, rode up the Tongue on June 9 to stampede the soldiers' horses. They failed, but so frightened the troops that their officers reported being attacked by Crazy Horse at the head of fifty to nine hundred warriors.[13]

Although very minor in terms of effect, the encounters with the soldiers along the Yellowstone and the upper Tongue told Crazy Horse and other leaders of the Rosebud camp that the attack on Two Moons's people was not an isolated event and that the army was intent on making war on them. The idea incensed and angered the bands and made them want to fight the whites. With so many of the free-living Lakota and Cheyenne gathered along the Rosebud, they also felt stronger than ever before and confident of victory if they should be attacked. "We supposed that the combined camps would frighten off the soldiers," Wooden Leg recalled. "We hoped thus to be freed from their annoyance. Then we could separate again into the tribal bands and resume our quiet wandering and hunting."[14]

BACKED BY CRAZY HORSE, Sitting Bull during the early spring of 1875 assumed the lead role among the free-living bands. Fed by the anger and confidence of his people, between May 21 and May 24, 1876, he climbed a butte above the Rosebud camp about seven miles above the stream's mouth to commune with Wakan Tanka. Seated on a rock, he prayed and meditated until he fell asleep. In the dream that followed he saw a great dust storm stirred by heavy winds approaching from the east. Drifting quietly to the west was a white cloud resembling an Indian village at the base of snowcapped mountains. As the storm neared the cloud, he could see line after line of soldiers with weapons gleaming in the sun. The storm crashed into the cloud. Thunder roared, lightning flashed, and great sheets of rain fell. Then the storm died, leaving the cloud intact until it drifted out of sight.

Returning to camp, Sitting Bull summoned the other chiefs and described his dream. He told them the storm was the soldiers and the cloud the Lakota and the Cheyenne. The soldiers were coming to wipe out their village, but would fail. The Lakota and the Cheyenne would win a great victory. Then he instructed the chiefs to send out scouts to watch for an army coming from the east.[15]

Soon afterward the camp moved up the Rosebud to the mouth of Greenleaf Creek, where Sitting Bull summoned White Bull, Jumping Bull, and a son of Black Moon. He asked the young warriors to accompany him to a nearby hilltop and listen to his prayer. After smoking with the young men, Sitting Bull rose, faced the sun, and started to pray:

> Wakan Tanka, save me and give me all my wild game animals and have them close enough so my people will have enough food this winter, and also the good men on earth will have more power so their tribes get along better and be of good nature so all the Sioux nations get along well. If you do this for me I will sun dance two days and two nights and will give you a whole buffalo.[16]

As he had promised, Sitting Bull called for a sun dance after the village moved up the Rosebud forty-five miles from its mouth on June 4. According to Standing Bear, members of every band came to dance. Crazy Horse, however, was not among them. He never took part in a sun dance. The dance began early the first morning, with a camp crier summoning the dancers: "Brave men, be ready, for your time has come. It is your time to do your duty now to send voices up to the Great Spirit. The religion we have now at will [sic] and we shall go forth and pray and repent."[17]

For two days the sun dance continued, affording Sitting Bull an opportunity to fulfill another vow. This one was to give flesh to Wakan Tanka. After purifying himself in a sweat lodge, Sitting Bull entered the dance circle, performed a pipe ceremony, and then sat down with his back against the dance pole. With White Bull seated nearby, Jumping Bull came forward, knelt down, and, with an awl, began to remove fifty bits of skin about the size of matchheads from each of Sitting Bull's arms. For a half hour the sacrifice went on while Sitting Bull cried out his supplication and the blood flowed freely onto the ground around him.

After the sacrifice, Sitting Bull began to dance, as he had vowed in his prayer. For many hours he danced around the pole while gazing at the sun, and then suddenly stopped and stood immobile, staring into the sun. Slowly his people gathered around him and gently eased him to the ground. Some sprinkled water on him. Eventually he opened his eyes to tell Black Moon what he had seen. A voice had told him to look just below the sun. There he saw soldiers and horses as numerous as grasshoppers riding down on an Indian village. They came upside down, their feet pointed toward the sky, their heads toward the earth, with hats falling off. A few Indians, too, were upside down. "These soldiers do not possess ears," the voice told him. "They are to die, but you are not supposed to take their spoils."[18]

Sitting Bull's vision told the Lakota and the Cheyenne that the soldiers were coming. They would attack their village and try to kill them. The Indians would win a great victory and kill all of the soldiers. Some of the Indians, those riding upside down, also would be killed. The Lakota and the Cheyenne, though, would win a great victory. But they must listen to the voice and not plunder the bodies of the soldiers. With troops coming from the north and the south, everybody knew the day could not be far off when soldiers would fall upside down into their camp.

FOLLOWING THE SUN DANCE, the Lakota and the Cheyenne broke camp and moved twelve miles up Rosebud Creek to a site near the mouth of Muddy Creek. For three rainy days, until June 12, they stayed at the location, and then moved another dozen miles to Davis Creek and the divide between the Rosebud and the Greasy Grass, known to the whites as the Little Big Horn. Trailing the buffalo, the chiefs decided to cross the divide to the Greasy Grass. On June 15 the women packed their lodges and the camp began moving west, toward the river.

From that night's camp, the Cheyenne sent out a scouting party of five warriors under Little Hawk. The next day the scouts found a herd of buffalo and killed a bull. They were cooking the meat when a herd of buffalo cows was spotted grazing nearby. Cow meat being more tender than the meat of a bull, they decided to leave Crooked Nose behind with the fire while they went off to kill a cow. As they were departing, however, they looked back to see Crooked Nose signaling them to return. When they reached Crooked Nose, he pointed to a hill and told them that he had seen two men looking over it.

Assuming that the men were Lakota scouts, as a joke Little Hawk suggested slipping around the hill and scaring them. The Cheyenne rode up a gully to the hill where the men had been spotted, and then Little Hawk dismounted and crept to the top, where he suddenly was confronted with a mass of troops, "as if the whole earth were black with soldiers."[19] The troops were those of General Crook, known to the Indians as "Three Stars," and were heading toward the Rosebud.

They numbered more than 1,000 and had with them more than 250 Crow and Shoshone warriors hungry for a fight with the Lakota that they felt certain of winning. Hastily, Little Hawk and the others retreated across the divide between the Rosebud and the Greasy Grass to find their people erecting lodges along Reno Creek. Howling at the top of their lungs, they raced through one camp circle after another, telling what they had seen on the Rosebud.

"Get all the young men ready and let us set out!" Little Hawk shouted.[20]

Fearful of another attack such as had destroyed Two Moons's village, many of the women began dismantling their lodges, while the young men painted and dressed themselves for battle, and the chiefs counciled. Soon the decision of the chiefs was announced by a crier: "Young men, leave the soldiers alone unless they attack us."[21] But it was too late. Wooden Leg recalled: "As darkness came on we slipped away. Many bands of Cheyenne and Sioux young men, with some older ones, rode out up the south fork [of Reno Creek] toward the head of the Rosebud. Warriors came from every camp circle."[22] About five hundred warriors rode off into the darkness. Unable to hold back the tide, Crazy Horse and Sitting Bull joined the throng. As the sun rose on the morning of June 17, 1876, they found themselves staring down on Crook's command camped along the big bend of Rosebud Creek.

COLD AND FOG made sleep difficult for Crook's men on the night the Indian force approached their camp. At about 3:00 A.M. the troops began to stir and build fires to brew coffee. As they saddled and loaded their horses and mules, Crook sent the white scouts to hurry the Crow and the Shoshone, who were just beginning breakfast. Aware of the power of the Lakota and the Cheyenne, the Crow and the Shoshone had stopped the joking and the singing that had earlier characterized their behavior. "It is evident that both tribes had a very wholesome respect for Sioux prowess," noted *Chicago Times* writer John F. Finerty, who was accompanying Crook's troops.[23]

At 6:00 A.M. the order was given to march. Two hours later, the troops halted to rest. Even though they were deep in "hostile" territory, no one bothered to put out a guard. But years of battling the

Lakota had taught the Crow and the Shoshone better. They sensed a fight coming. As Crook played whist and the troops unsaddled, built fires, and stretched out on the grass, the Indians rode down the valley to the north, where they quickly ran into a force of about a thousand Lakota and Cheyenne. In the fighting that followed, the Crow and the Shoshone managed to hold off the Lakota and Cheyenne warriors while the soldiers scrambled to form a battle line and counterattack.

Through the morning and well into the afternoon, the Battle of the Rosebud raged in a confusing melee of charges and countercharges. "Until the sun went far toward the west there were charges back and forth," Wooden Leg recalled. "Our Indians fought and ran away, fought and ran away. The soldiers and their Indian scouts did the same. Sometimes we chased them, sometimes they chased us."[24] Short Buffalo remembered:

> In the Rosebud fight the soldiers first got the Sioux and Cheyennes on the run. Crazy Horse, Bad Heart Bull, Black Deer, Kicking Bear, and Good Weasel rallied the Sioux, turned the charge, and got the soldiers on the run. . . . When these five commenced to rally their men, that was as far as the soldiers got. . . . Crazy Horse used good judgement in this Rosebud fight.[25]

Numerous writers have placed Crazy Horse at the head of a Lakota and Cheyenne force of fifteen hundred to four thousand warriors. As reflected in Short Buffalo's account, however, primary Indian sources do not ascribe such a role to him. Black Elk reported that "Crazy Horse whipped" Crook and sent him scurrying back to his base camp at Goose Creek near Sheridan, Wyoming. But Black Elk was a boy at the time and did not take part in the battle. Neither Iron Hawk nor White Bull, both of whom did fight at the Rosebud, mention anything of Crazy Horse's role as leader, which seems odd if he had been in charge of the Indian forces.

Given the independent manner in which the Lakota fought, it also is impossible to believe that the entire force would have followed Crazy Horse. They never had in the past. But, as is evident by Short Buffalo's remark, Crazy Horse did play a key role in stopping Crook's first charge. What happened before or after is impossible to determine. After Crazy Horse surrendered in the spring of 1877, he supposedly told a reporter for the *Chicago Tribune* that he had planned to draw Crook into a trap. He had often employed such a tactic in the past, and the numerous side draws that characterize the Rosebud battlefield were ideal for such a move, which probably had been his plan. The confused nature of the fight and the ingrained reluctance of the Indians to fight as a unit, however, prevented it from being realized.

As the sun slipped low in the west, the Lakota and the Cheyenne called off the fight and started back for their camp on Reno Creek. They were exhausted and hungry after their night ride and a long day of fighting. The Lakota lost twenty warriors, most to the Crow and the Shoshone, and the Cheyenne one. Both tribes also suffered many wounded. Crook lost nine soldiers, and the Crow and the Shoshone one man each. Twenty-three soldiers and seven Indian scouts also were wounded. Although he would proclaim victory in his report on the battle, Crook the next morning retreated to a camp he had left at the head of the Tongue, and then south to Goose Creek, where his men would spend most of their time over the next six weeks fishing for trout.

While Crook claimed victory, the Lakota and the Cheyenne were sure they had won. They had taken on a force at least twice their number, fought it to a standstill, and forced it to retreat. After burying their dead, they stopped to hold a feast before returning to their village, where they were greeted as victors. Then the next morning, June 18, the village moved down Reno Creek and into the valley of the Greasy Grass, where the people staged a celebration to honor their heroes. For the next six days the victors danced, feasted, and related stories of the battle while Indians from the agencies arrived to join them. By the end of the celebration the village had grown from 450 lodges housing 3,000 people and 800 warriors to roughly 1,000 lodges of 7,000 people and 1,800 warriors. Since the Battle of the Little Big Horn, white apologists have sought to justify Custer's defeat by portraying the village he attacked as immense. While certainly large, it was no more enormous than other Indian villages that periodically sprung up on the plains. Custer may even have attacked a larger village in November 1868 on the Washita River in Oklahoma.[26]

But the fight on the Rosebud was not the one that Sitting Bull had seen in his vision. The soldiers had not fallen into the village. The warriors had fought them far to the east of their camp. The fight Sitting Bull had seen remained in the future. Exactly when it might occur, nobody knew. But after the Rosebud, the warriors were confident that they could defend their village. The chiefs met and agreed to move their people farther up the Greasy Grass in search of buffalo. Then scouts brought word of antelope herds to the north and west beyond the Big Horn River, and the chiefs changed their plans. On June 24, 1876, the village moved eight miles down the Greasy Grass toward the mouth of Reno Creek, a pleasant site dominated by ragged bluffs, low grass benches, and thickets of shady cotton-wood trees.

VISIT THE LITTLE BIG HORN BATTLEFIELD off Interstate Route 90 east of Hardin, Montana, and chances are good that during one of the regularly scheduled programs on the period a park ranger will note that more ink has been spilled writing about the battle than the Indians and Custer's troops spilled blood fighting it. Support for that statement can be overheard in conversations on Custer Hill, where the "last stand" took place and amateur historians continue to refight the battle, bragging that they own or have read a hundred or more books on the fight and Custer.

Fascination with the Battle of the Little Big Horn began as soon as news of the Indian victory over Custer reached white America and spoiled its Centennial celebrations. That fascination has made Crazy Horse's actions during the fight among the best-documented events of his life, second only to those surrounding his death. Unfortunately, however, most of the best-known material is based on secondary sources, fictional accounts, the desire of some Indian participants to tell entertaining stories, and the need of many whites to justify Custer's defeat at the hands of "savages" by ascribing overwhelming numbers and almost superhuman abilities to his enemies, especially Crazy Horse, whose name is so well suited to the nineteenth-century white image of a wild, bloodthirsty Indian.

Recently, writers such as John S. Gray, Gregory F. Michno, Richard G. Hardorff, and Kenneth Hammer have attempted to cut through all of the myth and moralizing that still surround the battle to present the facts as best as they can ascertain. Gray and Michno also have sought to apply modern time-motion study techniques to primary source material and archaeological evidence to provide as accurate as possible a portrait of the battle and some of its participants. Working with primary Indian sources, Michno in particular provides a comprehensive, logical analysis of the fighting from the Indian side and the actions of such prominent warriors as Gall, White Bull, Wooden Leg, Sitting Bull, and Rain In The Face. In the process he also challenges many long-held beliefs involving some of those warriors, including Crazy Horse and his famous charge up Custer Hill from the north.

Although many writers place the opening of the Battle of the Little Big Horn at about 1:00 P.M., Sitting Bull's vision of soldiers falling upside down into camp did not begin to come true until about 3:00 P.M. on Sunday, June 25, 1876. It was then that most of the Indians saw the dust cloud of troops approaching and heard the first shots being fired. Red Feather saw Crazy Horse emerging from his lodge carrying his rifle and bridle shortly before 3:30 P.M. Some secondary sources attribute Crazy Horse's slowness to the fact that he had to properly prepare himself for battle, which seems odd, since the attack already was under way. He told Red Feather only: "Our ponies aren't in yet." Aware that there was no time to waste, Red Feather answered: "Take any horse." Then he rode off to join other warriors heading for the hills to the west.[27]

Roughly ten minutes later, Gall saw Crazy Horse riding his pinto pony through the Hunkpapa camp at the upper end of the village. The Hunkpapa were under attack from Major Marcus Reno's troops. Following Crazy Horse were a large number of warriors. As the warriors rode through the camp, they could see a band of Arikara scouts fighting alongside the soldiers. Angry to see other Indians fighting for the whites, they chased off the scouts, then went after the soldiers, who had dismounted and taken cover in the trees and brush along the river. *"Daycia! Daycia!"* [Here they are!], the women called from the top of the hill as more soldiers approached from the east, heading for the Cheyenne camp at the lower end of the village.[28]

West of Reno's position in the trees, Red Feather was wondering what to do next when Crazy Horse arrived in a cloud of dust. According to Black Elk, who was present at this fight, a "great cry went up out in the dust: 'Crazy Horse is coming! Crazy Horse is coming!' Off toward the west and north they were yelling 'Hoka hey!' [i.e., Take courage!] like a big wind roaring, and making the termolo; and you could hear eagle bone whistles screaming." Iron Hawk said:

> Crazy Horse, having collected his warriors, made a dash for the soldiers in the timber and ran into them. When the warriors assembling close to the bank saw this movement and heard the yells of Crazy Horse's men they also advanced furiously with great yelling, coming down on the flank. The soldiers broke and ran in retreat, the Indians using war clubs as the principal weapon, a few using bows and arrows, most of the execution being by knocking the troopers from their horses, the Indians moving right in among them.[29]

The attack on Reno's troops was the first in which Crazy Horse was involved. With the other warriors, he chased Reno's men to the river and pinned them against the opposite bank, which was about twelve feet high and steep. As the soldiers tried to climb the bank, Crazy Horse charged into their midst, striking many with his war club and pulling others off their horses into the water, where other warriors could get at them.[30]

As the surviving troops struggled up the bank and began digging in, Crazy Horse, Red Feather, Flying Hawk, Kicking Bear, and others rode across the crest of the hill, from where they spotted more soldiers heading for the lower end of the village. Crazy Horse pointed to the soldiers and then rode down the crowded bluff, recrossed the river, and headed off to meet the new threat. "Hoka hey!" the warriors cried as they raced down the river. "It's a good day to die!"[31] It was a few minutes after 4:00 P.M. Although Crazy Horse had no way of knowing it, the troops racing to attack the lower end of the village were those of Custer.[32]

On their way to the lower village, Crazy Horse and Flying Hawk stopped to help some wounded men to the Oglala camp. Then they rode down to the Medicine Tail ford below the camp. They could see Custer's troops on a high hill above the river. Along with many other warriors, Crazy Horse crossed the Greasy Grass above Calhoun Hill and headed up Deep Coulee. As the warriors splashed across the river, Custer turned and headed up Calhoun Hill. Crazy Horse and his men continued up Deep Coulee to a spot in the rear of the soldiers. On Calhoun Hill some of the troops dismounted to make a stand, while others continued along the ridge to Custer Hill.[33]

When Gall arrived on the scene shortly after 5:00 P.M., Crazy Horse was lying in a ravine north of the troops on Calhoun Hill, firing as fast as he could load. The soldiers were on foot "and most of their horses were in the upper part of the ravine where Crazy Horse was," Gall recalled.[34] At about the same time, White Bull, who had been impatiently riding back and forth in the ravine behind the lines, rode up to Crazy Horse and suggested that the two of them make a charge to capture some of the soldiers' horses. Crazy Horse declined. He actually may have agreed to charge, but then changed his mind, since White Bull complained in a 1930 interview that he "backed out."[35]

Whether Crazy Horse declined White Bull's entreatment to charge the troops on Calhoun Hill, or agreed to charge and then changed his mind, is not a reflection of his courage at the Little Big Horn. Indeed, he would more than prove his courage a short time later. According to Red Feather, most of the Indians who charged the troops that day were young men, inexperienced and reckless. Hungry for honors, they captured most of the soldiers' guns, ammunition, and horses, but also suffered the most casualties. The older warriors, according to Red Feather, held back for safety. At age thirty-five or thirty-six, Crazy Horse would have been counted among the older, wiser warriors. White Bull was about a decade younger. That certainly did not make him one of the youngest warriors on the field, but it would have made him young enough to crave honor in battle. In a 1932 interview White Bull also contradicted his statement that Crazy Horse "backed out" when he said that the war leader ran through the "infantry," meaning the dismounted troops.[36]

Growing impatient with the slow, sniping nature of the fighting, sometime shortly before 5:30 P.M., White Bull decided to charge. Whipping his pony toward a gap in the center of the soldiers' line, he raced between two troopers, cut behind one of them, and then dashed through a gap at the end of the line. Returning to the ravine, he pulled up next to Crazy Horse and shouted: "Hoka hey, brother! This life will not last forever!" Then he announced: "This time I will not turn back."[37]

Kicking his pony into action, White Bull headed back toward the soldiers' line. Perhaps goaded by his friend's reckless courage, Crazy Horse grabbed his own pony, blew his eagle bone whistle, and charged out of the ravine. "The soldiers all fired at once, but didn't hit him," Red Feather said. "The Indians got the idea the soldiers' guns were empty and charged immediately on the soldiers. They charged right over the hill."[38] White Bull recalled: "We charged them and the Dakotas were raked with a heavy fire. Many of us were killed by this volley. This made me very mad. They [the soldiers] left their horses and fled on foot. Some did not retreat but stood their ground. We overran their position, although the soldiers kept up a heavy fire."[39]

Amid the dust and confusion, the warriors rode down the soldiers fleeing on foot and pulled others from their horses. Many warriors counted coup. White Bull saw a soldier on a tired horse turning to fire at him. He grabbed the soldier by the shoulder of his blue coat and jerked him to the ground. The carbine fired into the air as the man fell, and Crazy Horse rode up to count second coup on him.[40] "Later [Crazy Horse] ran through all [of] them," White Bull said.[41]

ONE OF THE best-known events of the Battle of the Little Big Horn is the charge out of the north with Crazy Horse at the head of a thousand warriors—the charge that ended the life of Colonel Custer. Among the earliest writers to immortalize the charge was Cyrus Townsend Brady in his 1904 book *Indian Fights and Fighters*. Typical of many white writers, Brady attempted to put the best face possible on Custer and his men. Placing Crazy Horse in a ravine on Custer's right flank and Gall in a ravine on his left flank, Brady had the two warriors, as if they were communicating by radio and in two places at once, deciding that the time had come to end the battle, and then somehow charging out of the same ravine to simultaneously attack both flanks while other warriors hit the front of the troops. "Massing their warriors in the ravine," he wrote, "they fell on both flanks at the same time that Crow King and Rain In The Face led a direct charge against the front of the thinned and weakened line. They swept over the little band of men, probably now out of ammunition, in a red wave of destruction."[42]

The Santee Dakota Sioux Charles A. Eastman picked up the ball in his 1918 book *Indian Heroes and Great Chieftains*:

> Custer must have seen that wonderful dash up the sage-brush plain, and one wonders whether he realized its meaning. In a very few minutes, this wild general of the plains [Crazy Horse] had outwitted one of

the most brilliant leaders of the Civil War and ended at once his military career and his life. In this dashing charge, Crazy Horse snatched his most famous victory out of what seemed frightful peril, for the Sioux could not know how many were behind Custer. He was caught in his own trap. To the soldiers it must have seemed as if the Indians rose up from the earth to overwhelm them. They closed in from three sides and fought until not a white man was left alive.[43]

Mari Sandoz passed on the story in her 1942 fictionalized biography, *Crazy Horse: The Strange Man of the Oglalas,* and Stephen Ambrose in his 1972 dual biography *Crazy Horse and Custer: The Parallel Lives of Two American Warriors.* As Sandoz wrote,

With his heart singing the war song of the drums back among the helpless ones, his Winchester ready in his hand, the Oglala led his warriors through the river, around the end of the soldier ridge, and up a ravine behind it to cut off their retreat. And as he rode, more and more Indians fell in behind him, until the fresh war horse was the point of a great arrow, growing wider and longer, the dust of its moving standing in the air. They reached the head of the ravine just as the Indians from the river side pushed the soldiers to the crest of the ridge, and with a great whooping the fresh warriors charged the back of the retreating blue line, using mostly arrows, spears and clubs.[44]

Ambrose is even more dramatic and exact in his retelling:

The troopers were badly strung out. Hot, tired, dusty, thirsty, afraid, they were slowly working their way up the hill, trying meanwhile to maintain a steady volume of fire in order to hold back Gall's warriors. Just below Crazy Horse there was a small knot of men. Tom Custer was there, and Bos, and most of Custer's staff. Custer was at their head, not much more than twenty yards away from Crazy Horse. The officers were making their way to the top, probably looking in that direction, so it is possible that Crazy Horse and Custer looked into each other's eyes. If so, it was only for an instant. Crazy Horse and his men, making the air fearful with their battle cries, came sweeping down the hill. They crushed everything in their path. They swarmed among Custer's soldiers, killing them with arrows, clubs, lances, and bullets. . . . It was almost like buffalo hunting.[45]

The story of the charge is repeated in James Welch and Paul Stekler's 1994 book *Killing Custer* and in Larry McMurtry's 1999

minibiography *Crazy Horse*.[46] Examining Indian accounts of the battle in the light of terrain and time-motion issues, however, Michno
argues convincingly that Crazy Horse never made his famous charge
from the north. At the most, he believes, Crazy Horse may have
arrived on Custer Hill to confront the last of Custer's troops.[47] Flying
Hawk supports that claim when he tells of the last of Custer's men
running toward the river and being killed by the Indians who surrounded them. When Crazy Horse saw one of the soldiers running to
the east, he jumped on his horse and went after him. Flying Hawk
said the man got about a half mile from Custer Hill before Crazy
Horse brought him down. According to Flying Hawk, Custer and his
officers "were all killed before the soldiers ran for the river."[48] That
would seem to indicate that Crazy Horse arrived late on the scene.

Crazy Horse himself adds weight to the belief that he had very
little to do with Custer's "last stand" in a discussion he had with his
medicine man, Chips, a person from whom he would have had nothing to hide. During that talk, Crazy Horse focused on the fight with
Reno, not Custer. "Reno did not make much of a fight," he said.
"There was fighting with the Ree scouts; they made a charge and
killed two Indians. Reno did not make any fight of any importance."[49]

Depending on which way the political and social winds were
blowing, the story of the Battle of the Little Big Horn has been retold
in many different ways since it was fought on that dusty June afternoon in 1876. Because the Lakota and the Cheyenne came from a
preliterate culture, most of those retellings, among them almost all
early ones, have been from the white point of view and so, con-
sciously or unconsciously, have painted Custer and his men in a
more or less heroic light, bravely fighting for civilization in the face
of overwhelming numbers of savages. The earliest writers paid little
attention to the Indians and took no notice of their movements during the battle. Gradually, though, in some cases no doubt to enhance
Custer's image by enhancing the prowess of his opponents, white
writers began to paint a portrait of Crazy Horse as a supreme warrior
who instantly sized up the course of the battle and placed himself in
the perfect position to take by surprise one of the most famous officers in the history of the U.S. Army.

On the Indian side, the story of Crazy Horse's charge over Custer
Hill probably started with Gall on the tenth anniversary of the Little
Big Horn, when he told Edward S. Godfrey, who had been a lieu-

tenant at the battle, and David F. Barry, a writer and photographer, that Crazy Horse rode to the extreme northern end of the camp and "came very close to the soldiers on their north side." He said Crow King fired at the soldiers from the south, while Crazy Horse fired at them from the north.[50] But Gall probably was just telling the whites what he thought they wanted to hear. Generally affable, once Gall settled down on the Standing Rock Reservation, he often sought to ingratiate himself with the white authorities. Indian accounts of the battle fail to place Gall anywhere near Crazy Horse. Chips said: "After the Indians surrendered and got into intercourse with the whites Gall made some notable speeches and made quite a man of himself; but he was not looked upon among the Indians as a warrior at all."[51]

Although Crazy Horse most likely never made the legendary charge from the north that ended Custer's life, Indian accounts of the battle clearly reveal his bravery and the important role he played in pushing back Reno's troops and in overrunning the soldiers on Calhoun Hill. Except on the printed page or in the movies, he also probably never was aware of Custer's presence on the field. The idea that the two men stared into each other's eyes is absurd. Like Gall, Rain In The Face told many stories about the Battle of the Little Big Horn, but two months before his death confessed: "In that fight the excitement was so great that we scarcely recognized our nearest friends."[52]

25

KILLING LONG HAIR

As RENO AND HIS MEN, reinforced during the battle by three companies under Captain Frederick Benteen, lay dug in on a bluff above the Greasy Grass, the Indians danced and celebrated through the night. Then in the morning a party went out to relieve the warriors who had kept the soldiers from fleeing during the night. "We went up the back of the hill, where some of our men were, and looked over," Black Elk recalled. "We could not see the Wasichus, who were lying in their dug-ins, but we saw the horses and pack mules, and many were dead."[1] Though no record exists, it would seem certain that Crazy Horse at some time would have been among the warriors who were firing at Reno and Benteen's troops.

Throughout the day of June 26, 1876, the Indians kept up a harassing fire on Reno's camp. Then word arrived from scouts that more soldiers were making their way upriver. Hurriedly, the women packed the lodges, and then the camp started up the Greasy Grass. They traveled all night until they reached a dry creek, where they stopped to camp to have a feast. Then the next day they moved to Wood Louse Creek in the Big Horn Mountains. That evening, camp members were shocked to see soldiers riding abreast toward them. They turned out to be warriors dressed in the soldiers' clothes. The people built fires and danced and sang all night:

Long Hair has never returned, so his woman is crying, crying. Looking over here, she cries. Long Hair, guns I had none. You brought me many. I thank you! You make me laugh! Long Hair, horses I had none. You brought me many. I thank you! You make me laugh! Long Hair, where he lies nobody knows. Crying, they seek him. He lies over here. Let go your holy irons [guns]. You are not men enough to do any harm. Let go your holy irons![2]

For about a month, the victorious Lakota stayed near the Big Horn Mountains, watching for the soldiers. When troops failed to appear, a few people drifted back to their agencies, and the village moved onto Rosebud Creek near where the big sun dance had been held. From there, the village moved to the Tongue River and then across the divide to Mizpah Creek and the Powder River. As July drifted into August, word arrived that the soldiers again were coming. The Cheyenne broke off from the village and headed back to the Big Horns, while more Lakota started back for the agencies and others scattered up the Powder, the Missouri, and the Little Missouri. Among the bands that headed for the Little Missouri was that of Crazy Horse.

"The soldiers of Three Stars followed us," Black Elk said. "Our people set fire to the grass behind us as we went, and the smoke back there was wide as the day and the light of the fire was as wide as the night. This was to make the soldiers' horses starve. Then it began to rain, and it kept on raining for days while we traveled east. Our ponies had to work hard in the deep mud, and it must have been bad for the soldiers' horses back there with nothing to eat."

Chicago Times correspondent Finerty wrote of the effect of the weather and the fires on Crook's troops in the September 22, 1876, edition of the paper: "That night it blew great guns. It was our last chance under canvas for some time, and Old Boreas determined that we shouldn't enjoy it. Three-fourths of the tents were blown down, and so terrible were the clouds of dust and smoke blown from the burning prairies and wooded hills that suffocation was imminent with those who had the philosophy, or the necessary weariness, to sleep."

NEWS OF THE INDIAN VICTORY at Greasy Grass first reached the white public through an extra of the *Bozeman Times* dated July 3, 1876. The story was based on a dispatch sent from the scene by General Gibbon, who had reached the battlefield on June 28. "General

Custer's command met with a terrible disaster here on the 25th," Gibbon wrote. "Custer, with five companies, were so far as we can ascertain, completely annihilated except for two Crow scouts. . . . Roughly stated the loss of Custer's command is about one-half, say 250 men." Gibbon estimated the Indian force involved at 1,800 to 2,500 warriors. Not satisfied with reporting the facts from the scene, the *Times* started the nation down the long road of myth that continues to surround the battle by upping the number of killed to 315 and the size of the Indian force to between 2,500 and 4,000. Although nobody from the *Times* was near the scene, the paper also described the battlefield as a "slaughter pen."[3]

By the next day, as the nation celebrated the Centennial of the Declaration of Independence, news of the battle had been picked up by the *Helena Daily Herald* and, through the Associated Press wire service, newspapers in the East and as far west as Salt Lake City and San Diego. The most complete early account, the famous *Bismarck Tribune* story that frequently has been touted as the first to report of the Custer "massacre" by "red devils," did not appear until July 6.

Over the few next weeks, news of the battle spread across the nation, inspiring calls for revenge and immediately turning the event into a political football. "Killing a mess of Indians is the only recreation our frontier rangers want," announced the *Dallas Daily Herald.* "Texas deserves the honor of attempting to wipe out the Sioux," the *Austin Daily State Gazette* proclaimed. "In every case where an inoffensive citizen is slain, let 100 of these red brutes feel the power of a rope properly adjusted under their chins," wrote a *Chicago Tribune* reader. Closer to the scene, the *Black Hills Pioneer* noted: "There is but one sentiment on the Indian question here—the hostile Sioux should be exterminated."[4]

Democrats and the southern press, still smarting from the reconstruction policies of the Republicans, used Custer's death as an opportunity to attack the Grant administration. The "tragic events" on the Little Big Horn, stated the *Charleston Journal of Commerce*, were "hardly more than the logical results of the scandalous mismanagement of the army by our military President and the infamous frauds, peculation and inefficiency which flourished in the Indian Bureau." The *Richmond State* noted: "War with the Sioux is directly traceable to the Indian Bureau, and that Bureau is directly controlled by Mr. Grant and his personal friends." The *Wilmington* (N.C.) *Daily Journal* noted that the only reason the Republicans were interested in the Negro and not the Indian was because "the one could be made a voter, the other could not."[5]

As always amid the mass cacophony of the moment, though, a handful of reflective voices could be heard. The *New York Times*, in a July 12, 1876, editorial, said: "We must beat the Sioux, but we need not exterminate them." Chicago minister D. J. Burrell asked who should be held responsible for Custer's death: "The history of our dealings with these Indian tribes from the very beginning is a record of fraud, and perjury, and uninterrupted injustice. We have made treaties, binding ourselves to the most solemn promises in the name of God, intending at that very time to hold these treaties light as air whenever our conveniences should require them to be broken." Across the Atlantic *The Times* of London envisioned the Indians being exterminated and those who survived being driven to more distant and barren reservations. "The conduct of the American Government towards the Indians of the Plains has been neither very kindly nor very wise," it noted.[6]

ALTHOUGH THE ARMY, government officials, and whites living on the plains certainly knew about Crazy Horse before the Little Big Horn, his desire to avoid whites and his refusal to attend treaty councils generally kept his name out of the newspapers until early 1876. Even then, Sitting Bull garnered more press. In the *Omaha Bee*, for instance, a story appeared on September 9, 1875, in which it was reported that "about half of Sitting Bull's wild Indians have agreed to make a treaty." The September 13 edition of the paper announced that "runners have just arrived from the camp of Sitting Bull, who is recognized as chief of all the wild Indian bands." Stories in which Sitting Bull played a role also appeared in the February 7, March 1, May 5, May 9, May 13, and June 10, 1876, editions of the *Bee*.

In contrast, the *Bee* often treated Crazy Horse as junior partner in "Sitting Bull, Crazy Horse and Company." The paper makes no mention of Crazy Horse until its February 2, 1876, edition. Writing from the Black Hills, former Omaha marshal W. G. Hollins noted that Crazy Horse was camped on the Powder River.

Crazy Horse's name began to appear more prominently in the *Bee* after Reynolds's attack on Two Moons's camp on March 17. Based on Grouard's mistaken belief that the camp he led Reynolds to was that of Crazy Horse, the Omaha newspaper reported on March 27 that "General Crook has a Fight with Crazy Horse." The paper attributed the attack to Crook because he was Reynolds's commanding officer. It reported that Crook "had a fight with Crazy Horse and completely annihilated his force of about 500 men after a five hours fight." The story noted that four soldiers were killed and eight wounded, and concluded: "What Indians are not killed must starve, as all their provision stock and equipage was destroyed."

"Crazy Horse's Revenge," a story published in the May 15 edition of the *Bee*, appears to be among the earliest in which the war leader drew more than passing notice. It must be viewed critically, however, because of the insight it provides into Crazy Horse's thoughts, something even his best friends were privy to only on occasion. The story may be more a reflection of the correspondent's imagination than reality, but it is among the first to portray Crazy Horse as a legendary warrior. According to the story, after the survivors of the attack made their way to Crazy Horse's camp, "he told his people that he never made war on the white man's ground, but that he would now strike a blow that would be remembered by those who wanted his country to destroy what little was left to his people whose great misfortune seems to be their color. After Crazy Horse left his camp, he went to Red Canyon, where he attacked emigrants, and killed a party of one white woman and one colored woman and some men. The ball then commenced and is still rolling with but little hope of stopping, and all this done by one man."

Even after the Little Big Horn, Sitting Bull seems to have been the main focus of the white press. The weekly *Black Hills Pioneer*, which picked up stories from across the nation, confidently reported on July 22 that Crazy Horse was among the dead at the Little Big Horn. It identified Crazy Horse and Black Moon as two of the principal hostile chiefs. "The latter is first," the story noted, "Crazy Horse is second, and Sitting Bull third in rank and influence." In a July 22 special from Bismarck, the *St. Paul Pioneer-Press and Tribune* also reported Crazy Horse dead.

By August, though, Sitting Bull was dominating reports coming into the *Pioneer* office. The August 5 edition carried a story from the

Pioneer-Press in which Sitting Bull played a prominent role and another from the *St. Louis Globe-Democrat* that included a short profile of the Lakota leader. "His countenance is of an extremely savage type," the story reports, "betraying that bloodthirstiness and brutality for which he has been so long notorious. He has the name of being one of the most successful scalpers in the Indian country. There has been a standing reward of $1,000 offered for his head for the last eight years by the Montana people, who have special cause to know his ferocious nature, some of his worst deeds having been perpetrated in that territory."

Through the remainder of the summer and into the winter of 1876–1877, Sitting Bull's name repeatedly appeared in the *Pioneer.* Next to advertisements for the General Custer House, a new Deadwood hotel opened to take advantage of the publicity surrounding the Little Big Horn, stories by the *Pioneer* and other newspapers reported Sitting Bull in Montana, Wyoming, the Dakotas, Canada, and Minnesota, where one resident accused him of leading the Great Sioux Uprising of 1862. In contrast, Crazy Horse is mentioned in only a few stories immediately following the Custer fight, and then does not again appear in the newspaper until the February 17, 1877, edition, in a story titled "Another Artful Dodge of the Red-Skins." In that article Crazy Horse and his followers are said to be camped along the Tongue and about to be reinforced by Sitting Bull. The story goes on to report that the village wishes Spotted Tail would visit and bring tobacco to prove that the whites are sincere in their offer of peace. It describes Crazy Horse's people as being in a "suffering and destitute condition, and in immediate need of aid," concluding:

> That is the reason they are so anxious for peace, and they would embrace it now on almost any terms. But to the frontiersman, who has known and suffered by their treacherous ways, this is too thin, and we do not take any stock in their professions of friendship. If Mr. Spotted Tail can succeed in bringing them in, then let the government or its representatives at the agency see that the proper means are taken to effectually quiet these marauders—take their arms from them, and leave them no chance to again pursue their evil course, and murder unoffending white men with impunity.

AFTER MORE THAN two months of trying, Crook's troops finally caught up to the Lakota on September 9, 1876, at Slim Buttes on Rabbit Creek in northwestern South Dakota. At dawn on that rainy day, a cavalry detachment under Lieutenant Frederick Schwatka rode headlong into the sleeping village of American Horse: "Firing with pistols into the lodges. He chased the herd through it [the camp], knocking down and trampling over some lodges."[7] At about the same time, Schwatka's commander, Captain Anso Mills, ordered dismounted cavalry on the hills above the camp to open fire on the lodges, while other troops advanced toward the camp. With the bullets sounding like hailstones on the wet skins of the lodges, the Lakota warriors returned the fire. "They fought hard there in the rain," Black Elk said, "and the soldiers killed American Horse and chased the women and children out of their homes and took all of the papa (dried bison meat) that they had made to feed themselves that winter."[8]

Most of the Lakota retreated across swollen Rabbit Creek to the underbrush along the stream and the bluffs to the south and west of the camp. From there, they kept up a harassing fire on the troops, punctuated with an occasional charge by warriors attempting to recapture some of the camp's ponies. A reinforcing troop of cavalry arrived from Crook at about 11:30 A.M., at which time the soldiers began to collect everything of value from the camp. Among the items the troops found were relics belonging to Custer's men and passes signed by Indian agents. The passes, which described their owners as peaceful, particularly incensed the soldiers, who took out their anger on a group of men, women, and children hiding in a ravine. Among them was a wounded American Horse, who surrendered amid shouts from the soldiers of "No quarter!"

Correspondent Joe Wasson, writing in the September 26, 1876, *New York Times*, described the scene in the ravine when the troops thought one of the victims was white. "'Drag him out!' 'Cut him to pieces!' 'We'll burn him alive!' 'Show him to us,'" the troops shouted. "There was no white man, however. When the body was dragged into light, it proved to be that of a squaw whitened by death. She was frightfully shot. A bullet had torn her neck away, three had gone through her breast and shoulder, and two through each limb. Her body and clothing were one mass of mud and coagulated blood." After more bodies were pulled from the ravine they were all laid out, "and the curiosity of the command . . . [was] satisfied by an inspection of an hour or so."

From the Lakota captives, all of whom were women and children, Crook's officers learned that a camp of about three hundred lodges under Crazy Horse, He Dog, and Kicking Bear was nearby. The news caused apprehension among the officers, since Indians had been seen in the distance reflecting mirrors down on the troops. The soldiers began preparing for a fight. It came at 4:15 P.M., when Crazy Horse arrived at Slim Buttes "with a band of our warriors and chased the soldiers through the rain."[9]

Mounted on swift ponies, the warriors—estimated at six hundred to eight hundred—took up positions on the hills above the troops and opened fire while the soldiers set fire to the camp. After forty-five minutes of steady fighting, the troops were able to force Crazy Horse's warriors from the hills. The Lakota kept up a steady fire from a distance of five hundred yards to eight hundred yards. The troops returned the fire, but the distance was so great that neither side suffered many casualties. After another round of fighting near evening, the Lakota withdrew, and the soldiers set up camp on the ashes of American Horse's village.

At dawn the following day the Lakota briefly resumed the fight while Crook's men packed up and pulled out. "They fled southward toward the Black Hills, and many of their horses died in the deep mud," Black Elk said. "He [Crazy Horse] followed them a long way and made them fight as they fled."[10] Crook's men finally reached the Black Hills and a supply column on September 15, 1876. Although casualties were light on both sides and the Lakota continued to harass the troops along the way, the September 19 edition of the *Black Hills Pioneer* did not hesitate to proclaim victory to a white public hungry for revenge. "This is emphatically *the* event of the campaign so far as punishment for the Indians is concerned . . ." it announced, "for without a doubt the den of redskins so thoroughly rooted out has furnished shelter for more than one of the plundering savages who have annoyed us recently." The people of Deadwood and Crook City showered the troops with food and drink.

Although unbeaten, Crazy Horse and his people found no such relief. After Slim Buttes they started west, according to Black Elk,

and we were not happy anymore, because so many of our people had untied their horses' tails [stopped fighting] and gone over to the Wasichus. We went back deep into our country, and most of the land was black from the fire, and the bison had gone away. We camped on

The ordination of Spotted Tail as chief of the Sioux by General Crook at the Red Cloud Agency, on October 24, 1876.

the Tongue River where there was some cottonwood for the ponies; and a hard winter came on early. It snowed much; game was hard to find, and it was a hungry time for us. Ponies died, and we ate them. They died because the snow froze hard and they could not find grass that was left in the valleys and there was not enough cottonwood to feed them all. There had been thousands of us together that summer, but there were not two thousand now.[11]

In November, news reached Crazy Horse's camp that the Black Hills and the Big Horn country west of the hills had been sold to the whites by the agency chiefs in September after Congress refused to supply them with the food promised by treaty. Then on November 25, 1876, soldiers struck the Cheyenne Dull Knife's sleeping camp along the Red Fork of the Powder River in Wyoming. As with Two Moons's camp on the Powder and American Horse's camp at Slim Buttes, the soldiers fired into the lodges, and the people fled into the surrounding underbrush and hills as the warriors fought a holding action.

Freezing, starving, and nearly naked, survivors of Dull Knife's camp stumbled into Crazy Horse's village, looking for help. Some sources have reported that Crazy Horse turned away the Cheyenne. But Black Elk, who was part of Crazy Horse's camp, disputes that claim. He said the Lakota, who were hard pressed themselves, gave the Cheyenne clothing, "but of food we could not give them much, for we were eating ponies when they died." Short Buffalo added: "We helped the Cheyennes the best we could. We hadn't much ourselves." The Cheyenne eventually left to surrender at Camp Robinson. "So we were all alone there in that country that was ours and had been stolen from us," Black Elk said.[12]

Seeing the end near, Crazy Horse began acting even "queerer" than usual. "He hardly ever stayed in camp," Black Elk said.

> People would find him out alone in the cold, and they would ask him to come home with them. He would not come, but sometimes he would tell the people what to do. People would wonder if he ate anything at all. Once my father found him out alone like that, and he said to my father: "Uncle, you have noticed me the way I act. But do not worry; there are caves and holes for me to live in, and out here the spirits may help me. I am making plans for the good of my people."[13]

The time had come to make peace.

26

PEACE

As early as October and November 1876, several halfhearted attempts were made by authorities at Camp Robinson to open up negotiations with Crazy Horse and other leaders of the free-living bands who had fought at the Little Big Horn. Riders were sent out to the Powder, Tongue, and Yellowstone to inform the "hostiles" that if they did not come in, soldiers would be sent to destroy their camps. Until freezing temperatures and deep snow made effective military operations impossible, though, the messengers were just as concerned with locating the camps and guiding troops to them as persuading the bands to surrender.[1]

The first serious attempt at peace negotiations occurred in early December, when a delegation led by Important Man and Foolish Bear set out from the Cheyenne River Agency in the Missouri River country in search of Crazy Horse's camp. The terms they carried, however, were those of unconditional surrender, not negotiation. In return for his people coming in to an agency and surrendering their ponies and guns, Important Man and Foolish Bear told Crazy Horse no one would be punished for the Custer "massacre." It was an offensive offer that held no appeal for the war leader.

Recognizing that they had no choice but starvation and death in the end, Crazy Horse and other leaders of his camp actually decided to meet with the whites to discuss peace before Important Man and Foolish Bear appeared with their offer. On December 16, 1876, a delegation rode north from the camp to the mouth of the Tongue River and the cantonment of Colonel Nelson A. Miles, known to the Indians as "Bear Coat" for his manner of winter dress. As the peace-talkers neared Miles's camp, they sent out an advance party that included Gets Fat With Beef, Red Shirt, Hollow Horn, Drum On His Back, and another man. Drum On His Back was so well known to the whites that President Grant in 1875 presented him with an engraved rifle in recognition of his friendship to the United States.

Bearing two white flags of truce, the five men rode ahead of the main body of twenty to thirty Lakota and Cheyenne. To reach Miles's headquarters they had to ride through a camp of Crow scouts. As they entered the camp they were surrounded and attacked by the Crow. Miles wrote in a report to General Sheridan:

> The act was an unprovoked cowardly murder. The Crows approached them in a friendly manner, said "How!" shook hands with them, and when they were within their power and partly behind a large woodpile, killed them in a most brutal manner. . . . The only thing that can be said in defense of the Crows is that a false report was made by one of the Crow women that the Sioux had fired upon her, and that within the last few months some of their number had lost relatives killed by the Sioux in the vicinity of the Rosebud.[2]

Black Elk said of the incident:

> They went into the Crow camp and they had come as friends but the Crows surrounded them and seized them. Just before this Crazy Horse had whipped the Crows and killed one of the Crow women. This husband of the woman was there and he took out his pistol and killed Gets Fat With Beef as a revenge. There was hand-to-hand fight here. The three [four remaining] delegates tried to get away to the soldiers' camp, but they were all killed while fighting.[3]

Miles had warned the Crow the day before that they were not to attack any messengers from the Lakota. His men rushed into the Crow camp upon hearing the first shots, but it was too late. In the confusion that followed the killings, the guilty Crow jumped on their ponies and fled to their agency along the Big Horn. Furious, Miles ordered his men to disarm the remaining Crow and confiscate twelve of their horses and other personal items. The horses and other goods were sent to the Lakota, along with a letter assuring them that no white man had any part in the affair. But it was too late. Crazy Horse and others who favored continued resistance used the incident to prove that whites could not be trusted. On December 26 they sent out a raiding party that drove off about 250 head of stock. "They stole cattle and butchered them from the soldiers and this is what started the battle," Black Elk said. "Butchering of the soldiers' cattle was what started General Miles to coming down to fight them."[4]

Knowing that Miles's soldiers would be coming, and without any place "better to go," Crazy Horse prepared to fight by moving his camp to more advantageous terrain farther up the Tongue. Several days earlier, on about December 22, Important Man and Foolish Bear had found the camp. But the two peace-talkers could not have arrived at a worse time. The killing of the Lakota by the Crow had left the resisters in control of the camp. "We had a council and we checked the ones who wanted to go out to meet the soldiers . . ." Black Elk said. "Then we proceeded and went on the warpath."[5]

Before going to war, Crazy Horse and the other camp leaders agreed to send word to Miles that they had not started the war in which the two sides were engaged, but were determined to continue fighting as long as they possessed the means to resist. Not wanting to alert the army to his plans, Crazy Horse also warned Important Man and Foolish Bear that no one from the camp would be allowed to go back with them to the Cheyenne River Agency. When several small groups attempted to leave, Crazy Horse and the camp *akicita* (police) stopped them, killed their horses, and took away their guns.[6]

Crazy Horse and Dull Knife led the war party sent down the Tongue against Miles. The two sides fought a series of minor skirmishes on January 1, January 3, January 6, and January 7, 1877. Shortly before the January 7 skirmish, Miles's scouts captured four Cheyenne women and three children who had been visiting on the Belle Fourche River north of the Black Hills and were returning to their people on the Tongue. The women refused to answer questions from the officers, but that did not matter. Soon after their capture, scouts returned to inform Miles that Crazy Horse's main camp was just seventeen miles upriver.

Believing that the warriors would never allow his troops to get any closer to their village, Miles felt certain that the Lakota and the Cheyenne would attack the next day. His feeling became reality the following morning. While his men struggled to warm themselves and prepare breakfast in a foot of new snow, a voice called down in Lakota from the bluffs above: "You have eaten your last breakfast!"[7] Scouts who understood the Lakota language answered by calling the warriors women who would not put up much of a fight. Then Miles

MONTANA TERRITORY.—THE SIOUX CAMPAIGN.—THE BATTLE OF WOLF MOUNTAINS, JANUARY 8TH, BETWEEN THE COMMAND OF GENERAL MILES AND THE CONFEDERATE BANDS OF INDIANS UNDER CRAZY HORSE.—SKETCHED BY AN OFFICER OF THE EXPEDITION

The Battle of Wolf Mountains, January 8, 1877. From *Frank Leslie's Illustrated Newspaper*, May 6, 1877.

ordered his two cannons turned toward the heights as a mounted party of Indians opened fire from across the river.

Typical of fights between the plains tribes and the army, the Battle Butte Fight or Battle of Wolf Mountains on January 8, 1877, involved a series of individual actions by the Indians and tactical moves by the troops. Black Elk said the soldiers

> began shooting with the wagon guns that shot twice, because the iron balls went off after they fell. . . . Then the walking soldiers started up the bluff, and it began to snow hard and they fought in the blizzard. We could not stop the soldiers coming up, because we had not much ammunition. The soldiers had everything. But our men used spears and guns for clubs when the soldiers got there, and they fought hand to hand awhile, holding the soldiers back until the women could break camp and get away with the children and ponies.[8]

ALTHOUGH THE BATTLE BUTTE FIGHT pitted roughly 450 soldiers against 600 Lakota and Cheyenne warriors, casualties were light on both sides. The troops suffered 2 killed and 7 wounded. The Cheyenne lost 1 warrior and the Lakota lost 2. Nobody knows how many of the Indians were wounded. In the blizzard that began falling in the later stages of the fight, the Lakota and the Cheyenne fled back up the Tongue, and then over to the Little Powder. Some accounts have Miles's troops pursuing the retreating Indians for several miles, but that seems unlikely in a blizzard. After the weather broke, Miles started back for his base camp at the mouth of the Tongue. He arrived there on January 18.

"We got away," Black Elk remembered, "but we lost many things we needed, and when we camped on the Little Powder, we were almost as poor as Dull Knife's people were the day they came to us. It was so cold that the sun made himself fires, and we were eating our starving ponies."9

The suffering of the women and children, and the failure of the war party to defeat Miles, again stirred talk of surrender in Crazy Horse's camp. Those in favor of peace argued that it would be better to talk to the whites now than wait for them to send more soldiers. What had happened at Battle Butte showed that the soldiers were ready to fight, even in a blizzard. They would never give up. Then Sitting Bull appeared in the camp to announce that he was taking his people north to the Land of the "Grandmother," Queen Victoria. The news stunned those who wished to continue their resistance. Sitting Bull's dislike of the whites was as strong as that of Crazy Horse.

With less and less buffalo and other game available in the Tongue Valley, the camp that had hung together since the Slim Buttes fight began to break up during the last week of January 1877. Crazy Horse's Oglala and most of the Cheyenne moved west to the Little Big Horn, scene of their greatest triumph just six months earlier. The Miniconjou and the Sans Arc divided into small camps and moved to the Little Missouri, while others gave up altogether and headed for the Red Cloud, Spotted Tail, and Cheyenne River agencies, where they reported the sufferings of their people and the desire of many for peace.

Spurred by the news coming out of the "hostile" camps, white authorities moved to take advantage of the situation. Crazy Horse's uncle, Spotted Tail, was approached to travel to his nephew's camp with an offer of peace. Since the offer was the army's usual call for unconditional surrender, however, Spotted Tail balked. Instead, the army sent a delegation of about thirty Oglala under Sword. Their message was received favorably by a portion of Crazy Horse's camp, but many others felt they had nothing new to offer. Then, on February 9, two runners from the northern camps arrived at Camp Robinson to report many people willing to make peace, but only if Spotted Tail would come to them as a representative of General Crook. If Spotted Tail came with tobacco, it would be proof of Crook's sincerity and they would come in to the agencies. Interpreter Garnett said:

> According to the Sioux custom, packages of tobacco [were] wrapped in blue cloth and some in red cloth, a package [was] to be given to the chief of each band in Crazy Horse's camp. If these packages were opened the act was an acceptance of the proposition which the bearers announced as the object of their business; if they were returned unopened it was rejected. If the packages were opened, the tobacco was cut into small pieces and given around to the members of the band. If a chief had control over his band he could decide alone what to do; if he was afraid of opposition and did not wish to take the responsibility for a decision he assembled tribal leaders and submitted the proposition for ratification or rejection.[10]

ON FEBRUARY 13, Spotted Tail left Camp Sheridan near his agency in western Nebraska with a party of about two hundred warriors, several white men, and a pack train of mules loaded with gifts. The large number of warriors was designed to impress the "hostiles" with the seriousness of Crook's desire for peace, but not everyone was impressed. Spotted Tail, Black Elk said,

> was a great chief and a great warrior before he went over to the Wasichus. I saw him and I did not like him. He was fat with Wasichus food and we were lean with famine. My father told me that he came to make his nephew surrender to the soldiers, because our own people had turned against us, and in the spring when the grass was high enough for the horses, many soldiers would come and fight us, and many Shoshonis and Crows and even Lakotas and our friends, the Shyelas, would come against us with the Wasichus. I could not understand this, and I though much about it. How could men get fat by being bad, and starve by being good?[11]

Riders sent ahead by Spotted Tail found Crazy Horse's camp on Otter Creek, a tributary of the Tongue. They were on their way to surrender to Miles, who had sent peace-talkers out from his camp at the mouth of the Tongue. Miles and Crook did not like each other and were engaged in a competition to secure the surrender of the "hostiles" and the glory that would follow. When Spotted Tail's riders arrived at the camp, they sought to turn the people toward Camp Robinson by handing out ammunition and promising better treatment from Crook. They told Crazy Horse his people would be allowed to keep some of their guns and horses, and after a period have a buffalo hunt.

Sensing an opportunity to play one side against the other, camp leaders decided to send a delegation north to press Miles for a counteroffer. When Miles failed to match the offer made by Spotted Tail's riders, most of the delegation returned to Otter Creek. The camp then moved to the forks of the Powder to council with Spotted Tail.

For two days, the talks went on. Whether it was because of his long-standing reluctance to take part in councils, depression over the fate of his people, or a desire to avoid a face-to-face meeting with his uncle, Crazy Horse refused to take part in the talks. But through his father, Worm, he sent word that he would abide by whatever decision was made.[12]

Unable to agree on whether to surrender at the northern agencies or the southern agencies, the chiefs decided to allow the camp to divide into separate bands and each band to do as it pleased. The Cheyenne were undecided, but the Lakota were almost unanimously in favor of listening to Spotted Tail and going in to the southern agencies. Pleased with the decision, Spotted Tail hurried back to Camp Sheridan to report his success to General Crook. Spotted Tail arrived on April 5, 1877, after being gone for about fifty days. Soon afterward, small groups of "hostiles" from the camps began arriving almost daily at the Spotted Tail and Red Cloud agencies. Black Elk sadly recalled: "I heard that we would all go into the Soldiers' Town when the grass should appear, and that Crazy Horse had untied his pony's tail and would not fight again."[13]

To ensure that Crazy Horse would follow the promises made to Spotted Tail and come in to an agency, army authorities at Camp Robinson sent Red Cloud out to meet him with cattle and other provisions. The supplies were sent so that Crazy Horse's band would not have to stop along the way to hunt and give Crazy Horse an opportunity to change his mind about surrendering. During the big council that followed Red Cloud's arrival, a member of his party rose and told Crazy Horse and He Dog that Red Cloud had been sent by the president to lead them to a reservation that had been set aside for them and where they could live in peace. He Dog replied:

> We and other Indians were born and raised on this land. The Great Spirit of God gave us this land. He created animals which we catch and make clothing and shelter for our people, and also the sweets that grow on trees. God gave us this land to live on and protect as our own. You know what the Great White Father and his soldiers do to us? They make war, burn our homes, our tents, wherever we may be and kill our people. It is only right that we protect ourselves, our people, and our country. The only thing we can do is protect ourselves and fight with the soldiers. We do not fight because we want to, but because we have to, to stay alive. We do not want to spill blood, either ours or the white man's. Therefore, we agree with you. We will go back with you to live in peace with the white men, and learn their ways.[14]

Crazy Horse and He Dog then told Red Cloud that they would go to Camp Robinson.

ALTHOUGH CRAZY HORSE had promised to surrender, on the way in he had second thoughts. When Lame Deer announced that he and his followers had decided to turn back and hunt buffalo, Crazy Horse told He Dog that he was going to join them. He Dog said: "You think like a child. You smoked the pipe of peace the same as I. You promised to go back with Chief Red Cloud and to live in peace with the white men. Don't run away from our grandfathers. Do not do it. It is not good."[15] Crazy Horse said nothing. The next morning he left with Lame Deer's band, but returned after several days.

Responding to Crazy Horse and He Dog's request for food and other supplies, officials at Camp Robinson on May 1, 1877, sent out Lieutenant Rosenquest with ten wagons of supplies and a hundred head of cattle. In an interview recorded decades later, He Dog said that "White Hat," Lieutenant William Philo Clark, met Crazy Horse's band. But that probably is the result of the passage of time and the

confusion that often accompanies it. Contemporary newspaper
accounts report that Rosenquest carried the supplies to Crazy Horse
and that Clark did not meet the band until it was just a few miles outside of Camp Robinson. The fourteen-year-old Black Elk recalled of
the band's move to Camp Robinson: "We had enough to eat now and
we boys could play without being afraid of anything. Soldiers watched
us, and sometimes my father and mother talked about our people
who had gone to the Grandmother's Land with Sitting Bull and Gall,
and they wanted to be there. We were camped near Red Cloud's
Agency, which was close to the Soldier's Town. What happened that
summer is not a story."[16]

To a boy of fourteen who over the past year had experienced the
Battle of the Little Big Horn, starvation, and a winter of relentless
pursuit by the U.S. Army, the summer of 1877 might not have
seemed worth a story. But what happened behind the scenes at Camp
Robinson and the Red Cloud and the Spotted Tail agencies actually
was worthy of a Shakespearean drama. It started on the evening of
Crazy Horse's first day at Camp Robinson, when the traitorous scout
Grouard appeared at his lodge. With him was Crook's aide Lieutenant Bourke.

Even though Grouard had led Reynolds's attack on what he
believed was Crazy Horse's camp in March 1876, he approached the
lodge as the good friend whom, he would later claim, Crazy Horse
had taken with him to find his daughter's death scaffold and saved
from the wrath of Sitting Bull. As the two men neared the lodge,
Bourke recalled,

> a couple of squaws were grinding coffee between two stones, and pre-
> paring something to eat. Crazy Horse remained seated on the ground,
> but when Frank [Grouard] called his name in Dakota . . . at the same
> time adding a few words I did not understand, he looked up, arose, and
> gave me a hearty grasp of his hand. . . . The expression of his counte-
> nance was one of quiet dignity, but morose, dogged, tenacious, and
> melancholy. He behaved with stolidity, like a man who realized he had
> to give in to Fate, but would do so as sullenly as possible.[17]

Crazy Horse's greeting of Grouard as a friend indicates that he
did not know the scout had attempted to lead troops against him.

Grouard probably had visited Crazy Horse to assess his demeanor, determine if he had anything to fear from him, and look for ways in which he could turn the situation into an advantage for himself. So devious was his nature that even whites at Camp Robinson did not trust him. Camp doctor Valentine T. McGillycuddy said he "never had any use for Grouard."[18] The scout Baptiste Pourier called Grouard a coward to his face. "Every time we are up against anything dangerous," he told him, "you are always out of the way; you are a coward!"[19] The interpreter Louis Bordeaux said: "Grouard was afraid of Crazy Horse after having lived among his band for years as a refugee from trouble on the Missouri where he killed a schoolmate and had killed . . . mail carriers and robbed the mail and carried letters into the Indian camp and read them to Crazy Horse, the contents disclosing information as to the whereabouts and movements of the soldiers." Bordeaux also said that Grouard was afraid of Crazy Horse and the "northern hostiles, for he had been raised by them, and then deserted them and joined our troops under Crook in the spring of 1876 . . . he had a reason for wanting to get rid of Crazy Horse."[20]

Suspicion of Crazy Horse spread far beyond Grouard over the next couple of months. In hopes of appeasing the war leader and maintaining control over his followers, Lieutenant Clark, who had been given the responsibility of watching him, encouraged Crazy Horse to take Nellie Laravie, a young half-French, half-Indian daughter of a trader, as his third wife. Black Shawl at the time was suffering from tuberculosis. Clark and other officers let it be known, too, that white authorities wanted to make Crazy Horse chief of all the Lakota, but only if he visited newly elected president Rutherford B. Hayes in Washington.

Having no interest in political power, Crazy Horse refused to go to Washington. To encourage him to make the trip, Clark made him a noncommissioned officer in the U.S. Indian Scouts on May 15, 1877. Although the appointment paid well and carried quite a bit of prestige on the reservation, Crazy Horse still declined to go to Washington. Instead, he used the occasion to stress his desire for an agency of his own in Wyoming. Through a spokesman, he reiterated the request on May 25 during a council with General Crook in which the Lakota aired their concerns about plans to move them north to the Missouri River. Crook sought to calm their suspicions by promising to be open in his dealings with them and to make no decision about moving the agencies until the stragglers who were still out had come in and the new president had an opportunity to discuss the situation with the Lakota.[21]

Despite Crook's promise, Crazy Horse feared that if he went to Washington the army would move the agencies while he was gone. Having seen what had happened to the Lakota in past dealings with whites, he was so suspicious of the army's intentions that he refused to even place his mark on ration receipts. In June he made somewhat of a turnabout and declared that he would go to Washington after he was given an agency of his own in Wyoming. Army authorities put him off by arguing that they could only give him an agency after he visited Washington. Crook wanted Crazy Horse to go to Washington as proof that the Indian wars were over. The presence of such a determined "hostile" in the Lakota delegation would add to Crook's glory.

Soon afterward a sun dance was held on Beaver Creek near the Spotted Tail Agency. As usual, Crazy Horse did not dance, but he attended as an honored guest, mingling with relatives and friends whom he had not seen for months. Five dancers also sacrificed their flesh for Crazy Horse and the future. The manner in which the Lakota viewed Crazy Horse at that point can be seen in a comment by Bourke: "I never heard an Indian mention his name save in terms of respect."[22]

Since white authorities would never allow the Lakota to end the sun dance by sending out the traditional raiding party, five large rocks were rolled down off the top of Beaver Mountain to the dance site. The rocks were arranged in a V and dedicated to Crazy Horse and the warriors who had offered their flesh. The next day Crazy Horse rode to the top of Beaver Mountain and began a four-day fast.[23]

THE ATTENTION Crazy Horse received from the army and at the sun dance stirred the jealousy of some prominent Lakota who had long ago come into the agencies and adopted white ways. Among them were the powerful and politically savvy Red Cloud and Spotted Tail. Within a very short time the Red Cloud Agency and the Spotted Tail Agency, which stood roughly forty miles to the east, became hotbeds of rumors about Crazy Horse and his plans. Bourke wrote:

Crazy Horse began to cherish hopes of being able to slip out of the [Red Cloud] agency and get back into some section farther to the north, where he would have little to fear, and where he could resume the old wild life with its pleasant incidents of hunting the buffalo, the elk, and the moose, and its raid upon the horses of Montana. He found his purposes detected and baffled at every turn; his camp was filled with soldiers, in uniform or without, but each and all reporting to the military officials each and every act taking place under their observation. Even his council-lodge was no longer safe: all that was said therein was repeated by some one, and his most trusted subordinates who had formerly been proud to obey unquestionably every suggestion were now cooling rapidly in their rancor towards the whites and beginning to doubt the wisdom of a resumption of the bloody path of war.[24]

On July 27, 1877, a council was called at the Red Cloud Agency during which Lieutenant Clark read a message from General Crook concerning the trip to Washington. Eighteen of the best and strongest Lakota were to go to the city, where they could air their complaints about plans to move their people to the Missouri River. Crook also promised that all Lakota who wanted to could go on a buffalo hunt, provided that they would return to the agency in forty days and not cause any trouble while they were out.[25]

As was customary, at the close of the council, agent James Irwin offered the Lakota three head of cattle, sugar, and coffee for a feast. Young Man Afraid Of His Horses suggested that the feast be held at Crazy Horse's camp, which was near the Red Cloud Agency. Offended by the proposal, Red Cloud and his followers left the council and that night sent a delegation to Irwin and special agent Benjamin Shapp to express their displeasure at holding the feast at Crazy Horse's camp. Red Cloud's people told the agents that such a move was asking for trouble because it would increase the standing of Crazy Horse in the eyes of the Lakota while undermining the prestige and authority of Red Cloud, who had proven himself a friend to the whites. They warned Irwin and Shapp that Crazy Horse could not be trusted.

In his report on the meeting, Shapp wrote that as a matter of courtesy, Red Cloud wanted Crazy Horse to come to his camp for the feast. Red Cloud's people warned that Crazy Horse was an "unreconstructed Indian," Shapp noted,

he had constantly evinced feelings of unfriendliness towards the others, he was sullen, morose and discontented at all times, he seemed to be chafing under restraint, and in their opinions was only waiting for a favorable opportunity to leave the agency and never return. The time had come now. Once away on a hunt, he and his band of at least 240 braves, well armed and equipped, would go on the warpath and cause the government infinite trouble and disaster. The other Indians these men represented had no confidence in him. He was tricky and unfaithful to others and very selfish as to the personal interests of his own tribe. The ammunition that would be furnished them would be used for the destruction of the whites against whom they seemed to entertain the utmost animosity.[26]

Shortly after the council, in early August 1877, officers at Camp Robinson received word that the Nez Perce of Chief Joseph had broken out of their reservation in Idaho and were fleeing north through Montana toward Canada. To stop the Nez Perce at the least risk to white troops, General Crook planned to send a large contingent of Lakota warriors against them. In an effort to induce Crazy Horse to fight the Nez Perce, Lieutenant Clark offered him the powerful inducements of a horse, a uniform, and a new repeating rifle. But both Crazy Horse and the seven-foot-tall Miniconjou leader Touch The Clouds objected to the plan. Crazy Horse said that if he went, he wanted to take all of his lodges and hunt at the same time. Clark said the army did not want the women and children but only the warriors. Crazy Horse told Clark

> that when he came in from the north and met with the officers and others on Hat Creek he presented the pipe of peace to the Great Spirit there and said he wanted peace, he wanted no more war, and promised that he would not fight against any nation any more and that he wants to be at peace now; but only a day or two before this he had been called into a council at Fort Robinson with the officers, and they had asked him to go out and fight the Nez Perces; [but] that he did not want to do that for he remembered his promise to the Great Spirit not to fight any more. . . . However, he would do it; he would go and camp beside these soldiers and fight with them till all the Nez Perces were killed.[27]

Instead of translating "till all the Nez Perces were killed," however, Grouard, who was acting as the official interpreter, reported Crazy Horse as saying that he would "go north and fight until not a white man is left." Bordeaux immediately caught the misinterpretation and confronted Grouard, angrily accusing him of "willfully misinterpreting" Crazy Horse's words. "He represented him as saying that he would not go out to fight the Nez Perces," Bordeaux recalled, "but that he was going back to his country in the north and would take the warpath and fight the soldiers till they were all killed."[28] Touch The Clouds also spoke up against Grouard. But it was too late. White authorities at Camp Robinson began to look on Crazy Horse more suspiciously than ever.

Meanwhile, supporters of Red Cloud and Spotted Tail circulated rumors that Crazy Horse was going to use the buffalo hunt promised by Crook as an excuse to leave the reservation and resume hostilities with the whites. Based on those rumors, the sale of ammunition to the Lakota was halted on August 4, and the next day the buffalo hunt was postponed. Crazy Horse and others reacted with disappointment and anger to the news. When Crazy Horse was again approached about going to Washington to meet the Great White Father, he replied that he "was not hunting for any Great Father; his father was with him, and there was no Great Father between him and the Great Spirit."[29]

THE UPROAR OVER Grouard's misinterpretation grew until it reached all the way to General Sheridan, who ordered Crook to investigate the problem. Supporters of Red Cloud and Spotted Tail began passing on stories that either Crazy Horse or his family would be imprisoned or killed if the war leader made the trip to Washington. Crazy Horse responded on August 18 by informing Clark that he would not go to Washington, but instead would send several prominent men from his band. Thinking that Crazy Horse might listen to reason from a friend, the army sent He Dog to talk to him. He Dog told Crazy Horse that Red Cloud and Spotted Tail's people "have been telling you not to go to Washington because the army will kill you. It's not true, whatever they tell you. Do not believe them. They lie. They are jealous of you. I'm telling you that you should go with me."

"Two white men came to see me a while ago," Crazy Horse replied. "They gave me two pocket knives, with the blades open. They shook my hand."

Crazy Horse went into his lodge, brought out the knives, and showed them to He Dog. One was red and the other was blue. He said: "The two white men who gave me the knives wore gray clothes.

They told me they were army officers but since they were not in uniform I didn't think they were army men."

"I never said that they never told you to cross the White River," He Dog said. "These people have been saying that about me since you have refused to go to Washington with me. Maybe they meant these two knives as a bad sign of something to come. I don't know."[30]

FED BY A CONTINUOUS STREAM of rumors from the Red Cloud Agency, the crisis grew until many of Crazy Horse's followers began to move away from his camp. Noticing all the excitement, Agent Irwin inquired as to what was going on. He was told: "We moved our village together ten or twelve days ago to council upon the various subjects interesting to us. We have held councils everyday and done all we could to quiet Crazy Horse and bring him into a better state of feeling, but we can do nothing with him—he has not attended our council." Hearing the remarks, Irwin became more convinced than ever that Crazy Horse was planning to make trouble. He wrote the commissioner of Indian affairs, informing him:

> It now appears that Crazy Horse has not been acting in good faith with the army—He has all the time been silent—sullen—lordly and dictatorial and cruel with his own people and other bands of Sioux at this and at Spotted Tail Agency. He dictates the place for his agency up north and says he is going there—refused to sign receipts for his goods and made other demonstrations about the agency.[31]

The climax to all of the rumors and spying began on August 31, when Clark wrote Captain Daniel Burke, commander of Camp Sheridan, telling him that General Crook had left Omaha that morning for the Red Cloud Agency and that Crazy Horse, Touch The Clouds, and High Bear had informed him they were going north on the warpath. "I hope you and Lee can at least postpone any starting of the northern Indians," Clark wrote. "Crazy Horse has worked Touch The Clouds around to his way of thinking. Perhaps after he gets cooled off, and Spot [Spotted Tail] and the rest can get him, he will change; but it certainly shows that his reformation is not very deep."[32]

The next day, Touch The Clouds and High Bear were directed to report to Captain Burke's office, where they were questioned about their plans to go north with Crazy Horse and fight the whites. Speaking through Bordeaux, and with other interpreters listening to make sure no mistakes were made, Touch The Clouds accused Grouard of having lied about Crazy Horse wanting to go north and fight the whites. He said that when he and Crazy Horse had come into the Red Cloud Agency they had been promised peace, but now General Crook wanted them to fight the Nez Perce. Touch The Clouds pointed out that he had done everything he had been told since coming to the reservation, but that Crook and Clark now wanted him and Crazy Horse to put blood on their faces and go to war even though they had been promised peace. Although he and Crazy Horse had been deceived, Touch The Clouds said they would go north to fight the Nez Perce.

After Touch The Clouds finished, Burke and the other whites in the room turned to Grouard and asked if he now believed that Touch The Clouds and Crazy Horse planned to ride north and renew hostilities against the whites. Cornered, but still not willing to admit what he had done, Grouard responded: "I don't believe he intends doing so NOW."[33]

On September 2, Lieutenant Lee went to the Red Cloud Agency, where he found that Crook and Clark had lost all confidence in Crazy Horse, Touch The Clouds, and other members of the northern bands. Lee told them about the meeting with Touch The Clouds, Grouard's discomfort over what had been said, and his partial admission of having made a "mistake." Lee argued that a mistake clearly had been made as far as Touch The Clouds's intentions were concerned. Crook told him: "I don't want to make a mistake, for it would, to the Indians, be the basest treachery to make a mistake in this matter."[34]

To avoid a mistake, Crook headed off for a council that he had called with Crazy Horse and other Lakota leaders on White Clay Creek between the Red Cloud and Spotted Tail agencies. Crazy Horse had refused to attend. On the way to the council, Crook and his party were met by Woman's Dress, a nephew of Red Cloud who had long been jealous of Crazy Horse. "Where are you going?" Woman's Dress asked as he approached the advance riders of Crook's party. The interpreter Garnett told him that they were going to a council on White Clay Creek. "Don't you go there with General Crook," Woman's Dress warned. "When you hold this council at White Clay, Crazy Horse is going to come in there with sixty Indians, and catch General Crook by the hand, like he is going to shake hands, and he is going to hold on to him, and those sixty Indians are going to kill Crook and whoever he has with him."

As Woman's Dress was talking, General Crook arrived in an ambulance. Garnett told him what Woman's Dress had said. Crook asked: "What do you know about this Woman's Dress? Is he reliable? Does he tell the truth?" Garnett answered: "General, this is a big undertaking and I could not say—I am going to leave it up to Baptist Pourier, a man who is with me, and he will tell you." Pourier, who was related to Woman's Dress through marriage, told Crook that Woman's Dress was a truthful man and that whatever he said would be the truth. Crook thought for a moment and then said: "I never start any place but what I like to get there." Clark then spoke up and warned Crook against attending the council. "We have lost a man just like you, when we lost General Custer," Clark said. "We miss him, and we couldn't replace any man in his place alive. There is no use for you to start in there when you have no protection." When Crook asked what excuse he could use for not attending the council, Clark told him: "You leave that to me." Crook agreed and Clark told Garnett to ride ahead and inform the Lakota who had gathered for the council that a message had come for General Crook and he had to turn back for Camp Robinson.

At the council, the word about Crook was spread by American Horse, who afterward told Garnett to return to Camp Robinson and tell Crook and Clark that some of the Lakota at the council were coming to the post to talk with them.[35] The list included Red Cloud, Little Wound, Red Dog, Young Man Afraid Of His Horses, No Flesh, Yellow Bear, High Wolf, Slow Bull, Black Bear, American Horse, Three Bears, Blue Horse, and No Water, who had shot Crazy Horse in the dispute over Black Buffalo Woman.[36] During the meeting, Crook, according to his aide Bourke, told those present

that they were being led astray by Crazy Horse's folly, and that they must preserve order in their own ranks and arrest Crazy Horse. The chiefs deliberated and said that Crazy Horse was such a desperate man, it would be necessary to kill him; General Crook replied that would be murder, and could not be sanctioned; that there was force enough at or near the two agencies to round up not only Crazy Horse, but his whole band, and that more troops would be sent, if necessary; he counted upon the loyal Indians effecting the arrest themselves, as it would prove to the nation that they were not in sympathy with the non-progressive element of the tribe.[37]

Although Bourke reports that Crook was against the murder of Crazy Horse, Garnett, who was present at the meeting, says that Clark promised a reward of three hundred dollars and one of his best horses to the man who killed Crazy Horse.[38]

When Colonel Luther Bradley, commander of Camp Robinson, learned about the secret meeting, he called Garnett into his office and demanded to know what had taken place. In the office was He Dog, whose presence would seem to indicate suspicion among Crazy Horse's friends. Garnett refused to speak in front of He Dog. In private, he told Bradley that plans had been made to kill Crazy Horse, that Clark had offered a reward, and that ammunition had been drawn by the Indians involved in the plot. Bradley told Garnett to return to what he was doing and sent for Clark, who in turn called for Garnett and complained: "These Indians can hold nothing. Bradley has got hold of that council we had with the Indians today, so you go down to the Indian village right away, and stop them Indians from approaching Crazy Horse. When you go down, tell those Indians not to disturb Crazy Horse, but tell all to report to Fort Robinson before sun-up in the morning."[39]

Instead of the murder of Crazy Horse, orders were issued to surround his camp, disarm his band, and arrest him for transport to Omaha and then Fort Jefferson on the Far Tortugas south of Key West, Florida. When the plotters whom Bradley had stopped from murdering Crazy Horse arrived at Camp Robinson the next morning, September 3, they were issued ammunition and weapons and sent to arrest the war leader. As they neared Crazy Horse's camp, though, they learned that he had fled to the Spotted Tail Agency.[40]

TIRED OF ALL THE gossip and prying, Crazy Horse had decided to move his camp from the Red Cloud Agency to the Spotted Tail Agency because it had a reputation for being a peaceful place. Soon after he set up camp about three miles outside of the Spotted Tail Agency, a rider sent by Clark arrived at Camp Sheridan offering a two-hundred-dollar reward for any Indian who arrested Crazy Horse.

The messenger was followed by fifteen or twenty of Red Cloud's supporters who had been sent to bring Crazy Horse back to Camp Robinson. They caught up to Crazy Horse while he was riding with Black Shawl. When they demanded that he go back with them, Crazy Horse put them off by shouting: "I am Crazy Horse! Don't touch me! I am not running away!"[41]

Realizing that he had to talk to authorities at Camp Sheridan about his move, Crazy Horse later left his camp for the army post. He was escorted by Touch The Clouds and an estimated three hundred armed warriors, among whom were a number of informants, including White Thunder and Black Crow, who were determined to shoot Crazy Horse if there were any problems.

No sooner had Crazy Horse and his party arrived at Camp Sheridan than Spotted Tail appeared, backed by a large party of his own warriors. As the two sides faced each other, Spotted Tail greeted his nephew with less than affection: "We never have trouble here!" he announced. "The sky is clear; the air is still and free from dust. You have come here, and you must listen to me and my people! I am chief here! We keep the peace! We, the Brulés, do this! They obey ME! Every Indian who comes here, must obey me! You say you want to come to this Agency to live peaceably. If you stay here, you must listen to me! That is all!"

Spotted Tail's speech was greeted by much shouting and calls. One "frenzied northern Indian," thinking that Crazy Horse was about to be harmed, grabbed the arm of Captain Burke and said: "Crazy Horse is brave, but he feels too weak to die today. Kill me! Kill me!"

Both sides continued to eye each other suspiciously, but no shots were fired. After a few more exchanges of words the crowd began to disperse. Crazy Horse went into the office of Captain Burke. Lee recalled: "He seemed like a frightened, trembling wild animal brought to bay, hoping for confidence one moment and fearing treachery the next. He had been under a severe strain all day, and it plainly showed."[42]

During their talk, Burke sought to assure Crazy Horse that the army had no reason to harm him but that he had to return to Camp Robinson. Crazy Horse promised to go back to Camp Robinson the next day and allow the authorities there to decide if he must stay at the Red Cloud Agency or would be permitted to move to the Spotted

Tail Agency. He told Burke and the others present that he wanted to get away from the trouble at the Red Cloud Agency and had come to the Spotted Tail Agency to have his sick wife treated. He was told to repeat his words to the authorities at Camp Robinson, and then Burke made several of the warriors present responsible for Crazy Horse's safety during the night. He was told to report back to Burke's office at nine o'clock the following morning.

When Crazy Horse reported to the office the next morning, he informed Burke that he had changed his mind about going back to the Red Cloud Agency. He was "afraid something would happen" if he returned. He asked Burke and Lee instead to go ahead to the Red Cloud Agency to "fix up the matter for him and his people." Burke reassured Crazy Horse that the army had no plans to harm him and insisted that he owed it to his people to quietly and peacefully return to the Red Cloud Agency. Crazy Horse then agreed to go if Lieutenant Lee would accompany him and tell the soldiers at Camp Robinson everything that had happened at the Spotted Tail Agency, and tell the authorities at Camp Robinson that Crazy Horse was welcome at the Spotted Tail Agency if the district commander authorized the move. Lee and Burke also promised that Crazy Horse would be given an opportunity to tell his side of the story, "how he had been misunderstood and misinterpreted; that he wanted peace and quiet, and did not want any trouble whatever."[43]

Crazy Horse's request to ride horseback to Camp Robinson also was granted. He started back on the morning of September 5. Accompanying him were Lee, Bordeaux, Touch The Clouds, Black Crow, Swift Bear, Good Voice, Horned Antelope, seven friends of Crazy Horse's, and a few other Indians whom white authorities judged as reliable. "When about fifteen miles out," Lee said, "small parties of Spotted Tail's soldiers began to arrive, and when half way out (about twenty miles) I had over forty reliable Indian soldiers. Crazy Horse then realized that he was practically a prisoner."[44]

Although he was essentially a prisoner, Crazy Horse's spirit refused to give in. At one point on the trail to Camp Robinson, he dashed ahead over the brow of a hill, where he encountered a Lakota family heading for the Spotted Tail Agency. Lee thinks the family probably gave Crazy Horse a knife. When Spotted Tail's followers caught up to the war chief, though, he told them he had gone ahead to water his horse. The Indian soldiers responded by ordering him to ride behind Lieutenant Lee's ambulance. "He seemed nervous and bewildered, and his serious expression seemed to show he was doubtful of the outcome," Lee recalled. The lieutenant reassured Crazy Horse and his friends that he would do exactly as he had promised.[45]

When the procession was about fifteen miles outside of the Red Cloud Agency, Lee sent a courier ahead with a note asking if he should take Crazy Horse to the agency or to Camp Robinson. In the note, Lee also restated his promise that Crazy Horse would be given an opportunity to speak when he arrived at Camp Robinson. Bradley's reply reached Lee when the party was just four miles away from the Red Cloud Agency. Crazy Horse was to be taken to Bradley's office at Camp Robinson. The note said nothing about the promise made by Lee. Knowing that Bradley's office was next to the guardhouse, Lee concluded that Crazy Horse was to be imprisoned, "but I still hoped that he would be allowed to say a few words on his own behalf."[46]

AN ESTIMATED three thousand to six thousand Lakota had gathered at Camp Robinson to await the appearance of Crazy Horse. Upon arriving at the post, Lee immediately headed for Bradley's office, where he was met by the adjutant, who informed him that Crazy Horse was to be turned over to the officer of the day. Lee asked if Crazy Horse could speak to Bradley, and then had him dismount and enter the office. With Crazy Horse was Touch The Clouds, Swift Bear, High Bear, Black Crow, and Good Voice. Lee stationed an Indian guard at the door, and then went inside to talk to Bradley, who immediately informed him that there was no point in discussing the issue. He told Lee that the orders were "preemptory," that not even General Crook could change them, "and nothing further need be said, and the sooner Crazy Horse was turned over, the better." When Lee tried to explain what had been promised Crazy Horse, Bradley cut him short. Lee then asked if Crazy Horse could be heard in the morning. Bradley stared at him for a moment, and then ordered Lee to turn over Crazy Horse to the officer of the day. "Tell him to go with the officer of the day, and not a hair on his head should be harmed," Bradley said.[47]

Lee told Crazy Horse and his friends what Bradley had said. His remarks were greeted with "a joyous How!" Crazy Horse's face brightened. He stepped across the room and warmly took the hand of the officer of the day, Captain James Kennington. As a rumble spread through the crowd that had assembled outside, Crazy Horse then went with Kennington, two soldiers, and Little Big Man to the guard-house.[48]

Exactly what happened in the guardhouse will never be known, as credible witnesses are lacking. Probably, Crazy Horse either realized for the first time that he was going to be locked in a jail, or the reality of an expected imprisonment suddenly became unbearable to the recently free-living Lakota. He drew a knife that may have been given him by the Lakota family he had met on the trail, burst from the guardhouse, and swung the blade at Kennington and Little Big Man, who had grabbed his arms. "Let me go, let me go; you won't allow me to hurt anyone! You have done this before," he shouted at Little Big Man, and cut him across the wrist. Severely bleeding, Little Big Man dropped to the ground as other Indians rushed forward to subdue or help Crazy Horse. Swift Bear said: "We told you to behave yourself." Captain Kennington shouted: "Kill him! Kill him!" Some sources say he shouted: "Kill the son of a bitch!" To this, sentry William Gentiles, a forty-seven-year old native of Ireland who had served in the army for more than twenty years without rising above the rank of private, lunged with his bayonet and stuck Crazy Horse in the back, near the left kidney.

"He has killed me now!" Crazy Horse cried and collapsed to the ground.

As THE INDIANS drew their weapons and formed into two opposing groups, a detail of twenty guards moved in to surround Crazy Horse. Dr. McGillycuddy wedged his way through the crowd to find "Crazy Horse on his back, grinding his teeth and frothing at the mouth, blood trickling from a bayonet wound above the hip, and the pulse weak and missing beats." He immediately realized that Crazy Horse was "done for."

Without orders to the contrary, Kennington attempted to move the dying Crazy Horse into the guardhouse. He took one shoulder, asked McGillyciddy to take the other, and ordered two of his men to pick up the wounded man's feet. But Crazy Horse's followers objected, shouting that Crazy Horse "was a great chief, and could not be put in a prison." Then a "big northern Sioux" grabbed McGillycuddy by the shoulder, partly lifted him off the ground, and motioned for the white men to leave Crazy Horse alone.[49]

There the matter of what to do with Crazy Horse stayed as tension and confusion grew on all sides. Not knowing what else to do, McGillycuddy volunteered to discuss the situation with Colonel Bradley. "Please give my compliments to the officer of the day," Bradley said when McGillycuddy told him what had happened, "and he is to carry out his original orders, and put Crazy Horse in the guardhouse." McGillycuddy started back across the parade grounds for the guardhouse, about sixty yards away, when he saw American Horse. Seeking help, he told the Lakota leader that Crazy Horse was badly hurt and that Bradley wanted to put him in the guardhouse. As the other Lakota had shouted earlier, American Horse replied: "Crazy Horse is a chief and cannot be put in the guardhouse." McGillycuddy hurried back to the commander's office and warned Bradley that to place Crazy Horse in the guardhouse likely would result in the death "of a good many men and Indians." He suggested instead that Crazy Horse be placed in the adjutant's office. Bradley reluctantly agreed.

"I gave him hypodermics of morphine which eased his pain," McGillycuddy recalled, "he died about midnight, no one came to the adjutant's office that night and it was dismal and lonesome, the only ones present were Captain Kennington Officer of the Day, Lieutenant [Henry] Lemly officer of the Guard, Old Crazy Horse [Worm], the interpreter [John Provost], Touch the Clouds, and myself." As those present waited for the end, Worm wailed about the fate of his son and their people:

> We were not agency Indians; we preferred the buffalo to the white man's beef, but the Gray Fox [Crook] kept sending messengers to us in the north, saying come in, come in. Well, we came in, and now they have killed my boy; hard times have come upon us, but we were tired of fighting. Red Cloud was jealous of my boy. He was afraid the Gray Fox would make him head chief; our enemies here at the agency were trying to force us away, so probably we would have been driven soon back to our hunting grounds in the north.[50]

Dr. McGillycuddy gave morphine to Crazy Horse to ease his pain in the hours before he died.

At about 10:00 P.M., Touch The Clouds sent word to Lieutenant Lee that Crazy Horse wanted to see him. Lee went to the office, where he found Crazy Horse lying on the floor. He offered his hand. Crazy Horse took it and between moans told Lee: "My friend, I don't blame you for this. Had I listened to you this trouble would not have happened to me."[51]

Lieutenant Lemly reported that Crazy Horse gave a rather lengthy speech before he died. But he is the only one of the people who were present in the adjutant's office to report such a speech. It seems doubtful that a man in great pain, slipping in and out of consciousness, and heavily dosed with morphine could have made the speech that Lemly reported almost fifty years after the fact.

DESPITE THE TENSION that permeated the situation, the night passed without serious incident. Lucy Lee, Lieutenant Lee's wife, recalled Crazy Horse's father and mother crying and singing the death song until early morning, when they were granted permission to take Crazy Horse's body. True to the spirit of their son, the couple turned down an offer of an ambulance to transport the body. Instead, as the Lakota had done for generations, they lashed the body, which had been wrapped in a blanket, to a travois and carried it off to the Spotted Tail Agency, where it was laid on a small scaffold about a half mile above Camp Sheridan. "Whenever I go out of my quarters I see the red blanket in which the body is wrapped," Lee wrote in his diary for September 8, "and thus is recalled to my mind and heart Crazy Horse's pathetic and tragic end."[52]

Three days later, Crazy Horse's parents, who continued to mourn near the scaffold day and night, asked Lee if a fence could be erected around the body to keep the cattle away. Lee and the camp carpenter loaded a wagon with posts and rough planks, and in an hour built a crude fence around the scaffold.

At the same time, word of Crazy Horse's death was spreading across the nation. The *Omaha Daily Herald* broke the story of his stabbing in its September 6 edition. The paper had received a telegram about the stabbing so quickly that Crazy Horse was reported still alive and his condition improving. The death notice came the following day, along with an editorial that heartily praised Crazy Horse, something that often happened once an Indian was safely dead. The *Daily Herald* proclaimed Crazy Horse the

> master spirit of the Sioux Army, the bravest of his race. . . . From all we
> can gather . . . the death of the great warrior will go far to end all diffi-
> culties with the Sioux, and no higher compliment could be paid him as
> a brave and able leader than is contained in this single fact. It is proba-

NEBRASKA.—DEATH OF THE SIOUX CHIEF CRAZY HORSE, AT SYDNEY, SEPTEMBER 5TH.—THE FUNERAL PROCESSION PASSING THROUGH CAMP SHERIDAN ON THE WAY TO THE GRAVE.

The death of Crazy Horse. From *Frank Leslie's Illustrated Newspaper*, October 13, 1877.

bly true that Crazy Horse was one of the most remarkable men of his remarkable race and that as a warrior it is questionable whether it ever produced a greater.

The *Omaha Bee* in its September 6 edition called Crazy Horse "a bad, bold and treacherous chief" who was said to be "one of the big guns in the Custer massacre" and "lately grown very important in his own opinion." The *New York Times* noted in its September 7 issue: "In the tribe over which he ruled he was almost worshiped on account of his personal bravery; and yet he was greatly dreaded by his people, for his way was that of a despot. He had been a bad Indian ever since he had obtained manhood and been on the war-path nearly all the time for 12 years past." The *New York Tribune* of September 7 called Crazy Horse "a religious enthusiast. During his campaign in the Yellowstone Valley, he used to boast that he held communion with a spirit from above, that aided, sustained and directed him." In a September 11 story the *Tribune* added: "Crazy Horse was a brave man, reckless and foolhardy, of very little intelligence and had gained his notoriety through his brute courage and stub-born will."

Reporting that Crazy Horse was "born of poor but dis-honest parentage," a story in the September 12 *Omaha Bee* said he was

> not noted for his love for his fellow man. He never founded a hospital nor contributed to the furtherance of any philanthropic work, nor threw a nickel into the contribution box. He has contributed to the number of orphans and widows in the land, and has desolated many a home, and has left only deeds of wickedness to perpetuate his memory. . . . But now he is dead, he is harmless; he has gone to join Tecumseh, Captain Jack, Black Hawk, and a thousand other illustrious warriors, where in the happy hunting ground they can smoke their pipes and sit in the shade of their tepees, with no white man to molest or make them afraid.

In Chicago, the *Tribune* reported on September 14 that "Crazy Horse had been working to breed discontent among the Indians and urging them to go on the war-path, but he could not succeed. Among the northern Indians he had been pretty powerful, but when he came to this reservation he found so many Chiefs who were regarded his superiors that he lost all his influence and became angry and ill-natured." The *Army & Navy Journal* noted on September 15: "Death to him was preferable to captivity," and that the "wily Indian" had surrendered only "that he might fatten his ponies in peace, and pro-cure ammunition for fresh raids." The *New York Times* on September 19 claimed that "Red Cloud, and many other Sioux chiefs have all acted in the most praiseworthy manner during these troubles."

A few weeks after Crazy Horse's death a delegation of Lakota that included Red Cloud, Spotted Tail, Little Big Man, American Horse, Young Man Afraid Of His Horses, and He Dog traveled with General Crook and Lieutenant Clark to Washington, where they met with President Hayes on September 26. At that conference, the delegates again expressed their opposition to plans by the government to move them to the Missouri River. As in the past, their pleas were ignored. Winter supplies were shipped up the Missouri and dropped off, and the Lakota informed that they could either resettle along the river or starve.

On October 27 a caravan of about 4,600 Indians, 2 companies of cavalry, 120 wagons, 2,000 head of cattle, and assorted Indian office employees and traders began moving north from the Red Cloud and Spotted Tail agencies to the Missouri. About 75 miles into the jour-

"On this spot Crazy Horse Ogallala Chief was killed
Sept. 5 1877." Monument in Ft. Robinson, Nebraska.

ney, according to a report by Agent Irwin, about 2,000 northern Indians broke away from the Spotted Tail column and attempted to incite the other Indians to rebellion. "They brought with them the remains of Crazy Horse in order to madden our Indians," Irwin wrote, "but in this they failed, and the major portion finally struck off north."[53]

Caught by winter, Red Cloud's people reached the forks of the White River and refused to go on. Spotted Tail's people stopped on Rosebud Creek, a tributary of the White River and not the scene of the battle. Red Cloud's stopping spot eventually would become the Pine Ridge Reservation, and Spotted Tail's the Rosebud Reservation. In the Pine Ridge country, Crazy Horse's father and mother finally buried the body of their son. Some sources report that the site is along a small stream known as Wounded Knee Creek.

NOTES

CHAPTER 1. "CRAZY HORSE WITH US"

1. Thomas R. Buecker and Paul R. Eli, *The Crazy Horse Surrender Ledger* (Lincoln: Nebraska State Historical Society, 1994), p. 1.

2. *Chicago Times* (May 7, 1877).

3. Oliver Knight, "War or Peace: The Anxious Wait for Crazy Horse," *Nebraska History* (1973).

4. William Garnett interview, Ricker tablets.

5. Knight, "War or Peace."

6. *Chicago Times* (May 7, 1877).

7. Ibid.

8. Eleanor H. Hinman, "Oglala Sources on the Life of Crazy Horse," *Nebraska History* (1976).

9. *Chicago Times* (May 7, 1877).

10. Hinman, "Oglala Sources."

11. Ibid.

12. Garnett interview, Ricker tablets.

13. *Chicago Times* (May 7, 1877).

14. Hinman, "Oglala Sources."

15. Garnett interview, Ricker tablets.

16. *Chicago Times* (May 7, 1877).

17. Ibid.

18. Ibid.

19. Ibid.

20. Ibid.

21. Ibid.

22. Knight, "War or Peace."

23. *Chicago Times* (May 7, 1877) and Buecker, *The Crazy Horse Surrender Ledger*, p. 14.

24. *Chicago Times* (May 7, 1877).

25. Ibid.

26. Garnett interview, Ricker tablets.

27. *Chicago Times* (May 7, 1877).

28. Ibid.

29. Ibid.

30. Knight, "War or Peace."

CHAPTER 2. BUFFALO PEOPLE

1. James R. Walker, *Lakota Myth* (Lincoln: University of Nebraska Press, 1983), pp. 206–226.

2. The basic outline of Lakota Sioux history is drawn from Royal B. Hassrick, *The Sioux* (Norman: University of Oklahoma Press, 1964); George Hyde, *Red Cloud's Folk: A History of the Oglala Sioux Indians* (Norman: University of Oklahoma Press, 1957); *Spotted Tail's Folk: A History of the Brule Sioux* (Norman: University of Oklahoma Press, 1961); and Doane Robinson, *A History of the Dakota or Sioux Indians* (Minneapolis: Ross & Haines, 1956).

3. Raymond J. DeMallie, ed., *The Sixth Grandfather: Black Elk's Teachings Given to John G. Neihardt* (Lincoln: University of Nebraska Press, 1985), pp. 307–312.

4. Ibid., pp. 311–314.

5. Catherine Price, *The Oglala People, 1841–1879: A Political History* (Lincoln: University of Nebraska Press, 1996), pp. 41–42.

6. DeMallie, *Sixth Grandfather*, pp. 314–316.

7. Ibid.

8. David Lavender, *The Way to the Western Sea* (New York: Harper & Row, 1989), pp. 309–310.

9. Population figures for the Lakota come from Kingsley M. Bray, "Teton Sioux Population History, 1655–1881," *Nebraska History* (1994). Population figures for white America come from Gorton Carruth et al., *American Facts and Dates* (New York: Thomas Y. Crowell, 1979), p. 198.

10. Maxine Benson, ed., *From Pittsburgh to the Rocky Mountains: Major Stephen Long's Expedition 1819–1820* (Golden, Colo.: Fulcrum, 1990), p. xiv.

11. Francis Parkman, *The Oregon Trail* (Boston: Little, Brown, 1907), p. 134.

12. Ibid., p. 136.

13. George Catlin, *North American Indians* (New York: Viking Penguin, 1989), p. 205.

14. Luther Standing Bear, *My People the Sioux* (Lincoln: University of Nebraska Press, 1975), p. 14.

15. Catlin, *North American Indians*, p. 228.

16. Joseph Epes Brown, ed., *The Sacred Pipe: Black Elk's Account of the Seven Rites of the Oglala Sioux* (Norman: University of Oklahoma Press, 1963), p. 21.

17. Richard Irving Dodge, *The Plains of the Great West and Their Inhabitants* (New York: Archer House, 1959), pp. 297–298.

18. Mary Jane Megquier, *Apron Full of Gold* (Albuquerque: University of New Mexico Press, 1994), p. 46.

19. Parkman, *Oregon Trail*, p. 135.

20. James H. Howard, ed., *The Warrior Who Killed Custer: The Personal Narrative of Chief Joseph White Bull* (Lincoln: University of Nebraska Press, 1968), pp. 16–23.

21. Ibid., p. 13.

22. Standing Bear, *My People the Sioux*, pp. 4–5.

23. Evan S. Connell, *Son of the Morning Star: Custer and the Little Big Horn* (New York: Harper & Row, 1984), pp. 162–167.

CHAPTER 3. INDIAN BOYHOOD

1. Hinman, "Oglala Sources," and Chips interview, Ricker tablets. Also see Richard G. Hardorff, ed. *The Oglala Lakota Crazy Horse: A Preliminary Genealogical Study* (Mattituck, N.Y.: J. M. Carroll, 1985), p. 43; Mari Sandoz, in the notes to *Crazy Horse: The Strange Man of the Oglala* (Lincoln: University of Nebraska Press, 1961), sets 1841 or 1842 as the time of Crazy Horse's birth; see the introduction. Without taking into consideration Chips's remark that Crazy Horse was born in the fall, she subtracts He Dog's ninety-two years from the time of his interview in July 1930 and gets 1838. Then she adds, without giving sources, that "a checking of the old man's figures places the date about 1841–42." Other sources, such as Charles A. Eastman in *Indian Heroes and Great Chieftains* (Boston: Little, Brown, 1929), give the year as late as 1845, p. 83.

2. *New York Sun* (September 14, 1877).

3. Chips interview, Ricker tablets.

4. Firsthand information on Crazy Horse's lineage and childhood is extremely scarce for a number of reasons. Aside from the fact that the old Lakota did not possess a written language and many refused to talk to or were highly suspicious of white interviewers, most also did not like to talk about the dead. Also, according to David H. Brumble III in *American Indian Autobiography* (Berkeley: University of California Press, 1988), Indians generally did not consider childhood events as important and seldom talked about them. Instead, they preferred to recount their accomplishments in later life, such as coups, successful horse raids, and other acts that gave them standing in their culture. Consequently, several primary sources exist detailing Crazy Horse's deeds in battles and his death, though they always must be viewed with a certain caution because they were recorded decades after the events they report and could have been altered in translation. He Dog and Chips are the main primary sources on the early life of Crazy Horse. Eastman also provides information on Crazy Horse's childhood, but he did not actually know the chief. He reports collecting his information from old Lakotas he met while working on the Pine Ridge Reservation in the 1890s. Joe De Barthe, in *The Life and Adventures of Frank Grouard* (Norman: University of Oklahoma Press, 1958), appears to be the source for Crazy Horse's grandfather being named Crazy Horse. A trader and interpreter, Grouard lived in Crazy Horse's camp at various times, but is well known as a storyteller very interested in making himself look good, so his comments always must be viewed with extreme caution.

5. Several sources, among them He Dog, report that Crazy Horse's father changed his name to Worm. He Dog calls Worm a nickname. His birth in 1811 is supported by the *New York Sun* story on Crazy Horse's death. Chips reported that Crazy Horse's mother was a Miniconjou Lakota, but he did not remember her name. Mrs. Eagle Horse, the daughter of Crazy Horse's sister, identified her as Rattle Blanket Woman in a 1918 interview. Her birth in 1815 is reported by Mrs. Eagle Horse; see Hardorff, ed., *The Oglala Lakota Crazy Horse*, p. 37.

6. See Hardorff, ed., *The Oglala Lakota Crazy Horse*, pp. 27 and 39.

7. Catlin, *North American Indians*, p. 206.

8. George Catlin, *Letters and Notes on the North American Indians*, ed. Michael MacDonald (New York: Clarkson N. Potter, 1975), p. 211.

9. A detailed discussion of Crazy Horse's ancestry, including the Conroy letter, can be found in Hardorff's *The Oglala Lakota Crazy Horse*, pp. 27–32.

10. Ibid., pp. 29–30.

11. Chips interview, Ricker tablets, and Hinman, "Oglala Sources."

12. Neihardt, *Black Elk Speaks*, p. 85.

13. Carroll Friswold, *The Killing of Chief Crazy Horse* (Glendale, Calif.: The Arthur H. Clark Co., 1979), p. 68. Also see Chips interview, Ricker tablets, and Hinman, "Oglala Sources."

14. Chips, Ricker interview.

15. Tackett manuscript in the Fort Robinson Museum.

16. Hinman, "Oglala Sources."

17. Chips interview, Ricker tablets.

18. Hinman, "Oglala Sources" and Chips, Ricker interview.

19. John G. Neihardt, *Black Elk Speaks* (Lincoln: University of Nebraska Press, 1988), p. 85, and Chips, Ricker interview.

20. Neihardt, *Black Elk Speaks*, pp. 86–87.

21. Catlin, *North American Indians*, p. 462.

22. Parkman, *Oregon Trail*, p. 209.

23. Charles A. Eastman, *Indian Boyhood* (Lincoln: University of Nebraska Press, 1991), p. 56.

24. Ibid., p. 57.

25. Eastman, *Indian Heroes*, pp. 84–86.

26. Neihardt, *Black Elk Speaks*, p. 15.

27. Stanley Vestal, *Warpath: The True Story of the Fighting Sioux Told in a Biography of Chief White Bull* (Lincoln: University of Nebraska Press, 1984), pp. 6–7.

28. Neihardt, *Black Elk Speaks*, p. 15, and DeMallie, ed., *Sixth Grandfather*, pp. 147–149.

29. Eastman, *Indian Boyhood*, p. 61.

30. Eastman, *Indian Heroes*, p. 86, and Hinman, "Oglala Sources."

31. Hassrick, *The Sioux*, pp. 184–187.

32. Catlin, *North American Indians*, pp. 321–324.

33. Standing Bear, *My People the Sioux*, pp. 77–80.

34. Neihardt, *Black Elk Speaks*, p. 86.

35. DeMallie, ed., *Sixth Grandfather*, pp. 143–149, and Neihardt, *Black Elk Speaks*, pp. 53–57.

36. Eastman, *Indian Heroes*, p. 88.

Chapter 4. Manifest Destinies

1. Rush Welter, *The Mind of America: 1820–1860* (New York: Columbia, 1975), p. 21.

2. Ibid., p. 18.

3. Carruth, Gorton and Associates, eds., *The Encyclopedia of American Facts and Dates* (New York: Thomas Y. Crowell, 1979), pp. 198–226.

4. Welter, *Mind of America*, p. 36.

5. Robert F. Berkhofer, Jr., *The White Man's Indian* (New York: Alfred A. Knopf, 1978), pp. 92–94.

6. Ibid., pp. 6–7.

7. Ibid., p. 7.

8. Ibid., p. 21.

9. Ibid., pp. 19–20.

10. Ibid., p. 18.

11. Parkman, *Oregon Trail*, p. 242.

12. Horace Greeley, *An Overland Journey, from New York to San Francisco in the Summer of 1859* (New York: Readex Microprint, 1966), pp. 117–123.

13. Howard, *Warrior Who Killed Custer*, p. 11.

14. For a discussion on the plains Indians' relationship to the buffalo see Tom McHugh, *The Time of the Buffalo* (Lincoln: University of Nebraska Press, 1972); George Hyde, *Red Cloud's Folk*; and Dan Flores, "The Great Contraction: Bison and Indians in Northern Plains Environmental History" in Charles E. Rankin, ed., *Legacy: New Perspectives on the Battle of the Little Big Horn* (Helena: Montana Historical Society Press, 1996). George Catlin, Father Pierre-Jean De Smet, Francis Parkman, and other historical sources also provide information on the Indians' use of and relationship to buffalo. For quote see Hyde, *Red Cloud's Folk*, p. 62.

15. Catlin, *North American Indians*, pp. 59–60.

16. William E. Unrau, *White Man's Wicked Water* (Lawrence: University Press of Kansas, 1996), p. 36.

17. For details on the whiskey trade and its effects on the Lakota see M. I. McCreight, *Firewater and Forked Tongues: A Sioux Chief Interprets U.S. History* (Pasadena, Calif.: Trail's End, 1947); R. Eli Paul, ed., *The Autobiography of Chief Red Cloud: War Leader of the Oglalas* (Helena: Montana Historical Society Press, 1997).

18. Remi Nadeau, *Fort Laramie and the Sioux Indians* (Englewood Cliffs, N.J.: Prentice-Hall, 1967), p. 38.

19. Pierre-Jean De Smet, *Letters and Sketches: With a Narrative of a Year's Residence Among the Indian Tribes of the Rocky Mountains* (Philadelphia: M. Fithian, 1843), p. 123.

20. Paul, *Autobiography of Chief Red Cloud*, pp. 156–164.

21. Catlin, *North American Indians*, p. 205.

22. Unrau, *White Man's Wicked Water*, p. 2.

23. Ibid.

24. LeRoy R. Hafen and Francis Marion Young, *Fort Laramie and the Pageant of the West, 1834–1890* (Lincoln: University of Nebraska Press, 1938), p. 73.

25. The story of Fort Laramie is taken from several sources, mainly Nadeau, *Fort Laramie and the Sioux*; Hafen and Young, *Fort Laramie and the Pageant of the West, 1834–1890*; and David Lavender, *Fort Laramie and the Changing Frontier* (Washington, D.C.: National Park Service, 1983).

26. John J. Killoren, *"Come, Black Robe": De Smet and the Indian Tragedy* (Norman: University of Oklahoma Press, 1994), p. 139.

27. Nadeau, *Fort Laramie and the Sioux*, p. 40.

28. Chips interview, Ricker tablets.

CHAPTER 5. PRAIRIE TRAVELERS

1. The story of the migration west is taken mainly from Hafen and Young, *Fort Laramie and the Pageant of the West*; John J. Killoren, *"Come, Black Robe"*; Nadeau, *Fort Laramie and the Sioux Indians*; John D. Unruh, Jr., *The Plains Across: The Overland Emigrants and the Trans-Mississippi West, 1840–60* (Urbana: University of Illinois Press, 1979); Lavender, *Fort Laramie and the Changing Frontier*; John A. Garraty, *The American Nation: A History of the United States* (New York: Harper & Row, 1966); and Merrill J. Mattes, *The Great Platte River Road* (Lincoln: University of Nebraska Press, 1987).

2. Unruh, *Plains Across*, pp. 90–97.

3. Ibid., pp. 36–42.

4. *New York Daily Tribune* (March 9, 1843).

5. Unruh, *Plains Across*, p. 43.

6. Mattes, *Great Platte River Road*, p. 23.

7. Killoren, *"Come, Black Robe,"* p. 140.

8. John Bidwell, *A Journey to California*, quoted in Unruh, *Plains Across*, p. 183; also in Leroy R. Hafen and W. J. Ghent, *Broken Hand: The Life Story of Thomas Fitzpatrick, Chief of the Mountain Men* (Denver: The Old West Publishing Co., 1931), p. 72.

9. Unruh, *Plains Across*, contains an extensive discussion of Indian/migrant interaction derived from migrant journals and letters, pp. 156–200.

10. Ibid., pp. 159 and 162–163.

11. Ibid., p. 170.

12. Ibid., pp. 166–167.

13. Evan S. Connell, *Son of the Morning Star: Custer and the Little Big Horn* (New York: Harper & Row, 1984), pp. 380–381.

14. Such descriptions of Indian/migrant encounters can be found scattered throughout histories of the overland migration, among them Unruh, *Plains Across*, and Mattes, *Great Platte River Road*.

15. Unruh, *Plains Across*, pp. 186–187.

16. Mattes, *Great Platte River Road*, p. 260.

17. Unruh, *Plains Across*, pp. 194–197. The story of the Mountain Meadows Massacre is told in great detail in Anna Jean Backus, *Mountain Meadows Witness: The Life and Times of Bishop Philip Klingensmith* (Spokane, Wash.: The Arthur H. Clark Co., 1995).

18. Lavender, *Fort Laramie and the Changing Frontier*, p. 67.

19. Joel Palmer, *Journal of Travels over the Rocky Mountains*. (Ann Arbor: University of Michigan microfilm, 1966).

20. Unruh, *Plains Across*, pp. 184–185.

21. Howard, *The Warrior Who Killed Custer*, pp. 16–18.

22. Hardorff, ed., *Oglala Lakota Crazy Horse*, p. 31, taken from Garrick Mallory, "Pictographs of the North American Indians," *Fourth Annual Report of the Bureau of Ethnology* (Washington, D.C., 1889).

23. The political makeup of the Oglala at the time of Crazy Horse's birth is described in Price, *Oglala People*; Hyde, *Red Cloud's Folk*; and Larson, *Red Cloud*.

24. Parkman, *Oregon Trail*, p. 138.

25. Ibid., p. 139.

26. The death of Bull Bear is described in Price, *Oglala People*; Robert W. Larson, *Red Cloud: Warrior-Statesman of the Lakota Sioux* (Norman: University of Oklahoma Press, 1997); Hyde, *Red Cloud's Folk*; and Paul, *Autobiography of Red Cloud*.

27. Parkman, *Oregon Trail*, p. 139.

28. Paul, *Autobiography of Red Cloud*, pp. 64–70.

29. Larson, *Red Cloud*, p. 61.

30. Parkman, *Oregon Trail*, p. 145.

31. Quoted in Unruh, *Plains Across*, p. 386.

32. Mattes, *Great Platte River Road*, p. 82.

33. George Hyde, *Life of George Bent* (Norman: University of Oklahoma Press, 1968), pp. 96–97.

CHAPTER 6.   THE GREAT SMOKE

1. *Missouri Republican* (October 24, 1851).

2. Ibid. Chambers was assisted by B. Gratz Brown, a young lawyer who would later become governor of Missouri and a vice presidential candidate in 1872. Also see Killoren, *"Come, Black Robe,"* p. 151.

3. Killoren, *"Come, Black Robe,"* p. 158.

4. Francis Paul Prucha, *American Indian Treaties: The History of a Political Anomaly* (Berkeley: University of California Press, 1997), p. 237.

5. Ibid. Also see Killoren, *"Come, Black Robe,"* p. 131.

6. Killoren, *"Come, Black Robe,"* p. 119.

7. Ibid., p. 131.

8. Ibid., p. 107.

9. *Missouri Republican* (September 21, 1851).

10. Ibid. (October 24, 1851).

11. Ibid. (October 26, 1851).

12. Ibid. (September 21, 1851).

13. Ibid. (November 2, 1851).

14. Ibid. (October 1, 1851).

15. Ibid. (November 23, 1851).

16. Ibid. (November 30, 1851).

17. Ibid. (November 30, 1851).

18. Prucha, *American Indian Treaties*, pp. 239–240.

19. Carruth, Gordon and Associates, eds., *American Facts and Dates*, pp. 199–225.

CHAPTER 7. BUFFALO AND WAR

1. DeMallie, ed., *The Sixth Grandfather*, pp. 145–147, and Neihardt, *Black Elk Speaks*, pp. 53–60. Material on the Lakota's relationship to the buffalo also was taken from Hassrick, *The Sioux*; James LaPointe, *Legends of the Lakota* (San Francisco: Indian Historian Press, 1976); and Workers of the South Dakota Writers' Project, Works Projects Administration, *Legends of the Mighty Sioux* (Chicago: Albert Whitman & Co., 1941).

2. Standing Bear, *My People the Sioux*, pp. 21–23.

3. Catlin, *North American Indians*, pp. 252–253.

4. Neihardt, *Black Elk Speaks*, p. 57.

5. Vestal, *Warpath*, p. 8.

6. Hinman, "Oglala Sources."

7. Neihardt, *Black Elk Speaks*, p. 85.

8. Hassrick, *The Sioux*, p. 134.

9. Ibid., pp. 134–135.

CHAPTER 8. THE COW

1. Mattes, *Great Platte River Trail*, p. 31.

2. Unruh, *Plains Across*, pp. 119–120, and Mattes, p. 23.

3. Unruh, *Plains Across*, p. 119.

4. Quoted in Hafen and Young, *Fort Laramie and the Pageant of the West*, p. 210. The boat incident is related in many sources. Along with Hafen and Young, they include Killoren, "*Come, Black Robe*"; Price, *Oglala People*; Unruh, *Plains Across*; and Lloyd E. McCann, "The Grattan Massacre," *Nebraska History* (1956).

5. Hafen and Young, *Fort Laramie*, pp. 210–211.

6. Unruh, *Plains Across*, p. 222, and Killoren, "*Come, Black Robe*," p. 129.

7. Unruh, *Plains Across*, p. 222.

8. The story of the Mormon cow is told in a number of places, including Hafen and Young, *Fort Laramie*; Killoren, "*Come, Black Robe*"; McCann, *Nebraska History*; Price, *Oglala People*; and Lavender, *Fort Laramie*. The account is taken from those sources, as well as the Frank Salaway interview in the Ricker tablets.

9. Mari Sandoz, *Crazy Horse: The Strange Man of the Oglalas* (Lincoln: University of Nebraska Press, 1961). Sandoz places the young Crazy Horse at the Grattan incident. Accounts by individuals who knew Crazy Horse do not report him present at the incident. That, however, is not unusual, since the plains Indians generally did not consider what happened in childhood as important and when talking of the past preferred to relate coups, brave deeds, and other accomplishments that gave them status in their society. Being a fictionalized biography that lacks source citations, it is tempting to dismiss many things in Sandoz's book except for the fact that she may have personally heard the story while growing up in western Nebraska. Sandoz material must be used selectively and with a critical eye.

10. McCann, "The Grattan Massacre."

11. Ibid.

12. Ibid.

13. Ibid.; Salaway interview, Ricker tablets.

14. Ibid.; McCann, "The Grattan Massacre."

15. Ibid.

16. Ibid.

17. Ibid.

18. Ibid.

19. Ibid.

CHAPTER 9.   A DEATH AND A LIFE

1. American Horse interview, Ricker tablets.

2. Sandoz, *Crazy Horse*, pp. 39–41. Sandoz places Curly with the Brulés and has him seeing Conquering Bear on his deathbed, then seeking a vision. Stephen E. Ambrose, *Crazy Horse and Custer: The Parallel Lives of Two American Warriors* (Garden City, N.Y.: Doubleday, 1975), also has Curly seeing Conquering Bear, and then seeking a vision. However, he bases his report on Sandoz. Since Sandoz heard many stories from old Lakota when she was a girl growing up in western Nebraska, her tales cannot be dismissed. But they always must be viewed with a certain critical eye because she does not provide sources and it has been proven many times by many historians that the tales of old Indians can be wrong when compared to the actual historic record. The problem is compounded when a legendary individual such as Crazy Horse is involved.

3. Information on visions is available in many sources, including DeMallie, ed., *The Sixth Grandfather*; Hassrick, *The Sioux*; and Neihardt, *Black Elk Speaks*. Other sources include James R. Walker, *Lakota Belief and Ritual* (Lincoln: University of Nebraska Press, 1980), and Brown, *The Sacred Pipe*.

4. Neihardt, *Black Elk Speaks*, pp. 21–22.

5. Vestal, *Warpath*, pp. 12–15, and DeMallie, ed. *The Sixth Grandfather*, pp. 84–86.

6. The story of Curly's vision can be found in the William Garnett interview in the Ricker tablets. Garnett served as an interpreter and claims to have heard

the story from Crazy Horse in 1868. The Cheyenne John Stands in Timber, *Cheyenne Memories* (New Haven, Conn.: Yale University Press, 1967), also reports the images of the vision as he saw them on a sand rock drawing Crazy Horse supposedly made after the Battle of the Little Big Horn, p. 105. In addition, the vision is reported in Sandoz, *Crazy Horse*, pp. 104–105, and Ambrose, *Crazy Horse and Custer*, pp. 68–69.

7. Chips interview, Ricker tablets.

8. The comments of both He Dog and Red Feather appear in Hinman, "Oglala Sources."

9. Stands in Timber, *Cheyenne Memories*, p. 105.

10. Neihardt, *Black Elk Speaks*, pp. 86–87.

11. Chips interview, Ricker tablets.

12. Quoted in McCreight, *Firewater and Forked Tongues*, pp. 138–139.

13. Sandoz, *Crazy Horse*, pp. 41–43, and Ambrose, *Crazy Horse and Custer*, pp. 68–69.

14. Quoted in Killoren, *"Come, Black Robe,"* p. 202.

15. *New York Daily Times* (September 12, 1854).

16. Quoted in Killoren, *"Come, Black Robe,"* p. 202.

17. *New York Daily Times* (September 14, 1854).

18. Quoted in Killoren, *"Come, Black Robe,"* p. 204.

19. Logan's Lament: "I appeal to any white man to say if ever he entered Logan's cabin hungry, and I gave him not meat; if ever he came cold or naked, and I gave him not clothing.

"During the course of the last long and bloody war, Logan remained in his tent, an advocate of peace. Nay, such was my love for the whites, that those of my own country pointed at me as they passed, and said, 'Logan is the friend of the white man.' I had even thought to live with you, but for the injuries of one man, Colonel Cresap the last spring, in cold blood, and unprovoked, cut off all the relatives of Logan; not sparing even my women and children. There runs not a drop of my blood in the veins of any human creature. This called on me for revenge. I have sought it. I have killed many. I have fully glutted my vengeance. For my country, I rejoice at the beams of peace. Yet, do not harbor the thought that mine is the joy of fear. Logan never felt fear. He will not turn on his heel to save his life. Who is there to mourn for Logan? Not one." Quoted in Jim Schafer and Mike Sajna, *Allegheny River: Watershed of the Nation* (University Park: Penn State Press, 1993).

20. Quoted in Killoren, *"Come, Black Robe,"* pp. 203–204.

Chapter 10.   Blue Water

1. Sandoz, *Crazy Horse*, pp. 45–62. The story should be viewed skeptically because Sandoz does not supply a source and it fits too well with the heroic image of Crazy Horse that she constantly seeks to build.

2. The Brulés' actions after Conquering Bear's death are reported by many sources, including Hyde, *Spotted Tail's Folk*, p. 56, and *Red Cloud's Folk*, p. 77; Hafen and Young, *Fort Laramie*, p. 234; Killoren, *"Come, Black Robe,"* p. 205;

Mattes, *The Great Platte River Road*, p. 313; and Fred H. Werner, *With Harney on the Blue Water: Battle of Ash Hollow, September 3, 1855* (Greeley, Colo.: Werner Publications, 1988).

3. Quoted in Hafen and Young, *Fort Laramie*, p. 233.

4. Ibid., p. 234.

5. Ibid., pp. 233–235.

6. Ibid., pp. 235–236.

7. Ibid., p. 236.

8. Ibid., pp. 236–237.

9. The Brulés' actions during the summer of 1855 are recorded by several sources, including Hyde, *Spotted Tail's Folk*, p. 57; Mattes, *Great Platte River Road*, p. 314; Sandoz, *Crazy Horse*, pp. 69–70; and Ambrose, *Crazy Horse and Custer*, p. 70.

10. Sandoz, *Crazy Horse*, p. 70. The author bases the story on accounts by He Dog and Maglorie Alexis Mousseau, both part of Ricker tablets; a manuscript by Susan Bettelyoun, daughter of trader James Bordeaux, in the Nebraska State Historical Society; and her own recollections of stories she heard as a child.

11. Hyde, *Spotted Tail's Folk*, p. 57.

12. Hinman, "Oglala Sources."

13. October 31, 1932, letter from Walter S. Campbell to Eleanor Hinman. Campbell wrote several works of western history under the pen name Stanley Vestal. He was a friend of White Bull. The letter is in the Walter Stanley Campbell Collection in the Western History Collections of the University of Oklahoma.

14. The Battle of the Blue Water or Ash Hollow is reported by many sources, including Hyde, *Spotted Tail's Folk* and *Red Cloud's Folk*; Matte, *Great Platte River Road*; Ambrose, *Crazy Horse and Custer*; and Werner, *With Harney on the Blue Water*.

15. Hyde, *Spotted Tail's Folk*, p. 58.

16. Quoted in Matte, *Great Platte River Road*, p. 314.

17. Hyde, *Spotted Tail's Folk*, p. 59.

18. Quoted in Matte, *Great Platte River Road*, p. 319.

19. Hyde, *Spotted Tail's Folk*, pp. 60–61.

20. Matte, *Great Platte River Road*, pp. 320–329.

21. Ibid., p. 320.

22. Ibid., pp. 320–321.

23. Ibid., p. 321.

24. Ibid., p. 322.

25. Werner, *With Harney on the Blue Water*, p. 67.

26. Matte, *Great Platte River Road*, pp. 322–323.

27. Hyde, *Spotted Tail's Folk*, p. 61.

28. Quoted in Matte, *Great Platte River Road*, pp. 326–327.

29. Ibid., p. 327.

30. Ibid.

31. Sandoz, *Crazy Horse*, pp. 76–78 and 92. Also Ambrose, *Crazy Horse and Custer*, p. 73.

32. Werner, *With Harney on the Blue Water*, p. 53.

33. Quoted in Matte, *Great Platte River Road*, p. 331.
34. Ibid.
35. Werner, *With Harney on the Blue Water*, p. 82.
36. Matte, *Great Platte River Road*, p. 331.
37. Hyde, *Spotted Tail's Folk*, p. 63.

CHAPTER 11. CRAZY HORSE

1. Hyde, *Spotted Tail's Folk*, pp. 64–65. Hyde also provides an interesting comparison of the historic record to the various tales related by more modern Lakota, which maintain that fifteen warriors took part in the mail train robbery. Only five were ever arrested.
2. Letter reproduced in Werner, *With Harney on the Blue Water*, pp. 86–89.
3. Ibid.
4. Ibid.
5. Ibid.
6. Killoren, *"Come, Black Robe,"* pp. 205–206.
7. Ibid.
8. Hyde, *Life of George Bent*, p. 100.
9. The white version of the incident is told in several places, including Unruh, *The Plains Across*, p. 216, and Hafen and Hafen, *Relations with the Indians of the Plains*, pp. 15–18.
10. Hyde, *Life of George Bent*, p. 100.
11. Ibid., p. 10.
12. Hyde, *Life of George Bent*, pp. 101–102; Unruh, *The Plains Across*, p. 216; and Killoren, *"Come, Black Robe,"* p. 207.
13. Killoren, *"Come, Black Robe,"* p. 207.
14. Unruh, *The Plains Across*, pp. 216–217.
15. Hyde provides a detailed look at Lakota movement and white encroachment on their lands in the late 1850s in *Red Cloud's Folk*, pp. 83–98. Discussions of events at the time also can be found in Hyde, *Spotted Tail's Folk*; Killoren, *"Come, Black Robe"*; Unruh, *The Plains Across*; and numerous other works dealing with the period.
16. The Bear Butte council is reported in numerous sources. Lieutenant Warren's report on his encounter with the Lakota following the council was published in 1875 in *Explorations in Nebraska and Dakota*, reprinted in Robinson, *A History of the Dakota or Sioux Indians*, pp. 227–230. Information also in Hyde, *Red Cloud's Folk*, pp. 82–83, and *Spotted Tail's Folk*, pp. 78–79.
17. Chips interview, Ricker tablets.
18. The story of Curly's name change to Crazy Horse can be found in the Chips interview, Ricker tablets, and Hinman, *"Oglala Sources,"* pp. 9–10.

CHAPTER 12. THE WARRIOR

1. Thunder Tail was interviewed by Ivan Stars as part of an oral history project on the Pine Ridge Reservation in 1915. The interview manuscript is housed in Marquette University's Memorial Library. When compared to the his-

torical record, the interview contains some factual errors. Thunder Tail, for instance, is the only source who reports Crazy Horse with two brothers. However, many other things within it match the record. Whether Thunder Tail witnessed the events he reports or is just relating stories told by others is difficult to determine. At times, though, he refers to "we," which would seem to indicate that he was present at some of the events.

2. Eagle Elk's remarks are contained in a manuscript in the John Neihardt papers in the Western Historical Manuscript Collection of the University of Missouri/State Historical Society of Missouri.

3. Chips interview, Ricker tablets.

4. White Bull's remarks can be found in an October 13, 1932, letter to Eleanor Hinman from Walter Campbell, who wrote under the name Stanley Vestal. The letter is part of the Walter Stanley Campbell Collection in the Western History Collection of the University of Oklahoma.

5. Hinman, "Oglala Sources."

6. Blish, Bad Heart Bull manuscript.

7. The stories can be found in the Thunder Tail interview in Marquette University.

8. Hinman, "Oglala Sources."

9. Ibid.

10. McCreight, *Firewater and Forked Tongues*, p. 139.

11. Hinman, "Oglala Sources."

12. Ibid.

13. Eagle Elk manuscript.

14. Hinman, "Oglala Sources."

15. Stanley Vestal, *New Sources of Indian History, 1850–1891* (Norman: University of Oklahoma Press, 1934), pp. 320–321.

16. Eagle Elk manuscript.

17. Ibid.

18. Ibid.

19. Ibid.

CHAPTER 13. NATIONS DIVIDED

1. Hyde, *Life of George Bent*, pp. 105–109.

2. Quoted in Killoren, *"Come, Black Robe,"* p. 240.

3. The story of Indian/white relations at the beginning of the 1860s is told in many places, including Killoren, *"Come, Black Robe"*; Hyde, *Life of George Bent, Spotted Tail's Folk*, and *Red Cloud's Folk*; Price, *The Oglala People*; and Larson, *Red Cloud*.

4. Prucha, *American Indian Treaties*, pp. 269–270.

5. Hyde, *Spotted Tail's Folk*, pp. 83–84.

6. Price, *Oglala People*, pp. 45–46.

7. Richard Irving Dodge, *Thirty-three Years Among Our Wild Indians* (New York: Archer House, 1959), p. 91.

8. The basic story of the Great Sioux Uprising of 1862 was taken from the public television program "The Dakota Conflict."

9. Quoted in Hyde, *Red Cloud's Folk*, p. 102.

10. Eugene F. Ware, *The Indian War of 1864* (Lincoln: University of Nebraska Press, 1994), pp. 23–24.

11. Material on the behavior of troops and officers comes from Hyde, *Red Cloud's Folk*, pp. 102–104.

12. Material on the growing white encroachment and Lakota response was taken from Hyde, *Red Cloud's Folk*; Larson, *Red Cloud*; and Price, *Oglala People*.

Chapter 14. Love and War

1. Sandoz's *Crazy Horse*, pp. 131–134, is the source for the story of Crazy Horse falling in love with Black Buffalo Woman while in his late teens or early twenties. It is repeated in such works as Ambrose, *Crazy Horse and Custer*, p. 137, and Larson, *Red Cloud*, p. 77. Since Sandoz's *Crazy Horse* is more a work of fiction than biography, anything that appears in it must be viewed skeptically.

2. Hinman, "Oglala Sources," contains the primary information on Crazy Horse and Black Buffalo Woman. Ricker, Chips's interview, also mentions Crazy Horse's involvement with Black Buffalo Woman.

3. For a report on Lakota marriage customs see Hassrick, *The Sioux*, pp. 108–109 and 121–132.

4. Erik H. Erikson, "Observation on Sioux Education," *The Journal of Psychology*, 7 (1937), cited in Ambrose, *Crazy Horse and Custer*, p. 141.

5. Hyde, *Life of George Bent*, p. 118.

6. Bob Scott, *Blood at Sand Creek: The Massacre Revisited* (Caldwell, Idaho: Caxton Printers, 1994), pp. 13–17, and Hyde, *Life of George Bent*, pp. 110–111.

7. Larson, *Red Cloud*, p. 80.

8. Hyde, *Life of George Bent*, pp. 119–121.

9. Hyde, *Spotted Tail's Folk*, p. 88.

10. Hyde, *Life of George Bent*, pp. 122–123.

11. Ibid., p. 142.

12. Scott, *Blood at Sand Creek*, pp. 72–73.

13. Connell, *Son of the Morning Star*, pp. 162–163.

14. Scott, *Blood at Sand Creek*, p. 73.

15. Hyde, *Red Cloud's Folk*, pp. 108–109.

16. Hyde, *Life of George Bent*, pp. 151–152.

17. Scott, *Blood at Sand Creek*, pp. 151–153.

18. Ware, *The Indian War of 1864*, p. 309.

19. Quoted in Connell, *Son of the Morning Star*, p. 178.

20. Scott, *Blood at Sand Creek*, pp. 156–157.

21. Ibid., p. 159.

22. Connell, *Son of the Morning Star*, p. 178.

23. Quoted in Scott, *Blood at Sand Creek*, p. 181.

24. Ibid., p. 183.

25. Connell, *Son of the Morning Star*, p. 177.

26. Ibid.

Chapter 15.   Shirt-Wearer

1. Hyde, *Life of George Bent*, p. 171.
2. Ibid., p. 175.
3. Hinman, "Oglala Sources."
4. Hyde, *Red Cloud's Folk*, pp. 115–118.
5. See Hyde, *Red Cloud's Folk*, p. 118, and Hinman, "Oglala Sources."
6. Sandoz's *Crazy Horse* is the source for Crazy Horse's involvement with Caspar Collins. Typically, though, it contains no supporting sources for the information. Neither is support found in Agnes Wright Spring, *Caspar Collins: The Life and Exploits of an Indian Fighter of the Sixties* (New York: Columbia University Press, 1927).
7. Information on shirt-wearers comes from Hassrick, *The Sioux*, pp. 26–27.
8. Hinman, "Oglala Sources."
9. Garnett interview, Ricker tablets.
10. The general description of the business world at the time comes from Ron Chernow, *Titan: The Life of John D. Rockefeller, Sr.* (New York: Random House, 1998), pp. 97–99.
11. Paul L. Hedren, ed., *The Great Sioux War 1876–77* (Helena: Montana Historical Society Press, 1991), p. 103.

Chapter 16.   Platte Bridge

1. Information on the actions of the Lakota and the Cheyenne at the end of the Civil War comes from Hyde, *Red Cloud's Folk*; Hyde, *The Life of George Bent*; and Larson, *Red Cloud*.
2. Hyde, *The Life of George Bent*, p. 212.
3. Ibid., p. 213.
4. Ibid., pp. 218–219.
5. Ibid., pp. 125–126.
6. Sandoz, *Crazy Horse*, pp. 166–167.

Chapter 17.   One Hundred White Men Killed

1. Harlan's quotes and other information on the Northwest Peace Commission comes from Prucha, *American Indian Treaties*, pp. 270–271. Some information also is taken from Hyde, *Red Cloud's Folk*, and Killoren, "Come, Black Robe."
2. Quoted in Prucha, *American Indian Treaties*, p. 272.
3. Quoted in Killoren, "Come, Black Robe," pp. 267–273.
4. Hyde, *Red Cloud's Folk*, p. 139.
5. Quoted from Carrington report in Dee Brown, *The Fetterman Massacre* (Lincoln: University of Nebraska Press, 1971), p. 43.
6. Quoted in Larson, *Red Cloud*, pp. 92–93.
7. Brown, *Fetterman Massacre*, p. 44.

8. Ibid., pp. 78–79.

9. Quotes and story of the Gazzous woman's story come from Brown, *Fetterman Massacre*, pp. 78–80, who took them from Carrington's original report.

10. Ibid., p. 85.

11. Ibid., p. 147.

12. Vestal, *Warpath*, p. 59.

13. Brown, *Fetterman Massacre*, p. 150.

14. Ibid., pp. 155–156.

15. Ibid., p. 164.

16. Ibid., p. 166.

17. Vestal, *Warpath*, p. 54.

18. Hinman, "Oglala Sources."

19. Quoted in Brown, *Fetterman Massacre*, p. 169.

20. Ibid.

21. Ibid., p. 174.

22. Vestal, *Warpath*, p. 61.

23. Ibid., p. 67, and Brown, *Fetterman Massacre*, p. 181.

CHAPTER 18. WAGON BOX FIGHT

1. Quoted in Killoren, *"Come, Black Robe,"* p. 280.

2. Ibid., pp. 280–281.

3. Basic information on the events of early 1867 was taken from Hyde, *Red Cloud's Folk*; Killoren, *"Come, Black Robe"*; and Larson, *Red Cloud*.

4. Quoted in Killoren, *"Come, Black Robe,"* p. 282.

5. Ibid., p. 282.

6. Hyde, *Red Cloud's Folk*, p. 154.

7. Details on the Wagon Box Fight were taken from Larson, *Red Cloud*; Vestal, *Warpath*; and Jerry Keenan, *The Wagon Box Fight* (Boulder, Colo.: Lightning Tree Press, 1992).

8. Keenan, *Wagon Box Fight*, p. 11.

9. Ibid., p. 16.

10. Ibid., p. 18.

11. Ibid., pp. 23–24.

CHAPTER 19. VICTORY

1. General information on actions leading to the Fort Laramie Treaty of 1868 comes from Larson, *Red Cloud*; Hyde, *Red Cloud's Folk*; Killoren, *"Come, Black Robe"*; and Prucha, *American Indian Treaties*.

2. Quoted in Killoren, *"Come, Black Robe,"* p. 307.

3. Ibid., pp. 308–309.

4. Quoted in Ambrose, *Crazy Horse and Custer*, p. 305.

5. Hyde, *Red Cloud's Folk*, p. 171, and Larson, *Red Cloud*, p. 126.

Chapter 20. Love and Death

1. Hyde, *Red Cloud's Folk*, pp. 173–174.

2. Larson, *Red Cloud*, p. 128.

3. Ibid., p. 129.

4. Quoted in Hyde, *Red Cloud's Folk*, p. 177.

5. Ibid.

6. Ibid., p. 179.

7. Ibid., pp. 179–180.

8. Ibid., p. 184.

9. Hinman, "Oglala Sources," p. 13.

10. Ibid., pp. 16–17.

11. Ibid., p. 17.

12. Ibid.

13. Ibid., p. 19.

14. Ibid., p. 18.

15. Ibid., p. 33.

16. Ibid., pp. 15–16.

17. Ibid., pp. 14–15.

18. Ibid., p. 31.

Chapter 21. Agency Indians

1. The basic story of the Lakota after Red Cloud's return from Washington comes from Larson, *Red Cloud*, and Hyde, *Red Cloud's Folk*. Quote is from Larson, p. 139.

2. Hyde, *Red Cloud's Folk*, pp. 192–193.

3. Ambrose, *Crazy Horse and Custer*, p. 352.

4. Hinman, "Oglala Sources."

5. The *New York Sun*, September 14, 1877, mentioned in Hardorff, *Crazy Horse*, p. 34.

6. DeBarthe, *The Adventures of Frank Grouard*, pp. 181–182.

7. Larson, *Red Cloud*, p. 150.

8. Ibid., pp. 151–152.

9. Ibid., pp. 156–157.

10. Hyde, *Red Cloud's Folk*, p. 198.

11. Vestal, *Warpath*, p. 139.

12. Ibid., p. 140.

13. Ibid., p. 141.

14. Ibid., p. 142.

15. Ibid., p. 143.

CHAPTER 22.   CHIEF OF ALL THE THIEVES

1. The basic information on Gall's fight with Stanley comes from Robert M. Utley, *The Lance and the Shield: The Life and Times of Sitting Bull* (New York: Henry Holt, 1993).

2. Ibid., p. 111.

3. Sandoz, *Crazy Horse*, p. 275, and Ambrose, *Crazy Horse and Custer*, p. 362.

4. DeBarthe, *Frank Grouard*, pp. 52–53.

5. The story of the Yellowstone Wagon Road Association is taken from Utley, *The Lance and the Shield*, pp. 118–119; Addison Quivey, "The Yellowstone Expedition of 1874," *Historical Society of Montana* (1876), pp. 268–284; and James S. Hutchins, "Poison in the Pemmican: The Yellowstone Wagon-Road and Prospecting Expedition of 1874," *Montana the Magazine of Western History* (Summer 1958), pp. 8–15.

6. Quivey, *"Yellowstone Expedition,"* p. 275.

7. Utley, *The Lance and the Shield*, p. 118.

8. Ibid., p. 119.

9. The basic story of the Custer expedition and the Black Hills Gold Rush comes from Donald Jackson, *Custer's Gold: The United States Cavalry Expedition of 1874* (Lincoln: University of Nebraska, 1972) and Watson Parker, *Gold in the Black Hills* (Norman: University of Oklahoma Press, 1966), pp. 6–7.

10. DeMallie, *The Sixth Grandfather*, p. 164.

11. Parker, *Gold in the Black Hills*, pp. 6–7.

12. Quoted in Jackson, *Custer's Gold*, pp. 8–9.

13. Ibid., p. 14.

14. Ibid., p. 80.

15. Ibid., p. 81.

16. Ibid., pp. 87–88.

17. Ibid., p. 89.

18. Ibid.

19. Ibid., p. 90.

20. Ibid.

21. Ibid., p. 107.

CHAPTER 23.   PAHA SAPA

1. The basic stories of the flagpole and census incidents were taken from Hyde, *Red Cloud's Folk*, pp. 221–223.

2. Utley, *The Lance and the Shield*, pp. 119–120.

3. Quoted in Larson, *Red Cloud*, p. 169. The general story of the 1875 summit and the efforts to purchase the Black Hills comes from Ambrose, *Crazy*

Horse and Custer; Hyde, *Red Cloud's Folk;* and Robinson, *A History of the Dakota Sioux.*

4. Hyde, *Spotted Tail's Folk,* pp. 210–211.

5. *New York Tribune* (September 21, 1875).

6. DeBarthe, *Adventures of Frank Grouard,* p. 85.

7. Ibid.

8. Ibid., p. 86.

9. Ibid.

10. Ibid.

11. Ibid.

12. Quoted in Price, *The Oglala People,* p. 150.

13. Ibid., p. 151.

14. Ibid., p. 152.

15. Garnett interview, Ricker tablets.

16. Price, *The Oglala People,* p. 153.

CHAPTER 24.   GREASY GRASS

1. Hinman, "Oglala Sources."

2. Utley, *The Lance and the Shield,* pp. 128–129. Material on the situation in late 1875 and early 1876 also comes from Robinson, *A Good Year to Die;* Ambrose, *Crazy Horse and Custer;* and Hyde, *Red Cloud's Folk.*

3. DeBarthe, *Life and Adventures of Frank Grouard,* p. 97.

4. Ibid., p. 98.

5. Quoted in Vestal, *Warpath,* p. 182.

6. Hinman, "Oglala Sources"; Vestal, *Warpath,* p. 182. The quote is from Utley, *The Lance and the Shield,* p. 132.

7. Hinman, "Oglala Sources."

8. Ibid.

9. Quoted in Utley, *The Lance and the Shield,* p. 133.

10. Quoted in Robinson, *A Good Year to Die,* p. 56.

11. Figures are from Utley, *The Lance and the Shield,* pp. 133–135.

12. Hinman, "Oglala Sources."

13. Utley, *The Lance and the Shield,* p. 137.

14. Quoted in Robinson, *A Good Year to Die,* p. 123.

15. Sitting Bull's dream as told by One Bull is related in Utley, *The Lance and the Shield,* p. 136.

16. Ibid., p. 137.

17. Neihardt, *The Sixth Grandfather,* p. 173.

18. Quoted in Utley, *The Lance and the Shield,* p. 138.

19. Quoted in Robinson, *A Good Year to Die,* p. 139.

20. Quoted in Utley, *The Lance and the Shield,* p. 140.

21. Ibid., and Robinson, *A Good Year to Die,* p. 139.

22. Quoted in Utley, *The Lance and the Shield,* p. 140.

23. Quoted in Robinson, *A Good Year to Die,* p. 140.

24. Quoted in Utley, *The Lance and the Shield*, p. 141.

25. Hinman, "Oglala Sources."

26. For a discussion of the size of the village along the Little Big Horn see Gregory F. Michno, *Lakota Noon: The Indian Narrative of Custer's Defeat* (Missoula, Mont.: Mountain Press, 1997), pp. 3–20.

27. Richard G. Hardorff, ed., *Lakota Recollections of the Custer Fight: New Sources of Indian-Military History* (Spokane, Wash.: Arthur H. Clark Co., 1991), p. 82.

28. Michno, *Lakota Noon*, pp. 68–69.

29. Neihardt, *Black Elk Speaks*, pp. 110–111 and Hardorff, *Lakota Recollections*, pp. 64–65.

30. M. I. McCreight, *Firewater and Forked Tongues: A Sioux Chief Interprets U.S. History* (Pasadena, Calif.: Trail's End Publishing, 1947), p. 112.

31. Neihardt, *Black Elk Speaks*, pp. 120–121.

32. McCreight, *Firewater and Forked Tongues*, pp. 112–113.

33. Michno, *Lakota Noon*, pp. 145–146 and p. 165.

34. Ibid., pp. 177, 180.

35. Hardorff, ed., *Lakota Recollections*, p. 115.

36. Ibid. Also see Michno, *Lakota Noon*, p. 218.

37. Hardorff, ed., *Lakota Recollections*, p. 115.

38. Ibid., pp. 87–88.

39. James H. Howard, ed., *The Warrior Who Killed Custer: The Personal Narrative of Chief Joseph White Bull* (Lincoln: University of Nebraska Press, 1968), p. 58.

40. Hardorff, ed., *Lakota Recollections*, pp. 114–116, 207.

41. Ibid., p. 113.

42. Cyrus Townsend Brady, *Indian Fights and Fighters* (Lincoln: University of Nebraska Press, 1971).

43. Eastman, *Indian Heroes and Great Chieftains*, p. 100.

44. Sandoz, *Crazy Horse*, p. 329.

45. Ambrose, *Crazy Horse and Custer*, p. 442.

46. Welch and Stekler repeated the story while acknowledging that there is "pretty convincing evidence" against it.

47. Michno's story of the noncharge can be found in *Lakota Noon*, pp. 242–247, and in the article "Crazy Horse, Custer, and the Sweep to the North," *Montana: The Magazine of Western History* (Summer 1993).

48. Hardorff, ed., *Lakota Recollections*, p. 50, and McCreight, *Firewater and Forked Tongues*, p. 114.

49. Chips interview, Ricker tablets.

50. Michno, *Lakota Noon*, p. 246.

51. Chips interview, Ricker tablets.

52. Connell, *Son of the Morning Star*, p. 390.

CHAPTER 25. KILLING LONG HAIR

1. Neihardt, *Black Elk Speaks*, p. 128.

2. Ibid., pp. 129–130.

3. Rex C. Myers, "Montana Editors and the Custer Battle," *Montana: The Magazine of Western History* (Spring 1976).

4. The *Dallas Daily Herald, Austin Daily State Gazette*, and *Chicago Tribune* are quoted in Connell, *Son of the Morning Star*, p. 331. The *Black Hills Pioneer* quote is from the July 22, 1876, edition.

5. The *Richmond State, Charles Journal of Commerce, Austin Weekly Democratic Statesman*, and *Wilmington Daily Journal* are quoted in Brian Dippie, "Southern Response to Custer's Last Stand," *Montana: The Magazine of Western History* (Spring 1971).

6. Quoted in Connell, *Son of the Morning Star*, p. 332.

7. Quote in Jerome A. Greene, *Slim Buttes, 1876: An Episode of the Great Sioux War* (Norman: University of Oklahoma Press, 1982), p. 60.

8. Neihardt, *Black Elk Speaks*, p. 133.

9. Ibid.

10. Ibid., pp. 133–134.

11. Ibid., p. 134.

12. Ibid., p. 136, and Hinman, "Oglala Sources."

13. Neihardt, *Black Elk Speaks*, p. 136.

CHAPTER 26.   PEACE

1. For an account of the peace efforts see Harry H. Anderson, "Indian Peace-Talkers and the Conclusion of the Sioux War of 1876," *Nebraska History* (December 1963).

2. Fred H. Werner, *Faintly Sounds the War-Cry: The Story of the Battle Butte Fight, January 8, 1877* (Greeley, Colo.: Werner Publications, 1983), pp. 42–43.

3. Neihardt, *Sixth Grandfather*, p. 200.

4. Ibid.

5. Ibid., p. 201.

6. Anderson, "Indian Peace-Talkers."

7. Werner, *Faintly Sounds the War-Cry*, p. 19.

8. Neihardt, *Black Elk Speaks*, p. 137.

9. Ibid., p. 138.

10. Garnett interview, Ricker tablets.

11. Neihardt, *Black Elk Speaks*, p. 138.

12. Ibid., pp. 138–139.

13. Anderson, "Indian Peace-Talkers."

14. Carroll Friswold and Robert A. Clark, eds., *The Killing of Chief Crazy Horse* (Lincoln: University of Nebraska Press, 1988), pp. 52–53. He Dog was interviewed by his son, Rev. Eagle Hawk, long after his surrender. Quotes attributed to him should be read with those thoughts in mind. The time sequence in the interview also is somewhat confusing because of the Indian habit of telling stories out of sequence and probably also because of the time that passed between the event and the interview. I have tried to use the He Dog interview in conjunction with reports from the time to put together as accurate as possible a description of events surrounding Crazy Horse's surrender.

15. Ibid., pp. 54–55.

16. Neihardt, *Black Elk Speaks*, p. 139.

17. Quoted in E. A. Brininstool, "How Crazy Horse Died," *Nebraska History* (January 1929) from John G. Bourke, *On the Border with Crook* (New York: Charles Scribner's Sons, 1891).

18. Friswold, *Killing of Chief Crazy Horse*, p. 119.

19. Ibid., p. 96.

20. Louis Bordeaux interview, Ricker tablets, and Brininstool, "How Crazy Horse Died."

21. Edward and Mabell Kadlecek, *To Kill an Eagle: Indian Views on the Last Days of Crazy Horse* (Boulder, Colo.: Johnson Books, 1981), pp. 39–43.

22. Quoted in Brininstool, "How Crazy Horse Died."

23. Garnett interview, Ricker tablets and Hardorff, ed., *The Oglala Lakota Crazy Horse*, p. 22.

24. Quoted in Brininstool, "How Crazy Horse Died."

25. Hardorff, ed., *The Oglala Lakota Crazy Horse*, p. 22, and Kadlecek, *To Kill an Eagle*, p. 46.

26. Quoted in Kadlecek, *To Kill an Eagle*, p. 47. From a letter by agent Benjamin Shapp to the commissioner of Indian affairs.

27. Bordeaux interview, Ricker tablets.

28. Ibid. Also see Brininstool, "How Crazy Horse Died."

29. Quoted in Brininstool, "How Crazy Horse Died."

30. Friswold, *Killing of Chief Crazy Horse*, p. 61.

31. Quoted in Kadlecek, *To Kill an Eagle*, pp. 49–50.

32. Quoted in Brininstool, "How Crazy Horse Died."

33. Ibid.

34. Ibid.

35. Friswold, *Killing of Chief Crazy Horse*, pp. 77–78.

36. Ibid., p. 79.

37. Quoted in Brininstool, "How Crazy Horse Died."

38. Friswold, *Killing of Chief Crazy Horse*, p. 79.

39. Ibid., pp. 80–81.

40. Ibid., pp. 83–84.

41. Brininstool, "How Crazy Horse Died."

42. Ibid.

43. Ibid.

44. Ibid.

45. Ibid.

46. Ibid.

47. Ibid.

48. For a detailed account of Crazy Horse's final struggle based on modern homicide investigation techniques see James N. Gilbert, "The Death of Crazy Horse: A Contemporary Examination of the Homicidal Events of 5 September 1877," *Journal of the West* (January 1993). Also see Hinman, "Oglala Sources"; Ricker tablets, Garnett and Bordeaux interviews; Friswold, *Killing of Chief*

Crazy Horse; Hardorff, ed., *The Oglala Lakota Crazy Horse;* and Brininstool, "How Crazy Horse Died."

49. Friswold, *Killing of Chief Crazy Horse,* pp. 125.

50. Ibid., pp. 125–126.

51. Brininstool, "How Crazy Horse Died."

52. Ibid.

53. Ibid.

BIBLIOGRAPHY

Books

Ambrose, Stephen E. *Crazy Horse and Custer: The Parallel Lives of Two American Warriors.* Garden City, N.Y.: Doubleday, 1975.

Athearn, Robert G. *William Tecumseh Sherman and the Settlement of the West.* Norman: University of Oklahoma Press, 1956.

Backus, Anna Jean. *Mountain Meadows Witness: The Life and Times of Bishop Philip Klingensmith.* Spokane, Wash.: The Arthur H. Clark Co., 1995.

Benson, Maxine, ed. *From Pittsburgh to the Rocky Mountains: Major Stephen Long's Expedition 1819–1820.* Golden, Colo.: Fulcrum, 1988.

Berkhofer, Robert F., Jr. *The White Man's Indian.* New York: Alfred A. Knopf, 1978.

Blish, Helen. *A Pictographic History of the Oglala Sioux.* Lincoln: University of Nebraska Press, 1967.

Bordewich, Fergus M. *Killing the White Man's Indian.* New York: Doubleday, 1996.

Bourke, John G. *On the Border with Crook.* Lincoln: University of Nebraska Press, 1971.

Brady, Cyrus Townsend. *Indian Fights and Fighters.* Lincoln: University of Nebraska Press, 1971.

Brininstool, E. A. *Fighting Indian Warriors: True Tales of the Wild Frontiers.* Harrisburg, Pa.: Stackpole, 1953.

Brown, Dee. *Bury My Heart at Wounded Knee.* New York: Holt, Rinehart, & Winston, 1970.

——. *The Fetterman Massacre.* Lincoln: University of Nebraska Press, 1971.

——. *Fort Phil Kearny: An American Saga.* New York: G. P. Putnam's Sons, 1962.

Brown, Joseph Epes, ed. *The Sacred Pipe: Black Elk's Account of the Seven Rites of the Oglala Sioux.* Norman: University of Oklahoma Press, 1963.

Brown, Vinson. *Crazy Horse: Hoka Hey!* Happy Camp, Calif.: Naturegraph Publishers, 1994.

Brumble, H. David III. *American Indian Autobiography.* Berkeley: University of California Press, 1988.

Buecker, Thomas R., and R. Eli Paul. *The Crazy Horse Surrender Ledger.* Lincoln: Nebraska State Historical Society, 1994.

Carrington, Margaret. *Absaraka: Home of the Crows.* Chicago: R. R. Donnelley, 1950.

Carruth, Gordon and Associates, eds. *The Encyclopedia of American Facts and Dates.* New York: Thomas Y. Crowell, 1979.

Catlin, George. *Letters and Notes on the North American Indians.* Edited by Michael MacDonald. New York: Clarkson N. Potter, 1975.

———. *North American Indians.* New York: Viking, 1989.

Chernow, Ron. *Titan: The Life of John D. Rockefeller, Sr.* New York: Random House, 1998.

Clark, William Philo. *The Indian Sign Language.* Lincoln: University of Nebraska Press, 1982.

Connell, Evan S. *Son of the Morning Star: Custer and the Little Big Horn.* New York: Harper & Row, 1984.

Crook, George. *General George Crook: His Autobiography.* Norman: University of Oklahoma Press, 1960.

DeBarthe, Joe. *The Life and Adventures of Frank Grouard.* Norman: University of Oklahoma Press, 1958.

DeMallie, Raymond J., ed. *The Sixth Grandfather: Black Elk's Teachings Given to John G. Neihardt.* Lincoln: University of Nebraska Press, 1984.

Demos, John. *The Unredeemed Captive.* New York: Alfred A. Knopf, 1994.

De Smet, Pierre-Jean. *Letters and Sketches: With a Narrative of a Year's Residence Among the Indian Tribes of the Rocky Mountains.* Philadelphia: M. Fithian, 1843.

Dodge, Richard Irving. *The Plains of the Great West and Their Inhabitants.* New York: Archer House, 1959.

———. *Thirty-three Years Among Our Wild Indians.* New York: Archer House, 1959.

Eastman, Charles A. *Indian Boyhood.* Lincoln: University of Nebraska Press, 1991.

———. *Indian Heroes and Great Chieftains.* Lincoln: University of Nebraska Press, 1991.

Finerty, John F. *War-Path and Bivouac or The Conquest of the Sioux.* Norman: University of Oklahoma Press, 1991.

Friswold, Carroll. *The Killing of Chief Crazy Horse.* Glendale, Calif.: The Arthur H. Clark Co., 1976.

Froiland, Sven G. *Natural History of the Black Hills and Badlands.* Sioux Falls, S.D.: The Center for Western Studies, 1990.

Garraty, John A. *The American Nation: A History of the United States.* New York: Harper & Row, 1966.

Goble, Paul. *Brave Eagle's Account of the Fetterman Fight.* Lincoln: University of Nebraska Press, 1992.

Goldsmith, Barbara. *Other Powers: The Age of Suffrage, Spiritualism, and the Scandalous Victoria Woodhull.* New York: Alfred A. Knopf, 1998.

Greeley, Horace. *An Overland Journey, from New York to San Francisco in the Summer of 1859.* New York: Readex Microprint, 1966.

Greene, Jerome A. *Slim Buttes, 1876: An Episode of the Great Sioux War.* Norman: University of Oklahoma Press, 1982.

Hafen, Leroy R., and W. J. Ghent. *Broken Hand: The Life Story of Thomas Fitzpatrick, Chief of the Mountain Men.* Denver: The Old West Publishing Co., 1931.

Hafen, Leroy R., and Ann Hafen. *Relations with the Indians of the Plains, 1857–1861.* The Far West and the Rockies Historical Series, Vol. 9. Glendale, Calif.: The Arthur H. Clark Co., 1959.

Hafen, Leroy R., and Francis Marion Young. *Fort Laramie and the Pageant of the West, 1834–1890.* Lincoln: University of Nebraska Press, 1938.

Hardorff, Richard G., ed. *Cheyenne Memories of the Custer Fight.* Spokane, Wash.: The Arthur H. Clark Co., 1995.

———. *Lakota Recollections of the Custer Fight: New Sources of Indian-Military History.* Spokane, Wash.: The Arthur H. Clark Co., 1991.

———. *The Oglala Lakota Crazy Horse.* Mattituck, N.Y.: J. M. Carroll & Co., 1985.

Hassrick, Royal B. *The Sioux.* Norman: University of Oklahoma Press, 1964.

Hedren, Paul L., ed. *The Great Sioux War 1876–77.* Helena: Montana Historical Society Press, 1991.

Howard, James H., ed. *The Warrior Who Killed Custer: The Personal Narrative of Chief Joseph White Bull.* Lincoln: University of Nebraska Press, 1968.

Hyde, George. *Life of George Bent.* Norman: University of Oklahoma Press, 1968.

———. *Red Cloud's Folk: A History of the Oglala Sioux Indians.* Norman: University of Oklahoma Press, 1937.

———. *Spotted Tail's Folk: A History of the Brule Sioux.* Norman: University of Oklahoma Press, 1961.

Jackson, Donald. *Custer's Gold: The United States Cavalry Expedition of 1874.* Lincoln: University of Nebraska Press, 1972.

Johnson, Lowell, ed. *Fort Robinson Illustrated.* Lincoln: Nebraska Game and Parks Commission, 1986.

Josephy, Alvin M., Jr. *The Patriot Chiefs.* New York: Penguin Books, 1993.

Kadlecek, Edward and Mabell. *To Kill an Eagle: Indian Views on the Last Days of Crazy Horse.* Boulder, Colo.: Johnson Books, 1981.

Kammen, Robert. *Soldiers Falling into Camp: The Battle of the Rosebud and the Little Big Horn.* Encampment, Wyo.: Affiliated Writers of America, 1992.

Keenan, Jerry. *The Wagon Box Fight.* Boulder, Colo.: Lightning Tree Press, 1992.

Killoren, John J. *"Come, Black Robe": De Smet and the Indian Tragedy.* Norman: University of Oklahoma Press, 1994.

Kime, Wayne R., ed. *The Powder River Expedition: The Journals of Colonel Richard Irving Dodge.* Norman: University of Oklahoma Press, 1997.

King, Charles. *Campaigning with Crook.* Norman: University of Oklahoma Press, 1964.

LaPointe, James. *Legends of the Lakota.* San Francisco: Indian Historian Press, 1976.

Larson, Robert W. *Red Cloud: Warrior-Statesman of the Lakota Sioux.* Norman: University of Oklahoma Press, 1997.

Lavender, David. *Fort Laramie and the Changing Frontier.* Washington, D.C.: National Park Service, 1983.

———. *The Way to the Western Sea: Lewis and Clark Across the Continent.* New York: Harper & Row, 1988.

Levy, JoAnn. *They Saw the Elephant: Women in the California Gold Rush.* Hamden, Conn.: Archon Books, 1990.

Marcy, Randolph B. *The Prairie Traveler.* Bedford, Mass.: Applewood Books, 1993. Washington, D.C.: U.S. War Department, 1859.

Mattes, Merrill J. *The Great Platte River Road.* Lincoln: University of Nebraska Press, 1987.

McCreight, M. I. *Firewater and Forked Tongues: A Sioux Chief Interprets U.S. History.* Pasadena, Calif.: Trail's End Publishing, 1947.

McGillycuddy, Julia. *Blood on the Moon: Valentine McGillycuddy and the Sioux.* Lincoln: University of Nebraska Press, 1990.

McHugh, Tom. *The Time of the Buffalo.* Lincoln: University of Nebraska Press, 1972.

McMurty, Larry. *Crazy Horse.* New York: Viking, 1999.

Megquier, Mary Jane. *Apron Full of Gold.* Albuquerque: University of New Mexico Press, 1994.

Michno, Gregory F. *Lakota Noon: The Indian Narrative of Custer's Defeat.* Missoula, Mont.: Mountain Press, 1997.

Nabokov, Peter. *Two Leggings: The Making of a Crow Warrior.* New York: Thomas Y. Crowell Co., 1970.

Nadeau, Remi. *Fort Laramie and the Sioux Indians.* Englewood Cliffs, N.J.: Prentice-Hall, 1967.

Neihardt, John G. *Black Elk Speaks.* Lincoln: University of Nebraska Press, 1988.

Palmer, Joel. *Journal of Travels over the Rocky Mountains; to the Mouth of the Columbia River, Made during the Years 1854 and 1846.* Ann Arbor: University of Michigan microfilms, 1966.

Parker, Watson. *Gold in the Black Hills.* Norman: University of Oklahoma Press, 1966.

Parkman, Francis. *The Oregon Trail.* Boston: Little, Brown, 1907.

Paul, R. Eli, ed. *The Autobiography of Red Cloud: War Leader of the Oglalas.* Helena: Montana Historical Society Press, 1997.

Porter, Joseph C. *Paper Medicine Man: John Gregory Bourke and His American West.* Norman: University of Oklahoma Press, 1986.

Price, Catherine. *The Oglala People, 1841–1879.* Lincoln: University of Nebraska Press, 1996.

Prucha, Francis Paul. *American Indian Treaties: The History of a Political Anomaly*. Berkeley: University of California Press, 1997.

Rankin, Charles E., ed. *Legacy: New Perspectives on the Battle of the Little Big Horn*. Helena: Montana Historical Society Press, 1996.

Robinson, Charles M. III. *A Good Year to Die: The Story of the Great Sioux War*. New York: Random House, 1995.

Robinson, Doane. *A History of the Dakota or Sioux Indians*. Minneapolis: Ross & Haines, 1956.

Robinson, James M. *West of Fort Pierre*. Los Angeles: Westernlore Press, 1974.

Sandoz, Mari. *Crazy Horse: The Strange Man of the Oglalas*. Lincoln: University of Nebraska Press, 1961.

Scott, Bob. *Blood at Sand Creek: The Massacre Revisited*. Caldwell, Idaho: Caxton Printers, 1994.

Spring, Agnes Wright. *Caspar Collins: The Life and Exploits of an Indian Fighter of the Sixties*. New York: Columbia University Press, 1927.

Standing Bear, Luther. *My Indian Boyhood*. Lincoln: University of Nebraska Press, 1988.

———. *My People the Sioux*. Lincoln: University of Nebraska Press, 1975.

Stands In Timber, John. *Cheyenne Memories*. New Haven, Conn.: Yale University Press, 1967.

Unrau, William E. *White Man's Wicked Water*. Lawrence: University Press of Kansas, 1996.

Unruh, John D., Jr. *The Plains Across: The Overland Emigrants and the Trans-Mississippi West, 1840–60*. Urbana: University of Illinois Press, 1979.

Utley, Robert, M. *The Indian Frontier of the American West: 1846–1890*. Albuquerque: University of New Mexico Press, 1984.

———. *The Lance and the Shield: The Life and Times of Sitting Bull*. New York: Henry Holt, 1993.

Vaugh, J. W. *With Crook at the Rosebud*. Harrisburg: Stackpole, 1956.

Vestal, Stanley. *New Sources of Indian History, 1850–1891*. Norman: University of Oklahoma Press, 1934.

———. *Sitting Bull: Champion of the Sioux*. Boston: Houghton Mifflin, 1932.

———. *Warpath: The True Story of the Fighting Sioux Told in a Biography of Chief White Bull*. Lincoln: University of Nebraska Press, 1984.

Walker, James R. *Lakota Belief and Ritual*. Lincoln: University of Nebraska Press, 1980.

———. *Lakota Myth*. Lincoln: University of Nebraska Press, 1983.

Ware, Eugene F. *The Indian War of 1864*. Lincoln: University of Nebraska Press, 1994.

Welch, James, and Paul Stekler. *Killing Custer: The Battle of the Little Big Horn and the Fate of the Plains Indians*. New York: W. W. Norton, 1994.

Welter, Rush. *The Mind of America: 1820–1860*. New York: Columbia University Press, 1975.

Werner, Fred H. *The Dull Knife Battle*. Greeley, Colo.: Werner Publications, 1981.

——. *Heroic Fort Sedgwick and Julesburg: A Study in Courage.* Greeley, Colo.: Werner Publications, 1987.

——. *With Harney on the Blue Water: Battle of Ash Hollow, September 3, 1855.* Greeley, Colo.: Werner Publications, 1988.

West, Elliot. *The Contested Plains: Indians, Goldseekers, and the Rush to Colorado.* Lawrence: University Press of Kansas, 1998.

Workers of the South Dakota Writers' Project, Works Projects Administration. *Legends of the Mighty Sioux.* Chicago: Albert Whitman & Co., 1941.

ARTICLES

Anderson, Harry H. "The Controversial Sioux Amendment to the Fort Laramie Treaty of 1851." *Nebraska History* (1956).

——. "Indian Peace-Talkers and the Conclusion of the Sioux War of 1876." *Nebraska History* (1963).

Bray, Kingsley, M. "Teton Sioux Population History, 1655–1881." *Nebraska History* (1994).

Brininstool, E. A. "How Crazy Horse Died." *Nebraska History* (1929).

Gilbert, James N. "The Death of Crazy Horse: A Contemporary Examination of the Homicidal Events of 5 September 1877." *Journal of the West* (January 1993).

Hinman, Eleanor. "Oglala Sources on the Life of Crazy Horse." *Nebraska History* (1976).

Hutchins, James S. "Poison in the Pemmican: The Yellowstone Wagon-Road and Prospecting Expedition of 1874." *Montana the Magazine of Western History* (Summer 1958).

Knight, Oliver. "War or Peace: The Anxious Wait for Crazy Horse." *Nebraska History* (1973).

McCann, Lloyd E. "The Grattan Massacre." *Nebraska History* (1956).

Quivey, Addison. "The Yellowstone Expedition of 1874." *Historical Society of Montana* (1874).

UNPUBLISHED SOURCES

Walter S. Campbell Collection, University of Oklahoma Library, Western History Collection.

"The History of Crazy Horse as Told by Eagle Elk." Western Historical Manuscript Collection, University of Missouri Library.

Eli S. Ricker Collection, Nebraska State Historical Society and Susan Bordeaux Bettleyoun Manuscript.

Doane Robinson Papers, South Dakota State Historical Society.

Mari Sandoz Collection, University of Nebraska Library, Special Collections.

Thunder Tail Manuscript, Memorial Library, Marquette University.

INDEX